THE YEAR OF PERIL

TRACY CAMPBELL

The Year of Peril

AMERICA IN 1942

Yale

UNIVERSITY PRESS

NEW HAVEN & LONDON

Yale University Press books may be purchased in quantity for
educational, business, or promotional use. For information, please e-mail
sales.press@yale.edu (U.S. office) or sales@yaleup.co.uk (U.K. office).

Set in Scala type by IDS Infotech, Ltd.
Printed in the United States of America.

Library of Congress Control Number: 2019952877
ISBN 978-0-300-23378-0 (hardcover : alk. paper)
ISBN 978-0-300-25853-0 (paperback)

A catalogue record for this book is available from the British Library.

10 9 8 7 6 5 4 3 2 1

For Robin

CONTENTS

PREFACE

TWENTY-FIRST-CENTURY DATA MINING OFFERS a fascinating clue about what was at stake in the months following the attack on Pearl Harbor. Google Books Ngram Viewer is a search engine that displays the frequency with which a specific word or phrase has been used in printed material over the past centuries. It finds that one word was used more often in 1942 than in any other year since the United States was founded: more than in 1776, 1812, 1865, 1917, the years of the Depression, the Cold War, or after 9/11. The word is *democracy*.[1]

It is no accident that it was on the minds of so many people in 1942, when the future of democracy at home and abroad looked bleak. Government and military leaders warned that the U.S. could suffer more attacks and faced another World War I–like stalemate or even possible defeat. Adolf Hitler controlled much of Europe and the Atlantic, and Japanese forces dominated the Pacific. Nations that could be described as genuinely democratic were in increasingly short supply. In 1926, twenty-nine democracies had existed; by 1942, only twelve remained. Two years earlier, Winston Churchill had warned: "If we fail, then the whole world, including the United States, will sink into the abyss of a new dark age."[2]

I began thinking about this book in September 2008, when the world was on the brink of another abyss. The financial crisis was unfolding and the nation's economy teetered on the verge of collapse. Barack Obama and John McCain left the campaign trail to attend an emergency meeting at the

White House with President George W. Bush. The crisis was escalating to a point where no one seemed to know what to do, and the fragile bands of credit and commerce that held a capitalist economy together were ready to snap. During that period, the *New York Times* noted, "The prognosis for the American financial system was sliding from grim toward apocalyptic." Federal Reserve Board chair Ben Bernanke warned that without immediate government intervention, "we may not have an economy." He later wrote that the crisis could be a far worse economic nightmare than the Great Depression and "almost certainly the worst in human history."[3]

To save the financial system, on October 3, 2008, President Bush signed into law the $700 billion plan known as TARP (Troubled Asset Relief Program). The actual name of that legislation, the Emergency Economic Stabilization Act, recalled a moment when another president acted to provide stability to a precarious economy. To stave off runaway inflation in a time of unprecedented military spending, President Franklin D. Roosevelt signed Executive Order 9250, establishing the Office of Economic Stabilization. FDR's order stipulated that it was necessary not only to fight the "vast dislocations" that threatened the war effort, but also, in language that could have been borrowed from 2008, to protect "our domestic economic structure." Remarkably, he signed that order on October 3, 1942, sixty-six years to the day before Bush signed TARP.

The hammer-like blow to the national psyche brought by the Japanese attack on Pearl Harbor on December 7, 1941, is hard for modern audiences to fully appreciate. It was a singularly terrifying event in the life of the nation, one that presented dark scenarios that seem out of a dystopian novel. Beyond the immediate concerns about whether we would win the war, which Roosevelt had called the "Survival War," other questions arose. Could the nation unite in ways that transcended partisan, regional, racial, and ethnic divides? Would unprecedented spending bring ruinous inflation? Could democratic forms survive the necessities of "total war?"

Waging war simultaneously in Europe and over the vast Pacific required a collective effort in which the life of virtually every American was suddenly transformed. For some, it meant leaving home to serve and perhaps die in battlefields abroad; for others, it meant working in a defense plant or participating in scrap metal or rubber drives, buying war bonds, or contending with rationed food and gas. Americans were forced to confront terrifying realities in the early weeks of 1942. The attack on an American naval base demonstrated that the United States was no longer invulnerable to enemy invasion. What could be next?

Yet the hindsight of history has glossed over any sense of imminent catastrophe and reminds us of a more heroic era. When we think of the early days of World War II, it is customary to see it as a time of national unity, when petty divisions were quickly overcome by the desire to defeat a common enemy, and American society was led, in Tom Brokaw's words, by "the greatest generation any society has ever produced." Nostalgic memories of the early 1940s are reassuring because we know the outcome: the good guys prevailed. As time passes, even some essential facts of the war are fading from public memory. In a 2018 poll, over 60 percent of respondents in a citizenship survey could not identify the nations that the U.S. fought in World War II.[4]

Rather than reading history backwards, this book explores the year 1942 as it unfolded. We cannot, of course, erase from our minds the knowledge that the Allies would secure an unconditional victory in 1945; but we can better appreciate the severity of the national trauma if we see the year as the people alive experienced it. While some of that year's developments will sound familiar, others may seem alien to modern readers. In January, the last cavalry charge on horseback in U.S. history occurred in the Philippines; in December, the first sustained nuclear chain reaction took place under the football stands at the University of Chicago. In January, FDR proposed to spend $59 billion in the upcoming year, a figure larger than the nation's gross domestic product three years earlier. By year's end the highest federal tax bracket had increased to 88 percent. Coffee and gas were rationed, and federal employees regulated the price of everything from steel and lumber to biscuits and pork bellies. Bureaucrats deep within the corridors of power secretly discussed the nationalization of all private automobiles and taxing church property. Some large department stores, in an effort to discourage hoarding and black-market inflation, implored shoppers "not to buy too much," admonishing them to forego extravagance and focus on "what you really need." In these remarkable months, some considered what kind of society they wanted if the nation survived. If anything, it seemed certain that fundamental changes were on their way.

Yet in other ways, the world of 1942 was not so different. Many lamented the inadequate educational standards of public schools, the irresponsibility of teenagers, the inefficiency and overreach of government bureaucrats, endless spending and unprecedented government debt, and the inability of the nation's leaders to take the fight to the enemy. Charges of obstructionism and incompetency were often hurled at Congress and the administration, while rumors and misinformation spread like a contagion.

A fundamental premise of this book is that we can best understand a society by seeing it under its greatest stress, when its very existence is in peril. The stress that was omnipresent throughout the year revealed some of the best—and worst—characteristics of the United States. Every walk of life was disrupted, and many worried that new forms of terror could come to any town or community. At no time since the Civil War had the United States been more threatened than in the months following the events at Pearl Harbor.[5]

At its core, this is a story in which the protagonist is the country itself. It is about a vast landscape of people from all walks of life, many long forgotten, who played vital roles in these months. Some people in this book, such as Franklin and Eleanor Roosevelt, Walt Disney, and Douglas MacArthur, will be familiar to readers. Many others, such as Leon Henderson, Beardsley Ruml, Norma Greene, and Florence Nimick Schnoor, are essentially invisible. It is, at times, a heroic and inspirational story—at other times, one that is tragic and appalling. During these anxious days, the nation confronted what writer John Keane referred to as the "brittle contingency of democracy." In short, it was a time not unlike our own.[6]

ACKNOWLEDGMENTS

IN THE YEARS OF RESEARCHING AND WRITING, I accumulated many debts that I can never adequately repay. I thank the numerous dedicated archivists and librarians for their help, especially those at the Bancroft Library, University of California, Berkeley; the Special Collections Library, Clemson University; the Huntington Library, San Marino, California; the Archive of Folk Culture, American Folklife Center, Library of Congress, Washington, D.C.; the Women's Library Reading Room, London School of Economics; the New-York Historical Society, New York, New York; the New York Public Library and the Schomburg Center for Research in Black Culture, New York, New York; the Seeley G. Mudd Manuscript Library, Princeton University; the Franklin D. Roosevelt Presidential Library, Hyde Park, New York; and my friends at the Young Library and the Special Collections Research Center, University of Kentucky. I am grateful to Deborah Grubb of the Bedford Historical Society and Museum for opening the building on a Saturday morning so I could examine the Jack and Heintz Company records. My thanks also to Matthew Hanson at the FDR Library and Pia Jordan, director of the Tuskegee Army Nurses Project. Dr. Helma Harrington kindly allowed me to use one of her late husband's brilliant drawings.

Although I did not fully realize it at the time, I first became interested in the early months of World War II when I was a graduate student at Duke. In a class about modern America, Bill Chafe introduced me to the many domestic challenges of 1942, and he has remained a dear friend ever since.

Bill read parts of the manuscript and his razor-sharp suggestions reminded me of the era's political and economic relevance. I recall John Hope Franklin's outrage as someone who wanted to serve, but because of his race was treated with contempt by draft boards and other officials. He reached a point, as he later wrote, "beyond which even the most patient, long-suffering loyalist will not go." Ray Gavins introduced me to many concepts that are crucial to this book, and I regret that he did not live to see it finished. I wish that the late Larry Goodwyn could have read drafts and offered his advice. It would have made this a better book.

A number of colleagues and friends read all or parts of this book at various stages. They took time out of their busy schedules and their own writing projects to offer their advice and point out numerous errors. Don Ritchie, the historian emeritus of the U.S. Senate, kindly (and quickly) read the entire manuscript with his usual precision. I have relied on his remarkable storehouse of political history for many years and plan on doing so for many more to come. Tim Tyson's unflinching portraits of our recent past have had a profound influence, and I am grateful for his wise counsel and long friendship. Hank Klibanoff offered some of the best writing advice I have ever received, and I hope the final product is a fraction of what he envisioned. My thanks to Danielle McGuire and Paul Chamberlin for challenging me to redefine some crucial sections, and to George Herring for his suggestions and warm support over the years.

Colleagues at the University of Kentucky read various drafts and provided sound criticism and much encouragement. My thanks to Sarah Ballard, Terry Birdwhistell, Francie Chassen-Lopez, Eric Christianson, David Hamilton, David Olster, Karen Petrone, Jeremy Popkin, Gerald Smith, Mark Summers, Scott Taylor, and Tammy Whitlock. I received much support from fellow historian and dean Mark Kornbluh, as well as from Tina Hagee, who did at least a thousand things for me with her customary good humor and patience. My students have heard various versions of this book and their reactions helped me immeasurably.

My agent, John Wright, has been an enthusiastic champion of this project from the very beginning, and I am lucky to have him in my corner. Bill Frucht beautifully edited the manuscript with a deft understanding of the context of the year, and he allowed me the freedom to do some things that make working with him a special privilege. My thanks to Karen Olson for her expertise and perseverance with countless production issues, and to Robin DuBlanc for copyediting the manuscript with such care. My thanks also to Margaret Otzel and Ariana Bengston for their help in the final stages. Anonymous reviewers for Yale University Press asked penetrating questions and challenged me to refine the arguments throughout the book.

My son Alex and daughter-in-law, Delaney, have been there through the ups and downs of this project. I often thought of them as I considered the experiences of young people making their way both then and now. My youngest son Drew grew up with 1942 as a backdrop and accompanied me on several lengthy research trips. On one, after being informed by "the librarian with no soul" that he could not be with me in the research room, he patiently endured days of sitting in a stark lobby waiting for me to finish. My mother-in-law, Brooke Hicks, was five years old and living in Long Beach, California, when Pearl Harbor was attacked. She experienced area-wide blackouts, rubber shortages, fireside chats, and got lost on a visit to a nearby shipyard. Her memories helped me consider the role of children in times of crisis and how they are usually overlooked.

My mother turned fifteen in 1942 and was in high school at the time. In one of my last meals with her, I listened intently as she and some of her classmates recalled their memories of the war and its impact on their lives. When one of her friends casually mentioned that she had a job in Detroit inserting rivets on airplane wings, I am sure I startled nearby diners when I proclaimed: "You're Rosie the Riveter!"

My wife, Robin, has been the singular inspiration for this entire project. It simply would never have seen the light of day without her love and encouragement. In so many ways, this book has been a joint effort. She helped me examine archival collections from New York to California, read the entire manuscript with her keen editorial eye, and challenged me to rethink what I was doing all along. Her democratic spirit and her commitment to fairness and justice infuse every page. She is my brilliant and beautiful companion, and I look forward to completing many more projects with her by my side.

As I thought about this book, I sometimes looked at a photo of my late father, Alex, standing alongside an iron fence next to a body of water. On the back, he had written, "Lake Como, May 1945." He had been drafted in 1942 and served in the 103rd Signal Construction Battalion in North Africa and Italy. Like so many other veterans, he rarely mentioned his experiences in the war and left no records. The only clue I had were a few photos, all taken in the same general location. I wondered if I could find out where he was standing and perhaps learn something about his experiences. After scouring the internet for any leads, in 2015, Robin and I traveled to Lake Como and the magnificent grounds of Villa d'Este, where I found that same fence as my dad seventy years earlier. The emotional power of being there was overwhelming, as was the reception we received from Villa d'Este's managing director, Danilo Zucchetti, and a wonderful man named Emilio. When I showed them the photo, Danilo informed me that the hotel's history indicated that in May 1945, five hundred American soldiers, which I now knew included my father, were sent there "to enjoy themselves." Emilio summoned a young waiter from Poland and told him to listen carefully. After all, he said, "this is your history!" Danilo ordered champagne and we all toasted what my father and so many other soldiers had done to liberate Europe from fascism.

Although I had solved my original question, new ones arose. Why was my father among the five hundred singled out to stay in such a palace? What had he seen and experienced that merited such a reward? Who took the photos? And why had he never said anything about it? The magical afternoon on Lake Como reminded me that my father's story, like so many others whose worlds were turned upside down by the war, was one that guardedly revealed some of its secrets while leaving many others hidden.

THE YEAR OF PERIL

December 1941: "The Most Tremendous Undertaking"

WHEN SHE FIRST HEARD THAT PEARL HARBOR had been attacked, sixteen-year-old Elaine R. Engelson of Brooklyn was "amazed and ashamed" of her "weakness in facing a world crisis." She wrote to the *New York Times* the next day that although she, like many others, had "felt the inevitability of war" for some time, "the thought of it actually having come upon us was sudden." The horrifying events in Hawaii suddenly changed the rhythms of the teenager's life. She had grown accustomed to countless airplanes flying overhead, but on December 8, the sound of an approaching plane produced a new sense of dread. Although "the world has not yet come to an end by any means," she had the ominous feeling that "we are on the brink of a precipice overhanging a world of complete darkness." What was at stake, she said, was something she and many Americans had not fully appreciated until then: "We are fighting to save the world from a fate worse than death."[1]

For a stunned nation, it seemed impossible that the U.S. Pacific Fleet had been caught so unaware. Over twenty-four hundred Americans had died, and the navy had lost eight battleships, four destroyers, and 350 airplanes. Along with shock and anger came another reaction, shared by millions on both coasts. People wondered if Pearl Harbor was just a prelude to something far worse. In a Gallup poll taken shortly after December 7, 60 percent responded that it was "very likely" or "fairly likely" that the West Coast would be attacked in the next few weeks.

Though Americans could not know it at the time, the leader of the first wave of planes, Mitsuo Fuchida, wanted to return to Hawaii and bomb fuel tanks and other supply stations. Fleet Commander Vice Admiral Chuichi Nagumo was not persuaded, arguing that the American aircraft carriers *Lexington* and *Enterprise* still posed a threat to Japanese forces, and he refused to order a second air strike. Yet one Japanese flight deck officer succinctly expressed both the growing confidence of the Imperial forces and the fears of anxious Americans: "We're not returning to Tokyo; now we're going to San Francisco."[2]

After being informed of the attack, President Franklin D. Roosevelt summoned his cabinet to an emergency meeting at the White House, where Interior secretary Harold Ickes noted that the sullen crowds gathered near the gates "were responding to that human instinct to get near a scene of action even if they could see or hear nothing." The president told his cabinet that it was the most serious situation the nation had faced since 1861. He also asked congressional leaders for time to address a joint session the next day. Afterward, over a late dinner with journalist Edward R. Murrow, the president vented his frustration that U.S. planes had offered such easy targets: "On the ground, by God! On the ground!"[3]

As Roosevelt understood, nothing since the Civil War reached the magnitude of Pearl Harbor. The United States had escaped destruction on its own shores in previous wars, but it was now vulnerable to enemy planes. Recent events had made Americans aware of the chilling possibilities: the mustard gas used by Italian bombers against Ethiopians in 1935; the fascist bombing of Guernica, Spain, in April 1937, made famous by the Picasso mural; the Luftwaffe bombings of London in 1940 and 1941. Airplanes with such destructive power were a new and terrifying technology. In the United States, Orson Welles's radio broadcast *War of the Worlds* in 1938 had inspired panic among listeners. By the time the news of the Pearl Harbor attack reached the East Coast, Americans were besieged with a sense of dread. Paris and much of France were already occupied; England was preparing for imminent invasion; Poland, Czechoslovakia, China, and Southeast Asia had fallen; now, suddenly, America seemed vulnerable too.

As the nation struggled to understand how an American base could have been so exposed to a brazen attack, few heroes could be found. One sailor's courageous actions during the attack went largely unknown for months. Messman Third Class Doris "Dorie" Miller was a twenty-two-year-old African American from Waco, Texas, who found himself in the middle of the attack on the U.S.S. *West Virginia*. Because of the military's segregation policy, Miller could perform only kitchen duties. Yet not only did he risk his life by carrying his mortally wounded captain to safety, he manned an anti-aircraft gun, despite the fact that he had never used such weaponry. Miller likely downed at least one, if not more, enemy aircraft. In May, he became the first African American to be awarded the Navy Cross. News of Miller's heroics was widely disseminated throughout the African American community, and a song was sung in Harlem: "Dorie Miller, he's a killer—ask the Japanese."[4]

On Monday, December 8, FDR spoke before a joint session of Congress. Calling the 7th "a date that will live in infamy," he asked for a declaration of war against Japan. Summoning the "righteous might" of an angry nation, FDR promised a military response that would bring "absolute victory." Despite the rhetoric, many within the government and military understood the sobering reality. "This at once places at stake everything that is precious and worthwhile," wrote Secretary of War Henry Stimson in his diary, adding that "self defense" was "the key point for the preservation of each and all of our civilized institutions." The chances of defeat or stalemate were very real. William Batt, director of materials at the War Production Board, said it in the clearest of terms: "Not since the days of the revolution have we had much of a chance to lose a war. We have a chance to lose this one."[5]

Within the areas of the country most worried about new assaults, a common reaction on December 8 was to look guardedly at suspected enemies. Roosevelt had signed proclamations in the hours after Pearl Harbor designating Japanese, German, and Italians whom the FBI had deemed dangerous to American security in the United States as "enemy aliens." In Los Angeles, FBI agents and soldiers from nearby Fort MacArthur began taking "key" Japanese citizens into custody less than two hours after the attack, and some Italian Americans suffered the same fate. Filippo Molinari of San Jose, California, was arrested by the FBI on the night of the 7th, and soon found himself on a train bound for internment at Camp Missoula, Montana. When he arrived in Missoula, Molinari recalled, he was "still in his slippers, the temperature at 17 below and no coat or heavy clothes" to keep him warm.[6]

In Hawaii, the Justice Department established an internment camp at Sand Island to keep "enemy aliens" under control. New York mayor Fiorello La Guardia, who had been appointed director of the Office of Civilian Defense in May 1941, directed the city's Japanese nationals to stay confined in their homes, and known Japanese meeting places and restaurants were closed. The FBI had already compiled a "Suspect Enemy Aliens" list with help from the Census Bureau, and now used it to arrest over a thousand Japanese American leaders throughout New York. In San Francisco, Brigadier General William O. Ryan said "many planes" that were undoubtedly enemy aircraft had flown over San Francisco Bay. Western Defense Commander General John DeWitt warned that a Bay Area blackout was not sufficient and "a great many things will have to be corrected" in order to ensure the nation's safety. Blackouts in Southern California had the unanticipated consequence of killing four people in nighttime traffic accidents when cars could not use their headlights.[7]

In Washington, D.C., the floodlights illuminating the Capitol dome were turned off, and black drapes covered the White House windows. Large sand bins were scattered throughout the Capitol building in case of an incendiary attack. Two days before Christmas, curators at the National Archives removed the Declaration of Independence and the Constitution, carefully placing the documents between two sheets of acid-free manila paper inside a bronze container, and then secured it all inside a lead box with heavy padlocks. Guards took the box to the train station for a trip to Louisville, Kentucky, where the shipment was received by Secret Service agents and members of the Thirteenth Armored Division, stationed at nearby Fort Knox. They took the precious documents to the recently built Bullion Depository, where they remained for the duration of the war.[8]

Adolf Hitler declared war on the United States on December 11. The week earlier, the German government called for spending the equivalent of $150 billion over the next two years. Describing himself as "the head of the strongest Army in the world," the German Führer called the American president "the eternal Jew," who "aimed at world domination and dictatorship." In response, Roosevelt sent Congress another request, asking that

the U.S. recognize a "state of war" with Germany and Italy. Congress quickly gave its unanimous support, and the nation formally entered a truly
global conflict. The U.S. joined Great Britain and Russia in the Grand Alliance against Germany, Japan, and Italy (the Axis powers). "Every single
man, woman, and child," the president said in a fireside chat, "is a partner
in the most tremendous undertaking of our American history."⁹

It was a war that Roosevelt had long feared. Throughout the 1930s, he
had worried about the rise of fascism but faced strong congressional opposition to enflaming potential enemies. Even after the German invasion of
Poland in September 1939, isolationist sentiment ran strong throughout
the nation and in Congress. Many recalled the lessons of a Senate committee chaired by isolationist Gerald Nye of North Dakota, which had revealed
the outlandish profits taken by munitions makers during World War I.
When Hitler's armies had marched into Paris and bombed London in
1940, there were no united calls to enter the war. Even as he campaigned
for a third term in the White House in fall 1940, Roosevelt had famously
promised: "I have said it before but I shall say it again and again and again.
Your boys are not going to be sent into any foreign wars." The purpose of
any military buildup, he added, was to train a force "so strong that, by its
very existence, it will keep the threat of war away from our shores." Roosevelt's reassurances that the nation could avoid war helped him defeat
Wendell Willkie by a margin of 367 electoral votes.¹⁰

One reason for Roosevelt's reluctance to commit troops to Europe or the
Pacific was the state of America's armed forces. The military resources the
commander in chief had at his disposal at the beginning of World War II
were not what Americans today are accustomed to. In 1939, the U.S. Army
was ranked nineteenth in the world in size, with 187,886 troops in 8 divisions, smaller than the armies of Switzerland or Portugal. The German
Wehrmacht, in comparison, consisted of 3.7 million troops in 103 divisions,
the Italian Army had over 90 divisions, and the Imperial Japanese Army
had 1.7 million members. In 1940, the German Luftwaffe had 25,000
planes compared to just 2,665 aircraft in the Army Air Corps. American
infantry trained with wooden rifles and used trucks to simulate tank warfare, and horses pulled battlefield cannon. The standard rifle was the 1903
bolt-action Springfield that had been used in World War I.¹¹

The Army Air Force had but 18,000 airmen and 1,300 officers when war broke out in Europe. General Henry "Hap" Arnold understood that the U.S. followed "antiquated air doctrines" reminiscent of World War I, with "heroic pilots in dogfights." Now that planes "had broken down all boundaries of time and distance," Arnold believed Americans recognized that "even our own inland cities were within bombing range of the enemy." Arnold knew the task ahead was daunting: "Germany required ten years to create her Luftwaffe," while the U.S. had to "build our air force in one, and fight with it in four corners of the world at the same time."[12]

As the war raged in 1940, President Roosevelt and Congress began rebuilding the army and navy. One step was the Selective Training and Service Act of 1940, which required all American men between the ages of twenty-one and thirty-five to register for the draft. In October 1940, the nation held its first peacetime draft lottery, and by the time of Pearl Harbor, over 17 million Americans were registered and 921,000 men had been drafted. Over 12 million men received deferments, including 10 million who were listed as having "persons dependent upon them for support." Another 1,178,000 were "physically, mentally, or morally unfit," while just 5,710 registered as conscientious objectors. A decade of economic deprivation had its consequences: half of the first recruits for the U.S. Army were found to be unfit for service due to malnutrition and poor health care.[13]

In May 1940, to prepare the nation for the worst, FDR had set an outlandish production goal of fifty thousand planes. The Lend-Lease Act, passed by Congress in March 1941, called for an additional $7 billion worth of planes, ships, and other goods that would serve as a lifeline to Great Britain. In case of American entry into the war, the military worked secretly on a variety of overall strategies. In September 1941, the administration settled on a "Victory Program" calling for a 10-million-man army that would not be fully ready to confront Hitler's forces until mid-1943. Word of the secret plan was leaked to the isolationist *Chicago Tribune* and the *Washington Times-Herald* the first week of December 1941. In its issue of Saturday, December 6, the *Tribune* warned readers of the Roosevelt administration's secret "blueprint for total war."[14]

The fear of more attacks led one of the world's leading private insurers, Lloyd's of London, to cancel all policies protecting American property from enemy destruction. Many U.S. insurance companies followed suit. The Insurance Executives Association, a lobbying group, suggested that another entity should assume the loss in case of war. Two New York insurance executives, Clement L. Despard and Isaac Witkin, sent a plan to the Reconstruction Finance Corporation outlining how the federal government should underwrite losses in the case of "invasion, revolution, insurrection, rebellion, civil war, bombardment," and damage caused "by the operation of martial law, military or usurped power in connection with foregoing perils."[15]

The government did not take long to respond. On December 13, 1941, President Roosevelt chartered the War Insurance Corporation, capitalized with $100 million, to provide protection against losses resulting from enemy attacks. Three months later, the agency was renamed the War Damage Corporation (WDC) and authorized to underwrite policies worth up to $1 billion. In the event of enemy attack, all claims had to be approved by the secretary of commerce and the president. More than five hundred private companies served as the WDC's agents, and within a year nearly 4 million policies had been issued, insuring a total of $94 billion. The federal government in 1942 collected premiums totaling over $218 million. The policies covered buildings and structures as well as crops and orchards, but excluded losses due to "blackout, sabotage, capture, seizure, pillage, looting, use and occupancy," as well as lost "rent, rental value or other indirect loss." Jewelry, furs, paintings, antiques, and stamp or coin collections could be insured for up to $10,000, and museums and art dealers could insure their collections for up to $100,000. Policies would not be extended to anyone "who, in the opinion of the President, [is] unfriendly to the U.S." The tangible fear of inland attacks was revealed by companies such as the Matlaw Corporation of Hammond, Indiana, which bought a policy for $104, insuring a commercial building located twenty-three miles south of Chicago.[16]

While the West Coast braced for more Japanese air raids, the East Coast readied for attacks from the German Navy. Shortly after Hitler declared war on the U.S., German admiral Karl Dönitz's U-boats began attacking ships in the Atlantic Ocean as far west as the U.S. coastline. Long before American ground troops could be deployed in Europe or the Pacific, the war would be fought in the waters of the Atlantic, and for the time being the Germans held a clear advantage. Given their control of the ocean, it seemed likely that their planes would soon bomb eastern cities or unleash chemical warfare.[17]

Air raids became a part of everyday life in many American cities. The Office of Civilian Defense (OCD) hastily issued some "rules." First, "remain calm and do not be frightened. Much more damage can be caused by panic than by falling building materials or even the bombs themselves." In addition to avoiding subways and telephones, citizens were advised that "if bombs should fall, lie down, whether at home or outside, and keep as far as possible from windows." Parents were told that if an air raid occurred while their children were at school, "see to your own safety, stay home, do not try to reach the school. You could accomplish no good. You could do a great deal of harm by such action." The OCD acknowledged that "this is hard advice," but "it is for your best interest and for the welfare of your children." New York City teenagers met at the Triangle Ballroom to volunteer for service in a citywide air-raid drill, performing such tasks as acting as couriers to deliver food and clothing and rendering first aid. One scoutmaster who attended the meeting warned, "If any of you are here seeking telephone numbers or dates, go right home and remain there. This is not a social affair, but the grim business of war." When she was told to prepare for an air-raid drill at her elementary school in New York City, one young girl was not quite sure what to do. She likely knew little about the details of what had happened nearly five thousand miles away in Hawaii, but after seeing how the adults in her life were responding, she sensed that something awful had occurred. She asked her teacher, "Is this when I cry?"[18]

Some within the Roosevelt administration proposed having the War Department take over "Home Defense" in order to adequately prepare for enemy attacks. Secretary of War Stimson rejected the idea. "We have burdens enough," he said. He hoped to keep his department focused on fighting the war abroad and to avoid the public outcry that could occur if the U.S. mainland suffered an attack. Yet he admitted that an attack "in the immediate future" on American soil was "likely."[19]

If fear of conventional bombings provoked anxiety throughout much of the country, so did the fear of chemical warfare, something that anyone knowledgeable of World War I knew well. Some U.S. military officials thought that massed squadrons of planes dropping mustard gas, chlorine, or lewisite could cause "a complete revision of how we wage war." Despite international agreements, no nation had abandoned the production of chemical weapons, and the United States maintained a massive supply. Although gas was rarely used in combat in World War II, U.S. Navy researchers conducted experiments on sixty thousand U.S. sailors, in part to see if the effects of mustard gas differed according to one's race.[20]

One place that did not panic after Pearl Harbor was Wall Street. After the Dow Jones Industrial Average closed at 115.9 on Friday, December 5, the first day of trading after the attack saw only a slight decline, to 112.52. There was no rush by investors to convert their equities to gold or cash. Rather than worry about stock prices, Wall Street was more focused on its physical structure. The insurance bonds that covered its trading rooms contained a war risk exclusion, and firms began negotiating for a new indemnity bond that would also cover enemy bombing. One financial firm trained its workers to pile trays of paper securities into a vault, and those on the trading floor were advised to keep their papers in fireproof steel boxes.[21]

The reaction of pundits and political observers to any national tragedy usually includes a call to end partisan bickering. Throughout the nation that December, opinion makers counseled that politics should take a back seat to a united effort against the common enemy. Basil Brewer, publisher of the *New Bedford (Mass.) Standard-Times,* published an editorial that read: "ABANDON POLITICS in preparedness program FROM THE PRESIDENT DOWN," followed by "Stop beating the OLD CLASS HATRED TOM TOMS. The welfare of ALL is threatened." In addition to an end to red tape and giving "dollar a year men" authority, Brewer called for building factories and airports underground. He implored the nation to "SACRIFICE THE DEMOCRATIC PROCESS AS LITTLE AS POSSIBLE, BUT AS MUCH AS NECESSARY."[22]

President Roosevelt welcomed calls to end partisan sniping and began considering the full extent of his powers in total war. During the Civil War, Abraham Lincoln had suspended the writ of habeas corpus and assumed extraordinary executive power. In 1918, Woodrow Wilson had signed the Sedition Act, which outlawed "disloyal, profane, scurrilous, or abusive language" about the government, flag, or armed forces of the United States. No president exercised similar power until 1933, when Roosevelt, declaring that the American people wanted "vigorous action" to combat the Depression, asked

Congress for "broad Executive power to wage a war against the emergency, as great as the power that would be given to me if we were in fact invaded by a foreign foe." Eight years later, the nation confronted those foes.[23]

On December 16, 1941, after two hours of debate and a voice vote, Congress passed the War Powers Act, giving the president authority to redistribute and establish executive agencies, impose government censorship, and award war contracts without competitive bidding. It also authorized the president to order surveillance "when deemed necessary to the public safety." Having declared war, Congress entrusted the conduct of the war abroad and at home to the chief executive. The *New York Times* felt the legislation gave FDR "almost unlimited powers to regulate the nation's emergency war effort at home," and the *Wall Street Journal* lamented that FDR "now holds greater powers over life and property than any President before him." One Democratic congressman from Virginia, John W. Flannagan Jr., argued that in some way the nation "needed a Pearl Harbor—a Golgotha— to arouse us from our self-sufficient complacency." Flannagan felt that Pearl Harbor produced a "righteous wrath" so powerful "that our differences and divisions and hates melted into a unity never before witnessed in this country."[24] Time would soon test Flannagan's observations.

With massive war spending imminent, congressional leaders began considering how to combat the inflation that they believed was certain to follow. During the Civil War, prices had risen 120 percent, and during and immediately after World War I they had risen more than 170 percent. Considering what the nation now confronted, similar inflationary levels could prove disastrous to the war effort and wreck the nation's economy as well. The budgetary challenges also gave the president's opponents an opportunity to drastically cut domestic spending. Over the preceding decade, conservatives in both parties worried that the administration's response to the Depression, a vast system of government work programs and regulatory agencies termed "the New Deal," was misguided. While his most vocal opponents considered it a socialistic experiment that prolonged the economic downturn and generated government waste, others worried it had created a vast bureaucracy that produced dependence on government. After Pearl Harbor, New Deal programs that conservatives had long hated were among the first to be targeted. Led by budget hawk Virginia senator Harry Byrd, a joint committee named Reduction of Non-Essential Federal Expenditures suggested cutting over $1.7 billion, mostly in programs ranging from the Civilian Conservation Corps to the Farm Security Administration. A minority report, led by Wisconsin senator Robert LaFollette, rejected the committee's proposals, saying that the cuts would fall "on the very lowest income groups among our population" and would cripple national morale.[25]

By the last week of 1941, more bad news came from the Philippines with the bombing of Manila, followed by additional Japanese attacks on Guam, Wake Island, Thailand, and Hong Kong. Senator Burton K. Wheeler of Montana was clear about how he felt toward the Japanese: "One can come to only one conclusion from the action of the Japanese," he said, "and that is that they are an inhuman and half-civilized race." Wheeler, an isolationist who had made the famous declaration that the passage of Lend-Lease would "plow under every fourth American boy," added that "the tragedy is that we have given away so much of our material that we cannot retaliate and bomb Tokyo, Kobe, Yokohama, and Nagasaki." Senate majority leader Alben W. Barkley of Kentucky struck a less racist but more vengeful tone, noting that as "Manila is suffering, with its 600,000 helpless inhabitants huddled under the rain of Japanese missiles," Japanese leaders should "think of Tokyo, with ten times as many inhabitants, when the inevitable day of destruction comes, as our bombers swoop down upon the city."[26]

On New Year's Eve, FDR predicted that in the coming year, half of the national income would be expended on the war. While he would not specify exactly how much spending he would ask Congress to approve until a subsequent address in early January, estimates among Washington insiders reached as high as $50 billion, more than the nation's GDP in 1939. To place that sum in context, in 1939, when Roosevelt asked for a $309 million increase in military spending over the previous year's appropriation of $1 billion, the request had prompted some isolationists in Congress to object to the "enormous outlay."[27]

As the new year approached, Columbia University historian Allan Nevins admonished Americans that the coming year was "destined to be one of the most critical—perhaps the most critical—in the history of the United States." He called for a "heroic mood" that could be achieved only if "the whole people be enlisted on as nearly an equal basis as possible" to stave off the "grumbling, rumor-mongering and passive resistance that will become the vocation of large groups." Nevins also hoped that the war could produce "a new and sounder world organization, which can make fresh advances toward the preservation of peace, the equalization of economic opportunity, and the promotion of liberty." Another scholar, W. E. B. Du Bois, writing just days after Pearl Harbor, was less hopeful: "War, like every other human ailment, tends to leave the body politic folded along ancient creases and festering in old sores."[28]

January: State of the Union

THE BIGGEST FOOTBALL GAME ON NEW YEAR'S DAY 1942 was the Rose Bowl, Oregon State versus Duke. But it was not played in the Rose Bowl itself, the massive stadium in Pasadena, California, because that city was just twenty miles from the Pacific Ocean. Instead, the game was played twenty-five hundred miles away, at Duke's stadium in Durham, North Carolina. Following Pearl Harbor, Lieutenant General John DeWitt had asked California governor Culbert Olson to cancel the game because he thought the Rose Parade, which attracted a million spectators, and the game itself, in a stadium that seated over ninety thousand people, were easy targets. Rather than cancel the game, Duke invited Oregon State to play in the presumably safer confines of central North Carolina. The game proceeded without incident, and on a rain-soaked New Year's Day, Oregon State won, 20–16. More than seventy players and coaches from both teams would soon join the military, including Duke's forty-nine-year-old head coach, Wallace Wade. In 1944, one of the Duke players, Charles Haynes, was gravely wounded in Italy but was carried to safety by Frank Parker, who had played for Oregon State.[1]

On New Year's Day, Franklin Roosevelt and his guest for the holidays, British prime minister Winston Churchill, attended church before laying a wreath at the tomb of George Washington at Mount Vernon. Later that evening they signed a declaration, along with twenty-six other nations allied against the Axis powers, that built upon the Atlantic Charter signed months before off the coast of Newfoundland. Using a term that would become an institutional reality four years later, the "United Nations," the declaration concluded that a "complete victory over their enemies is essential to defend life, liberty, independence, and religious freedom," and affirmed their opposition to the "savage and brutal forces seeking to subjugate the world." Soviet ambassador Maxim Litvinov and Chinese foreign affairs minister T. V. Soong also signed the document, pledging to "preserve human rights and justice in their own lands as well as in other lands."[2]

As the nation nervously celebrated New Year's Day, news from foreign battlefields brought home the worsening plight of the American military. On January 2, the Japanese took Manila, forcing U.S. troops in the Philippines to retreat to a peninsula facing the South China Sea whose name would soon be familiar—Bataan. In the intense fighting, the struggling American troops found themselves outgunned and unprepared. The backwardness of the U.S. Army was in full evidence on January 16, when the last horse-mounted cavalry charge in American history took place in the village of Morong. The troops holding out in Bataan found their backs truly against the wall.

Football games could be moved to accommodate worries about new attacks, but the nation's capital could not, and the city quickly went on the defensive. One observer noted that Washington, D.C., "is a town where barricades suddenly appear in streets that bore heavy traffic. Soldiers stand guard at doors . . . fences are suddenly erected to block off sidewalks . . . anti-aircraft guns sprout on roofs where starlings roosted." When America entered World War I, the city's population was thirty-eight thousand; by 1942 it was a quarter million. "Here is a strictly artificial city," noted *Life*, "the only major capital in the world that produces nothing but government." The capital was already the most expensive city in America to live in. According to the Bureau of Labor Statistics, a four-person family required $1,633 a year to afford basic "maintenance living" costs for food, clothing, and housing in Washington, compared to $1,628 in New York City. Washington's housing costs were the highest in the nation, followed by another city overrun with war workers—Detroit. Washington already was home to one hundred thousand jobholders, and another eighty-five thousand would arrive soon. So many people moving to Washington created a massive housing shortage and escalating prices. A *New Yorker* cartoon depicted three men sharing the same bed, one asking another, "Planning to be in Washington long, Mr. Bellow?"

At a late January press conference, Roosevelt lamented the "parasites" in Washington who had no real war duties but liked the district's schools and lived in large homes. He warned that if they did not leave town to relieve the housing crisis, he might use his emergency war powers to take over office buildings, hotels, and even private homes. *New York Times* columnist Arthur Krock mused that if FDR could not find a solution to the "parasites" in D.C., "it might be suggested that the entire 'headache' be turned over to General Hershey and the Selective Service for analysis and remedy."[3]

The White House itself quickly became a sealed fortress. Guards were stationed at every gate, and the Secret Service's ring around the chief executive grew. To protect the president, Treasury secretary Henry Morgenthau suggested building an immense, five-story windowless building on Pennsylvania Avenue connected to the White House by tunnels to serve as a shelter in case of enemy attack. When Roosevelt got wind of the plan, he rejected it as "crazy as hell." But the president already had a secure destination to go nearby. A seven-hundred-foot-long tunnel was hurriedly built in late 1941 that connected the White House to an eleven-hundred-square-foot shelter deep under the Treasury Building, which was stocked with water, two hundred pounds of food, and twelve beds. Shortly after Pearl Harbor, construction also began beneath the new East Wing of the White House on a sixteen-hundred-square-foot shelter protected by seven-foot-thick concrete walls and a nine-foot-thick ceiling. Secret Service agents could wheel Roosevelt there quickly in case of an attack. It eventually became the Presidential Emergency Operations Center, the primary location to which all subsequent presidents could be evacuated in the event of an emergency.[4]

The talk in Washington during the first week of January concerned the president's upcoming State of the Union address. While FDR's speech of December 8, 1941, reverberates down the years, few remember the longer speech he gave to Congress in January, which laid out the details of how the nation would wage and pay for the war. In terms of policy, it was one of the most significant State of the Union addresses ever. Shortly after noon on January 6, FDR ignored the Secret Service, which was advising him to deliver the speech from the White House, and went to Capitol Hill to do it in person. In a thirty-six-minute oration that was seldom interrupted by applause, Roosevelt declared, "The militarists of Berlin and Tokyo started this war. But the massed, angered forces of common humanity will end it." The president said that the nation must outproduce the Axis powers—"The United States must build planes and tanks and guns and ships to the utmost of our national capacity."

What he meant by "utmost" was astounding. Rather than speak in general terms about production goals, the president set specific targets: 60,000 planes, 45,000 tanks, 20,000 anti-aircraft guns, and 6 million dead-weight tons of merchant ships—in 1942 alone. His targets for 1943 were even more ambitious—125,000 planes, 75,000 tanks, 35,000 anti-aircraft guns, and 10 million tons of ships. As he announced these numbers, gasps could be heard in the House chamber. Roosevelt offered the overwhelming production figures, he said, in order to "give the Japanese and the Nazis a little idea of just what they accomplished in the attack at Pearl Harbor."[5]

In a policy that would echo through the century down to the present day, Roosevelt wanted to build a military force of such magnitude that it would overwhelm the enemy. One magazine reported that if the tanks Roosevelt envisioned being built in the next two years were placed front to back, the line would extend from New York to Salt Lake City. While that was an exaggeration, British general Frederick Morgan wrote in *Life* magazine that the Americans had "decided to make the biggest and best war ever seen."[6]

If the numbers of planes and tanks produced gasps among members of Congress, the amount of money Roosevelt proposed to spend was equally shocking. The president said the federal budget for the next fiscal year would require $59 billion in total spending (of which war spending accounted for $52.7 billion), almost twice the size of the previous fiscal year's budget. Roosevelt wanted to manufacture the arms necessary not only for American troops "but also for the armies, navies, and air forces fighting on our side."

Such numbers were outlandish, unheard-of. The *Economist* described Roosevelt's budget as "stupendous" and "astronomical." During the 1920s, the federal government had spent roughly $3 billion per year, and in the mid-1930s, budget hawks were dismayed when the federal budget rose to

$8 billion. These new sums, the *New York Times* editorialized, were "too huge to carry any real meaning to the mind." Roosevelt's first wartime budget worked out to $1,550 per household, an amount greater than the yearly income of two-thirds of American families. He proposed to spend $21 billion more than the total value of all the securities on the New York Stock Exchange, and an amount equal to the dollar value of all the products turned out in 1939 by all 184,000 of the nation's factories.[7]

He added that the budget deficit for the year would be approximately $35 billion and that the accumulated federal debt would exceed $110 billion by the end of the fiscal year. Roosevelt reiterated that "we cannot outfight our enemies alone unless, at the same time, we outproduce our enemies." Rather than merely making a "few more" tanks and ships, the president wanted to "outproduce them overwhelmingly, so that there can be no question of our ability to provide a crushing superiority of equipment in any theater of the world war."[8]

Roosevelt's prose was no more restrained than his wallet. A victory for Hitler would mean that "the Holy Bible and the Cross of Mercy would be displaced by *Mein Kampf* and the swastika and the naked sword." The nation's war objectives repeated his Four Freedoms speech of 1941: "establishing and securing freedom of speech, freedom of religion, freedom from want, freedom from fear everywhere in the world." Compromise with evil, the president told his listeners, was not acceptable, "only total victory" would suffice. FDR also warned against "complacency," and urged Americans not to be defeatist or divided: "We must be particularly vigilant against racial discrimination in any of its ugly forms. Hitler will try again to breed mistrust and suspicion between one individual and another, one group with another, one race and another."[9]

Many members of Congress were deeply impressed with the president's performance. It was "worthy in all respects of the greatest crisis this nation has faced," said Democratic senator Joseph O'Mahoney of Wyoming. Carl Vinson, chair of the House Naval Affairs Committee, called it "one of the greatest messages ever given by the President to a Congress." House majority leader John W. McCormack went even further, declaring it "one of the greatest speeches of all times," adding: "Without regard to our religious convictions, we can all thank God that in this crisis he gave us as our leader

Franklin D. Roosevelt." Some Republicans were not as impressed. Senator Charles McNary of Oregon felt it was a "scrappy speech" but underscored how the war ahead was "going to cost a mountain of money." Representative James Wadsworth of New York was appalled by the amounts of money Roosevelt intended to spend, saying "it's too astronomical for me." Wadsworth thought the president "doesn't ever intend to quit spending money."[10]

The president's speech was heard by a larger radio audience than any other midday broadcast, except for the Pearl Harbor speech. *Life* noted how the war had given Roosevelt a "honeymoon" with his political opponents, but warned that soon enough, "the dead cats and the low punches will fill the air again and under the cover of honest criticism the men who hate Roosevelt will throw everything they've got into a desperate effort to un-horse him."[11]

At the moment, however, even business leaders were reluctant to "un-horse" the president. Although Roosevelt and many titans of industry despised each other—in 1936, he had called them "economic royalists" who had "created a new despotism and wrapped it in the robes of legal sanction"—in 1942 he needed their experience and, most important, their production facilities. They, in turn, tended to forget the eternal virtues of laissez-faire economics and limited government when massive military contracts became available. The relationship the two sides forged in the early days of the war provided the blueprint for war production and an uneasy alliance between government and business that would long survive the war. Rather than build an industrial foundation from scratch, the government mostly relied on the existing foundation devoted to consumer goods, which could be retooled and converted to producing armaments. This unique approach, a planned economy jointly directed by Washington bureaucrats and large corporations, was the essence of the American military production effort, and it showed how industrial capitalism and democracy could coexist, to each one's benefit, in the war crisis.

One American industrialist, Henry Ford, found himself in an awkward position after America entered the war. Not only had Ford staunchly opposed the New Deal, he had a long history of embracing far-right causes. In the early 1920s he had written *The International Jew: The World's Foremost Problem,* a meandering anti-Semitic rant claiming, among other things, that "poor in his masses, [the Jew] yet controls the world's finances." In *Mein Kampf,* an admiring Adolf Hitler had referred to Ford as a "great man." Ford apologized in 1927 for "the harm I have unintentionally committed" with his writings, but his company maintained a plant in Cologne, Germany, and in 1938, Ford was awarded the Grand Cross of the German Eagle, the highest honor bestowed by Hitler to a foreigner. By the early 1940s he had distanced himself from Hitler, and after Pearl Harbor he supported the American war effort. He soon graced the cover of *Time* as a "Mass Producer," a vital figure in making the planes and tanks necessary for victory. Yet few knew that when the nation entered the war, the German Army was using over 350,000 Ford trucks.[12]

Another business leader desperately wanting to be perceived as patriotic was IBM's Thomas J. Watson, who took out a full-page ad in national magazines proclaiming:

> The Japanese attack on the United States instantly changed our trend of thought in this country. Before that attack, some of us thought in terms of "I," others in terms of "we." Neither of those terms expresses our feelings today. "I" represents only one person. "We" may mean only two or a few persons. Our slogan now is WE-ALL, which means every loyal individual in the United States. We are facing a long, hard job, but when the U.S. decides to fight for a cause, it is in terms of WE-ALL, and nothing can or will stop us. . . . Our commander in chief can be certain that WE-ALL are back of him, determined to protect our country, our form of government, and the freedoms we cherish.

Perhaps one reason Watson made such a public display was that the punch card machines used by the German government in census taking and locating Jewish citizens were manufactured by a Berlin-based IBM subsidiary, Dehomag. When the Berlin plant was dedicated in 1934, IBM executives stood by Dehomag's founder, Willy Heidinger, who boasted that the company was like "a physician" who "dissects, cell by cell, the German cultural body." The cards Dehomag created, Heidinger said, could be used by his nation's "Physician, Adolf Hitler, with the material he needs for his examination." Dehomag was proud that its work helped Hitler "take corrective procedures" if he found the health of the German people to be jeopardized, and concluded, "Our characteristics are deeply rooted in our race." The German people must cherish those racial traits "like a holy shrine which we will—and must—keep pure." In 1937, in recognition of the assistance provided by Watson and Dehomag, Hitler had awarded him the Grand Cross medal. Watson returned the medal in 1940 and began working to repair his damaged image at home.[13]

FDR sent his actual budget to Congress on January 7. He wanted to finance the war with "a balanced financial program" and did not shrink from the obvious. In calling for an additional $7 billion in federal taxes, Roosevelt used words that would be barely conceivable from a modern president: "I am confident that all Americans will be proud to contribute their utmost in taxes." He saw taxes not just as a revenue producer but also as a way to decrease inflation: less money in taxpayers' pockets meant less demand for goods. To help with the effort, Treasury secretary Morgenthau commissioned Irving Berlin to write a song supporting the new taxes. Berlin's "I Paid My Income Tax Today" proved not as popular as another of his songs that was recorded that year (by Bing Crosby in May), "White Christmas."[14]

Yet even in the midst of the emergency, FDR was concerned with enlarging some social programs. He called for a $2 billion increase in old-age, disability, and hospitalization payments, to be paid for by raising employee and employer contributions to Social Security. Even the conservative columnist Ralph Robey was on board with the administration's tax policies, though he cautioned, "If every single penny of income of every person in the United States who makes $5,000 or more a year were taken by the government, it would not be as much as the President asked for in new taxes." Robey believed a national sales tax would be necessary, but he warned: "Even if we get the $9 billion, that leaves $35 billion to be borrowed, a sum almost 50 percent greater than the entire amount borrowed by the U.S. Government during the whole of the last war." The ultimate enemy, according to Robey, was inflation: "Even bombing causes less suffering to a people than runaway inflation."[15]

FDR's call for the largest tax increase in history aroused little opposition in Congress. Virginia senator Carter Glass, the powerful Appropriations Committee chair, said, "We will make every appropriation the President asks for," adding "Congress will do anything that is necessary to smash the Axis." In the first week of 1942, Congress seemed ready to accede to the president's wishes. The Republican leader in the House, Joseph W. Martin Jr. of Massachusetts, told a national radio audience on January 12 that "there are no partisan lines in this determination of the American people to win this war." He then suggested the president "might do well to avail himself of the splendid talent and experience of men like former President Herbert Hoover, Wendell Willkie, Alf Landon, and Thomas E. Dewey." Hoover, Martin suggested, should be appointed head of Price Control, since that "would give the Nation greater confidence than those who now exercise that control."[16]

Instead of his political opponents, Roosevelt preferred more conventional appointees. On January 13 he named Donald M. Nelson, a former executive with Sears and Roebuck, to head the newly created War Production Board (WPB), with authority to make the final decisions on matters relating to procurement and production. On that day, Nelson recalled, "the awful realization was slowly coming over the country that America was losing a war." Supporters and critics of the administration seemed to agree that Nelson's appointment solved one of their overriding concerns over the diluted and dysfunctional effort the administration had made so far. The *New York Times* editorialized that Roosevelt's executive order gave Nelson "powers and responsibilities as great as those given to Bernard M. Baruch as director of the War Industries Board by President Wilson in the first world war," and that it was his "greatest delegation of power since 1933." After his appointment to head the WPB, Nelson abolished the Office of Production Management (OPM), saying, "Debating societies are out—we are going to have action!" But his powers were actually less than they seemed. The Office of Price Administration still controlled prices, and the military purchasing bureaus refused to relinquish their considerable authority to a civilian. To succeed, Nelson would have to maneuver through a variety of military and bureaucratic minefields. In no uncertain terms, Nelson understood a sobering truth: "We were really in trouble."[17]

Raymond Moley, a former Roosevelt aide who became a staunch critic of the administration, was shocked by FDR's budget proposals. "Simply put, the core of this philosophy is that dollars have ceased to have meaning in our great emergency," he wrote. "We might as well talk about ergs or foot-pounds as dollars in discussing what we are going to expend on the war. . . . Like the witches in Macbeth, we'll do and do and do. Just what we'll do we don't exactly know, but we shall be very earnest and self-sacrificing about it." Suggesting that the president's numbers were wildly unrealistic, Moley reminded his readers that "finance is not the handmaiden of war or a shady camp follower of armies. It is a legitimate spouse, an integral part of order and law. Our minds must comprehend it. For while dollars do not make life, dollars, as measure of value, help us to plan life."[18]

Emil Schram, the president of the New York Stock Exchange, was more muted in his assessment. "The millions of people in this country must be made to understand why our free enterprise system deserves to be perpetuated." He knew what kept investors awake at night: "They fear that we may lose some of our cherished liberties instead of preserving them" and that "our private economy may be radically altered or impaired" by the war. Schram got to the point that would justify much of the mobilization effort: "I am aware of the claims which are already being made—that it will be an all-powerful government and not industry which will be responsible for the results which finally will win the war." Roger Babson, the Prohibition Party presidential candidate in 1940, dismissed early complaints about commodity shortages and taxes, warning, "We ain't seen nothing yet." Like many others, Babson called 1942 "the most important year in our nation's history."[19]

The war intruded on a nation in which white supremacy was deeply ingrained in every walk of life. Despite pleas from African American leaders, Army Chief of Staff General George Marshall and Secretary of War Henry Stimson refused to consider desegregating the military. Marshall thought overturning a practice that had been "established by the American people through custom and habit" would hurt the "morale" of white troops. Stimson, who believed the nation was "suffering from the persistent legacy of the original sin of slavery," wrote in his diary that he was satisfied to create "colored divisions" even though his own experience had taught him the "incompetency of colored troops." "What these foolish leaders of the colored race are seeking is at the bottom social equality"—a vain hope, he thought, due to the "impossibility of race mixture by marriage." He agreed to an "all-Negro" division of the army, to be trained at Fort Huachuca, Arizona, and a "Negro aviation squadron" that would be trained at Tuskegee, Alabama. Nor did Roosevelt support changing the racial makeup of the military, although he had told civil rights leader A. Philip Randolph in 1940 that he saw no reason African Americans should not be musicians on board naval ships, "because they're darned good at it."[20]

One of Stimson's assistants, Judge William Hastie, hosted a meeting of African American leaders to consider the problems facing "Negro Citizens in a World at War" that included NAACP executive secretary Walter White, National Council of Negro Women founder Mary McLeod Bethune, and Negro Employment and Training Branch director Robert Weaver at the Harlem YMCA in mid-January. Lester B. Granger of the National Urban League told delegates that certain southern Democratic congressmen were "using their power of appropriation to force out of the government persons who have shown they were free of racial prejudice." Hastie asked his audience how many thought African Americans were "whole-heartedly, unselfishly, all-out in support of the present war effort?" Only five of the fifty-six attendees believed this to be true, producing a backlash of anger and ridicule from African American newspapers, which claimed that the vote did not accurately portray the sentiment of most American blacks. George Schuyler of the *Pittsburgh Courier* wrote that African Americans were "100 percent" behind the war effort because they had no other choice. Yet the vote was more revealing than Schuyler wanted to admit. Later in the month, the *Crisis,* the official paper of the NAACP, declared it would not endorse the war effort: "Now is not the time to be silent about the breaches of democracy here in our own land. . . . If all the people are called to gird and sacrifice for freedom, then it must be for freedom for everyone, everywhere, not merely for those under the Hitler heel." Claiming that a "lily-white army cannot fight for a free world," that paper called upon the U.S. to fight "for a world in which lynching, brutality, terror, humiliation, and degradation through service and discrimination shall have no place."[21]

The racial realities within the nation's military were on display that month in Alexandria, Louisiana. The trouble began outside an all-black movie theater in Alexandria's "Little Harlem" section on January 10, when a white MP arrested an African American soldier. When two African American MPs arrived, an argument ensued between the white and black MPs. The anger boiled over into violence, and over sixty MPs with the Fifth Army, dozens of city police, and at least ten state police were called in to contain a riot over a four-block area. Before it was over, thirty people had been shot or beaten. Over three thousand black troops were rounded up and restricted to their military barracks in Camps Livingston and Claiborne. A preliminary War Department finding concluded that "although a show of force may have been justified to disperse the excited crowd which gathered when a colored soldier resisted arrest by a military policeman," the incident escalated because civilian and military police indulged "in indiscriminate and unnecessary shooting." The FBI concluded, "The Southern Negro soldier is not as retiring or subservient as would be expected." Local black citizens disputed the official army finding that no one had been killed, claiming that as many as ten black soldiers died in the violence. One black soldier at Camp Claiborne decried "the way these Southern MP's treat us," and vowed he would "rather desert and be placed before a firing squad and shot down before fighting for America."[22]

The mixing of white and black soldiers was one thing, but the distribution of the nation's blood supply was another. After Pearl Harbor, Americans feverishly wanted to contribute in some way, and donating blood seemed a natural reaction. There had been twelve hundred individual blood donations in the weeks before Pearl Harbor but fifteen thousand in the first weeks of 1942. At Red Cross centers across the nation, African Americans were told they could not donate blood because white soldiers preferred to have blood transfusions from their own race. The Red Cross, President Roosevelt, and the military were besieged with criticism: soldiers might die needlessly because 15 million potential blood donors had been refused. One editor asked, "What fifth columnist could Hitler possibly hire to do a job equal to that?" Reacting to the public outrage, on January 21 the Red Cross announced a change in its policy. The organization would permit African Americans to donate blood, but the white and black blood supplies would be segregated "so that those receiving transfusions may be given plasma from blood of their own race." Even after the *Journal of the American Medical Association* noted that there was no scientific evidence to suggest that the blood plasma of one race was any different from that of another and called the policy "a grievous affront to the largest minority group in our country," the Red Cross stood by its decision.[23]

The matter of separate blood supplies was an issue of dire national importance to Congressman John Rankin from Mississippi, one of the nation's most vocal white supremacists. Calling the Red Cross "the greatest institution of its kind the world has ever seen," Rankin lavishly praised the organization for opposing the effort to "pump Negro blood into the veins of our wounded white boys, regardless of the direful effect it might have on them or their children." On the House floor, Rankin warned of another danger to national security: "Members of the police force have told me repeatedly of the communist dances they have witnessed and of seeing these communist women dancing with Negro men, while the male communists danced with Negro women."[24]

If the military and the Red Cross remained resilient to desegregation, perhaps another area of American life could be transformed. The war industries that began to dot the landscape provided an opportunity for African Americans to contribute to the war effort and, in the process, fight for equal pay and hiring practices. In 1941, as the European and Pacific wars escalated, A. Philip Randolph had pressed FDR into signing Executive Order 8802, which prohibited racial discrimination in defense plants, yet this hardly changed employment opportunities in many areas of the country. The Bureau of Employment Security reported that between September 1941 and February 1942, more than half of the available job openings nationwide were closed to African Americans.[25]

At a small arms manufacturing plant in St. Louis, only 3 percent of the 20,500 workers were African American, and there were no African American women employed at all. The company responded to protests by saying it would hire one hundred black women as "plant matrons," assigned to clean the lavatories. Stories like this moved Randolph to comment that many war industries "trade in the dangerous business of race hatred as usual." He urged African American communities in Washington, D.C., and Chicago to conduct their own "blackouts" to show their "resentment against the Negro status of half-man in America."[26]

On January 25, Cleo Wright, a thirty-year-old African American cotton mill worker, was arrested in Sikeston, Missouri, for assaulting a white woman. The victim said Wright had stabbed her, and when police officers tried to arrest him, a struggle ensued, and an officer shot Wright three times. The wounded prisoner was taken to a local hospital and treated before being jailed. When word spread throughout Sikeston of Wright's arrest, alongside rumors of his "confession," a mob of some three hundred men took Wright from the jail, tied his feet to the back of a truck, and dragged him through the "Negro district" of Sikeston. Afterward, they poured gasoline on his naked body and set it on fire. The *Sikeston Herald* noted that the town "stands charged before the world with permitting a mob to take a prisoner away from officers, dragging him to death," but defended the "passions of those people who were aroused by a most atrocious crime committed against one of our unoffending and helpless women." Nothing, the paper claimed, that the mob "could have inflicted on the human beast who entered the house of Mrs. Sturgeon could be too severe," adding defiantly that, if anything, "we are guilty of not keeping clear the lines which must separate the white and black races from each other." A columnist in the *Sikeston Standard* wrote, "It gives us the gripe in our bowels to read in some papers that the lynching of a negro brute in Sikeston was a blot on the State of Missouri and that Sikeston should hang her head in shame. ... We are making no excuses for the act, as Sikeston citizens must protect the wives of soldier boys who are in the Army." Anyone condemning the lynching or advocating that the law should "take its course," the columnist went on, "is not fit for the dogs to use as a post."[27]

In the wake of Wright's lynching, the NAACP sent a team of investigators to the town to document the racial "attitudes" among the town's white residents. Their portrait could have applied to countless other communities. Local whites were openly upset that a young African American clerk at a Sikeston drugstore had not waited to be spoken to by a white customer, but had initiated conversation directly. Several whites warned, "That boy is just looking for a lynching." Friends of the clerk took him out of town for his own protection. Other white residents commented that "Negroes are naturally vicious" and that "violence is necessary to keep them subservient." The investigators found in Sikeston a widespread sentiment that "killing a Negro is not a crime like killing a white man."[28]

Walter White of the NAACP alerted the president to Wright's murder and demanded a federal response. "This is a most crushing blow to Negroes which could top repeated rebuffs, segregation, and discrimination suffered by Negroes in the war effort." He hoped FDR would propose legislation to make lynching a federal offense. Previous efforts to get the president to support anti-lynching legislation had always failed because Roosevelt did not wish to antagonize southern Democrats in Congress. (Throughout the twentieth century, federal anti-lynching legislation failed over two hundred times. As of 2019, the most recent attempt passed the U.S. Senate but had not made it to the floor of the House.) Yet in the wake of the Wright murder, some African Americans wondered what the point was in fighting the war. James Rodgers of Spartanburg, South Carolina, wrote to the president that he wanted "to know what the Negro is fighting for in this war. They fought in the last war" only to return home to "lynchings and racial prejudice." James Stewart, president of the Universal Negro Improvement Association, told a crowd in Cincinnati, "We will remember Missouri, then Pearl Harbor."[29]

In a time of patriotic fervor, African Americans who appeared unsupportive of the war risked charges of disloyalty or even treason, yet pledging blind support in a time of racial repression seemed hypocritical. The dilemma was captured in a letter to the *Pittsburgh Courier* in late January by twenty-six-year old James G. Thompson of Wichita, who wondered, "Should I sacrifice my life to live half American? Would it be demanding too much to demand full citizenship rights in exchange for sacrificing my life?" He suggested that in addition to adopting the "V" sign for victory, African Americans should adopt the "Double V" sign: "victory over our enemies from without, the second V for victory over our enemies from within." After the *Courier* promoted the Double V campaign, African Americans all over the country endorsed the effort, and it became a symbolic marker for people supporting the war effort but fighting for civil rights at home.[30]

After being labeled "enemy aliens" shortly after Pearl Harbor, many Italian Americans bristled at the suggestion they were not patriotic. In 1940, there were over 1.6 million Italian-born people living in the United States, and almost a million of them had obtained American citizenship. In January, trade union leaders asked FDR to remove the "intolerable stigma of being branded as 'enemy aliens'" from Italian nationals who had "formally declared their intention of becoming American citizens before Pearl Harbor." The resolution, for the time, fell on deaf ears within an administration struggling to define which groups within the nation posed realistic threats to national security. Within weeks, Attorney General Biddle announced that all Japanese, German, and Italian "enemy aliens" were being removed from the coastal areas around Los Angeles and San Francisco to zones fifty miles inland. Over ten thousand Italian Americans on the West Coast were forced to leave their homes, and six hundred thousand others had strict curfews.[31]

The nation's racial tensions unfolded at an ominous juncture in the war. On January 20, in a villa outside Berlin named Wannsee, Reinhard Heydrich and Adolf Eichmann gave official sanction to the term *final solution* to denote the German government's plan to exterminate 11 million European Jews. In the United States, the Committee for a Jewish Army, whose members included radio commentator Lowell Thomas and theologian Paul Tillich, stated that "Jews of the world over should be given a chance to express and to demonstrate their solidarity with the great American nation" and be allowed to "form an army of Palestinian and stateless Jews" to fight alongside the Allies in the Middle East.[32]

In mid-January, the war in the Atlantic was demonstrating how far the American military effort had to go before it could ever launch an offensive campaign against Germany. Dönitz had dispatched five U-boats, each with between fourteen and twenty-two torpedoes, to the East Coast of the United States, as well as at least ten additional boats. Within two weeks, nearly three dozen U.S. ships, totaling over two hundred thousand tons, were sunk between Newfoundland and Bermuda, and on January 19 a single German boat sank eight ships in New York Harbor in a span of twelve hours. German boats used the lit silhouettes provided by the skylines of cities, from New York to Miami, to find their targets, and nothing seemed to stand in their way. One of the U-boat commanders, Reinhard Hardegen, brought his vessel into New York's Lower Bay, and on January 14 stood on the ship's bridge to behold the spectacular New York City skyline. "I cannot describe the feeling," he recalled, "but it was unbelievably beautiful and great." Hardegen added, "I would have given away a kingdom for this moment if I had one," for the honor of being the first German to see "the coast of the USA." Hardegen died in June 2018 at the age of 105.[33]

For millions living in major cities along the coasts, these boats were a serious threat and demonstrated how Germany's control of the Atlantic could have catastrophic consequences. Many were certain that the terror that had befallen London would eventually come to the United States. William L. Shirer, author and radio commentator, told a luncheon gathering at New York's Biltmore Hotel that he believed Hitler would launch a "token" bombing of the city with 150 bombers that would take off from France. The fear of air attacks launched from Europe or from German boats led the Metropolitan Museum of Art to lease a private house as a refuge for some of its priceless art collections during the war. The museum's director, Francis Henry Taylor, refused to divulge the location of the house but noted it was "built of the most modern steel and concrete construction." (After the war, the refuge's location was revealed: Whitemarsh Hall outside of Philadelphia.) Fear was palpable elsewhere on the East Coast as well, especially in Washington, D.C., where the Phillips Collection sent forty paintings to the William Rockhill Nelson Gallery of Art in Kansas City, including Renoir's *Luncheon of the Boating Party* and works by Picasso, van Gogh, and Matisse. A painting that Edward Hopper completed on January 21, *Nighthawks*, a portrait of four anonymous figures inside a New York City diner late at night, would become one of the most iconic images of the twentieth century. Although the memory is of a nation coming together in a time of war, Hopper's depiction of urban detachment is one that endures. "Unconsciously," Hopper said, "probably, I was painting the loneliness of a large city." *Nighthawks* was purchased months later by the Art Institute of Chicago for $3,000.[34]

The Southern Governors Conference in Miami received warnings from officials with Civilian Defense and the Office of Production Management. "It is possible and probable," one administrator told the governors, "that Nazi planes will pay us a visit in the not-distant future." Reed Landis, an assistant to Civil Defense director Fiorello La Guardia, was certain that German planes would concentrate their attacks on large cities rather than industrial centers. The point, he reasoned, was to cause "hysteria" and depress morale in a nation where Landis already saw "unmistakable signs of fifth column activity." Another official said suspicious markings had been found on rooftops and in cornfields "with no explanation forthcoming," adding to the fear that the enemy had agents deep within the countryside. John H. Ohly, a special assistant to the undersecretary of war, warned that every American should be prepared for an imminent attack. "The next blackout may not be a practice one," he said. The fears were compounded when a Dornier 217, a new Nazi bomber with a range of forty-five hundred miles, crashed over northeastern England on January 19. British crews got a close look at the plane's seventy-two-foot wingspan. In addition to being able to bomb deep inside Russia, the plane was capable of reaching the American mainland from a takeoff point in occupied France. Meanwhile, the publisher E. P. Dutton encouraged citizens to buy the *Air Raid Safety Manual* because "many authorities believe the disruptive value of an air raid against American homes is worth a desperate gamble on Hitler's part." If people did not know what to do in case of an air or gas attack, "it is simply American horse-sense as well as your sacred duty to your family and your country to find out."[35]

Colonel George J. B. Fisher, of the War Department's Chemical Warfare Service, worried that Americans were not prepared for the terror awaiting them. On January 13, he told a national radio audience, "Anyone who has heard the whine of an aerial bomb, falling at a speed that mounts to 600 miles per hour, has felt the urgent need of a bomb-proof shelter." He described how new, heavier bombs required more sophisticated shelters and explained the scientific aspects of a bomb's detonation in chilling detail: "This detonation is, technically, the reaction occurring when a suitable stimulus is applied to a relatively large quantity of trinitrotoluene, amatol, or other high explosive. . . . The entire mass is converted, almost instantaneously, into other more stable substances, principally gases," a reaction that "subjects the bomb case to heat as high as 20,000 degrees centigrade; it distends the case to one and a half times its normal size; and when the limit of expansion is reached, splits the case into a shower of sharp-edged splinters or fragments which may run, on the average, to about the size of a man's thumb." He declined to explain how worried listeners could build a satisfactory bomb shelter, suggesting they consult the Office of Civil Defense for the latest advice.[36]

Despite the incessant anxiety, life went on. People still went to restaurants and movies, and some even took vacations. The City of Miami did its part to try to attract tourists from the frozen North—"Above all," a national ad read, "the city of Miami knows how to do one job surpassingly well—to take our God-given warmth and sunshine, and to convert it into rest and recreation and healthful living for the benefit of thousands of visitors." The pitch ended, "As war's strain and worry grow, there'll be an ever greater need for a warm, wholesome place where those who have earned a brief respite can come to relax. . . . We think it's important to keep on supplying the best vacations in the world to those who need and deserve them."[37]

While government and military leaders anguished over how to pay for and wage the war, some government officials considered what the nation and the world should look like when it was over, assuming the Allies won. The National Resources Planning Board, chaired by Frederic Delano, the president's uncle, distributed a pamphlet written by Harvard economist Alvin H. Hansen titled *After the War—Full Employment.*" Hansen wrote: "The fact is that many people dread to think of what is coming." In his view, "a military victory for democracies is not enough" because if those nations then "muddle through another decade of economic frustration and mass unemployment," the results could be "social disintegration" and more war. While Hansen was careful to say, "We do not want government to run the whole show" and that he did not advocate "a totalitarian state," he argued for a society that invested in "urban redevelopment, flood control, reforestation, public health programs, express highways, federal aid to education, and old-age pensions." By doing so, he hoped, the nation could approach full employment and also "safeguard political freedom." Hansen was confident that war could produce technological developments and new products and processes that would ultimately improve the postwar standard of living.[38]

The National Labor Relations Board, building on Hansen's work, issued a report to Congress in January predicting that pent-up demand from saving and rationing could create a "post-war boom." The most important component, the board believed, to "a better life for all" was "full employment," which was "the key to national prosperity." Without it, once the war ended and the war production machine ground to a halt, the nation could well return to the Great Depression. The lofty goal of "full employment" would not generate much opposition in theory; the issue was how to achieve it. Some advocated public jobs to fill the void in recessions, while others wanted the government to allow markets to determine the level of employment and wages. The *Wall Street Journal* worried that the administration would use the war emergency to "make permanent changes in American social and economic institutions" and, alarmed by the rising level of government spending such programs promised, warned that "there are no places to which these planners will not go." If government were not curbed, the paper warned, "every American man and woman may be a college graduate at public expense!"[39]

After a decade of high unemployment (still at 7 percent in January 1942), organized labor briefly considered the wage gains that the war promised. But from the president's standpoint, higher wages threatened to ignite runaway inflation. On January 12, FDR signed an executive order establishing the National War Labor Board (NWLB). Created in response to a seminal labor-management pact in which leaders of the American Federation of Labor and the Congress of Industrial Organizations agreed to a no-strike pledge for the duration of the war, the NWLB had a mandate to settle labor disputes in ways acceptable to both sides. The board was composed of twelve commissioners appointed by the president, of whom four represented the general public, four represented employees, and four represented employers. FDR's order gave the NWLB authority to impose arbitration in labor disputes, and if arbitration failed, the president could seize plants and factories. When he initially agreed to the no-strike pledge, CIO president Philip Murray said his members were "ready and eager to do their utmost to defend our country," but that they also "expect reciprocity, and that no selfish advantage will be taken" by their employers. With the wage freezes and production increases that were soon to come, that initial patriotic pact between labor and management collapsed. Despite the "no-strike" pledge, in 1942 there were 2,938 strikes involving nearly 850,000 workers, equating to the loss of more than 4 million idled workdays.[40]

The commodity most crucial to the war effort was a mundane substance that most took for granted. As the *New York Times* reported, rubber was essential to almost every aspect of the war:

Tanks have rubber treads; the sharp edges of their interiors are cushioned with sponge rubber. Planes take off on rubber tires, have self-sealing, bulletproof gas tanks and fuel lines made of rubber. Airmen wear rubber-lined, electrically-heated suits for high-altitude bombing. Parachutists have special inner soles of foamed rubber to break the shock of dropping to earth at sixteen miles per hour. A battleship has 80 tons of rubber in her makeup . . . pontoon bridges are built on rubberized floats; gas masks made by the millions are fashioned of rubber. Our army has ordered miles of a new kind of assault wire sheathed with rubber—wire lighter and more flexible than any known before, so signal men can keep close behind advancing infantry. Soldiers march on millions of rubber heels; the Army is supplied by hundreds of thousands of rubber-tired trucks.

Ninety-eight percent of the rubber used in American factories—nearly 750 million tons in 1941—was imported from the Dutch East Indies and British West Indies. The sudden halt of these imports was one of the dire consequences of Pearl Harbor and the Japanese domination of the Pacific. The U.S. had produced just twelve thousand tons of synthetic rubber in 1941, and its stockpiles of about five hundred thousand tons would be depleted by midsummer. Since a new plantation needed at least seven years to become productive, three things were obvious from the beginning: rubber would have to be severely rationed, scrap rubber was desperately needed, and new ways to produce synthetic rubber would have to be found very soon.[41]

The nation suddenly found itself scrambling to save every pound of rubber. The production of rubber bands and pencil erasers was halted, and the rationing of automobile tires soon followed. On January 3, motorists were prohibited from buying new tires unless they could provide a certificate explaining how the new tires were essential for health or safety. Food delivery trucks pooled their supplies, and even requests for retreads soon required a certificate. For dozens of other everyday items such as gloves, hoses, and floor mats, Americans soon learned to live without or make do with what they already had. For one commodity, used or homemade products would simply not do, and a black market soon developed for condoms.[42]

In case anyone doubted how far the government would go in planning the war economy, in mid-January the OPM announced a program for rationing 450,000 new cars and 200,000 trucks. The federal government had first claim on these vehicles, then doctors, police, and others whose operations were considered essential. The National Automobile Dealers Association responded that forty-four thousand dealerships and five hundred thousand employees accepted the restrictions "as part of war." Meanwhile, state and local tire rationing boards began parceling out the month's allotment of 356,974 new tires, less than 10 percent of the number that had been produced monthly in 1941. These tires went to "essential" vehicles, which ruled out passenger cars, even hearses. Daniel J. Tobin, president of the International Brotherhood of Teamsters, thought the plan was "the most unreasonable program that has yet been devised by any government agency." A member of the Westfield, New Jersey, tire-rationing committee had his tires stolen while attending a committee meeting.[43]

In January the government also discussed a basic instrument of daily life. The notion of altering clocks for economic purposes had been controversial for many years, with farmers often opposing any changes that disrupted the rhythms of nature. The outbreak of war ended that discussion, and on January 20, FDR signed the National Daylight Savings Act. With an extra hour of daylight, experts predicted, the nation would save 736 million kilowatt hours of electricity. When railroad and airline companies wanted a different name for the new time rather than "daylight savings time," Roosevelt suggested "war time."[44]

Consumers reacted to FDR's war plans by stockpiling goods they suspected would soon be in short supply. Store managers across the nation watched customers purchase loads of linens, children's clothes, and women's corsets (which contained rubber). Sales in many department stores were 30 percent higher than in January 1941, and the Federal Reserve Bank estimated that stores in New York had increased sales by 17 percent in just the first week of 1942.[45]

As the nation's consumers adjusted to war, the upcoming baseball season presented its own challenge. Baseball commissioner Kenesaw Mountain Landis had written FDR asking whether the season should even go on. Roosevelt replied that it should, since "there will be fewer people unemployed and everybody will work longer hours," and they would need an enjoyable diversion. Many major leaguers, he knew, would be called into military service, but he thought the diminished quality of play would not "dampen the popularity of the sport."[46]

Baseball continued, and so did motion pictures. In addition to making a host of war-related movies aimed at boosting national morale, many Hollywood stars volunteered for service, while others worked to aid the war effort in different ways. One of the first casualties was a popular actor and friend of the president's who had attended a fireside chat broadcast in 1940. On January 16, a chartered plane carrying Carole Lombard crashed thirty miles southwest of Las Vegas. She was returning to California after helping sell defense bonds in Indianapolis. Her husband, Clark Gable, rented a plane to go to the crash site where a search was under way for survivors. He soon joined the Army Air Force.[47]

In the first weeks after Pearl Harbor, the nation's lawmakers should have had the sense to avoid self-serving political actions. Yet on January 21, Congress approved what *Life* called "the most ill-timed piece of legislation ever passed," the Civil Service Retirement Act. The bill, signed by Roosevelt three days later, gave pensions to members of Congress and the executive branch. Yet another pension bill, which would have provided benefits to widows, children, and parents of veterans, remained stalled in the Senate. At least one senator, Harry Byrd of Virginia, understood how this looked. "We are placing ourselves in a very unfortunate position," he told his colleagues, "if we vote ourselves pensions." The backlash was immediate. "American soldiers were dying in the grim siege of Bataan," wrote Roger Butterfield in *Life*, while Americans "read in their newspapers that Congress had voted itself a pension out of the U.S. Treasury." In Spokane, angry voters sent packages of old dentures and prosthetics to "indigent Congressmen." One poll showed that 83 percent of Americans opposed congressional pensions, and Congress repealed the act just two months later. But the political damage had been done, and with elections coming later in the year, the memory of the bill remained. Undersecretary of the Navy James Forrestal told Harold Ickes he was "truly nervous about the wartime setup" and worried that "unless things soon begin to go better here in Washington, citizens might march on the city to express their indignation."[48]

While Congress and the president exercised their wartime powers, one government official wielded a different kind of power that soon dominated the economic life of every American not in the military. To combat inflation, controls on the economy were necessary, and on January 27, the White House gave Office of Price Administration (OPA) director Leon Henderson the power to ration all retail goods. A few days later, his authority was extended to price and rent ceilings. The *New York Times* noted, "Mr. Henderson . . . will decide what civilians may buy for the duration of the war." Baselines were established at prevailing prices of goods between October 1 and 15, 1941, and Washington was quickly consumed with the issue of what constituted standard prices that would serve as reference points, or "parity." Maximum prices for, say, wheat, could not be set until wheat reached 110 percent of parity as well as several other restrictions. Henderson's rationing program began in earnest with the creation of eight thousand local rationing boards throughout the nation. Who got to sit on these local boards became an increasingly thorny issue as the year unfolded.[49]

Henderson had one of the most powerful and difficult jobs in Washington. American wartime history was not encouraging for those tasked with fighting inflation. During the twenty months that the U.S. was active in World War I, food prices increased 80 percent, while clothing prices more than doubled. In just six months in 1941, wholesale prices had risen 13 percent. If the massive war spending of 1942 brought runaway inflation, the effect on the domestic economy could be horrific, and the interest rates the government paid on its massive borrowing could be ruinous. After December 7, the OPA had begun to issue directives, such as asking sugar producers and refiners not to raise prices and requesting ceilings on egg and wheat prices. This was an early taste of what was to come.[50]

A Gallup poll taken in mid-January showed how many Americans supported Henderson's overall aims. When asked if government should have the power to determine what products should be made by individual businesses and what prices they could charge, 78 percent responded favorably. Two-thirds thought government should be able to tell workers which jobs they should perform, as well as decide their pay and how many hours they worked. A smaller but still sizeable majority, 61 percent, believed the government possessed the authority to order farmers to grow specific crops and determine the prices they would receive.[51]

Henderson knew it was important for the OPA head to be "humanized" in order to minimize anger at the agency's rules and regulations. The *New York Times* noted that he "has done so many things that at least one of them is almost certain to have aroused some resentment." That resentment was not long in coming. Addressing a convention of auto dealers in mid-January, Henderson laid out their prospects under rationing with brutal frankness: "Without question, some dealers will fall by the wayside. Some will fail, many employees will be dismissed. For the present their jobs will be liquidated." But, he added, "I anticipate that before long there will be work in defense production for every unemployed man." While he denied that the government might ration used cars or "commandeer" private automobiles, many dealers left the meeting feeling they had attended their own funeral. One of Henderson's proposals was that 130,000 cars produced in January should be held in storage for a year and the tires and rubber tubes they contained turned over to the OPA. The president of the dealers association called this "outrageous."[52]

In the first weeks after the declaration of war, Republicans struggled to function as the opposition party. At the New York Young Republican Club dinner in late January, thirty-nine-year-old Thomas E. Dewey, the district attorney of Manhattan who was introduced as the "next governor of New York," spelled out how he thought his party should approach the war: they would "agree that politics is at an end but will point out deficiencies, call for necessary changes and oppose unsound measures. Freedom is never served by the absence of opposition." In a sign of the bipartisan support for Roosevelt's war plans, on January 23 the House passed a military appropriations bill allocating $12 billion, mostly to airplane construction, without a dissenting vote.[53]

The war crisis demonstrated to many that the nation was woefully unprepared, and some business leaders blamed the country's public education system. H. W. Prentis Jr., former president of the National Association of Manufacturers, told an audience of college administrators that the nation's schools had not adequately equipped Americans to deal with its daunting challenges. "With all our emphasis on materialism," Prentis said, "education has been compelled to follow the crowd and teach concrete facts designed to help us make a living rather than emphasize the abstract principles that underlie and in the long run determine the whole course of human existence. But if our Republic is permanently to survive, I am convinced that our schools and colleges must now impregnate the minds of our citizens not only with knowledge of our political institutions, their history and how they work, but also with faith and pride in what these institutions stand for, whence they came and with how much travail of body and spirit they were created." He hoped that colleges would require more courses in American history and government. "Would that the present crisis might stir as many vigorous patriotic pens into action as have been wielded by the collectivist brethren of the academic world in decrying the achievements of the American Republic and advancing their own starry-eyed theories of government and economic organization!"[54]

The need for military personnel produced its own share of challenges. Before the war, the peacetime draft registration program had contained over 17 million names of male citizens between twenty-one and thirty-seven years old, and the American military in early 1942 had approximately 2 million personnel. In order to reach an army of 10 million, the War Department announced it would increase the size of the draft by registering everyone between the ages of twenty and forty-four, generating an additional 9 million names. The plan was to have 3.6 million soldiers in uniform by the end of the year.

Military leaders debated the ideal age from which to draw infantrymen. No paratroopers were currently over twenty-three years old. "The consensus appears to be that males under 21," wrote Frank Kluckhohn in the *New York Times*, "lacked sufficient sense of responsibility and tire more quickly than most in the 21–28 year range." That meant that American men born between 1914 and 1921 were the best candidates for military service. General Lewis B. Hershey, the director of the Selective Service, said that married men would continue to receive deferments in order to maintain "the family as the basic social unit" until the need to draft them "becomes much greater than it is at present." Hershey hoped to protect vital industries such as agriculture, but he added that industry should consider the "gradual but constant substitution of women for men who are fit to fight."[55]

The Army Recruiting and Induction Service ran ads telling "Men of 18 and 19" that they would "get a break" if they enlisted before the age of twenty. "A new Army ruling makes it possible for you to pick out any one of the eight combat branches in which you want to serve." Enlistees could choose the air force, armored force, cavalry, coast artillery, engineers, field artillery, infantry, or Signal Corps. "Whichever one you choose," the ad said, "you'll enjoy the comradeship of a splendid group of men."[56]

Even in the early days of the war, some industries were not ashamed to tout their wares with patriotic appeals that seemed to stretch reality. The New York Dress Institute ran an ad in which Martha Washington visits her husband at Valley Forge. The year 1778, the ad noted, "was a bitter winter of war. The newborn United States of America had undertaken what seemed to the world an impossible task." To aid in this task, Mrs. Washington "packed what luggage she could. Packed it with dresses, charming, colorful, feminine. At the very sight of her, fresh and lovely, in that desolate camp, new courage sprang up in the hearts of General Washington and all around him." In italics, the institute told its readers that Mrs. Washington's appearance provided *courage that made this country a nation.* Fashion's importance to the war effort was reiterated at the Millinery Merchandising Executives Association meeting at the Waldorf-Astoria in New York City, where a Columbia marketing professor, Paul Nystrom, stressed that in times of war, the products of the fashion industries "create interest and inspire courage and morale." The war should remind everyone, he noted, that the "national need is for interests in life and in the things worth living for."[57]

Exactly how a woman could go to a store and purchase clothing that fit properly was a mystery to many. In late January, the Department of Agriculture adopted a new, ostensibly simpler and more efficient system of sizing women's clothing. The department based its efforts on a study by Ruth O'Brien and William C. Shelton, *Women's Measurements for Garment and Pattern Construction*, published just a month earlier. The authors had worked with nearly fifteen thousand volunteers through a Works Progress Administration grant in an effort to establish a scientific method of sizing for the clothing industry, for which "wrong size" caused up to 40 percent of women's garments to be returned. O'Brien and Shelton believed that height and weight combined, rather than bust size alone, would be the most useful criterion in formulating sizes. While their study did not produce the unified system they hoped for, their calculations of "stature and bust girth, stature and abdominal-extension girth" became the foundation of the modern system of sizing women's clothing.[58]

Not all Americans were thriving in the war economy. Some regions were in as dire shape as they had been in the depths of the Depression. In the Pennsylvania counties of Northumberland and Schuylkill, out-of-work coal miners appeared before the Federal Anthracite Investigating Committee to describe what had befallen "the forgotten people of America." The region's anthracite coal production had decreased by half since the Depression, and whereas 160,000 miners had once worked in the mines, by 1942 that number was fewer than 90,000. Tax receipts had dwindled, hundreds of homes were foreclosed, and some teachers had gone eight months without being paid. In Mahanoy City, residents described how they were losing their battle against bankruptcy and were close to "obliteration." Public school systems were breaking down in Northumberland County as teachers prepared to strike for back wages, and a local minister, the Rev. Joseph J. Petrovitz, declared that "communism was feeding lavishly upon the widespread discontent." Two suggestions came from the hearings: the government should bring war industries to the area, and it should curtail its use of oil in favor of coal. "We are not asking money for not mining coal," said a local banker. "We are asking for an opportunity to work."[59]

On January 30, President Roosevelt celebrated his sixtieth birthday. He had already served as the nation's chief executive longer than anyone before or since, and the toll of those years was showing. He developed darkening circles under his eyes, and the polio that had ravaged his legs and his heavy smoking were also aging him. Yet he remained larger than life, as indispensable to the American war effort as Churchill was to Great Britain's. His administrative style, featuring overlapping agencies that sometimes competed with each other, exasperated many in Washington. FDR admitted as much in the spring of 1942: "You know I am a juggler," he said, "and I never let my right hand know what my left hand does." He was willing "to mislead and tell untruths if it will help win the war."[60]

"No one who hasn't had the experience can realize what it was like to enter the Oval Room and see Franklin Roosevelt behind that fabulous desk," wrote Donald Nelson, adding, "There is no other experience in the world quite like it." Portraits of Roosevelt hung in a place of honor in countless American homes. The privileged child born into fabulous wealth on the banks of the Hudson River had become a champion of the poor, the voiceless, and those who felt forgotten. In his classic book *Christ Stopped at Eboli*, the Italian painter and anti-fascist writer Carlo Levi remembered that many homes in the small southern Italian village of Eboli contained two portraits—one of the Virgin of Viggiano, the other of Franklin Roosevelt. "To see them there, one facing the other," Levi wrote, "they seemed the two faces of the power that has divided the universe between them." Opposite the Virgin's image, Roosevelt seemed "a sort of all-powerful Zeus, the benevolent and smiling master of a higher sphere." The *New York Times* later wrote, "Men will thank God on their knees a hundred years from now, that Franklin D. Roosevelt was in the White House."[61]

The task facing the president would have aged anyone. The alliance with Russia and Great Britain was filled with tension and mistrust. At home, he faced a number of competing forces: those who wanted revenge on Japan and opposed focusing on Hitler and Europe; farmers and workers who wanted limited intrusion into their daily lives; military leaders demanding a major offensive on the European continent; administration officials who wanted more authority over the domestic economy and business groups that wanted free rein; and political opponents in both parties who had grown weary of the three-term president and hoped for major victories in the November elections.

A fundamental tension underlying these conflicts was, ultimately, a disagreement about the role of capitalism and democracy in war. A *Fortune* editorial stated in clear terms what free enterprise confronted: "We are now, like business itself, face to face with the fact that there won't be an industrial civilization or any kind of civilization at all if this war is not won. . . . Victory cannot be bought. Not billion dollar appropriations but the hard task of organizing machines, materials, and manpower is crucial in the war of production." Noting that many were predicting federal budgets as high as $150 billion, the magazine concluded: "If the program is successful, the price is cheap."[62]

The massive changes awaiting the nation were already being felt. Shutting down production of consumer cars and retooling plants to make the weapons of war was one of the first signs. *Time* described the scene: "At 3:18 on a snowy afternoon in Flint, Michigan, a little knot of men stood around a shiny black Chevrolet coupe in assembly plant #2. Someone had scrawled on its rear window 'Last Chevrolet off January 30, 1942.' The men grinned, joked, washed up and wandered outside to line up before the pay window. Some current of emotion—half abashed, self-conscious, a sentiment that seemed a little ridiculous when dedicated to inanimate machinery—moved through the crowd, finding its horseplay, the offhand talk, the what-the-hells with which American workmen cover up what they feel." The workers watched in amazement as the auto industry "literally died and was being reborn" into "something greater than anything Detroit has ever seen in 40-odd years of the motor industry." Donald Nelson knew that many industries, "in fact, the entire economy, shivered under the impact of conversion." What was occurring in hundreds of factories and shops throughout the nation, Nelson understood, "was not so much industrial conversion as industrial revolution."[63]

2

February: "The Worst Week of the Century"

EARLY ON THE MORNING OF VALENTINE'S DAY 1942, twenty-four-year-old Florence Nimick Schnoor asked her husband, Richard, to drive her to the train station in White Plains, New York, where she would take the train to New York City for a day of shopping. Florence and Richard, the sergeant at arms in the New York State Assembly, had been married just a week. After seeing her off, Richard drove back to his home in Armonk where he was surprised to receive a call from his wife later that morning. Florence said she was not feeling well and wanted Richard to pick her up at the Wood-lawn Station in Mount Vernon. When he arrived, he was shocked to find her ashen and feverish. He immediately took her to St. Joseph's Hospital in Yonkers. By 4:00 p.m., she was dead.

Florence was the grandniece of Andrew Carnegie and the daughter of Alexander K. Nimick, a millionaire Pittsburgh industrialist whose inheritance originated in a will his mother wrote on stationery from the Waldorf-Astoria. Born in 1917, she had been raised in an affluent neighborhood in Greenwich, Connecticut, and attended private schools in Stamford. After her mother died in 1924, she lived with guardians while her father remained abroad. Several times during her teen years, she went on extended trips to France and Italy. At the Gray Court School, sixteen-year-old "Flo" was known for her turtleneck sweaters and her love of tennis. She graduated from the Gray Court School in 1935.[1]

Little is known of Florence's education or work life afterward. She met Richard in September 1941, and the couple eloped in early February 1942. They kept their marriage a secret, and on Valentine's Day Florence held another secret, which she apparently kept even from Richard. She was pregnant. She went to New York that day not to shop but to get an abortion.

Despite being related to one of the wealthiest figures in the nation's history, Florence found herself in the same desperate situation that confronted the poorest American woman. In 1942, contraception was illegal in many states and abortion was treated as a heinous crime. The few qualified physicians who dared offer abortions risked stiff prison sentences, such as Dr. Emory Klein, who had recently been found guilty of running an "abortion ring" on East Sixty-Third Street in New York City and sentenced to nineteen years in prison. He was the eighth physician that year to have been convicted of providing abortions. In May, New York governor Herbert Lehman signed a bill saying that any medical professional who referred patients to an "abortionist" was "equally guilty" of a crime, no less than the physician performing the procedure. An editorial in the *Catholic Telegraph-Register* saw "the advocates of birth control" engaged in an effort that was "harmful to the nation" and warned that once birth control received "moral sanction and social approval," it would "not even halt at national suicide."[2]

The matter of legalizing abortion had been discussed at a recent medical conference in New York. Dr. Alan F. Guttmacher, an obstetrician from Johns Hopkins, citing a special prosecutor's estimate that upwards of 250,000 abortions were performed in New York City each year, blamed the medical profession for "patent hypocrisy and [a] holier-than-thou attitude" that he found "revolting." At least in "therapeutic" cases in which pregnancy threatened the life of the mother, Guttmacher told a *Times* reporter, he hoped the profession would "relax its barriers" so as to "cheat the criminal abortionist." Eighty-five percent of the women who obtained abortions, Guttmacher noted, were married, and the methods of illicit abortionists could be "medieval."[3]

A telling decision came just weeks after Florence's death, when the Connecticut Supreme Court of Errors, in a 3–2 ruling, upheld a law that prohibited physicians from providing contraceptive advice to married women even if pregnancy threatened the woman's life. The court added that there was "another method, positive and certain" that would prohibit pregnancy: "It is abstention from intercourse." The following year, the U.S. Supreme Court upheld the Connecticut decision. The court eventually ruled contraception legal in 1965.[4]

Florence Nimick Schnoor was one of many American women who felt they had no other option but to submit to illegal abortions. At some point, she had obtained the name of someone in New York who would perform the abortion. Investigators later concluded that she likely paid $40 for the procedure. After an autopsy, the medical examiner concluded that Florence's abortion had been "particularly brutal and inept." Before she died, doctors had begged her for the identity of the person who performed the operation, but that was another secret Florence would take to her grave. The only clue was her address book, which contained approximately two hundred names. Police contacted all two hundred people but came up empty.[5]

Even as the events of Pearl Harbor reverberated, some reformers were busy trying to change a legal and cultural barrier that forced many American women to resort to desperate measures. Just two weeks before Florence died, the Birth Control Federation of America (BCFA), led by Margaret Sanger, had met at the Waldorf-Astoria, where advocates proclaimed planning parenthood was "a democratic ideal; forced parenthood is a slave ideal." One result of the conference was that the BCFA officially changed its name to Planned Parenthood Federation of America. For some opponents, such as Father Charles Coughlin, the battle between "Mary and Margaret," or the conflict between the Virgin Mary and Margaret Sanger, presented a stark choice for the nation since "Mary wants babies, as do all Christian wives." On February 17, Florence Nimick Schnoor's funeral took place in Greenwich, Connecticut. The next day, she was buried in a family plot in Allegheny County, Pennsylvania. No one was ever arrested for her death.[6]

On Sunday, February 1, those attending religious services in New York City heard a variety of sermons dealing with the war crisis. At St. Patrick's Cathedral, Archbishop Francis J. Spellman declared that the "heart of the Holy Father is filled with sorrow and crushed with the sufferings and the miseries of all his children"; at the West Side Jewish Center, Rabbi Leo Ginsburg delivered the address "The Lord Is a Man of War"; at the Riverside Baptist

Church, the Reverend Harry Emerson Fosdick gave the sermon "Being Rich without Knowing It"; at the Broadway Presbyterian Church, the Reverend Paul C. Warren offered "How Shall We Pray in a Time of War?"; and at the Bronx Free Fellowship Unitarian Church, the Reverend Leon Rosser Land's sermon was "What Is God Doing in This War?" At the Congregation Kehilath Jashurum on East Eighty-Fifth Street, Rabbi Joseph H. Lookstein told his congregants, "President Roosevelt is not only a champion of democracy, but a prophet. . . . Long after the tyrants of our day are forgotten and their tyranny is but an ugly smudge upon the face of history, the Atlantic Charter, which is the handiwork and the brain child of our President, will continue as an immortal blessing of humanity."[7]

Thousands of young Americans were volunteering for military service. The young men who stood in line at the U.S. Marine Corps Recruiting Headquarters on Church Street in New York City had a range of motivations. Some knew the draft was approaching and wanted to join their preferred service, while others came out of a patriotic fervor to avenge Pearl Harbor or to defeat Nazism. One recruit, John Michael Gusko of Bayonne, New Jersey, stood a good chance of receiving a deferment because he worked in a defense factory, but he nonetheless signed up for military service because he wanted "to help out." When asked if he preferred to fight in Europe or the Pacific, Gusko offered, "I guess I'm most angry at Hitler. . . . He started this sort of mess." Jay Nollman had been a student at Yale before becoming a metallurgist at U.S. Steel. He knew he could possibly receive a deferment for his knowledge of metallurgy but said, "I'm not the kind of fellow to try to duck anything." Nollman, who was engaged at the time, expressed what many felt upon entering the war: "What I'd like to do is to get it over with, come back, get married, have a couple of kids and be like John Doe." When Leonard "Jack" Larsen of West Seneca, New York, left his pregnant wife for basic training at Fort Pickett, Virginia, he told her, "I only hope that if I see action, I can face it as you did when I departed." His wife responded, "I hope and pray you'll never see action, but if you do, I hope God will bring you home safe to me." Nollman married his fiancée in June 1942 and died in 1988. After serving in France, Larsen returned home in 1946, and he and his wife lived together until his death in 1999. Gusko was not as lucky. He died on June 5, 1945, fighting in the Pacific with his Marine division.[8]

In the days after Pearl Harbor, the desire for revenge seemed to unify the nation. James Reston wrote in the *New York Times*, "The deep divisions which marked this country's entrance into the wars of 1776, 1812, 1861, 1898, and 1917 were absent. . . . Overnight, partisan, personal, and sectional differences were shelved." Yet Reston's assessment told only part of the story. In some respects, Americans came together in ways they never had before: volunteering for military service, supporting rubber or scrap metal drives, serving in air-raid watches, buying war bonds. This collective desire to "do something" infected the entire nation. Yet while the crisis of war united some communities, others were ripped apart. The trauma of war brought to light bitter resentments and prejudices, and in no area were these greater than when it came to race.[9]

When Pearl Harbor was attacked, one of the first reactions of many Americans was to lash out against all things Nikkei.[10] That intense anti-Japanese sentiment manifested itself in films, books, government pamphlets, and newspaper cartoons. The enemy in the Pacific was often portrayed as slant-eyed and buck-toothed, sometimes with satanic-looking hairy hands and grotesque fingernails. Some aspects of these caricatures resembled the anti-German caricatures that flourished in 1917–18. Everywhere along the West Coast, fears of new attacks prompted blackouts and civil defense preparations.

Yet the hatred of the enemy went much further than depictions in newspapers and motion pictures. In early 1942, approximately 127,000 Japanese Americans resided in the United States, 112,000 of them on the West Coast. In the first weeks of the year, whites along the coast warned government officials of the treachery of "alien enemies" of Japanese descent. As General John DeWitt, who had famously said, "A Jap is a Jap," warned War secretary Henry Stimson, "There are indications they are organized and ready for concerted operation." In a remarkable leap of logic, DeWitt argued that even if Japanese Americans had not yet committed any sabotage, that only proved they were biding their time. Along with California attorney general (and future U.S. chief justice) Earl Warren, DeWitt saw only one option: mass evacuation and incarceration. As the public mood for such steps intensified, one California official with the Social Security Board, Richard M. Neustadt, was worried about the abuses that might occur and was certain that only the federal government could oversee the operation. If it were left to the state, he told a Washington official, "Alien enemies would commit suicide rather than go to state offices." Neustadt understood the intensity of the hatred that Japanese Americans confronted: "You have no idea of the prejudices that are involved."[11]

Those prejudices were not hard to find in California. A couple from San Fernando wrote FDR that "Japs" were "nasty, dirty, sneekie people." They added that they "always did hate them." J. Violet Sims told the president that she had always been friendly to "these people," but in her experience, although such "foreigners" possessed "an innocent and almost helpless appearance generally," they were not to be trusted. Sims believed they were "obedient to and carrying on a system" that "had its feet in Japan, and still has." Roosevelt heard from a California resident who complained, "For years, we people on the western coast have preached about the menace" presented by Japanese Americans, "but no one believed us." The answer was obvious: "We must get rid of all Japs in California." That sentiment was echoed by Frank Miller of Montgomery, Alabama, a place he said was composed of "a homogenous people." Miller wrote FDR that he and his neighbors were "amazed that the federal government is treating aliens so leniently." He felt that "every one of them should be put in a concentration camp." Japanese Americans were similar to "Indians—the only good Indian is a dead Indian."[12]

Although many Nikkei were American citizens and some had family members serving in the American military, their loyalty to the nation did little to blunt the suspicion. Despite loud condemnations of a general evacuation (led by U.S. attorney general Francis Biddle), the pressure on Roosevelt to take some measure to protect the mainland intensified. Some angry Americans called for his impeachment. Agnes Waters of Chicago, a member of the "We, the Mothers" organization, which claimed a membership of twenty thousand, told a public gathering on February 24 that for failing to defend the nation against attack, Roosevelt "ought to be killed!" The president told Harold Ickes that he was surprised there had been "so few attempts at sabotage" to date and worried that war plants would soon be targeted by enemy spies. Two of Congress's most virulent racists upped the ante. Representative Martin Dies claimed in early February that he had evidence of a planned joint German-Japanese invasion and urged that all

Japanese Americans five hundred miles inland from the West Coast be removed to detention areas. On February 18, Representative John Rankin declared, "This is a race war," and claimed it was vital to "get rid of every Japanese, whether in Hawaii or the mainland." In case that was not clear, he added how he really felt: "Damn them! Let's get rid of them now!"[13]

The president's compliance the next day was not as draconian as martial law, but it marked a profound turning point in the lives of Japanese Americans and the role of civil liberties in wartime. Executive Order 9066, signed on February 19, directed the secretary of war to "prescribe military areas" where "any and all persons may be excluded." The order was greeted with approval from Congress. Representative Albert Gore of Tennessee said, "The President has his sleeves rolled up and is determined to do his utmost . . . to use the power of his office to safeguard us against Fifth column work from inside our own country." The order affected not only Japanese Americans, but also German and Italian Americans. General DeWitt was given authority to designate the western half of Washington, Oregon, California, and southern Arizona as "military areas" where over one hundred thousand evacuees would be housed. While the term *concentration camps* was replaced with *internment camps*, the reality was the same.[14]

Among the first instances of "compulsory evacuation" of Japanese Americans under the new order came as hundreds of Nisei were moved from Los Angeles to Manzanar, California. A typical case was that of Seijiro Suchiya, who had migrated to the U.S. in 1920, joined a fishing fleet in Terminal Island, and raised three sons. One of his sons, Takeshi, said, "When we stop to think it over, most of us understand the necessity for evacuation. But the immediate reaction is, we've got to have *some* rights." The *Christian Century* told readers that with the internment camps, the nation was "headed toward the destruction of constitutional rights" and added that America seemed intent on "the establishment of racial discrimination as a principle of American government."[15]

While Japan posed the greatest threat to the West Coast, fears of German and Italian American "enemy aliens" persisted. To those subjected to removal fifty miles inland, the notion that the U.S. considered them security threats seemed absurd. High school student Alex Frediani of Samoa, California, sometimes manned on nearby sand dunes a two-story tower alongside veterans of the previous world war to watch for Japanese invaders. Despite working to protect his community, Frediani and his Italian American family faced their own share of suspicion. He recalled that a neighbor came to his house in early February 1942 and told his father, "You gotta get out of town right now!" The neighbor had heard a rumor that anyone refusing to leave would be arrested and thrown into a "concentration camp." Frediani's father, who worked at a lumber mill in Eureka, was incredulous: "Gee, I just don't believe they'd do that in this country."[16]

Persuading anxious Americans to deny people who looked like the enemy their basic constitutional rights was easy compared to persuading them to pay higher taxes. Treasury secretary Henry Morgenthau understood what he was up against, so he asked Walt Disney to make a short film to help the cause. Titled *The New Spirit*, the eight-minute cartoon opens with Donald Duck eager and willing to do his part for the war effort, yet disappointed to hear a radio voice tell him: "Your country needs you by paying your income tax!" He grumbles about the task until he understands that average citizens could help by paying their taxes on time. This is not merely about funding government services. Rather, in a phrase Donald endorses, it is something more—"Taxes to beat the axis." When Donald realizes his taxes will pay for an unstoppable military machine, he cannot wait to do his part. Approximately 32 million people saw the film, and in a Gallup poll, 37 percent responded that it had a positive effect on how they saw the issue of paying their taxes.[17]

Not all were pleased with the government's role in producing the film. The U.S. House of Representatives was angered by Disney's $80,000 price tag, and on February 10 it voted 259–112 to eliminate any further similar expenditures. Representative John Taber of New York said he hoped the Treasury Department would not "get into any more such situations" like "the Donald Duck operation." "Can you think of anything that would come nearer to making people hate to pay their taxes," he asked his colleagues, "than the knowledge that $80,000, that should go for a bomber, is to be spent for a moving picture to entertain people?" Morgenthau, however, told reporters he would do it again if he had the chance. "I don't know of any better way to bring to seven million new taxpayers the pleasant announcement that they have to pay their taxes."[18]

If paying taxes did not stem the inflationary tide, the government could use compulsory savings. The Treasury Department, whose sales of war bonds in January exceeded $1 billion, argued that compulsory savings would provide a "cushion" of pent-up spending power after the war. Department officials suggested collecting the savings and paying a nominal interest rate redeemable after the war. The idea was not well received by labor unions and farm groups—or by members of Congress, who preferred to avoid the issue until after the November elections.

One segment of American business felt left out of the drive to produce the American war machine. The Senate Small Business Committee was particularly angry at War Production Board director Donald Nelson for favoring large, established businesses. On February 5, Senator James E. Murray of Montana criticized Nelson's appointments at the WPB as "the same four big business executives who headed similar divisions previously in the OPM," and charged that during Nelson's time at the OPM, "very little was accomplished for small business." A report from the committee warned that small businesses in the U.S. faced "bankruptcy and chaos along a wide front" unless more war contracts came their way. For the time being, the focus of war conversion was on the larger industries and their plants, while some smaller businesses would be allowed to focus on civilian needs and, in some cases, subcontract for larger plants.[19]

On February 19, Ernest Kanzler, chief of the WPB's automotive division, announced at a Detroit press conference something that the small-business owners had suspected from the beginning. The "Big Three" automakers—GM, Ford, and Chrysler—would soon receive new government orders totaling $10.5 billion, an amount two and a half times greater than in 1941. When they reached full production, Kanzler estimated, the auto factories converted to war would need around 1 million workers, compared to the 550,000 workers required by the car companies in peacetime. Additionally, the Detroit plants would not get to full productive capacity "until women are trained and out on war work." The auto industry had been completely shut down since February 10, leaving nearly 300,000 workers temporarily unemployed. General Motors president Charles Wilson felt confident the war production plans that FDR had demanded would be accomplished "in the same old way we used to run the auto business." C. C. Carlson, president of the Automotive

Parts and Equipment Manufacturers, was hostile to UAW leader Walter Reuther's proposal for joint labor-management control of the industry; Carlson said the war "was not being fought for or against any labor union," but was being waged on behalf "of the one union, the Federal Union."[20]

In early February, Congress went about approving the massive appropriations bills needed to fund FDR's war budget. The House quickly approved $26 billion for the navy on February 4 and the Senate passed it unanimously. Navy secretary Frank Knox, the 1936 Republican vice presidential nominee, confided to his wife, "It represents a colossal responsibility and I shall have to take additional safeguards to keep greedy, unscrupulous fingers out of the cash drawer." He quickly learned to keep his opinions to himself after he caused outrage among America's Pacific allies by calling Hitler and Germany the country's chief enemy. Following that statement, presidential secretary Stephen Early announced that all cabinet members and federal administrators would submit public remarks to Archibald MacLeish, the head of the Office of Facts and Figures, for approval. Early was careful to say that the move was not meant to "censor" administration officials but to help them "avoid remarks they themselves did not want to make." Airports were ordered to use code when discussing weather reports because some short-wave radios could overhear the transmission from the airport towers to pilots.[21]

While Congress was busy spending like never before, some on the War Production Board openly worried about the president's expressed production goals for the year. In ways that foreshadowed how the space industry in the 1960s labored under President John F. Kennedy's deadline for landing a man on the moon, government and industry leaders worked under enormous pressure to reach FDR's goals by the end of 1942. Some even wondered if "spare" planes could count in the sixty-thousand-plane goal. After agreeing that only new, completed planes would be included in the final figures, Nelson admitted to administration officials that he was worried about the stated goals but was reluctant to ask the president to lower them.[22]

Few federal agencies in American history have confronted the challenges imposed on the Office of Price Administration. In World War I, the Wilson administration had delayed controlling prices until January 1918, when

Bernard Baruch was named to head the War Industries Board. Baruch later estimated that inflation had added $15 billion to the cost of waging that war. If similar inflation occurred in 1942, it would put the prospects of victory in serious jeopardy. The very act of establishing price and wage ceilings was extraordinarily difficult from an economic and political standpoint, but it would have been impossible to control the wartime economy without it. Despite its unpopularity, the OPA created a sense of security among competing economic groups and forces. By keeping inflation to a minimum, it reduced hoarding and speculation, and helped keep the price of war goods at a consistent level.[23]

For most Americans, the OPA was personified by its director, Leon Henderson. If people wanted to buy a new tire, a gallon of gasoline, a shirt, a pair of shoes, or a can of navy beans, or hoped to ask for a raise or rent an apartment, or wanted to go bowling or buy a pretzel, they were affected by Henderson's decisions. Although he was widely recognized at the time, he is mostly unknown today. He has not been the subject of a biography or even a scholarly article. His historical anonymity is remarkable, especially considering that *Life* magazine opined that Henderson "had as much real influence on the economic policies of the New Deal as any man except the President himself."[24]

Henderson, born in 1895 in Millville, New Jersey, attended public schools and then worked his way through Swarthmore College, earning a degree in economics in 1920. He was profoundly influenced by Millville's small-town environment, and even while working in Washington and New York he maintained a home and a bank account there. *Life* magazine speculated that when Henderson thought about consumers, "the mental picture [he has] is probably a composite of Millvillians."[25]

Henderson taught at the University of Pennsylvania's Wharton School and at the Carnegie Institute of Technology before joining the Russell Sage Foundation in New York in 1925. There he became a consumer advocate and helped secure legislation in several states to restrict usurious lending. He went to Washington in 1934 to join the National Recovery Administration as head of the research and planning division, and following Roosevelt's landslide victory, he worked at the Works Progress Administration as an economic advisor to presidential confidant Harry Hopkins. In 1937,

Henderson drafted a prescient memo to Hopkins in which he argued that prices were rising too fast and that within the year, purchasing power would decline so far that workers would start losing their jobs. Not long after, FDR grew worried over the increasing federal debt, and he made a fateful decision to cut government spending and contract the economy. When the nation fell into the "Roosevelt Recession" of 1937, Henderson's fears became reality.

Columnist Drew Pearson noted that Henderson's rise was due "to the fact that he can say 'no' when it would be easier to say 'yes.'" Pearson described him as "an ardent liberal but no radical," a "hard-fisted, hard-boiled regulator, and Wall Street doesn't like him." One of Henderson's allies, Texas representative Wright Patman, defended him against charges that he was a "Russian Communist who came over here to try to change our form of government." Patman assured his House colleagues that Henderson was "a Mason, a Democrat, and the son of a preacher." Bernard Baruch also defended him against red-baiting, saying, "If Henderson is a communist, then I am a fellow traveler." Baruch considered him "the most informed man in Washington on what we did in the last war" and "the best man in the country for his job."[26]

Henderson was profane, complained of his bad back, smoked an endless chain of cheap cigars, and often spit out of windows. His staff members had to brush off ashes from his jacket before he left for important meetings, and they lavished praise on their boss when he wore a new suit or tie. On one trip to New York, he got into several fistfights: with two taxi drivers, a truck driver, and a spectator at a football game. One White House official noted that Henderson "has an almost religious willingness to fight for what he thinks is right," adding, "That's what the president likes in him."[27]

In 1939, acting on the advice of former New Deal "brain trusters" Thomas Corcoran and Ben Cohen, FDR named Henderson to the Securities and Exchange Commission. In January 1941, when FDR created the Office of Production Management, Henderson was angered that the president had reduced his price division to a minor player in the new agency. He left Washington for a vacation after warning Hopkins that if inflation were not brought under control, it would imperil the entire defense program. His views obviously got the attention of the president, who in April 1941 named him the first director of the OPA, a position one writer described as "the most difficult ever tackled in a free economy," which was to prevent "'the little man' of inflation from parking on our stairs again; or, if unable to do that, at least to keep our economic dt's within bounds." Behind Henderson was a small army of three thousand government workers toiling in temporary two-story gray buildings along Independence Avenue. His immediate staff contained economist John Kenneth Galbraith, attorney Paul Porter, and General Counsel David Ginsburg. The *Saturday Evening Post* concluded, "It is no exaggeration to say that the future of our economic system, the real value of all wages, savings, government bonds, insurance policies, rests as much upon Henderson as upon any other one person."[28]

In the summer of 1941, Henderson and Donald Nelson coauthored an article for the *Harvard Business Review* in which they argued that "price administration means government interference with the exercise of individual business judgments," and that such interference "amounts to a temporary partial loss of what we are striving to preserve." But the two individuals upon whose shoulders would rest the ability of the American economy to confront the crisis of war wanted the business community to know that "we have set out upon a road . . . full of pitfalls." Included in their outlook was the need for increased taxes and strong price and rent controls. Writing shortly after the war, Harvey C. Mansfield remarked that the foundational idea Henderson brought to the OPA was straightforward: "In a money economy, the profit motive, the expectation of making a gain from business," was "the main incentive to be relied upon in war as in peace." Despite what some may have suspected, Mansfield concluded, Henderson operated "well within the framework of traditional capitalism."[29]

In early 1942, Henderson received his first taste of national notoriety when he rode a "victory bike" made of recycled rubber and other materials for newsreel and print reporters along the Washington Mall, with his ever-present cigar in his mouth and his stenographer sitting in a basket on the front of the bicycle. The bicycle's metal parts contained no copper or nickel, and its tires were made of 90 percent reclaimed rubber. The bicycle industry hoped to produce 750,000 of them in 1942. Henderson's awkward attempt to look like an everyday person backfired. One citizen, George E. Shaw of Los Angeles, asked FDR, "What has Leon Henderson got that many of our true Americans haven't?" Shaw said that he, like many Americans, was "getting sick and tired of your support of a Radical. . . . What has he ever done to deserve your support to the point of alienating the love and affection of your people?" Some of Henderson's critics thought he had ambitions far beyond the OPA, possibly including running for the White House someday. In a poll taken in early 1942, 46 percent of Americans had a favorable opinion of Henderson; 44 percent did not.[30]

Before spring, Henderson grew worried about the inflationary spiral that seemed to be emerging in the American economy. He warned that unless the government could "siphon off" at least $11 billion of an anticipated $15 billion in new national income, drastic rationing and "severe price controls" would have to be implemented in order to stave off inflation. There were three ways, he suggested, that the government could perform this "siphoning": compulsory savings, a withholding tax or, the method he preferred, higher income taxes on middle brackets and corporations.[31]

In Chicago on February 20, Henderson described himself as an "orthodox economist" who suddenly found himself in strange waters. In his new role, he told the crowd, it might seem strange that he was the nation's chief "price fixer and rationer" or that "a Chicago mail order executive should be the top man in production, and that a Hyde Park gentleman farmer should be the head of this glorious state." Henderson found this situation "the symbol of democratic America, an America whose course is still guided by facts and realities." The reality, as he saw it, was the threat of explosive inflation, and he challenged the crowd to remember that simple fact: "It is the reason why we must tax and tax and tax until it hurts. It's the basic reason why you must save and save and save. It explains why wages must be kept under control, why farm prices must be kept under control, why profits must not be allowed to skyrocket, and why the rise in the cost of living must be fought at every crossroads."[32]

The next day, Henderson told a meeting of Iowa farmers that while he supported the general idea of farm parity prices, farmers would have to live with price curbs in order to prevent catastrophic inflation. "I am not arguing against any change in the distribution of the pie," Henderson said, "but I am stressing the fact that it is going to be a smaller pie and that it is our job to see to it that the cuts in the pieces come where they can do the least harm to our national strength and national morale." He told the farmers that while taxes and price controls would stave off inflation, "voluntarily accepted restraints by a free people in this emergency were more important." While that might not be popular, Henderson ended, "the boys in the fox-holes at Bataan and on Corregidor come first." "Great sacrifices are involved for all of us," and "everyone in the community must share the burdens."[33]

A glimpse of Henderson's power came when he issued ceiling prices for all passenger automobiles. Saying the move was meant "to protect buyers and secure reasonable profits" for car makers, the OPA set maximum prices dealers could charge, to go into effect on February 12. A Chevrolet Fleetmaster coupe cost $815, a Ford Special Six cost $780, and a Cadillac Series 75 five-passenger sedan was $4,060. The least expensive car on Henderson's list was a Crosley convertible coupe, which cost $412, and the most expensive was a Packard 1520 LeBaron limousine for $5,690. By early April, the new rules were on display on ads for new 1942 Oldsmobiles, which assured readers the cars were "for sale" but then added in smaller print, "provided, of course, that [buyers] secure from the local rationing board a certificate of purchase which OPA says they may secure, because they are contributing to the war effort." Those in eligible occupations included traveling salesmen of food or medical supplies, physicians, ministers, police personnel, and licensed taxi operators.[34]

In interviews at war factories, defense workers revealed some of the tensions that existed on the shop floor and throughout an anxious nation. A CIO member said: "What I really think should happen is that the government should take over all the shops during the war—that way a man would feel that he was really working for the country." If a worker felt he was merely "working for the company," the union member said, "his heart isn't in it much." A poll of hundreds of war workers revealed that over half expected a depression after the war. When asked what one reform they wanted to see enacted after the war, 22 percent wanted guaranteed employment, and nearly 10 percent wanted "fairer distribution of wealth." A Seattle ship worker boiled it down: "A man's got a right to a job, to have social security, to know that he can work and eat. Why should corporations profit off a man's work and starve him?"[35]

Meanwhile, the news from the Pacific continued to grow worse. On February 15, the British surrendered to Japanese troops in Singapore, a loss described by a devastated Winston Churchill as a "heavy and far-reaching military defeat" and nothing less than "the greatest disaster to British arms which our history records." The fall of Singapore had once seemed unthinkable. The British had fortified the city with eighteen-inch guns, and except for London and Liverpool, it had been the most heavily defended city in the British Empire. The capture of Singapore darkened an already dismal mood in America. Joseph Goebbels wrote in his diary on February 15, "When one surveys the overall situation critically one becomes convinced that there is a deep moral and political depression in London, as well as in Washington."[36]

Time's issue of February 23 editorialized that the previous week "was the worst week of the war." Even more than the fall of France, what had occurred over the preceding days made it "the worst week of the Century." Such a week "had not come to the U.S. since the blackest days of the Civil War. Now, as in 1864, the fate of the nation was plainly in the balance." In addition to the fall of Singapore, the magazine reported the partial capsizing of the eighty-three-thousand-ton former French liner *Normandie*, which suffered a fire on February 9 in New York Harbor. At one time, the ship had been the world's largest passenger liner, and when France entered the war in 1939, it was kept in New York out of range of German U-boats. After Pearl Harbor, FDR seized the ship from the Vichy government and ordered the navy to convert it to a troopship. The *New York Times* reported that crews used so much water to extinguish the blaze that it caused the ship to list so that it lay "grotesquely on her side in her West 48th Street slip." Tens of thousands of onlookers came to see it, and its sad ending came at a point when the nation was especially anxious over its ability to wage war.[37]

In the same issue, *Time* published photos of "the new order" in Hitler's Poland, with starving babies and Jewish corpses. The "sadism as applied by the Nazis to the Jews," *Life* warned, displays "the kind of thing the fighting foes of Nazism may expect if they really 'lose the war.'" A group calling itself the Committee to Defend America, from Lancaster, Pennsylvania, saw "enemy aliens" at work: "In view of such disasters as Pearl Harbor and the burning of the *Normandie*," the organization warned, "incredible calamities" were likely to continue at the hands of such people. Rather than feeling confident that Pearl Harbor had awakened the American giant, the *Nation* noted, "the first step toward winning the war is the realization that we have a good chance of losing it." Considering what the nation was up against, it is little wonder that three out of ten Americans polled in mid-year favored a negotiated settlement with Hitler rather than risk waging a war the country could not win. Few disagreed with WPB head Donald Nelson, who wrote in *Life*, "This year, 1942, is the critical year in the existence of the United States."[38]

The news from Singapore sent a sobering reminder to millions of Americans that what had happened at Pearl Harbor could be just the start. In Louisville, Kentucky, the editor of a women's magazine noted that "never since Pearl Harbor and the fall of France have I been so shaken." After searching for someone to blame—Roosevelt, Churchill, perhaps Congress—the writer suggested, "I wonder if we as American women cannot start from here and carry some of the responsibilities and some of the burden of this war?" She urged women to buy less, save more, and "be cheerful," adding, "Hitler surely loves us when we are downhearted, grouchy, blue, and sure that we will lose this war." The fear of imminent danger did not subside after FDR held a press conference on February 17. When asked about possible air attacks, the president suggested that "under certain conditions," enemy ships could bomb New York or Detroit at any time, maybe even "tomorrow night." Suspecting that the president might know something, air-raid watchers went on high alert.[39]

In considerations of a nation at war, children are usually left out of the discussion. In the early 1940s over 30 million Americans under the age of fourteen made up almost a quarter of the population. How children dealt with the war and the ways in which parents and teachers tried to inform them of their changed world were matters of profound importance. Some experts believed that the developing psyches of the young should be shielded from the war's harsher aspects. Elizabeth Woodruff Clark, executive director of the National Association of Day Nurseries, warned parents to conceal their fears and anxieties from their children. Cautioning that terror had injured more children in Europe than bombs, she maintained that "physical protection is not enough" and "too many very young children are suffering from the war of nerves. This should not be. Day nurseries are successfully cushioning any possible fright by making a novel game of air-raid drills, by concentrating on nerve-strengthening diets, and by helping children lead normal, unexcited lives. No matter what parents may fear," Clark added, "their supreme duty in 1942 will be to conceal this fear from their children."[40]

Not everyone shared this view. In a *New York Times* magazine article, "War Need Not Mar Our Children," anthropologist Margaret Mead wrote, "Americans have been reared in the belief that any contact with the facts of life and death is dangerous to children." In her view, American children were "needlessly overprotected from every unpleasant aspect of life," but she understood that Pearl Harbor had drastically changed the circumstances of the "urban classes." "Suddenly, and for the first time in our lifetime, there is the possibility that mothers and teachers and welfare workers will not be able to protect children from such things, that bombs may fall and people will die before their eyes." At the root of it all, Mead understood, was that "people continue to believe, as they have been taught, that contact with death will maim their children's minds for life." She recounted a story from American Samoa in which village children watched "a post-mortem Cae-sarian operation" performed in an open grave. "No one shooed the children away, no one suggested that they weren't able to watch quietly, as their elders. The simple facts of life and death, as they occur in war or peace, in the community, do not hurt children." That lesson was not well understood in the United States, where "we have been overprotecting children for fifty years." If children were not included "within the community circle as the community faces what disasters may come, the children will be hurt, not by bombs, but by the isolation thrust upon them as their parents tersely put them off with feeble fibs and tales that the blackout is to keep the naughty Japs from stealing their toys."[41]

Editor Pauline Rush Fadiman agreed. "If there is one outstanding fact we have learned from England about how children take war, it is that their attitudes are almost completely set by the attitudes of the grown-ups around them, especially their parents." Fadiman found it "surprising how many parents think that they should protect their children from war by not talking about it in their presence, and by listening to news broadcasts only when the children are out of the room. .... American parents have been criticized, and not unjustly, for a tendency to shield and overprotect their children, at all costs, from the more disagreeable aspects of life, so that they are unprepared for reality." In the end, however, "this war is one reality from which we cannot protect them."[42]

At the Elementary School of Hunter College in New York, children expressed some of their concerns about war through art. Dr. Ruth Conkey, a psychologist, examined the paintings and found "a surprising lack of manifest fear." The children, she observed, drew air raids and bombings as they would "rocket ships, Indians or jungle adventures," without "being emotionally moved by these representations." For these children, war was an abstract reality, and none of their depictions showed children themselves being harmed. Even more interesting were the ways in which children represented the war through humanitarian aspects such as the Red Cross or ambulances carrying the wounded to safety. "Children are concerned about war as long as they can do something about it," Conkey concluded, and hate was rarely on display. Instead, children often demonstrated remarkable insights. One young girl drew Uncle Sam holding the hand of Germany. When asked what it meant, the girl said the picture could come true: "If Germany would promise not to fight anymore, and she would see that she should not rule everything. The United States would say, 'you promise?' And if Germany would promise the United States would wait a whole year and then would say, 'let's be friends.' And we will have to teach German children, who were taught war by Hitler and were not allowed to read books. They would believe us. They would like to be free." Conkey emphasized that parents should talk freely to their children about the war, show seriousness but not fear, and encourage "a humorous viewpoint; nothing is so good as laughter for banishing fear." Many of the children's artworks displayed humor, she wrote, mostly in depicting Hitler and other dictators as rats or other animals, thus using ridicule to disarm frightening personalities they saw in newspapers or newsreels.[43]

In a draft of an article that the *New York Times* had asked Mead to write about how adults should react to war, Mead wrote that New Yorkers were a "very mixed bag of people." Recent air-raid drills had drawn varying reactions in the city, and Mead thought that the explanation was simple: "Our hetero-geneity is at once our weakness and our strength." The differing populations, she wrote, were emblematic of a city without a true "people": "New Yorkers are not one kind of people, in the same sense that the inhabitants of Coventry, Cracow, or Rheims were one kind of people." Understanding how different "peoples" react was crucial. "Once this great point is recognized, and Americans learn to have neither too high nor too low an opinion of their fellow Americans, learn to expect neither British stolidity nor the pitiful stampede into which the deceived and confused French population fell, we will have laid a basis for making positive plans about preparing people to deal competently with panic-threatening situations."[44]

Mead's editor at the *Times* was disappointed with her advice. Lester Markel wrote that he hated to "seem persnickety, but apparently I haven't made myself clear about that piece." He had wanted "a discussion of panic, its causes and cure," but "what we have now is still a piece on New York's likelihood to fall into a state of panic. Whether you meant to say it or not, the reader gets the impression—or, at least, this reader does—that it is probable New York will panic in case of an air raid. . . . I wonder, frankly, whether it is advisable to say that at this time." Markel refused to publish Mead's article.[45]

The dire situation facing the country had, of course, political implications. Understanding that the November election presented opportunities, Republicans worked to find the right balance of criticism and patriotism. At the National Republican Club dinner in New York, gubernatorial candidate Thomas Dewey drew extended applause when he dismissed any call for a negotiated peace with Hitler. "We have but one course," he stated, and "every suggestion of compromise must be rejected." He carefully situated the GOP in a stance that demanded "competence of the war effort of our national administration," adding, "Never in our history has there been so great a need for vigilant, patriotic opposition." Dewey had recently resigned as national chairman of the USO Fund Drive, and was succeeded in that post by Prescott Bush, a member of the banking firm of Brown Brothers, Harriman. Bush, later elected to the U.S. Senate from Connecticut, was the father and grandfather to two American presidents.[46]

The Republican nominee for president in 1940, Wendell Willkie, sounded a similar tone in his Lincoln Day address in Boston. Willkie wanted the GOP to "be a free party—a party free to develop its own policies; free to stand on the side of sound thinking." He suggested that General Douglas MacArthur be summoned from the Philippines to assume command of all U.S. armed forces, reporting directly to the president. "Bring Douglas MacArthur home," Willkie implored, "place him at the very top. Keep bureaucratic and political hands off him. Give him the responsibility and the power of coordinating all the armed forces of the nation to their most effective use." With MacArthur in such a position, Willkie asserted, "the people of the United States will have reason to hope that skill, not bungling and confusion, directs their efforts."[47]

Other members of the GOP struggled to find the right tone. RNC chair Joseph W. Martin outlined the party's wartime approach: "Only through the bi-party political system of operation can the Bill of Rights be protected and vitalized. Wherever one party secures and retains control of government, it means mono-party government. And mono-party government means dictatorship." Former presidential nominee Alf Landon thought New Dealers were treating the war as "just another political alphabetical project," and worried they were leading the nation toward "totalitarian collectivism." *Newsweek* concluded that despite the perceived unity after December 7, "the national consolidation that arose from the smoke over Pearl Harbor was threatened with dissipation in the winds of political oratory."[48]

Not all the criticism was Republican. Senator Harry Byrd of Virginia, a conservative Democrat, was also critical of the administration: "The executive branch must end the fantastic and increasing confusion and strip the government of nonessentials so we can devote all our energies to winning the war." The proliferation of executive agencies had created, in Byrd's words (which also echoed Franklin Roosevelt's), "thousands of nonessential parasites."[49]

Willkie's proposal to bring MacArthur back as commander of American forces grew out of a larger criticism of the American military, which had long complained that except for the commander in chief, there was no official organization for the leaders of army, navy, and air forces (the U.S. Air Force became a separate branch in 1947). The same military officials believed that civilians, including the secretary of war, did not have the necessary background to make recommendations to the president directly. On February 20, FDR responded by establishing a "unified tactical command" or, as it would be known, the Joint Chiefs of Staff. Led by Admiral Harold Stark, General George C. Marshall, Admiral E. J. King, and Lieutenant General Henry "Hap" Arnold, the chiefs met regularly with the president to formulate military strategy. The new structure would have far-reaching consequences. As historian George C. Herring noted, "The emergence of the military into a key policymaking position brought enduring changes in civil-military relations and the formulation of national security policy."[50]

Some of the criticism launched toward the Roosevelt administration concerned the role of organized labor, and although labor had made a "no-strike" pledge at the start of the war, conservatives were not pleased that unions retained a voice in the upper levels of the White House. With the national effort geared toward all-out production, the slightest shop floor problem involving labor unions could escalate into a national argument. One such problem occurred on February 11 at Ford's River Rouge plant in Detroit. The auto factory had been converted to make machine tools for bombers, and a labor dispute on the factory floor resulted in a series of work stoppages over a forty-eight-hour period. R. J. Thomas, president of the local and a national vice president of the CIO, eventually ordered "all loyal union members" to return to work. Military officials were outraged that such stoppages continued while "soldiers were dying in the Far East." That the River Rouge walkout occurred during the week labeled "the worst" in American history only added fuel to the backlash against organized labor and its administration allies.[51]

Other embarrassing items also fueled conservatives' anger. The Office of Civil Defense came under fire for two hires made by First Lady Eleanor Roosevelt, who had been named assistant OCD director by her husband. Still stinging from public rebuke of the congressional pension bill, members were anxious to be seen as vigilant against administration officials' use of the war for personal ends, and with news that Mrs. Roosevelt had hired actor Melvyn Douglas and dancer Mayris Chaney to posts within the OCD, House Republicans moved quickly. Stories that Chaney had danced semi-nude fanned the flames, and Representative Clare Hoffman of Michigan suggested that the hires constituted "Bundles for Eleanor." The House voted 88–80 to withhold funds from the OCD for "instructions in physical fitness by dancers." One outraged Ohio woman wrote to Eleanor Roosevelt: "People aren't giving up their sons, working long hours, buying defense bonds . . . to have you making a Roman holiday with a Communist movie actor and a dancer." When Congress learned that Chaney was earning $4,600 a year for her government work, the indignation escalated. Representative Philip Bennett of Missouri said if Chaney were worth $4,600, then a striptease artist he knew in the Ozarks should get $25,000. Then, when it was disclosed that Douglas earned $8,000 for his efforts, Representative Charles Faddis of Pennsylvania said it was repugnant that he made the same salary as General MacArthur. Chaney and Douglas soon resigned, followed shortly by Eleanor, but the notion that the Roosevelts were using wartime agencies to reward their friends was gaining traction. As the first political scandal to emerge since Pearl Harbor, the Chaney-Douglas episode was a foretaste of how the New Deal's critics sharpened their blades even during wartime. Any hint of using the war to advance social causes was met by angry protests that invoked the sacrifices made by soldiers and families. As Hillary Clinton discovered fifty years later, for a president's spouse to assume official duties always provokes criticism, and Eleanor understood that it was not prudent "for a vulnerable person like myself to try a government job."[52]

The criticism directed at Chaney and Douglas notwithstanding, the motion picture industry itself was seen in a different light. The head of the Selective Service, General Lewis Hershey, announced that moviemaking was "an activity essential in certain instances to the national health, safety, and interest" and ruled that draft boards in California could grant deferments to "actors, directors, writers, producers, cameramen, sound engineers, and other technicians." Some prominent actors, including Jimmy Stewart, Tyrone Power, Henry Fonda, and Clark Gable, volunteered anyway, while others, most notably John Wayne, used their deferments to make westerns and war movies on Hollywood back lots. Whether theatrical performers should also receive deferments was on the mind of actor Maurice Evans, who asked for a decision before his troupe set out on a tour with *Macbeth*. When some members of Congress questioned the loyalty of stage actors, Eddie Cantor and Chic Johnson responded that they hoped Congress would reject "isolating people in the entertainment industry from their fellow Americans."[53]

A larger criticism came from administration opponents, who worried that New Dealers within the administration were not being fully candid with the American people on the progress of the war. Arthur Krock was among the loudest of those who thought the administration was squandering money to pursue "social economic schemes without regard to war necessities." Krock was also critical of the general American reaction to the first weeks of war. The nation, he believed, was overconfident and lacked the "spirit of urgency and alarm" he thought was necessary. In a February poll, 71 percent responded that Americans were not sufficiently alarmed about the war. James Reston wrote in the *New York Times*, "The Anglo-Saxon peoples will not make the revolutionary sacrifices that are now necessary until they understand that the position of their countries in the war is not only bad but desperate." Reston went on: "Never in our history has the outlook been so grim and so dark."[54]

Another worry was consumer hoarding. If left unaddressed, hoarding could have disastrous consequences for the nation, and if it made essential goods scarcer, many would go without and prices for the remaining supplies would increase, adding to inflation. Nine New York department stores, including Macy's, Bloomingdale's, and Saks Fifth Avenue, saying they were acting "in the interest of intelligent buying and patriotic behavior," took out an ad in the *New York Times* with a cartoon Hitler pinning an Iron Cross on the chest of consumers who were hoarding merchandise. Hoarding served the needs of the enemy, the ad noted, because it led to "great dissatisfaction among the millions of people who cannot afford to build up reserves of merchandise and who would be content to endure mild deprivations if 'everyone was in the same boat.'"[55]

By mid-February, administration insiders perceived a looming crisis. Leon Henderson sent a memo about crude rubber supplies to an administration economist with the note, "If you are really prepared to have your blood run cold, I suggest you look at it. . . . It will show that at our present rate of use the [Allies] will be entirely out of crude by June of next year." Another estimate was even worse: current supplies would be exhausted well before the end of 1942. While the specifics of the rubber situation were closely held within the administration, Henderson admitted to the Chicago Better Business Bureau, "I am scared about this war, and I don't mind your knowing it." He added that he wished he could see into the future and find "America glorious and triumphant at the end, and perhaps as an orator I would do so," but he could not do that, "because I don't know that in this country every person is doing something every day which will further the war effort."[56]

The rubber shortage led the United States Rubber Company to run ads in late February imploring Americans to consider an "important patriotic thing you can do: *keep your car running for the duration of the war.*" To preserve the tires currently on their cars, each driver should "cut in half the weekly driving of himself and his family." This would result in the "saving of new rubber practically equal to the entire present American rubber stockpile." Rather than buy new tires, the company urged drivers to see "a responsible tire dealer" and "find out the mileage left in your tires. Then, budget those miles to last just as long as possible for *necessary* driving."[57]

If the nation's war factories were to reach Roosevelt's goals, they could not ignore their employees' morale and well-being. In their efforts to find new ways to serve their employees, over twenty-five hundred companies used a report by O. C. Cool, a labor relations consultant, finding that in order for companies to operate with the greatest efficiency, management must "pay greater heed to the small grievance and the seemingly insignificant irritation" of the worker. When one Pennsylvania tool manufacturer underwent a production decrease of nearly 30 percent, the Cool surveyors located the origin of the problem. An employee in the chemical department had asked a foreman for rubber gloves with which to dip metal into a vat of dangerous chemicals but had been refused. Without any recourse, the workers exposed their bare hands and production slumped. Once the workers' grievances were heard and they were given protective gloves, productivity returned to normal levels. In a New England plant, workers grumbled over the rumored salaries and benefits received by management. The Cool Company's response was to publish a factory newspaper in which salaries and profits were openly discussed. Despite such measures, the Cool report concluded that the nation's industrial slowdowns were largely due to there being "many executives [who] are still neophytes in the art of collective bargaining."[58]

Perhaps no factory symbolized how the war offered new visions of the industrial workplace more than the Jack and Heintz plant ("Jahco") in Bedford, Ohio. Starting with fifty employees in 1940, by 1942 the airplane component company held contracts with the Army Air Force totaling over $216 million and had a workforce of over four thousand. Owner William Jack referred to all employees as "associates" and offered them a litany of benefits that included free health care and life insurance; complimentary hot meals, vitamins, and recreational areas where tired workers enjoyed a massage or a Turkish bath; and paid vacations to Honeymoon Isle off the west Florida coast. Jack wanted Jahco to be "an absolutely democratic association," which he felt "enlarges acquaintanceship. It restrains selfishness. It creates confidence. It removes suspicion. It drives away fear." In words that echoed FDR, Jack stated that "freedom from fear" drove his management policy: "Fear of the boss is avoided by our democratic mode of operation. Fear of unjust dismissal is avoided by the union committee. Fear of discrimination is avoided by the medium of the goodwill ambassadors. Fear of illness, either for self or family, is relieved by insurance coverage. Fear of toothache is avoided by having a dental department available for emergency care."[59]

In return, employees at Jahco worked grueling twelve-hour shifts seven days a week. Yet Jack boasted that the company's absenteeism rate was well below the national average and in February there were no unauthorized absences at all. The company's production rates per worker were among the highest of any factory in the nation and waiting lists for job openings at the plant reached thirty-four thousand people.

The company spent over $150,000 for "welfare" facilities such as dental clinics and a hospital, which treated 473 workers in 1942. The hospital saw thirty abdominal operations, four amputations, eighty-three tonsillectomies, and fifty-three births. One woman working at Jahco told Jack, "You have treated me as though I meant something to the good of your company." Another employee said, "I'm not sure there is another place like this in the wide world and not another boss like Bill." A former employee who had joined the Marines wrote that Jahco "has the best working conditions in the United States, conditions that will be more general by the time the war is over."[60]

Men who came to work for the company started out at 95 cents per hour (substantially higher than the national average pay for new male workers, which was just 58 cents per hour), while women earned 75 cents for the same job. Not all of Jack's principles were democratic or visionary. Jack encouraged associates to discipline workers arriving late by subjecting them to humiliating "wolf calls," and to combat the worry that enemy agents might be nearby by encouraging all employees to consider themselves "FBI agents to protect the interests of the American flag and Jack and Heintz." Jack underscored how the experiment in allowing women to work at the plant had serious limitations. "Each woman understands that when this war is over and her husband returns," Jack said, "that he will take his old job and the wife will no longer be with us."[61]

When the company reported before-tax profits in 1942 of over 1,770 percent more than in 1941, not everyone was impressed. Representative Carl Vinson's Naval Affairs Committee questioned Jahco's lavish bonuses and salaries, including a $39,000 bonus Jack gave his secretary and $145,000 he gave himself. Congressional investigators were concerned that the bonuses were just a way for Jack to avoid corporate excess profits taxes. Jack responded that the profits were directed toward a reserve fund "for postwar readjustment." *Time* reported that other area factories thought "the customs and working habits at J and H are as preposterous as the bonuses," which totaled over $2 million in 1942. In response to congressional scrutiny and criticism from other area factory owners, Jack and Heintz agreed to limit its profits to 6 percent, renegotiated contracts with the Army Air Force and returned $11 million to the government. The salaries paid to the owners were reduced from $100,000 to $15,000.

To its workers, the Jahco experiment offered a bold vision of labor-management relations. To its critics, it offered a case study of how massive government contracts produced reckless spending that could not be repeated in peacetime. The workplace culture that Jahco tried to implement would become dated by the 1960s and was not tried again until the tech boom of the 1990s, when a labor shortage (this time of skilled tech workers) again made for a strong correlation between a company's overall work culture and high productivity.[62]

At other plants near Cleveland, a different culture was emerging that displayed how communities reacted to the needs of total war. Over three hundred white-collar professionals, including lawyers, teachers, architects, and businessmen, volunteered their services at various Cleveland plants to relieve war workers after normal work hours. These volunteers, after working a full day in their regular occupations, did four-hour shifts in the evenings, one from 4:00 to 8:00 p.m., the second from 8:00 to midnight. Called "half-shift men," they helped out in areas like packaging, shipping, and other office tasks that required no special training. The experience of Jahco and other Cleveland-area factories displayed some of the possibilities the war provided, as well as how some deeply ingrained notions were not going away.[63]

The *New York Times* noted that "the most discouraging aspect of the record of the last two months has been the ability of our enemies to strike hard blows, which we seem incapable of parrying. . . . Change must come if the war is to be won, and that change can only come if we equip the enormous manpower of the Nation with strong weapons of attack." The only answer to the news coming from Pearl Harbor, Singapore, and Bataan "is a tremendously increased tempo of production." Meanwhile, the paper provided some welcome distractions. On February 15, it offered its first Sunday crossword puzzle, written by Charles Erlenkotter. Two weeks after Pearl Harbor, Margaret Farrar, who became the editor of the Sunday crossword, had told publisher Arthur Hays Sulzberger, "I don't think I have to sell you on the increased demand for this type of pastime in an increasingly worried world." Among the clues in the first puzzle was a nine-letter query, "Donald Nelson gives out these." The correct answer was "contracts."[64]

In the first months of the war, the American people's one real connection with the fighting was through the president himself. Although Roosevelt had used fireside chats throughout the 1930s, the war provided another reason for these chats to reach a vast audience in a personal way. In anticipation of a nationally broadcast speech he would give on February 23 outlining the progress of the war, FDR asked Americans to get a world map so they would be able to follow along as he discussed major developments. Stores reported that world maps sold out in just hours. In response to criticism that the administration was withholding the true extent of the human and military damage caused by the attack on Pearl Harbor, FDR said, "Your government has unmistakable confidence in your ability to hear the worst, without flinching or losing heart. You must, in turn, have complete confidence that your government is keeping nothing from you except information that will help the enemy." Even while discussing the foreign theaters of war, Roosevelt returned to the theme of mobilization. His mammoth production goals might have seemed "fantastic" to "Axis propagandists," he said, but just weeks into the effort, he was certain the goals would be reached.

"This generation of Americans," Roosevelt declared, "has come to realize that there is something larger and more important than the life of any individual or of any individual group—something for which a man will sacrifice, and gladly sacrifice, not only his pleasures, not only his goods, not only his associations with those he loves, but his life itself." It was one of Roosevelt's most significant fireside chats since the banking crisis in the early days of his presidency. "Never before," he concluded, "have we had so little time in which to do so much."[65]

That same evening, as the president tried to calm anxious citizens, a Japanese submarine surfaced near Goleta, California, and lobbed fifteen to twenty-five shells toward an oil refinery near Santa Barbara. Although the attack caused very little damage, a "yellow alert" was sounded, the region was blacked out, and all traffic was stopped on U.S. 101 between San Francisco and Los Angeles. Radio stations quickly went off the air rather than serve as possible beacons for enemy ships and planes. *Newsweek* commented: "And so the war came to America itself."[66]

The "war" that came to California inflamed many passions. Search planes crossed the skies for days, and a state legislative committee heard reports that "fifth-column" activities in the area were being directed by something called the Black Dragon Society. Worried that the Japanese had deliberately timed the attack to coincide with FDR's address, the White House decided that it would not announce the president's speeches more than two days in advance. Local authorities in the southwestern region

of the country built more camps to accommodate additional "visitors"—
Japanese Americans suspected of aiding the enemy. Meanwhile, the lack of
"aliens" to work the region's farms and fields led to increased prices for let-
tuce and celery, although a delegation headed by a local justice of the peace
advocated a plan that allowed aliens to work in the artichoke farms in day-
time under armed guard. To help protect San Diego and the peninsula, the
U.S. government permitted Mexican soldiers to cross the border. *Life* reported that "wherever they went," the foreign soldiers "were greeted cor-
dially by the Americans." American officials even gave a dinner in honor of
the Mexican soldiers at La Caverna, near the border.[67]

The Santa Barbara attack put an already nervous California even more on
edge. On February 25, thinking that Japanese planes had been spotted over
the city, skittish observers handling anti-aircraft guns fired over fourteen
hundred rounds at the suspected targets in the night sky over Los Angeles.
The shells and tracer bullets offered, in the words of the *New York Times,*
"the first real show of the second world war on the United States mainland," and the city remained in a blackout throughout the night. Some citizens manning the guns reported they had seen two hundred planes in the
sky. Yet the next day, it was apparent that no planes had been shot down, no
enemy bombs had fallen on the city, and the only casualties were two residents who suffered heart attacks and three more who died in traffic accidents due to the blackout. The Western Defense Command issued a terse
statement: "The aircraft which caused the blackout in the Los Angeles area
for several hours this morning have not been identified." The only physical
damage came from unexploded anti-aircraft shells that damaged some
houses and a bank. After reviewing the evidence, Navy secretary Frank
Knox admitted there were no Japanese planes, but Secretary of War Stimson contradicted him, claiming that some fifteen aircraft of mysterious
origin, which "may have come from commercial services operated by enemy agents," had flown over the city. Representative Leland Ford, a Republican from Los Angeles, was critical of the administration's response. "Our
people ought to know whether this was a practice raid," Ford said, or "a
political raid." Californians were "not jittery and were not hysterical, but
they are beginning to believe the Army and the Navy are." The *New York
Times* asked, "Is it possible that our whole system of supervision is so lax

that a group of 'enemy aliens' can casually take off from their own planes on nearby American airfields and fly over our cities at night?"[68]

On the other side of the nation, the events in California raised new concerns. New York City mayor Fiorello La Guardia warned of the vulnerability of Times Square, saying that if all signs were not rewired so they could be quickly extinguished, he would order that they be darkened permanently. New Yorkers were further worried when a German U-boat sank an American destroyer, the *Jacob Jones,* off the New Jersey coast on February 28, killing 125 sailors. Former governor Al Smith warned that New York could easily be attacked by "hit and run" bombers and asked citizens to purchase "health bonds" that would be used to finance hospitals and clinics to meet such an emergency. Archbishop Francis Spellman agreed to purchase the first such bond.[69]

Although it would be a few weeks before the country knew it, February 20 produced one of the first authentic American military heroes of the war. Lieutenant Edward O'Hare, piloting a Grumman F4F-3 Hellcat with low ammunition supplies, single-handedly warded off nine Japanese bombers attacking his carrier, the U.S.S. *Lexington.* A correspondent who witnessed O'Hare's heroics described what he saw: "He darted recklessly into a hail of anti-aircraft fire and clipped off one Japanese straggler. Then he leap-frogged over his victim and knocked off at least two others."[70] In all, O'Hare shot down five enemy planes and severely crippled another; because the enemy aircraft were forced to release their bombs early and missed their target, he undoubtedly saved his carrier. In April, President Roosevelt awarded O'Hare the Medal of Honor, and the citation stated that he had accomplished "one of the most daring, if not the most daring, single action in the history of combat aviation." O'Hare would be killed in action in 1943. Six years later, the airport at Chicago's Orchard Depot was renamed in his honor.

The president's and War Department's refusal to desegregate the armed forces struck many African Americans as a fundamental betrayal that threatened any notion of national "unity." Author Pearl Buck wrote an open letter to the nation's black citizens, published in various African American newspapers and the *New York Times* on the last day of February, in which she noted, "The division between colored and white peoples in our own country is dangerous." She did not dismiss the "injustices and cruelties" African Americans suffered but advised, "When you remember the suffering, which you have not deserved, do not think of vengeance as the small man does." Instead, "stand by this great mass of your white countrymen in this imperfect democracy of ours, where, nevertheless, the hope of democracy is still clearest." Then she wrote of another "fear" that gripped America: "If you are aware of the struggle of the average white person, you will be patient with him as he gropes toward the meaning of freedom and human equality. It is a difficult and unfamiliar road for most white people, and they are fearful because they are being driven along it by the trends of world events."

The same day Buck's letter was published, the reality of the racial divide hit home. In Detroit, the heart of the war production effort, a riot broke out at the Sojourner Truth housing Project at Fenelon and Nevada Avenues. Some African Americans who were scheduled to move into the previously all-white project were met by twelve hundred angry whites, many carrying rifles, shotguns, or clubs. The previous night, a cross had been burned in a nearby field. While whites held signs reading, "Don't Let Negroes In or White Standards Will be Lowered," African Americans countered with signs reading, "What About Some Democracy in America?" Although nearly two hundred police officers tried to disperse the white protestors with tear gas, shots were fired and several people were stabbed. *Life* magazine ran a photo of a young black man standing amid a cloud of tear gas, telling a reporter, "The Army is about to take me to fight for democracy." But, he said, he would rather stay home and "fight for democracy right here," because in Detroit "we are fighting for our own selves." Eventually 40 people were injured and 220 were arrested. In reaction, the Detroit Housing Commission decided against altering the racial makeup of the city's housing projects. The 1942 riots foreshadowed what would happen the following year in Detroit, when an even bloodier race riot erupted, causing thirty-four deaths. In light of the evidence, Pearl Buck's patronizing admonition to be "patient" with white people had no relevance. African Americans in Detroit and around the nation struggled to define democracy at home while fighting for it abroad.[71]

In Alabama, near Fort Deposit, a white posse searched for Roosevelt Thompson, an African American laborer who worked for a white landowner, Charley Hartsell, who accused Thompson of attempting to rape his wife. When the posse found Thompson they shot him dead on the spot. An investigation of the murder conducted by the Association of Southern Women for the Prevention of Lynching found that the real reason Thompson had been killed was his demand that Hartsell pay him $80 in back wages. Alabama governor Frank Dixon rejected the claim that a "lynching" had occurred and warned that the Ku Klux Klan would ride again if the federal government did not allow the states to control their own destinies.[72]

The pervasive feeling among people of color was expressed by Mordecai W. Johnson, the president of Howard University, who told Senate majority leader Alben Barkley, "In my travels around the country I find that the colored people are deeply distressed about the employment situation in general." Johnson echoed the nation's growing distress but then spoke of an even deeper concern, one that struck at the very core of a democratic society fighting for its survival. In addition to concerns about housing and employment, he said, the average African American felt a basic apprehension about his or her "long-range outlook as a human in the United States."[73]

3

March: Total War

IN MARCH, DOCTORS SCRAMBLING to find an answer to a life-threatening situation helped produce one of the most far-reaching consequences of World War II. In a hospital in New Haven, Connecticut, a thirty-three-year-old patient named Anne Miller had miscarried and developed a severe blood infection. She remained in a delirium and near death for several days as her fever reached dangerous levels. After using a variety of drugs without success, her doctors tried a small amount of a drug called penicillin. It had been discovered in 1928 by Alexander Fleming but had never been widely used or even available. The next day, Miller's fever broke and she ate a full meal. With her recovery, Anne Miller became the first patient ever to be successfully treated with the new drug. She lived until 1999, dying at the age of ninety.[1]

A few weeks after Miller's recovery, researchers at Oxford University reported that they had found the drug one hundred times more fatal to bacteria than sulfa drugs, but they warned that since the new drug was produced from cultures of fruit fungus, supplies would be limited. The Oxford researchers had come to the U.S. in 1941 to try to convince American pharmaceutical companies that they should mass-produce it, but industry leaders were not persuaded. After Pearl Harbor and Anne Miller's recovery, however, and with the U.S. government subsidizing the effort, production skyrocketed. In the first five months of 1942, companies around the world manufactured a total of 400 million units of pure penicillin, enough to treat only a few hundred patients for a staph or strep infection. By 1945, U.S. pharmaceutical companies were producing 650 billion units a month. It would be impossible to estimate how many lives have been saved by penicillin, but among all the events of 1942, the experience of Anne Miller may have done the most to change health care around the world.[2]

In early March, readers of *Life* saw a photo of the first "German missile to land in the western hemisphere," an unexploded torpedo that settled on a beach on the Caribbean island of Aruba. Although it was a thousand miles from the U.S. mainland, the sight of a German bomb so near to American waters produced more worries within a nation on edge. As military and political leaders debated whether American troops would be better utilized in Europe or the Pacific, they were forced to consider the Japanese presence along the West Coast and the German presence along the East: should U.S. troops be deployed abroad, or were they better utilized at home, protecting valuable American assets?

Army Chief of Staff George Marshall was worried by the "deluge of requests for the employment of Federal combat troops not only to protect our coastal communities, but to guard installations throughout the United States." Some members of Congress had urged Marshall to protect Mississippi River bridges and the Keokuk Dam in Iowa. In December and January, Marshall said the U.S. had deployed troops to such locales because it was "wise to reassure the public," but "the time has now come when we must proceed with the business of carrying the war to the enemy and not permitting the greater portion of our armed forces and our valuable materiel to be immobilized within the continental United States." He acknowledged that the U.S. should expect some isolated air attacks, but he hoped they would not derail the nation from "engaging and defeating the enemy in theaters distant from our shores."[3]

In the Pacific, the news grew worse. General Douglas MacArthur's hold on the Philippines was slipping, and after he retreated to his command post on the island of Corregidor on March 11, some of the soldiers who remained on Bataan gave him the nickname Dugout Doug. Approximately seventy-five thousand U.S. and Filipino troops were left on their own on Bataan without fresh food, water, or sanitary facilities, facing a Japanese army and navy that controlled the Pacific. Despite the defeats his forces suffered, MacArthur remained a hero to many Americans. Columnist Ernie Santos wrote that he courted "danger with a reckless abandon unknown among American generals except 'Stonewall' Jackson or Jeb Stuart." If MacArthur were killed or taken prisoner, Santos believed, it would "be worse than the disaster of Pearl Harbor many times over."[4]

In early 1942, MacArthur was the military figure most Americans identified with the war, and the only one who rivaled FDR in popularity. Few Americans possessed as lengthy and impressive a military background. He had been an aide-de-camp to Theodore Roosevelt, risen to the rank of brigadier general during World War I, and then served as the superintendent of West Point. MacArthur had won the Silver Star seven times, and after he left Corregidor on March 12 and eventually made it to Australia, was awarded the Medal of Honor for his "defense" of the Philippines. In one of the most famous promises of the war, the general had told Filipinos, "I shall return." *Life* gushed that when MacArthur escaped to Australia, a "thrill shivered the anti-Axis world," proving that "here was the first great national hero of the age." In March, thirteen newborns in New York City were named after him, a fact that, the *New York Times* noted, "ought to be as good as a Gallup Poll on when the general became a hero in the plain, ordinary households in New York." In New York City, Councilman James A. Phillips introduced a bill that would change the name of LaGuardia Field to MacArthur Field. Phillips said: "Mayors may come, mayors may go, but the outstanding feats of generals remain in history. As LaGuardia Field in Queens is the world's greatest airport, so General MacArthur is the world's greatest hero." The general's universal popularity extended to children, who could go to Hearn's Department Store in New York and find a MacArthur Soldier Suit, "the pride of every youngster," on sale for $2.97. The suit included a khaki uniform, a cap, flap pockets, and four-star insignia on the shoulders, as well as a photo of the general himself.[5]

Parents who bought that uniform for their children did not know that MacArthur had recently accepted a $500,000 payment for his services in the Pacific from Philippine president Manuel Quezon. Members of MacArthur's staff split an additional $140,000 from Quezon. Historian Carol Petillo, the first scholar to uncover the documents that revealed these payments, writes of the effect they may have had on MacArthur's conduct in the Philippines: "It is significant that after several statements arguing that Quezon could not be safely evacuated, MacArthur, one day after the transfer of funds was ordered, reversed his position and decided that the president's evacuation could indeed be achieved." President Roosevelt and Secretary Stimson apparently knew of the payment but chose not to interfere. When Quezon offered General Dwight Eisenhower a $60,000 bonus later in the year, Eisenhower refused, realizing the "danger of misapprehension or misunderstanding" that could arise if he accepted funds from a foreign government in a time of war.[6] To FDR's mind, MacArthur's gallant image needed to be protected on behalf of a nervous country in need of heroes.

In a national radio address on March 2, WPB director Donald Nelson reminded his audience of FDR's ambitious production goals for the year, which he termed "the greatest production job in history." Already the clock was ticking. "We have but ten months to go—304 days—in which to strengthen our striking power to a point where victory can come within our grasp," said Nelson. "In the lives of men now living, those 304 days immediately ahead can shape the whole course of history for a thousand years, and shape it to our way of life." He implored all Americans to redouble their efforts to reach Roosevelt's goals, asking, "Could any right, privilege, profit or material possession of which we voluntarily deprive ourselves during those 304 days to gain our end compare with what we gain by so doing?"[7]

Companies in the war industries scrambled to find adequate personnel. Want ads proliferated in major and minor newspapers. "Production Manager for War Products Plant," read one, asking for applications from those "who by long experience and a demonstrated record of accomplishment are fully competent to take charge of operations in a plant of thousands of employees." The ad did not name the plant but promised bonuses "based on accomplishments" and "liberal separation pay if the executive cannot later be brought into our peacetime organization."[8]

Office personnel had few machines beyond primitive adding devices at their disposal. Human labor did the job that computers and robots could easily replicate decades later. Although the earliest computers were still largely in the design phase in 1942, the theoretical dilemmas posed by these new machines were already on the minds of some. In March, a twenty-two-year-old science fiction writer delineated some of these dilemmas in a short story that appeared in *Astounding Science Fiction*. Centered around a robot named Speedy who accompanies two astronauts to Mercury in 2015 to restart an abandoned mine, Isaac Asimov's "Runaround" contained, for the first time, what became known as the "Three Laws of Robotics": (1) a robot may not injure a human being or, through inaction, allow a human being to come to harm; (2) a robot must obey the orders given it by human beings except where such orders would conflict with the first law; and (3) a robot must protect its own existence as long as such protection does not conflict with the first and second laws. Although Speedy is trapped between obeying its orders and self-preservation, in the end the first law outweighs the others and Speedy protects its human creators.[9]

With no progress against their enemies in sight overseas, in early spring Americans turned to their own country, where they saw the foundation of an industrial colossus under construction. *New York Times* correspondent A. H. Raskin reported from Detroit that "a sense of desperate urgency grips this mass production capital," where "what amounts to a new industrial revolution is being carried forward." Raskin saw factories "being torn apart with no consideration for anything except how quickly the way can be cleared for pouring out guns, tanks, planes and shells in sufficient volume to annihilate the Axis forces." By far, the "most breathtaking of the new enterprises is the Ford bomber plant at Willow Run." In a place that had recently served as a camp where underprivileged youths "scratched its surfaces for cabbages and radishes," a massive $60 million factory was being built that eventually would employ eighty thousand people. When Raskin asked someone waiting for a bus if Detroit could get the tanks and planes rolling in time, the man glowered at the question—"Of course, Detroit will make the grade. It will take a little time, but once old Henry Ford gets his teeth into the Germans it will be all over but the signing of the armistice."[10]

While the auto industry's conversion received the most attention, countless other companies that had been making consumer goods quickly transformed themselves into military manufacturers. Metal cans became ammunition boxes, watches became time fuses, locomotive boilers became track shoe links for tanks, nylon stockings became parachutes, vacuum cleaners became gas masks, and Louisville Slugger baseball bats became rifle stocks.

The way the government awarded defense contracts displayed how the war took precedence over concerns about inefficiency or waste. For the Willow Run plant, the government covered all costs and gave Ford an additional 8 percent profit. These "cost plus" contracts assured companies that they would not lose money once the complexities of the job were undertaken. Secretary Stimson had counseled Roosevelt to approve such arrangements, adding famously, "If you are going to war in a capitalist country, you have to let business make money out of the process or business won't work." Ford hated the idea of making armaments and was a staunch enemy of the president's basic economic philosophy; his cooperation on such a massive scale proved Stimson's point. Ford's, of course, was not the only Detroit auto company retooled for war. Chrysler, the second-largest auto producer, had thirty major war contracts, including ones for making the Sherman tank, forty-millimeter anti-aircraft cannons, and a variety of military trucks and pontoons. The company anticipated that its war contracts would require more than 145,000 workers.[11]

The editors of *Time* grasped that a transformation was under way: "Something is happening that Adolf Hitler does not yet understand—a new reenactment of the old American miracle of wheels and machinery, but on a new scale. This time it is a miracle of war production, and its miracle-worker is the automobile industry. Even the American people do not appreciate the miracle, because it is too big for the eye to see in an hour, a day or a month." Once the Detroit facilities were fully readied, "they will pour out such a flood of war machines as no man has ever imagined." Yet Wall Street was gloomy. In late March, the Dow Jones Industrial Average fell to 98.3, 14 percent under the high it reached earlier in the year. Market analysts surmised that investors were worried about higher taxes.[12]

The massive new war plants could not dispel a profound sense of urgency. Donald W. Mitchell wrote in the *Nation* that "any realistic evaluation" of the war would show it to be "critical in the extreme. . . . We are losing the war today, and by the middle of the year it may have been definitely lost." If the rubber shortage worsened and German and Japanese forces held their ground, defeat or negotiated peace might be in America's future. "The darkest hours of American history," he warned, "probably lie ahead." James Reston of the *New York Times* noted the American people's misconceptions about the war, including the possibility that the U.S. could not lose. "Nothing is more falla-cious in time of war than the illusion that money is power," he wrote, adding, "We may be able to solve most of our difficulties with it in peacetime, but one cannot stop a tank with a hundred-thousand-dollar bill." Representative John W. Boehne Jr. of Indiana told the Bronx Real Estate Board, "Every one of us needs to be awakened to the grave peril that confronts this Nation. We need to be told again and again of the humiliating defeats that we have suffered in the first three months of this war. . . . We need to be told that we can lose this war, and are consistently losing it now."[13]

Thomas J. Wallner, president of the Southern States Industrial Council, was even clearer: "This war cannot possibly be won—ever—and may be irrevocably lost—this year—unless there is an immediate and extremely far-reaching reversal of policy" by the Roosevelt administration. The funda-mental reason why "America is losing the war," he wrote, was "the attempt by the administration to simultaneously fight a foreign war and wage an internal economic revolution." Despite many Americans' fears that eco-nomic ruin awaited unless government controls were extended and health care and jobs were guaranteed, Wallner had hit on the Republican answer to FDR and the Democrats in wartime. The GOP would advocate focusing all of the nation's energies on winning the war and put all other domestic issues aside—a way of ending the New Deal once and for all.[14]

The fear did not go unnoticed by advertisers. An ad by Warner and Swasey Turret Lathes asked Americans, "Did you ever face the sobering thought that your country may not win this war? Victory will go to the side with the most tanks, planes, guns, and shells, and so far the enemy has more than we. The weapons of war are made on machine tools, and tool production has been trebled. But tools can't make guns. Only the men who use the tools can do that." The ad encouraged each worker to increase out-put by 10 percent, which might bring the war to a successful end. "Some social theorizers say that if American workmen speeded up, they'd work themselves out of a job that much sooner. Yes, the speed-up we're suggest-ing would work them out of a job—the job of slaving for German and Jap masters at ten cents an hour."[15]

After the Japanese overran Burma on March 9, the situation seemed almost hopeless. As journalist Frederick Gruin wrote, "In a little more than three months, the aggressors in the East had won one million square miles of territory inhabited by more than 100 million people." In addition, the Japanese military "held the world's most important sources of rubber, tin, quinine, and hemp, as well as rich oil fields, inexhaustible supplies of foodstuffs, valuable iron, manganese, and copper deposits."[16]

It was not much better in the Atlantic. German U-boats sank 375,000 tons of tankers in March alone, and since the beginning of the year had sunk 1.25 million tons. At any given time, a dozen or so German U-boats cruised in the Gulf of Mexico and along the East Coast. German naval leaders calculated that each month, they could destroy as much tonnage as the American war machine could produce. Beaches in New Jersey and North Carolina were plagued by oil spills originating from sunken tankers. There was little the U.S. Navy could do. Three months after Pearl Harbor, the navy had only sixty-seven Coast Guard cutters and eighty-six planes to cover the East Coast, and Hitler's U-boat commanders had free sailing. Roosevelt complained to Churchill, "My navy has been definitely slack in preparing for this submarine war off our coast." The president blamed the situation on naval leaders, who "declined in the past to think in terms of any vessel of less than 2,000 tons."[17]

As American forces suffered continual setbacks that spring, Dr. Henry Shoskes, formerly a banker in Warsaw, told a gathering in New York that the Nazis in Poland had "deliberately managed to create such a condition in the ghettoes as to annihilate the inhabitants in the shortest possible time." Unless they were stopped, Shoskes warned, "there will be no more Jews in Poland." After the Wannsee meeting in January, the extermination of European Jews had begun in earnest. In March 1942, almost three-fourths of all the eventual Holocaust victims were still alive. By the end of the year, almost three-fourths had been slaughtered.[18]

At home, feelings of vulnerability were on open display. The Salamagundi Club in New York, which included a number of artists and painters, was uneasy with the artistic depiction of American soldiers. Club president George Lober worried that the pictures and drawings he had seen did not do justice to the "virility" of those serving in the armed forces. He agreed with the navy's Lieutenant Commander Griffith Baily Coale that artists should use more models who had actually served in the military, in order to portray them as properly "rugged." The navy planned on allowing some of its sailors to be loaned out to club members twice a week so that more acceptable portraits could be made.

Some advocated informing complacent adults about the dangers of war through their children. Office of Civilian Defense captain Donald S. Leonard suggested, "If the children could be taught the truth as to the peril latent in the present status of the war, they would carry this message home, where it is needed to stir adults into the desperate seriousness of the situation we are in." He added: "Some people still don't realize that we can lose the war." Given the continuing losses in the Pacific, Leonard concluded that Japan was "winning the war, and we should not fool ourselves to the contrary. . . . The minds of children should be impressed with this fact."

New York University chancellor Harry Woodburn was shocked that any government official would consider "saying that the American people were so complacent that school children ought to be told to carry home to their fathers and mothers word that the war might be lost." Leonard's suggestion, he said, made him wonder "just what sort of an unreal world such bureaucrats live in." He added: "If this war is lost, it will not be lost by the American people, it will be lost behind office desks in Washington, by the bureaucrats and the politicians."[19]

On March 2, Congress appropriated $32 billion for war, the largest single appropriation it had ever made. The enormous expenditure, and the certain knowledge that it was just the beginning, made questions of paying for the war a growing national concern. With the end of the fiscal year fast approaching, the House Ways and Means Committee waited until the following day to begin considering new tax legislation. Treasury secretary Henry Morgenthau told the committee that the administration planned to raise $7 billion in new taxes. His proposals doubled the tax bills of a vast majority of taxpayers. The new taxes "will be severe," the secretary warned, yet he reminded everyone that "it is a million times cheaper to win than to lose" a war. Morgenthau also asked for authority to order collection "at the source" through payroll deductions. This would not be an additional tax, merely a means of collecting the huge new levies. He reiterated the administration's opposition to a general sales tax, emphatically insisting that such levies were both inflationary and regressive. "The very lowest income earners," he said, "have all they can do to feed and clothe themselves and their families." He abandoned his earlier suggestion to tax all profits above 6 percent and instead called for an additional $1 billion in Social Security taxes, which would help in the fight against inflation and provide a pool of money to be used after the war for broader health and unemployment benefits. The sharpest blow for corporations was Morgenthau's proposed boost of the new corporate surtax from 6 percent to 31 percent, which would raise an additional $3 billion. If Congress enacted the proposed tax program, *Newsweek* reported, it "would impose upon American businesses and upon the middle and upper income groups a tax load probably heavier than that borne in any democratic nation. On the other hand, low income groups here would still pay a much smaller tax than in Canada or Britain."[20]

Taxation had been at the heart of social and political conflicts since the founding of the republic. In its early years, the relatively lean federal government did not have to confront the need for significant revenue, but during the Civil War, with the Union itself threatened, the White House and Congress resorted to a new tax on income. The first such tax, introduced by Representative Justin Morrill of Vermont, was a relatively modest levy of 3 percent on incomes above $800. By the end of the war, the rate had increased to 5 percent on incomes between $600 and $5,000, and 10 percent on incomes over $5,000. By 1865, approximately 10 percent of Union households were paying income taxes. Yet these taxes were seen as an emergency effort, and in 1872 Congress refused to renew them. By the eve of the twentieth century, one-third of federal revenues came from excise taxes on alcohol and tobacco, with tariffs providing most of the rest. Discussions for renewing the progressive income tax were thwarted in 1895 when the U.S. Supreme Court declared it unconstitutional.[21]

During the Gilded Age, when corporations and robber barons accumulated tax-free fortunes, the reliance on property and excise taxes struck many as galling. Debt-ridden farmers paid taxes on their property while Wall Street giants paid nothing on their enormous incomes, and as wealth disparity escalated, progressives called for a "graduated income tax." The ratification of the Sixteenth Amendment in 1913 made federal income taxes legal, but they remained a small part of the federal revenue picture. The Revenue Act of 1913 called for a tax rate of just 1 percent on incomes over $3,000, a level that required payment from just 2 percent of American households.[22]

When the U.S. entered World War I, in April 1917, the need for massive sums jolted the federal government into rethinking the whole matter of taxation. In 1918, rates for most taxpayers remained nominal, but the highest bracket increased to 77 percent. To fund the war in Europe, the federal government adopted an "excess profits" tax on corporate profits above a "normal" rate of return. This tax outraged business leaders but won praise from workers and unions. The nation's brief foray into World War I cost $38 billion in all, including 28.6 percent of GDP spent on the war in the last three months of 1918. After the war, federal taxes returned to their relatively low prewar levels. In 1926, people making up to $4,000 paid only 1.5 percent in taxes, and the highest bracket was 25 percent. The upper rate increased to 79 percent in 1936, but this affected only a tiny number of earners. In 1939, only 7 percent of workers paid any income tax at all.[23]

Raising the staggering amounts required by Roosevelt's mobilization plans demanded far more than bonds or small rate increases. After Pearl Harbor, the president and Morgenthau turned to increasing taxes, especially on corporations and wealthy Americans. In March, taxpayers got the first gleanings of the new rates.

Morgenthau's tax tables revealed the progressivity of the administration's revenue plans. Only forty-eight thousand taxpayers in 1942 made more than $2,500. The minimum wage stood at 30 cents per hour, meaning that someone who worked for such a wage would likely not make more than $700 a year even with overtime. Lower- and middle-income groups accounted for nearly 80 percent of the national income in 1941. Morgenthau's proposals for the upper brackets took already high levels to a degree that economist Thomas Piketty labeled "confiscatory." A single person making $50,000 would find his or her tax rate increased from 40 percent to 56 percent; for someone making $100,000, the rates would go up from 53 percent to 73 percent. In the highest bracket, incomes of $1 million and higher, the rate would go from 73 percent to 88 percent. As Congress began

Table 1. Proposed federal income tax rates, March 1942

Income ($)	Single taxpayer		Married taxpayer	
	Present tax	Proposed tax	Present tax	Proposed tax
800	3	8	0	0
1,000	21	40	0	0
1,500	69	128	0	0
2,000	117	230	42	80
3,000	221	470	138	285
5,000	483	1,023	375	805
10,000	1,493	2,720	1,305	2,435
15,000	2,994	4,888	2,739	4,535
50,000	20,882	27,715	20,439	27,145
100,000	53,214	69,625	52,704	68,965
500,000	345,654	429,610	345,084	428,935
1,000,000	733,139	879,610	732,554	878,935

Sources: Time, March 9, 1942; *New York Times,* March 4, 1942.

considering these proposals, the Treasury Department sponsored an ad of a man proudly depositing his tax returns in the mail, while nearby a woman beamed, "I'm so proud of you!"[24]

In the three months since Pearl Harbor, Congress had largely complied with the administration's requests, passing War Powers legislation and approving a variety of administrative agencies. The tax bill, however, presented a challenge to senators and representatives who hoped for reelection in eight months. Wishing to delay the issue and avoid angry constituents, Congress balked, and months would go by without any resolution, eventually prompting a showdown between the legislative and executive branches of the federal government.

As the tax bill stalled, another Treasury Department proposal drew immediate fire. Its suggestion that married couples file mandatory joint returns was attacked at a House Ways and Means hearing on March 25 by representatives of several women's groups, who thought the proposal might return women to the "status of chattels." One of the witnesses was district judge Sarah T. Hughes of Texas, who presided over divorce courts in Dallas. Hughes said mandatory joint returns would increase divorces and weaken the "stability of the family and the home." She thought the proposal was unconstitutional and was about far more than taxes: "It concerns individual freedom, that thing for which the people of the democracies are fighting."[25] Judge Hughes was eventually named to the federal bench by President Kennedy, and on November 22, 1963, swore in fellow Texan Lyndon Johnson as president aboard Air Force One.

On March 5, OPA director Leon Henderson appeared before a Senate committee and made declarations that caught the attention of the nation's 30 million motorists. For all intents and purposes, he told them, they were driving on the last set of tires they could purchase for at least three years. The rubber situation had grown so grave that the government might even commandeer tires from passenger automobiles. Gasoline rationing was in sight as well, Henderson warned, in order to decrease tire wear. Motorists who drove faster than forty miles per hour should be seen as "slackers," he added, and the "bootlegger in tires" was far worse than the people who sold liquor during Prohibition. Senator Harry Truman, who for the past year had headed a Senate committee looking into waste and corruption in U.S. war production, asked Henderson, "If we do not take care of our tires and they run out, do you mean that we won't get anymore?" Henderson replied: "That is the simplest way to put it." No one could criticize his own choice of automobile. He drove a used car he had bought for $300 and had tires that the *New York Times* described as "almost treadless."[26]

Henderson did not help his cause when, a few days after his Senate appearance, he decided to take a poorly timed vacation to Puerto Rico. His first stop was Miami, where he spent an evening visiting nightclubs. Considering the sacrifices he had just demanded of millions of Americans, his partying was not well received. The *Miami Daily News* noted that Henderson was seen with "an imposing roll of banknotes," and while he had nothing to say to reporters, he was nonetheless interested in "seeing as much of Miami's night life as possible."[27]

Henderson's night out rankled Joy Bowerman, a Miami stenographer, who wrote to FDR, "I am just one of the rank and file of the masses and am told every day by either the radio or the press that I am complacent and don't seem to be able to grasp the meaning of the fact we are at war." Bowerman said she "deeply resented" the OPA director's club-hopping and added, "Doesn't it appear as if Mr. Henderson might be the complacent one and the one who is not able to grasp the meaning of the fact that we are at war? . . . If Mr. Henderson should run out of places to go, General MacArthur could give him a few pointers."[28]

Henderson's public behavior did not endear him to many on either side of the political aisle. Ohio state senator Murray S. Parker, a Republican, deplored "Confusion Henderson's" trip and suggested, "Many people wish that a job might be found for him in Rio." The *Miami Herald* noted that with "millions of our youth under arms, thousands of them under enemy fire, the price administrator, who poses readily for the cameras, would do himself and the country a service by showing more delicacy and discretion and less gusto for display in his fun-seeking." A father of a soldier in the Army Air Corps hoped his son never saw the story of Henderson's escapades.[29]

Representative Martin Dies of Texas, the chair of the House Un-American Activities Committee, noticed as well. Dies and Henderson had tangled before, when Henderson testified before a committee in 1941 that the Texan was not a "responsible member of Congress." In 1942, Dies asserted that Henderson had been affiliated with Communists. Henderson angrily denied the allegation and offered to eat, on the steps of the Treasury Building, any evidence that connected him with any subversive organization. Dies, never one to worry about evidence, charged Henderson with being a "technocrat." Henderson rebuffed that charge by saying simply, "Try again, Mr. Dies." As long as he had the backing of the president, Henderson could dismiss the charges by his detractors, even powerful ones.[30]

Given the brewing discord, Henderson's image needed cultivating. The *Women's Home Companion* ("Understanding Women Is Our Full-Time Job!") ran an ad showing Henderson's image above his words: "Housewives are the frontline troops in the war against waste!" Noting that "every American homemaker is working earnestly in defense of her home and family," the magazine offered itself as the place where women could get the "practical help" necessary in fighting the war against household waste that would impress Henderson.[31]

FDR knew that Henderson's and the government's struggle to control inflation needed a boost. On March 9, he told a radio audience that the fight against "ruinous inflation . . . is not fought with bullets or with bombs, but it is equally vital." The economic war at home required not only "good will" among citizens but "unflagging vigilance and effective action by the government to prevent profiteering and unfair returns." The president noted that various sectors of the American economy might not be aware of what others were doing, which presented opportunities for resentment: "Labor, says the evil whisper, is sabotaging the war program with strikes and slowdowns, and demands for higher wages. Business, it says, is gouging the country with unconscionable profits. And the farmer is using the war to grab all he can." Acknowledging the black markets that had formed for some goods, he said he was certain 90 percent of the nation was cooperating in the national effort, and "if less than 10 percent of the population is chiseling we still have a pretty good national record."[32]

The president's words were soon quoted in an ad for the John Wanamaker Store in New York and Philadelphia. "Everything the President said about the dangers of serious inflation in his splendid speech," the ad read, "fits exactly with the basic principles of our entire economic program." Wanamaker's was lowering its profit margins and eliminating waste, and it hoped its customers would help the nation avoid "the pitfalls of serious inflation." The ad displayed some of the store's sale items, including men's tweed suits for $30 and flannel slacks for $6.50.[33]

Within the OPA, anxiety over inflation was growing. The cost-of-living index was rising 3 percent a month. OPA director of research Richard V. Gilbert warned Henderson in early March that "the price situation is now so serious that only drastic measures taken simultaneously on all fronts can prevent the development of an utterly unimaginable situation." Describing the brewing situation as "explosive," Gilbert noted that although the pending tax program would alleviate the government's fiscal imbalance, "we are faced with a prospect of $21 billion of excess purchasing power." The only solution, he believed, was some sort of compulsory savings program. He confided to another staffer, John Kenneth Galbraith, that Congress would like nothing better than to have Henderson advocate widespread rationing, which "Congress and the country will certainly regard as a screwball idea."[34]

One of the people most inclined to think that ideas coming from the OPA were "screwball" was former Kansas governor Alf Landon, the Republican

Party's 1936 presidential candidate. In a national radio address, Landon told listeners what he believed was to blame for the crisis: "I am convinced that those who continue to push forward new and untried changes in our social and economic system are the real creators of dissension in this country." Consequently, he claimed, the nation was "reaping the fruits of cynical 'debunking' and running down of all the old mooring posts in our national life. . . . Education and political philosophy have been turning out a generation that have not remembered the Creator in the days of their youth. Neither have they remembered the youth of the republic. As a result, we lack mooring posts to tie to. We have been cynically setting aside the political philosophy of our founders, and disregarding maxims as old as the race." Landon took dead aim at the New Deal: "Under the guise of social progress we have been educating the people to believe that government should support the people rather than that the people should support the government."[35]

By March, some of the restrictions issued by the war agencies had begun to affect the details of daily life. The WPB issued over two dozen clothing restrictions that changed the sartorial habits of some fashion-conscious men. Cuffs, pleats, double-breasted tuxedos, full dress coats, and the "fancy-back jacket" popularized by Clark Gable in *It Happened One Night* were prohibited to save cloth. Manufacturers had until the end of the month to make the changes, and tailors an additional two months. The WPB estimated that the restrictions, such as limiting the size of a belt on a size 37 sackcloth coat to twenty-nine and three-quarters inches, would reserve between 40 and 50 million pounds of raw wool a year for the armed forces. Similar restrictions on women's fashions drew the cautious disapproval of Edna Woolman Chase, the editor of *Vogue:* "Fashion is born out of the deep needs of all of us to look our best, and to feel better because we do. . . . The women of America would clothe themselves in sackcloth if it would help win this war, . . . but now we are learning that doing without may harm a nation as greatly as having too much." *Vogue's* readers were inspired by a "1942 uniform," a black wool suit "to make you look efficient and feminine" for $125.[36]

Stores did their best to adapt to the new clothing requirements, sometimes resorting to appeals that boggle the modern imagination. "So What?" asked an ad for Crawford Clothes, a major men's clothing chain, urging its customers to curtail their impulse to purchase new clothes. "Why? Why all the rush? Actually, little is gained in buying clothes if you don't need them now." The ad called buying more than one needed "not only unpatriotic but unwise and unnecessary."[37]

The federal government's authority to make such changes penetrated every aspect of American life. When eight hundred members of the American Bankers Association met in New York on March 4, many expressed their unease with the new rules of economic life. Henry Koeneke, the president of the organization, said, "It is an unpleasant fact that in modern, total war, great powers must be given to the central government so that it may take such steps as become necessary and act quickly as military necessity requires." Koeneke used the example of the auto industry, which just a few months before had been "flourishing," but now no longer existed "except as an adjunct of the armed forces of the nation. That is what the government can do when the nation is in peril." Other bankers criticized the navy for having been "slothful" at Pearl Harbor and mentioned that the fire on the *Normandie* was aided by people "not mentally on their toes." The bankers were resigned to a planned economy run by unelected people in executive agencies, but considered it their clear duty to "see to it that every great power given to the government includes a provision for its termination as soon as the war is ended."[38]

Later in March, at a meeting of mortgage bankers, delegates were informed that the war was having a transformative effect on wealth and housing. Marcus Nadler of NYU told the audience that future demand for "luxurious single-dwelling homes" would diminish and the needs of "a new middle class of skilled labor will increase the importance of more modest housing." The war was causing population to shift to where defense plants were erected, and those changes were "probably" permanent. The bankers understood that the massive demographic changes, coupled with higher taxes, were "bringing about a redistribution of wealth." They were right: as income was redistributed to lower brackets, the incomes of bankers and those in the financial sector fell throughout World War II.[39]

The New York Stock Exchange broke with tradition and in March officially recommended a security—U.S. Defense Bonds. Emil Schram, the president of the exchange, noted that since the founding of the NYSE in

1792, it had recommended a security only once before, when it placed its stamp of approval in 1917 on Liberty Bonds. In 1942, war called again, and the exchange hoped its members would invest "in national security today and in personal security for tomorrow." Schram believed that by urging investors to buy bonds, "this open market place of the system of American free enterprise is, in a sense, speaking in the interest of all sound securities."[40]

The worsening plight of American forces in the Pacific led to increasing pessimism at home. On March 19, two days after MacArthur had reached Australia, Office of Facts and Figures chief Archibald MacLeish warned that the real enemy was "the American defeatist who would rather lose the war, and with it everything America has been or can become, than make the terrible effort victory demands." He described the various kinds of "defeatists": "The idle women whose dinner hours have been altered and who call their country's struggle for its life 'this wretched war'; the sluggish men on the commuters' trains who have never fought for anything but golf balls in their lives; the American who fears or hates our allies in this war more than he trusts and loves his fellow-citizens; the partisan who would win his partisan victories at any cost of suffering or defeat to his own country." MacLeish warned of newspaper editors who "undermined the peoples' confidence in their leaders in a war, to infect their minds with suspicion of their desperately needed allies, to break their will to fight." The comment was an unsubtle dig at Robert McCormick's *Chicago Tribune*. Roosevelt wrote MacLeish that McCormick, along with Joseph Patterson (*New York Daily News*) and his sister Cissy Patterson (*New York Times Herald*), "deserve neither hate nor praise—only pity for their unbalanced mentalities." MacLeish confided to David Lilienthal, "McCormick and his unbelievable relative, Mrs. Patterson, use the privilege of 'criticism' as camouflage to cover a vicious propaganda resembling in many notable aspects the propaganda put out by the Nazis."[41] How MacLeish, as the nation's censor, would deal with such "unbalanced" editors exercising their First Amendment rights in wartime was a test that would be played out on a daily basis.

Another lingering tension between the administration and its political opponents seemed finally to be settled in March. Ever since June 1936, when the president spoke of business leaders as the "economic royalists" whose greed jeopardized American democracy, New Dealers within the administration had hungered for serious antitrust litigation against major corporations. Now, however, after Pearl Harbor and the nation's entry into the war, the administration needed the immediate aid of large manufacturers. Leading the effort against corporate power was the head of the antitrust division of the Justice Department, Assistant Attorney General Thurman Arnold, a devoted New Dealer who fiercely resisted the idea of companies using the war to their advantage. Yet on March 20, 1942, FDR approved the suspension of antitrust suits in cases that clearly impeded the war effort. The reasoning behind this decision was clear. The war "must come first and everything else must wait." If the war were lost, "the anti-trust laws, as indeed all American institutions, will become quite academic."[42]

If antitrust advocates had to face the reality of war, so did unions. The wartime "no-strike" promise that organized labor had made to the president was also made to the House Naval Affairs Committee on March 26, when CIO president Philip Murray appeared alongside American Federation of Labor president William Green and promised that no strikes or other work stoppages would be undertaken during war. "For the first time in the history of our government," Murray said, "labor has voluntarily yielded its right to strike. I hope you realize what that means. . . . The only weapon labor had for redress of wrongs that might be perpetuated upon it has been laid down, given to the President."[43]

By early spring, total war had come to every community in America, and each dealt with it in its own way. One was Durham, Connecticut, located about twenty miles northeast of New Haven and with a population of 1,087. It had only 324 homes, and its citizens mostly farmed but some had already found work in defense plants in Hartford or New Haven. One hundred and sixty-eight of its residents volunteered to watch for enemy planes at a local observatory, and the air-raid warden had trained twenty deputies. The churches and the town hall were prepared to serve as evacuation centers in case of an attack. One reporter, observing "the way of life for which Americans are fighting," noted how "women come afoot to the store to market and to get the morning mails," while "a mother, who was a bride in 1917 opens a letter with trembling fingers—a letter postmarked Air Training Center, Moffett Field, California."

Cities along the coasts had scheduled blackouts throughout the spring to judge their effectiveness in case of an actual attack. Boston organized two, while Portland, Maine, and Galveston, Texas, each conducted one that was considered "99 percent effective." When nearly a million people in the Bronx participated in a blackout in late March, reporters were impressed by the way the entire borough "became a virtually dead city, with great blocks of blackness marred by not a single touch of illumination." Yet the exercise was not met with universal approval. Three youths were given suspended sentences after they were ordered by air-raid wardens to extinguish their cigarettes. The youths complied but began shouting to local tenants to turn on their lights. Chastened after their sentencing, they promised to take future air raids more seriously. Mayor La Guardia was pleased with the overall effort and was confident that if the bombs actually arrived, "the city will be as dark as Hitler's heart."[44]

By late March, the rough outline of total war was in place, but whether Roosevelt's audacious production goals could be reached was still anyone's guess. There was some agreement among the WPB's leadership that the production totals would be met by the end of 1942, but they didn't know exactly where things stood because the administration worried that the precise information would be of interest to the enemy. Donald Nelson, no doubt already feeling pressure, asked in early March for an increase of 25 percent in machine tools. He called the arms effort "the most gigantic job any country has faced in all history," adding that upon its success rested "the whole course of history for a thousand years."[45]

The looming challenges and sense of shared sacrifice complicated the rules of personal finance and negotiation. Joe DiMaggio, the New York Yankees outfielder who in 1941 had a hit in a record fifty-six consecutive games, won the American League's Most Valuable Player Award, and led his team to a World Series championship, entered into negotiations with the Yankees in 1942 at the start of spring training. The Yankees planned to reward his 1941 season, arguably one of the greatest any player has ever had, with an increase of $2,500 from his previous salary of $37,500. Refusing to play with his team in "Grapefruit League" games until the Yankees agreed to a higher salary, DiMaggio told reporters that "all things considered, I feel justified in looking for an increase. I do not consider $2,500 a fair raise." He would not name a figure, but it was widely believed he would sign for $45,000. He remained in his penthouse on Lido Beach as the Yankees beat the Cardinals in St. Petersburg. Having held out for a week, DiMaggio returned to the field after agreeing to a reported salary of $42,500 (about $2.1 million in 2018 dollars). He quite likely could have gotten more, but perhaps he was aware how bad it would look for an athlete to hold out for a better contract at a time when millions were sacrificing life and limb for the war, and millions more were dealing with wage and price ceilings. Another reason may have been his parents, who came from Sicily and had lived near San Francisco for forty years but had not become American citizens. There was no suggestion that they presented a threat to the nation, but General DeWitt had said he wanted DiMaggio's parents evacuated and jailed—"no exceptions." While officials were able to keep the DiMaggios from jail, they were not allowed to use their private fishing boat or operate their restaurant on Fisherman's Wharf.[46]

Baseball would continue, but other sports struggled to decide whether to hold their 1942 seasons. In Georgia, canceling football at the University of Georgia and Georgia Tech was suggested in March by L. W. Roberts, chair of the state's Board of Regents. When told of a possible ban on football, Governor Eugene Talmadge replied: "We're doing everything for winning the war, if it takes putting our debutantes to hoeing potatoes," but he would not say whether such patriotic fervor extended to canceling football. The two men had worked together in 1941 on an effort to oust some faculty members the governor thought were trying to introduce "racial co-education," but whether he would support Roberts on the football issue was another matter.[47] Eventually, Roberts's proposal failed, and the Georgia Bulldogs won all but one of their games in 1942 and were crowned the national champions when they beat UCLA in the 1943 Rose Bowl. Most other sports continued as well, although the quality of competition was lessened by the number of athletes who entered the military. Byron Nelson won the Masters golf tournament and Shut Out won the Kentucky Derby. The major cancellation of the year was the decision by the United States Golf Association to cancel the U.S. Open.

With the approach of spring, some worried that improved weather conditions might make it easier for German or Japanese bombers to attack the

U.S. mainland. After the scares along the West Coast in February and the air raids along both coasts, a more clear-headed assessment of what was possible was undertaken in early 1942 by Hanson W. Baldwin, a Naval Academy graduate and military editor for the *New York Times*. Baldwin noted that considering the limits on military planes and the distances they would have to fly across the two oceans, an attack on the East Coast was far likelier. He based this assessment on a *Foreign Affairs* article by Edward Warner, who argued that, as a general rule, aircraft should plan on flying two and a half times the distance to a specific target in order to fully account for wind speed, fuel, and payload. A transatlantic flight, then, should use nine thousand miles as a base in considering an attack on New York or Washington. While no German or Italian planes had that capability, this did not rule out one-way suicidal flights or those that could take off or refuel at bases in Greenland or Labrador. Planes could also take off from aircraft carriers, but the carriers would have to sail through many miles of ocean undetected. The primary benefit for the Germans would be the "panic, confusion, and disruption" an attack would create, and the subsequent reallocation of resources to the home front and away from offensive actions in Europe. Baldwin concluded that the enemy could mount sustained attacks on the American mainland only if it captured new lands and bases close to North America, or developed bigger, longer-range bombers like the American B-19.[48]

Major metropolitan areas continued to prepare for the worst. The Manhattan Civil Defense Volunteer Office listed notices that advised New Yorkers "What to Do in an Air Raid." If on foot, "walk—do not run—into a nearby building." If their children were at school, parents were told not to go to the school but stay at home because the teachers "are trained to take care of them." There was also advice on what to do if in a car or a bus. The committee was adamant about one thing: "Never shout, scream, or run! If others do, don't you do it!" The enemy was likely trying "to create a panic— as dangerous as bombs." The local effort reflected the Office of Civilian Defense's approach led by James Landis, who traveled throughout the country warning every American to remain vigilant against imminent attack. He told thousands at the Cotton Bowl in Dallas that German planes bred "terror," while members of the Texas home guards entertained the crowd by bayoneting effigies of Hitler and Mussolini.[49]

The evacuation of Japanese Americans on the West Coast continued, and on March 18, FDR signed Executive Order 9102, establishing the War Relocation Authority (WRA) with the responsibility to "formulate and effectuate a program" of evacuation and internment. He appointed Milton Eisenhower, an Agriculture Department official and the brother of General Dwight Eisenhower, as its head. Just four days later, on March 22, the first group of Japanese Americans arrived in Manzanar, California, to begin the "relocation" process. Five hundred locals, nervous about having ten thousand Japanese Americans interned nearby, signed a petition urging they be kept behind barbed wire. A local barber said, "We ought to take those yellow tails right down to the edge of the Pacific and say to 'em, 'Okay boys, over there's Tokyo. Start walking.'" Those sent to the camps had to sell their property quickly, and San Francisco city leaders adopted an anti-gouging ordinance to keep them from being exploited. Despite the ordinance, Japanese Americans sold everything from stores to automobiles at pennies on the dollar. Milton Eisenhower proved a reluctant overseer of the internment camps and lasted just ninety days in the job. The reality of the situation was expressed by former army judge advocate W. A. Graham, who wrote that since February 19, when the president signed Executive Order 9066, "though the public generally does not realize it, we in California are living under conditions of martial rule."[50]

The day after Roosevelt established the WRA, the House select committee investigating "national defense migration," known as the Tolan Committee, released its preliminary report. The members of the committee supported Roosevelt's February Executive Order 9066, but understood there were some considerable challenges to removing and possibly interning millions of people with varying German, Italian, and Japanese backgrounds. While General DeWitt had initially planned on treating all three enemy groups the same, the sheer numbers of German and Italian Americans forced officials to rethink the matter. In 1942, almost 9 percent of the nation's population were of German or Italian descent and were scattered all across the continent. The committee wrote, "It is encouraging . . . that Gen. DeWitt proposes to postpone the movement of Germans and Italians until his organization has gained experience with the Japanese." If the War Department undertook the effort of gathering an estimated 300,000

German aliens and 675,000 Italian aliens, plus the possibility of including nearly 2 million more naturalized Germans and Italians, the committee concluded, "it is doubtful whether our war effort could bear the consequences of shifting them all from their present residences to new settlements." The fundamental issue, even in the crucible of war, was clear: "This is a nation of alien peoples."[51]

4

April: "General Max"

ON APRIL 6, EIGHT PAINTINGS BY Thomas Hart Benton were unveiled at the Associated American Artists Gallery on Fifth Avenue in New York City. Benton had been at work since Pearl Harbor on a series titled *The Year of Peril*, meant to show the enemy's genocidal nature. A native of Missouri, he originally intended to display them at Kansas City's Union Station, but after he finished the first few, Abbott Laboratories paid him $20,000 for the series and worked with the Office of War Information (OWI) to distribute the images on posters and pamphlets. One of the most striking, titled *Again*, showed Jesus Christ suffering on the cross, shot from the air by an enemy plane and stabbed in his side by modern soldiers. "Over and over again," Benton said about the painting, "evil people with mad dreams of power have driven the centurion's spear into His side."

Two paintings depicted the horror on American soil. One, entitled *Invasion*, is an apocalyptic vision reminiscent of Picasso's *Guernica*. On a midwestern American farm, marauders inflict horrifying violence on a family, killing a man and raping a woman, while a wounded young boy reaches for a red wagon. In another, *The Harvest*, enemy planes fly away as a distraught woman stands next to the dead bodies of a young child and an older man, holding her face in a way reminiscent of Edvard Munch's *The Scream*. Benton's nightmarish scenes captured the somber mood of the nation, and he warned that if the scenes he imagined took place "because of halting production measure at home," then "the war will be lost." Like many Americans,

Benton worried that the year foretold the impending collapse of Western civilization. Edward Alden Jewell, the art critic for the *New York Times,* felt that Benton had "loosed unreservedly his wrath and his deep-throated sirens of warning." "For all its melodramatic shrillness and luridness," Jewell wrote, "this is an urgent message that deserves to be read." In the first weeks after the New York opening, seventy-five thousand people viewed the paintings, but the OWI soon stopped distributing the series out of fears that soldiers might go AWOL if they saw the terrifying pictures.[1]

These apocalyptic visions were shared by many of the nation's evangelical ministers, who saw the world crumbling before them. Secularism, Catholicism, and the war were the usual culprits, but a more ominous force at home worried them just as much as Axis troops—the "terrible octopus of liberalism" centered in the White House and the New Deal policies of Franklin Roosevelt. When over a hundred preachers met in St. Louis on April 7, including Harold Ockenga of Boston and Bob Jones Sr. of South Carolina, they expressed general agreement that FDR and his administration posed a dire threat to Christianity. William Ward Ayer of New York's Calvary Baptist Church, for instance, railed against the "radicals in high places in our government life." The pastors agreed to form the National Association of Evangelicals for United Action, and as its first president, Ockenga told his colleagues, "I see on the horizon ominous clouds of battle unless we are willing to run in a pack." The organization, representing over 1 million parishioners, would become an inspiration to young ministers like Billy Graham and would grow into a potent force in American politics, standing in opposition to "big government" programs that its members felt encouraged secularism, gender and racial equality, and socialism.[2]

The news from the war fronts was relentlessly bad. Throughout April, the Japanese swept across Southeast Asia, and after defeating the British at Singapore they took Malaya, Java, and Borneo. American forces in the Philippines had retreated to Bataan, and as historian George Herring writes, by the spring of 1942, "From Wake Island in the Central Pacific to the Bay of Bengal, Japan reigned supreme." Hitler's grip on Europe tightened and his divisions had driven deep into Russia. German troops under Erwin Rommel threatened the Suez Canal and had routed British forces throughout the Middle East. Hitler controlled one-third of the world's population and mineral resources, and the possibility of some kind of negotiated peace lingered in the minds of observers on both sides of the Atlantic. In the United States, frustration mounted that no serious offensive steps had been undertaken against an enemy that seemed increasingly invincible.[3]

On April 9, the War Department announced that 11,500 Americans and 64,000 Filipinos fighting in Bataan had surrendered. Although the nation would not know the full details until later in the war, what occurred next was one of the darkest moments in American military history. The victorious Japanese, who considered surrender disgraceful, subjected the Allied soldiers to an eighty-mile trek in tropical heat to a prisoner-of-war camp near the base of the peninsula. In what became known as the Bataan Death March, the Japanese forces denied water to the prisoners, bayoneted stragglers, and committed unspeakable acts of brutality. Historian David M. Kennedy described it as "one of the cruelest episodes" in a war that would "grotesquely add to history's already extensive annals of cruelty." Six hundred Americans died on the march, and many more died in the camps. The rocky fortress of Corregidor, an island at the mouth of Manila Bay commanded by Lieutenant General Jonathan Wainwright, was the lone U.S. holdout in the Philippines. War secretary Henry Stimson noted to FDR, "Our troops were outnumbered and worn down by successive attacks as well as lack of food and the diseases peculiar to the tropics. Their lines were finally broken. . . . I don't know what happened, but it is evident that Bataan has been overthrown. Corregidor is still fighting." Unlike Stalin or Hitler, who insisted that their forces fight to the bitter end even if that meant certain death, Roosevelt gave Wainwright the sole authority to decide whether to continue fighting or surrender.[4]

After the president gave his cabinet the news from Bataan, Interior secretary Harold Ickes commented in his diary: "I used to wonder how rulers of a country could stand it to have their people killed, wounded, or captured, their lands ravished, their property destroyed, and their women raped." After four months of war, Ickes discovered "that those responsible for the welfare of a country cannot allow any considerations" to weigh on them "except the accomplishment of final victory. . . . We have to go ahead on the theory that there is no price too great to pay for the privileges that we enjoy as Americans." In a nation that battled with "great valleys of poverty and social injustices," Ickes found the "prejudices and passions between different elements and sets" were "infinitely to be preferred to such slavery as exists in Germany." In the end, "we have to be indifferent to the cost, not only in money, but in human lives."[5]

The events in Bataan had devastating consequences for one Kentucky county. Sixty-six soldiers from Mercer County, all of them part of the 192nd Tank Battalion, had not been heard from since April 9. The battalion had landed in the Philippines in November 1941 and was among the first to do battle with the Japanese. *Life* proclaimed that in the county seat of Harrodsburg, the terrifying consequences of war had come early: "Harrodsburg is one of the first towns in the entire country to taste the last full measure of war." The men who sat regularly outside the county courthouse hoped their young men were still fighting the Japanese, but then the local paper began giving instructions on how readers could send letters to prisoners of war. One such reader was J. T. Gentry, who owned a four-hundred-acre farm and whose son, William, was a first lieutenant in the battalion. Gentry said he was proud of his son and "wouldn't want a slacker in my family," and when his other son, Dick, volunteered for aviation training school, Gentry said, "The government's got both of my boys and that's all right. I only wish I had some more to give." "No man likes to have his sons go to war," he added, "but it's right they do and we are with them all the way." In time, the residents of Mercer County learned that twenty-nine of their sons died in the attack on Bataan. The other thirty-seven would survive the death march. One of these, William Gentry, was awarded two Silver Stars and a Purple Heart. He lived until April 2000.[6]

The conversion to a total-war economy continued. Refrigerators, typewriters, radios, vacuum cleaners, and metal office furniture were no longer being made, and consumers understood that soon there would be no new lawnmowers or sewing machines. The endless automobile assembly lines that had produced Fords, Pontiacs, and Plymouths had been modified with new lines and machinery to produce bombers, jeeps, and tanks. In early April, the government announced that the manufacture of golf clubs would be halted by the end of May, in order to save 3 million pounds of steel and one ton of aluminum each year. The manufacture of golf balls had been halted on April 1.[7]

Yet victory required more than armaments. Runaway inflation could esca-late the price of those armaments, make the tax increases meaningless, widen domestic political divisions, and ultimately, perhaps, make victory impossible. Well aware of the perilous economic conditions that faced the nation and the Allied cause, administration officials continued to discuss a dizzying array of economic proposals aimed at raising revenue while containing inflation. Throughout the spring, Americans heard about plans that involved freezing all prices, rents, and wages; curtailing consumer credit; initiating an excess profits tax of 100 percent combined with a compulsory savings program of 20 percent; placing a $50,000 ceiling on individual incomes; lowering indi-vidual tax exemptions; implementing a national sales tax; and creating a war consumption tax of 5 percent. Whether any of these measures would be en-acted remained to be seen, but everything, whether revealed to the public or not, was on the table. Taxpayers and Congress, meanwhile, were growing in-creasingly frustrated with administration "bureaucrats" who seemed to wield power along the lines of czars and monarchs.[8]

In April, historian Allan Nevins wrote about the array of national chal-lenges, saying that the U.S. was in a far different state than when it entered World War I. Following Pearl Harbor, wrote Nevins, the nation "savagely denounced all politics, timidity, and executive mollycoddling, and it clam-ored for that concentration of authority which was once feared." But behind the apparent unity were looming issues: "Do we have sufficient unity of the more exacting kind: the kind that will enable farmers, workers, capitalists, and professional groups to work together with sympathy and comrade-ship?" Major constituencies of the American economy would have to adjust their activities. Farmers "will have to cease demanding high advances over parity, workers to cease asking for inordinate wage rises, and business-minded editors to cease printing Wake-Up America editorials which attack farmers and workers while saying practically nothing about capitalist prof-its." If those groups did not endorse shared sacrifice, Nevins warned, "we shall have that equality of sacrifice seen in Poland, Greece and occupied France—where everybody has lost practically everything."[9]

An unlikely source revealed the state of American war production at the time, with a quarter of the year already past. House Speaker Sam Rayburn told a crowd in Sulphur Springs, Texas, that the U.S. was currently making thirty-three hundred planes a month and would be able to reach the president's stated goal of sixty thousand by the end of the year. "Without divulging military secrets," he added, "I can say that one factory alone is turning out each day an entire trainload of tanks." Rayburn assured his audience that "your son is not being sent to battle until he is the best trained and equipped soldier that ever went to war." The president himself, he reminded people, had four sons in the armed forces, and the popular Texas pol was clear about where his support lay: "Trust your leadership. The country cannot win this war and the President lose it. Do not allow us to be divided." Representative Clarence Cannon of Missouri added to the promising narrative, claiming that the volume of war production "borders on the miraculous."[10]

The real numbers were not quite what Rayburn and Cannon were telling the public. While the U.S. actually produced 3,495 planes in April, a few more than what Rayburn had stated, the total for the first quarter was just over 13,000. At that rate, the number of planes built in 1942 would fall 21,000 short of the president's goals. Considering that the same factories would have to turn out 5,875 planes a month beginning in May to reach Roosevelt's figures, some within the War Production Board and the Office of Price Administration hoped to persuade FDR to lower his original estimates. Richard V. Gilbert complained to Leon Henderson that "a defeatist campaign is on to cut the war production program by 30 percent or more," adding that the president's goals were being criticized "by the bright angels who first acclaimed it." Gilbert warned that publicly slashing Roosevelt's goals "courts military and political disaster."[11] In the meantime, the real figures would be kept secret, and officials could either massage the numbers by counting other planes in the total, or else hope that the factories could increase their output so that the president would not be embarrassed at year's end.

On April 8, Henderson went to the White House for a meeting with President Roosevelt, budget director Harold Smith, and Federal Reserve chair Marriner Eccles. Afterward, Roosevelt and Henderson lunched alone. Henderson would not reveal the specifics of what was discussed, but he told reporters that new taxes would be necessary to control inflation. The general price level was still "of a highly explosive character but has not been touched off." The *New York Times* predicted that the OPA might freeze all wholesale and retail prices that were not already under a price ceiling.[12]

Henderson privately anguished over the specter of runaway inflation. On April 24, after the Bureau of Labor Statistics found that the cost of living had increased 15 percent since September 1939, he informed the president that "the price situation is getting out of hand," but he still cautioned that freezing wages "is a drastic measure" that should not be "proposed lightly." The political implications were not lost on the OPA director: such a freeze "may make it more difficult for some unions to hold their membership, let alone increase it." Henderson also underscored the importance of placing a ceiling on income at $50,000 for individuals and $100,000 for families, which he felt would "dramatize the equality of sacrifice, which is essential in a general program as drastic as the one we propose." The OPA's program represented "a call to the colors on the civilian front," and if the government failed to control inflation, it would be a "defeat in one of the decisive battles of the war."[13]

Adding to the inflationary pressure was even more war spending. On April 24, budget director Smith announced that FDR's previous estimate of $56 billion in war outlays had been revised to $70 billion for the fiscal year beginning July 1. The mounting debt and its consequences worried many financial observers, including some within the administration. Treasury Department economist Harry Dexter White wrote to Secretary Morgenthau that when the war ended, the interest on the debt would create "a serious obstacle to government expenditures for socially desirable purposes in the post-war period." Unless steps were taken to reduce the debt, there would be "a substantial redistribution of the national income in the wrong direction," resulting in the emergence of "a new economic class" composed of government bondholders "who are bound to consolidate and create a new and powerful vested interest." In addition to more short-term borrowing, White proposed a system of compulsory savings bonds that would yield 1 percent upon maturity. Others were also worried about the federal debt. Emil Schram, president of the New York Stock Exchange, estimated that the total federal debt could reach $150 billion by 1944, and if the war lasted longer, could top $200 billion. (That amount would come to $24.8 trillion in 2018 dollars. The federal debt at the end of 2018 was somewhat less, approximately $22 trillion.) Yet, Schram said, "whatever the cost of victory may be, the American people are prepared to pay it."[14]

With further rationing of consumer goods soon to come, Americans went on a spending spree over Easter weekend. *Newsweek* called it "the last free and unfettered shopping spree for the duration." Men bought two or three suits instead of one to beat a deadline after which all pants had to be cuffless and all double-breasted suits vestless. Stores ran ads begging customers to buy less, yet shoppers ignored their pleas. J. C. Penney earned $6 million more in April than it had in January, and F. W. Woolworth's nearly $5 million more.[15]

Whenever supplies were cut or goods were rationed, the OPA grew concerned about black-market economies that could escape official records and increase consumer spending. Historian Caroline F. Ware wrote in her 1942 book *The Consumer Goes to War* that "every black market is Hitler's ally" and "every bootleg tire helps the Japs." Citizens were asked to keep their eyes open to such activities, but the OPA had little ability to enforce its policies. Whether neighbors would resort to reporting on each other remained to be seen, but a palpable tension was brewing among consumers and merchants.[16]

Retailers remained convinced that more drastic government price controls were coming soon. An "exceptionally well-posted retail executive," according to the *New York Times*, warned on April 12 of an imminent announcement in the "terrific" battle against inflation: "The price ceiling is coming and it will be a stiff dose of medicine for retailers." The executive also warned that many retailers would go out of business, not necessarily because of price ceilings but because they could not "get merchandise." A Gallup poll in mid-April showed that two-thirds of Americans already favored price and wage freezes to stabilize the economy. The states that favored the new regulations the most were Iowa (72 percent) and Texas and New Jersey (68 percent each). The state most opposed to controls was New York, where 34 percent disapproved and 9 percent were undecided. Nationwide, support for the controls ran at a 2–1 ratio. "If a national plebiscite were held," stated Gallup, "it would be found that the people are far ahead of their government."[17]

While we may think of the wartime economy as one in which every factory produced tanks and guns, the reality was far different. Across the country, nearly 125,000 factories produced nothing toward the war, and the *New York Times* described the worrying landscape for these companies—they faced "the alternatives of making essential civilian goods, changing to war economy, or strangling slowly." Among the nation's smaller manufacturers, many felt that they were being left out of government contracts, and that without help they would soon be out of business entirely. Their worries only increased when the WPB announced that in the first four months of war, 85 percent of the approximately $100 billion in war contracts had been given to just 350 companies, mostly large, established concerns. With the government trying to reduce consumer spending and with raw materials increasingly hard to come by, the outlook for some of these smaller companies was grim. Donald Nelson told a news conference in April that industrial "casualties" were "just inevitable." Harold Ickes worried that even if the U.S. won the war, it could still "lose the peace" because of the "manner in which big business is being coddled." In Salt Lake City, a frustrated small businessman complained that "all the government has got to do is just keep taxing and they'll have every damn business in the country out of business. . . . You'd think a small businessman is a criminal they way they go after him."[18]

Leaders of large corporations struggled to avoid the appearance of profiting from the war as small companies languished. General Electric president Charles Wilson said his company's income in 1942 would be approximately $1 billion, yet the company "has no intention of profiteering on war business." On April 14, IBM's Thomas J. Watson, already worried about his public image as a possible Nazi sympathizer, asked his board of directors to reduce his share of the profits from 5 percent to 2.5 percent. (In 1941, Watson's salary was $462,519.) Meanwhile, the U.S. Chamber of Commerce proposed a new $10 billion tax plan that would tax all war profits at 100 percent and institute a retail sales tax of 10 percent. While a sales tax would disproportionately affect lower income brackets, a majority of Americans polled in the spring of 1942 favored a federal sales tax of 2 percent but opposed anything higher.[19]

Amid the various pressures on Nelson and the WPB, morale within the agency began to suffer. Few business leaders seemed pleased with the WPB or with Nelson's leadership. To gauge what those within the WPB were really feeling, a secret survey was conducted among a thousand employees, including "dollar a year" appointees and general staff. Most were confident in Nelson's leadership but believed he was not fully exercising his considerable powers. The nation, they thought, was "ready for the strongest measures that may be needed rather than a gradual transition that results in uncertainty and bad morale." Most within the WPB thought it needed to become a "functioning business-like organization with definite lines of authority and powers." Whether it could ever achieve such efficiency seemed doubtful unless changes were authorized from the White House.[20]

Other businesses strove to justify their very existence. The American Motion Picture Industry ran an ad in the April 16 *New York Times* with the headline "Morale Is Mightier Than the Sword!" The film industry, the ad stated, could not "build combat planes or bombers," but it could "give America the hours of carefree relaxation which will make its work hours doubly productive." While some industries existed to "keep 'em flying, keep 'em shooting," movies would "keep 'em smiling."

Hollywood had begun producing war-related films even before the U.S. entered the war. In the spring, Twentieth Century–Fox released *To the Shores of Tripoli,* which proved to be the studio's biggest-grossing film of the year. The film was in post-production when the attack on Pearl Harbor occurred, causing the producers to reshoot the ending. Rather than have the former Marine, played by John Payne, marry the navy nurse (Maureen O'Hara), the new version has the soldier proudly reenlisting when he hears of the news of the attack.[21] Some of the film's fans thought its patriotic fervor helped the Marine Corps in its recruitment.

Walt Disney, smarting from the embarrassment caused by the $80,000 he accepted from the Treasury Department to promote the Donald Duck tax propaganda film, *The New Spirit,* devoted his time to a new film that would have a significant impact on American culture and would produce even more outrage. The animated film about a small deer, *Bambi,* would be released that summer. Despite its seemingly innocent themes, some hunters found the movie's portrayal of gun owners downright offensive. Raymond J. Brown, editor of *Outdoor Life,* said the film "was the worst insult ever offered to American sportsmen and conservationists." *Time* noted that "Disney's indictment of men who kill animals for sport is so effective that U.S. sportsmen who have seen the picture are gunning for him."[22]

Although President Roosevelt had issued an executive order in 1941 requiring companies producing war goods to be unbiased in their hiring, racial and religious discrimination remained the rule. Many companies simply would not change. On April 12, the President's Committee on Fair Employment Practices ordered ten such companies to cease their discriminatory policies. Among those cited were the Buick Aviation plant in Melrose, Illinois, the Studebaker branch factory near Chicago, and the Allis Chalmers Corporation of Milwaukee, all of which the committee charged with refusing to "employ Negroes or Jews, or both, but chiefly the former." The companies had asked private employment agencies for only white or "Gentile" workers and had advertised for employees who were only "Protestant" or "white." They denied they were in violation of Roosevelt's order, but were required to furnish evidence that their hiring practices were in line with "the national policy."[23]

The growing tension between white and African American soldiers boiled over yet again, this time at Fort Dix, New Jersey. In the preceding months, the *New York Times* reported, "there has been considerable tension between the white and Negro soldiers of the camp." An argument over the use of a pay phone at the Military Sports Palace, just off the base, escalated into a gun battle that killed a white MP and two African American soldiers. Five other black soldiers were wounded, but the base commander ruled it was "merely a brawl with no racial significance." As historian Lizabeth Cohen writes, "Black soldiers surely were angered at being denied access to a commercial service, particularly in a northern state."[24] Whether in armament production or serving in the military, African Americans confronted a racial code that was not ready to change, even for national survival.

The news came first from a Japanese radio station: "Just after noon on the 18th, the first enemy planes appeared over the city of Tokyo." The reports gave little information but indicated the attack "inflicted damage on schools and hospitals." No confirmation was forthcoming from Washington. In the next hours, reports of air attacks from planes with American insignias came from Kobe, Nagoya, and Yokohama. Journalists and experts scrambled, wondering if American planes had actually bombed the Japanese capital. How had it been done? With Japan's control of the Pacific, the Japanese home islands seemed impervious to American bombers simply because they were too far from any American bases. If the planes had taken

off from aircraft carriers, how had the ships sailed so far without being detected? The first reports indicated the planes were likely American B-25s,
which only added to the mystery. B-25s were probably too bulky to take off
from a carrier and certainly too large to land on one. Considering that the
U.S. Navy had a total of just seven carriers, would it risk one or more on a
raid that Hanson Baldwin of the *New York Times* thought "could have no
decisive effect upon the war's course"? Instead, Baldwin offered his best
guess: "It seems quite possible that planes based on a Chinese field conducted the first air raid in history on metropolitan Japan."[25]

For three days, the raid on Tokyo remained shrouded in mystery. The
origins of the planes, their mission, and where they went were sources of
endless speculation among knowledgeable observers in Washington. Not
until President Roosevelt held a press conference on April 21 did the public
learn the news: American planes had indeed attacked Japanese cities. An
obviously pleased FDR recalled that during a recent White House dinner, a
"sweet young thing" asked, "Where did those planes start from and go to?"
Roosevelt told the reporters that he responded, "They came from our new
secret base at Shangri-La." That coy answer hid a secret plan that had been
in the works for months. Sixteen B-25 bombers had taken off from the carrier *Hornet* just eight hundred miles from the Japanese coast. The plan
called for the pilots to bomb various inland targets and parachute to safety
in China before their planes ran out of fuel. Most of the crews made it to
China, while one landed north of Vladivostok and two were forced down in
Japan. The attack had been a daring gamble that brought little military advantage but did wonders for American morale and showed the Japanese
that their island was vulnerable in ways they had never considered. The attack provoked the Japanese high command to retaliate brutally in its occupied Chinese areas and to reconsider its overall Pacific strategy. It also gave
Americans a new hero: the leader of the raid, Lieutenant Colonel Jimmy
Doolittle.

The daring attack provided Americans a sense that Japan would pay for
Pearl Harbor. Secretary of War Stimson had been "a little bit doubtful"
about the raid because he worried it would "only result in sharp reprisals"
from the Japanese, but he relented because it was "a pet project of the President's." Historian David M. Kennedy described Doolittle's daring raid as

"a hare-brained stunt," but one that "set in motion a chain of events with momentous implications." After the raid, Japanese leaders recognized the threat posed by the "Midway slot" and over the next weeks focused their efforts on capturing Midway Island, which they saw as a precursor to the eventual capture of Hawaii. The series of events set off by the Doolittle raid would prove a turning point in the war.[26]

Americans could only guess at other secrets Roosevelt knew. One was that he had approved, well before Pearl Harbor, a massive project to develop an atomic bomb. Three years earlier, the question of whether Hitler's scientists could produce a weapon that harnessed nuclear power frightened American scientists enough to convince Roosevelt that the U.S. should begin its own research campaign. In a famous letter to the president written in August 1939, Albert Einstein had warned that it might be possible to produce a chain reaction within "a large mass of uranium, by which vast amounts of power" could be generated, and the need to develop such a weapon before German scientists did so required "quick action on the part of the administration." Roosevelt began pouring federal money into the vast effort. By the time the U.S. entered the war, some within the government may have known such plans were in the works, but they had no idea of their scope. A. I. Elder of the WPB told a meeting of the American Chemists Society in Memphis in late April that the nation's greatest secret weapon was its "inventive genius." Hitler and Hirohito, said Elder, should expect "some secret weapons to appear."[27]

By late April, increasingly frustrated by congressional inaction on inflation, FDR appealed directly to the American people in a fireside chat on April 27 to convince them of the need for immediate action. The speech was the culmination of several meetings that had started with the lunch between Roosevelt and Henderson. "We realize that the war has become what Hitler originally proclaimed it to be—a total war," said Roosevelt. That war would require the nation to spend "a lot of money, more money than has ever been spent by any Nation at any time in the long history of the world." He added the nation was already spending "about $100 million every day," but that figure would be doubled by the end of the year. In language that endeared him to millions, Roosevelt said, "You do not have to be a professor of mathematics or economics to see that if people with plenty of cash start bidding against each other for scarce goods, the price of those goods goes up. . . . Because rises in the cost of living which came in the last war were not checked in the beginning, people in this country paid more than twice as much for the same things in 1920 as they did in 1914." To avoid a recurrence, the nation had to "face the fact that there must be a drastic reduction in our standard of living." If left unchecked, the president warned, inflation could reach 90 percent within one year.

Roosevelt highlighted a "seven-point program" for controlling the economy: (1) higher taxes; (2) ceilings on prices and rents; (3) stabilization of wage rates; (4) stabilization of farm prices; (5) more investment in war bonds with less consumption of goods; (6) rationing of scarce commodities; and (7) less installment buying and more repayment of debt. He went even further: "In time of this grave national danger, when all excess income should go to win the war, no American citizen ought to have a net income, after he has paid his taxes, of more than $25,000 a year." (This was equivalent, in 2018, to approximately $385,000.)[28]

Roosevelt's speech struck a chord with his audience, and he resorted to powerful appeals that he had not used in either the December 8 speech or his State of the Union address: "The price for civilization must be paid in hard work and sorrow and blood. The price is not too high. If you doubt it," then

ask the workers of France and Norway and the Netherlands, whipped to labor by the lash, whether the stabilization of wages is too great a "sacrifice." Ask the farmers of Poland and Denmark, of Czechoslovakia and France, looted of their livestock, starving while their own crops are stolen from their land, ask them whether "parity" prices are too great a "sacrifice." Ask the businessmen of Europe, whose enterprises have been stolen from their owners, whether the limitation of profits and personal incomes is too great a "sacrifice." Ask the women and children whom Hitler is starving whether the rationing of tires and gasoline and sugar is too great a "sacrifice."

In addition to calling for higher taxes and a maximum income, Roosevelt made it clear that he wanted something that most politicians would be loath to demand: "rigid self-denial, a substantial reduction for most of us in the scale of expenditure that is comfortable and easy for us." He made it clear that "we cannot have all we want, if our soldiers and sailors are to have all they need," but he refused to label this program "sacrifice." "I have never been able to bring myself, however, to full acceptance of the word 'sacrifice,' because free men and women, bred in the concepts of democracy and wedded to the principles of democracy, deem it a privilege rather than a sacrifice." It was more accurate to "call this total effort of the American people as 'equality of privilege.' "[29]

The next day, the administration released the details of the new policies, called the General Maximum Price Regulation, or General Max, that set ceilings on virtually every daily consumer item and regulated the economy in ways that would shock modern Americans. If rising prices were left to themselves, Henderson warned, "the inevitable result would be inflation, a defeat on the home front that could not fail to be reflected on the battlefields abroad." Henderson asked the American people "over the next few weeks to be tolerant," adding, "It will take time for the government to adjust its own machinery." He hoped people understood that the significant sacrifices involved were necessary: "This is a war measure, just as the Selective Service is a war measure."[30]

General Max touched everything from tobacco to infant food, clothing, household items, hardware, and fuel. Historian Meg Jacobs notes that it "was the first time the U.S. government had attempted to regulate and codify consumption by dictating retail prices throughout the economy." Henderson admitted that the orders were "of such magnitude that even we who have been busy framing them for the last few weeks cannot fully visualize their ramifications." *Newsweek* had no problem clarifying the ramifications: "Mr. and Mrs. John Brown are about to find totalitarian economic control has entered their democratic American way of life." To the *New York Times,* the directive was further evidence that Henderson was "the most potent figure in Washington today so far as the average citizen is concerned." On a deeper level, the directive was a watershed moment in American economic history, one that the *New York Times* decreed "forecast a degree of control of the nation's economy" that was "unprecedented in American history. Traditional rights of private enterprise, a cherished heritage of the country from the days of the earliest settlers, seemed foredoomed at least for the duration" of the war. General Max sent shudders through Wall Street. On the day it was announced, the

Dow Jones closed at 92.92, nearly 19 percent lower than where it had been in early January, and the lowest level since the depths of the Great Depression or afterward. In fact, Henderson warned that within fifteen months, the nation's standard of living could be as low as it was in 1932. Yet the directive had an immediate impact. From May to June 1942, the cost of living index dropped one-tenth of 1 percent, the first decline in nineteen months.[31]

While General Max hit consumers hard, its major weakness concerned agricultural prices. In a concession to the political power of the farm bloc, price ceilings on farm products could not occur until prices reached 110 percent of parity, and many foods were not covered at all. Over the next four months, prices on uncontrolled foods rose 10 percent. On April 27, FDR had asked that Congress amend the price-control law concerning farm prices, but the farm bloc resisted any changes.[32]

In addition to freezing many prices and wages, FDR took on a cause that would be unthinkable in just about any other situation. In calling for a maximum after-tax income of $25,000, Roosevelt introduced a bold idea that he felt was justified by the shared sacrifice of war. While modern readers are used to the concept of a minimum wage, the idea of a maximum income, where the government confiscates 100 percent above a certain level, seems to come from a dystopian novel. Yet even more surprising may be the concept's popularity in 1942. *Newsweek* commented that the president's plan "has met with enthusiastic approval of the common man. Even the Republicans admit it was a master political stroke." In the midst of total war in which many in the military would pay with their lives, the notion of taxing all income over a certain amount was applauded by those who remembered the "Profiteers" of World War I. But an income tax of 100 percent, for any bracket, seemed to run counter to the American ideal of free enterprise. To the nation's founders, after all, high taxes were seen as the lynchpin of tyranny. Yet this was not the first time FDR had championed the idea of limiting incomes. In the summer of 1941, he had proposed to the Treasury Department the idea of limiting personal income to $100,000 and taxing the rest at 99 percent. "Why not?" he asked, since "none of us is ever going to make $100,000 a year."[33]

Roosevelt was not the first reformer to call for income limits. The idea had been floated in 1880 by the moral philosopher Felix Adler, who in response to enormous wealth inequality had suggested a graduated income tax "up to 100 percent on all income above that needed to supply all the comforts and refinements of life." In the early days of the Depression, Senator Huey Long of Louisiana had proposed a "Share Our Wealth" plan that limited income to $1 million, then more than three hundred times the average family income. Long bristled at critics who called his plan "socialistic," arguing that it would actually create more millionaires by preventing massive concentrations of wealth. His plan was echoed by "radio priest" Father Charles Coughlin, who declared that in "the event of war for the defense of our nation and its liberties, there shall be a conscription of wealth as well as a conscription of men." At his height of popularity in the late 1930s, Coughlin commanded a listening audience of 30 million. Roosevelt's call for a confiscatory tax came in a context in which limiting incomes was no moral call for redistribution but a popular demand that no one should be immune from shared sacrifice or earn disproportionate profits from the war. Yet the very idea was sure to generate a backlash from conservatives wary of allowing government to establish such a principle, even in war.[34]

The first test of Roosevelt's plan came from House Ways and Means Committee chairman Robert L. Doughton of North Carolina, who claimed there was no "feverish demand" for limits on incomes. The Senate was more receptive. Harry Byrd of Virginia favored a "reasonable salary limit," and two senators on the finance committee, Democrat Joseph Guffey of Pennsylvania and Republican Arthur Capper of Kansas, said they favored FDR's plan. Republican Senator Robert Taft of Ohio, on the other hand, opposed the idea entirely, asking why the president had not made the limit $2,500 or some other arbitrary figure.[35]

It should be noted that in 1942, most American workers made less than $2,000 a year. According to the Securities and Exchange Commission, the highest salary in the United States in 1941, $704,425, was that of film executive Louis B. Mayer. Gun inventor and manufacturer Carl G. Swebilius was second with $628,839, and Eugene Grace of Bethlehem Steel made over $522,000. Several of the largest incomes in the country were not revealed since many came from sources other than wages. But the SEC report listed the salaries of many well-known Hollywood figures, such as Clark Gable ($357,500), Darryl Zanuck ($260,000), and Ginger Rogers

($215,000). Business executives on the list included George Washington Hill of the American Tobacco Company ($288,144), C. W. Deyo of Woolworth ($252,000), Harry Bracey of Kroger Grocery ($249,600), and Charles E. Wilson of General Electric ($175,000).[36]

One Wall Street insider dismissed the idea that salary limitations would do anything to limit inflation, while another noted that defending high salaries would only ensure the passage of the act, a remark that acknowledged the anti-capitalist sentiment in many corners of the nation. Defenders of the plan, such as Bernard Baruch, privately admitted they could live off the income from their savings and investments. Support for the plan came not only from defense workers and recently drafted soldiers; the head of a billion-dollar utility company anonymously told the *New York Times* that he supported the president's plan, adding that he could "see no economic justification for salaries in the $300,000 to $500,000 range." The corporate leaders accepting such salaries, the executive suggested, "are just helping to pull down the whole structure of free enterprise."[37]

Outside of Wall Street, the president's plan was popular, especially as one went down the income range. A government survey found that 64 percent supported the plan while 24 percent opposed it. Just three years earlier, *Fortune* magazine had reported that 72 percent of lower- to middle-income respondents opposed any measures limiting incomes. According to the government survey, Roosevelt's call for a maximum income had suddenly become "a symbol of the idea of equality of sacrifice."[38] Whether this support would translate into policy remained to be seen.

On the same day that General Max was announced, General Brehon Somervell, commander of the Army Service Forces, wrote to Henderson about the growing rubber crisis. Considering the desperate shortage, Somervell suggested that the army should purchase all available stocks of tires from civilian automobiles in order to ensure that tires remained available for military purposes. The casual way in which Somervell made the plea struck at a deeper problem that had plagued civilian war mobilizers from the start. In the end, who was responsible for purchasing or rationing scarce materials, the government or the military? Presidential appointees such as Henderson and Nelson found themselves constantly having to overrule men in uniform, while military officials such as Somervell dismissed administration officials as meddlesome bureaucrats who did not understand the reality of war. The president refused to be drawn into the dispute, leaving it to his subordinates to fight it out. After Somervell said he "appreciated" the impact of such a program on "civil transportation," the OPA director phoned Somervell and said he would not issue any such directive.[39]

The price controls, coupled with little progress on the war front, only served to increase the public angst. The November elections loomed, but the *New York Daily News* repeated the rumor that congressional elections might not even be held. The *New York Post* offered two-to-one odds on whether the elections would take place. For Roosevelt's supporters, the elections posed a threat to their congressional majorities. Democrats worried that voters were irritated with government rationing and the lack of an offensive against the enemy. Democratic national chair Edward Flynn urged the party faithful, "Stand by the president—don't plague him during the war with an opposition House." Many Republicans understood that millions were feeling disenchanted in the aftermath of Pearl Harbor and were tired of the growing bureaucracy in Washington, whose actions sometimes bordered on the absurd. An interoffice memo in April from the War Department captured it well: "The Divisions of Resources Branch will hereafter be known as the Branches of Resources Division."[40]

While the Democrats faced darkening prospects, Republicans had to walk a fine line between supporting the war effort and offering an alternative approach. *Newsweek* explained the political dynamics at work: "Surprising as it sounds, many an important Republican is privately expressing hope that the GOP doesn't win a House majority this fall. They feel that if a GOP House should get out of hand, embarrass the Administration, and lay itself open to charges of obstructing the war effort, it might wreck GOP hopes for 1944. An ideal condition would be for the Republicans to win enough seats so that they could, in combination with conservative Democrats, control the House but still avoid responsibility."[41]

As the month came to a close, a new era began outside Washington. At 8:00 a.m. on Thursday, April 30, employees of the Army Ordnance Department began moving into the new War Department headquarters in Arlington, Virginia. Before Pearl Harbor, the War Department had been spread all over Washington in myriad buildings, some temporary and others outdated. To centralize the needs of the military, Congress approved construction of a massive new building in 1941, on a site selected by the president himself. The five-sided structure would be the largest office building in the world, covering twenty-nine acres and containing over 6.5 million square feet and seventeen miles of corridors. Ground was broken on September 11, 1941, and after Pearl Harbor the building became an urgent priority. The construction, overseen by Somervell and Colonel Leslie Groves, was done at breakneck speed, and the building was ready for use in just seven months. It would be completed in January 1943. Secretary of War Stimson sat behind the desk used by Robert Todd Lincoln when he held the post under Presidents Garfield and Arthur, and on the desk was a direct line to the White House. Shortly after the first workers began moving in, its official name changed from War Department Building to the one that thousands of workers were already using: the Pentagon.[42]

While the new building's name was readily apparent, what to call the war itself was not. The world has long recognized the conflict between 1939 and 1945 as "World War II." For those involved in it, placing it in a category with the Great War was not immediately evident. In April, Roosevelt said he had been looking for the right name to describe the momentous undertaking before the nation. He said he had settled on the term "Survival War." Though it was quickly forgotten, the name gives modern observers a glimpse of how Americans saw the world in 1942. FDR believed the nation was fighting for "the survival of our civilization, the survival of democracy, the survival of a hemisphere. . . . Survival is what our problem is, survival of what we have all lived for." The American public was not entirely sold on Roosevelt's term. In a Gallup poll taken in April, most respondents preferred "World War II," or "Second World War," while some favored "War of World Freedom" or the "Anti-Dictator War." The president of the Advertising Federation of America had another idea—"The War That Business Helped to Win." While "Survival War" was quickly forgotten, its wider implication should not be.[43]

5

May: "These Fascist Economic Measures"

IF ANY AMERICAN SEEMED LOST IN THE political wilderness of 1942, it was former president Herbert Hoover. During his successful 1928 campaign, he had predicted that economic growth would soon bring about "the day when poverty will be banished from this nation." Had the economy continued as it had in the 1920s, Hoover might have been considered one of the nation's greatest presidents. Instead, the Depression began just months into his term, and he never found a way to control the economic misery. He failed to convey sympathy with the struggles of the American people, who saw him as detached and disconnected, and his name became synonymous with failure. After losing to FDR in 1932, Hoover did not go away quietly but spent the next decade defending his record and railing against Roosevelt and the New Deal, which he termed "National Regimentation." In 1934, he warned that "the methods of planning progress cannot be through governmental determination of when and how much a factory may be operated." Roosevelt's agenda, he said, "steps off the solid highway of true American Liberty into the dangerous quicksand of governmental dictation."[1]

As the nation geared for war in the early 1940s, Hoover continued to disparage the president's policies. He opposed Lend-Lease and criticized Roosevelt's Four Freedoms speech because it lacked a "Fifth Freedom": free enterprise and the right to "accumulate property." After Pearl Harbor, Hoover hoped his experience could be put to use in some way, and Bernard Baruch suggested to FDR that he make Hoover head of economic mobilization.

Roosevelt quickly dismissed the idea: "Well, I'm not Jesus Christ," he said. "I'm not going to raise him from the dead."[2] Hoover and Roosevelt's mutual contempt made what Hoover said on May 20, 1942, even more remarkable.

Speaking before a meeting of the National Industrial Conference Board in New York, Hoover made a breathtaking suggestion: "To win total war, President Roosevelt must have complete dictatorial economic powers. . . . There must be no hesitation in giving them to him and upholding him in them." Hoover added that once the war was over, "these Fascist economic measures" should be "immediately abolished." If liberty "is to live, the nation must secure recovery of all suspended liberties after the war."[3]

One person who found Hoover's suggestion implausible was Adam Clayton Powell, pastor of the Abyssinian Baptist Church in Harlem and a member of the New York City Council, who would be elected to Congress in 1944. In February 1942, he launched the first edition of the *People's Voice,* which advertised itself as a "militant newspaper" and "America's Greatest Negro Newspaper." In addition to Powell's editorials, the paper featured the drawings of Ollie Harrington, which highlighted the bleak realities of the nation's racial landscape. Responding to Hoover's suggestion, Powell wrote: "Dictatorial powers for the President or anyone else would mean the cessation of democracy," and giving up aspects of a democratic system in order to win the war was the equivalent of "winning the whole world and losing your soul."[4] That a conservative Republican and a "militant" Democrat could take such positions on the question of how much power should be given a popular Democratic president in wartime revealed how, that spring, the world seemed upside down. It also showed how a frightened nation struggled to define the limits of democracy as it fought for survival.

By the first week of May, Americans were beginning to see the rough outlines of what "total war" meant. Besides the millions who had been drafted or joined the armed forces, millions more had moved into the booming war industries. Most families were learning how to maintain the semblance of a normal life while dealing with rations, price ceilings, and the effects of a managed economy. The government labored to fight inflation and pass a tax bill, and the November elections were approaching. Since the beginning of the year, the unemployment rate had fallen a full point, to below 6 percent, and the promise of more jobs seemed endless.[5]

Except for the symbolic bombing of Japan by Jimmy Doolittle's raiders, there was little to relieve the widespread anxiety over the course of the war. "Never has the Allied cause seemed in such mortal peril," wrote columnist Frederick Gruin, adding that the armies of Germany and Japan had conquered "the rich tip of Southeast Asia; the Indies; much of the fertile Don Valley and the northern Caucasus," and "stood at the gates of Australia, India, Egypt, and the Middle East." Another push by enemy forces might "break the ramparts of Central Asia." If that occurred, "the Allies would be cut into fragments" and there "might fall the twilight of democracy and international order."[6]

Though there had been no more Pearl Harbors, the pervasive fear continued along both coasts that more attacks were on the way. In Seattle, rumors spread that "the Japs are planning to blow up the water mains," according to one local resident, who was outraged that the federal government did not "understand these little Oriental cunning tricksters." The onslaught by German U-boats in the Atlantic further raised the fear of a Nazi invasion. One person claimed an FBI agent had told him, "Any minute now there will be explosions and disorders all over the country."[7]

Franklin Roosevelt understood that the lack of concerted offensive action by Allied forces was not sitting well with the public. On May 6, he sent a memo to military leadership on how he envisioned the overall strategy. The best that could be hoped for in the Pacific, he wrote, was "a holding operation" in which "defense of all essential points in the Pacific is the primary objective." In the Atlantic, "the principal objective is to help Russia. . . . It must be consistently reiterated that Russian armies are killing more Germans and destroying more Axis materiel than all the twenty-five united nations put together." Maintaining the flow of goods to Russia was essential, as was "the organization of a second front to compel the withdrawal of German air forces and ground forces from the Russian front." Above all, the president told his military leaders, "The necessity of the case calls for action in 1942—not 1943!"[8]

Adding to Roosevelt's frustrations was that on that same day a valiant yet exhausted General Wainwright had surrendered his troops to Japanese military authorities on the island of Corregidor. The emaciated general wrote a final letter to his commander in chief: "With profound regret and with continued pride in my gallant troops I go to meet the Japanese commander," concluding, "Goodbye, Mr. President."[9]

FDR was also disappointed with the output of America's factories. Although the production figures were not released to the public, secret reports authorized by the WPB showed that airplane production through the end of May would total seventeen thousand, a considerable accomplishment but nowhere near enough to reach Roosevelt's goal of sixty thousand by the end of the year. The "feasibility" issue was much studied within the administration, and economists Mordecai Ezekiel and Simon Kuznets warned that the president's goals for 1942 and 1943 were "significantly larger than can be attained." By year's end, "it seems most likely that the objectives for munitions and construction for 1942 will not be reached by a fairly substantial margin." The report reiterated that short of some drastic change, reaching FDR's targets was "wholly impossible."[10]

Despite what those who studied the situation had come to know, there was no chance that Roosevelt might publicly alter his goals. On May 1, he reminded Donald Nelson "that the concept of our industrial capacity must be completely overhauled under the impulse of the peril to our Nation. I am apprehensive that the schedules established at that time, for 1942, with such modifications as have been made in the interim, are not being met and I am convinced that a more determined effort must be made at once if the requisite objectives are to be accomplished." That the ambitious figures Roosevelt had promised might not be attained only added to the overall military impasse. Unless things changed by November, the political fallout could be immense to both the Democratic Party and the president himself.[11]

Part of the problem was procuring raw materials. While Nelson on paper was a sort of mobilization czar with widespread authority, he actually possessed far less power. He often found himself competing with General Brehon Somervell for materials, as well as with the navy and several other procurement boards. In the words of historian James MacGregor Burns, "Merchant ships took steel from the Navy, the Navy took aluminum from aircraft, rubber took valves from escort vessels and petroleum, the pipelines took steel from the ships, new tools, and the railroads."[12] The incessant bureaucratic infighting led to more delays, and many blamed the president himself. Roosevelt's well-known management style of dividing authority among competing individuals was not playing well with Congress, the military, or an increasingly frustrated public.

Many American corporations understood that they needed to be seen contributing to the war effort, not merely earning money for their shareholders. Some combined profits and patriotism in unique ways. It became hard to find an advertisement for any product that did not show a soldier or a war worker touting its benefits. R. J. Reynolds, the maker of Camel cigarettes, was proud that for "these men who fly bombers, it's Camels all the time." "Yes, in times like these, when there's added tension and strain for everyone, there's nothing like a Camel for steady smoking pleasure." Another ad showed a beaming young woman saying, "In my new defense job, I appreciate Camels more than ever!" It was in 1942 that Reynolds put up the iconic billboard in New York's Times Square with a two-story-tall image of an American soldier saying, "I'd Walk a Mile for a Camel" and blowing smoke rings over the fascinated throngs. Another ad, for North American Aviation of Ingelwood, California, boasted that Doolittle's raiders flew the company's B-25s. North American's ad showed a man with a morning stubble reading the *Los Angeles Times*' headline "Tokyo Bombed!" and saying, "Yes sir, that's my baby." Shrewdly tying patriotism to the company's bottom line, the ad also exhorted citizens to buy more war bonds, which would then be used to produce even more planes. "The next time you read about B-25s, just say 'I helped build that plane' the way we say it here."[13]

Everywhere one turned, there was the message, repeated in magazines, newspapers, and motion pictures, that life's everyday travails could be eased and improved with a cigarette. President Roosevelt himself had declared tobacco an essential wartime material and even granted military exemptions to growers. Ads for Julep cigarettes touted their new "miracle mint" that, when added to the tobacco, "freshens the mouth at every puff." "Even if you chainsmoke," the ad claimed, "your mouth feels clean, sparkling all day long." Other ads displayed the beneficial effects of smoking. "Old Gold fans" Betty Thompson and Patti Hill were shown under large hair dryers getting a light for their cigarettes. "Patti," asked Betty, "isn't it wonderful having a swell permanent and calmly smoking a new Old Gold?"

Customers of Philip Morris could take comfort that "eminent doctors" found that other popular brands contained four times more "irritant." "Be sure of your cigarette," the ad cautioned, since "all smokers inhale." An ad for Chesterfield informed readers that "whatever you do for Uncle Sam, Chesterfield will help make your job more pleasant."[14]

Cigarettes were not the only commodity that would later be proven lethal that was touted as a healthy way to deal with the anxieties of war. Another was offered as a conduit to a brighter future that touched many aspects of daily life. The Keasbey and Mattison Company of Ambler, Pennsylvania, publicized itself as the "Best in Asbestos" and foresaw a time when the material would be commonplace. "Our research laboratories," company ads promised, "continue to search for new uses of asbestos, in order that this strangest of minerals may be of still greater service, when peace has come again. Tomorrow's drinking water will get safe conduct in asbestos-cement water mains. Town Fathers of tomorrow will not relish digging up sections of ailing water main when K&M's long-lived, always-healthy asbestos-cement pipe can be had. No doubt about it—the post war era will find K &M 'Century' Pipe in even greater demand than ever before." Although it would be decades before the full effects of asbestos exposure were better known, the hints were already there by 1942. In the late 1930s, an assistant U.S. surgeon general warned of the dangers that high levels of exposure of asbestos posed, and in 1941, a memo from the head of the Navy's Division of Preventive Medicine wrote, "We are having a considerable amount of work done in asbestos" and worried "that we are not protecting the men as we should." Yet those early concerns were overcome by the navy's shipbuilding needs. In 1942, the WPB secured over 14 million pounds of asbestos pipe insulation to be used in new ships. A single battleship carried over 450 long tons of asbestos thermal insulation. Shipyard workers and naval personnel were especially prone to diseases caused by asbestos exposure, and by 1987 researchers concluded, "The shipyards of World War II, where asbestos utilization . . . [was combined] with minimum controls and minor precautions, left a legacy of disease and death."[15]

The necessities of war changed much about American life, most dramatically for women. Many are familiar with the image of "Rosie the Riveter," a

term that originated with a 1942 song written by Redd Evans and John Jacob Loeb. The term was applied to 4 million women who went to work in
defense plants and performed every job that had once been seen as "man's
work," including welding, operating cranes and, of course, riveting. Yet to
focus only on the "Rosies" misses the many women who contributed to the
war effort in ways that did not require them to help build bombers or tanks.
When a shortage of taxi drivers in New York developed, women began driving cabs. While Leon Henderson could issue price and rationing directives
from Washington, women in neighborhoods and communities, as historian Lizabeth Cohen notes, "were the shock troops for the OPA." In Newark,
New Jersey, over two hundred female volunteers staffed the local OPA office, and five hundred others checked rents in apartments and rooms to
ensure they were within the established ceilings. When the Office of War
Information needed to train "block leaders" to go door to door in Newark
giving people pertinent war information, 349 women volunteered. Cohen
writes that women in 1942 were busy "living creatively and nutritionally
with shortages, observing price controls and rationing regulations, recy-
cling and collecting scrap and fat. . . . Good citizenship and good consum-
ership were promoted as inseparable."[16]

Companies exploited the new demands and burdens on women. The
H. J. Heinz Company claimed that "on a thousand fronts our women are
enrolled in winning the war," but noted that "Mrs. America" still had a job
to do in "thirty million kitchens providing the health and happiness of her
family." Heinz ketchup, pickles, baby food, and other prepared foods saved
women valuable time. "It would take hours to duplicate Heinz foods," and
these "precious hours can be devoted to the needs of the nation." Sunsweet
prune juice advised that women working "behind the guns" could get
"Three Way Help" from its juice in the form of vitamins, minerals, and
laxatives.[17]

Yet domestic duties were not what some women had in mind. For some,
the only way to properly serve their nation meant military service. On May
15, President Roosevelt signed legislation establishing the Women's Army
Auxiliary Corps (WAAC), and two months later established the naval equivalent, the Women Appointed for Voluntary Emergency Service (WAVES).
Army Chief of Staff George Marshall had supported the expanded role for

women in the army, writing that "there are innumerable duties now being performed by soldiers that can actually be done better by women." Congress's approval of the WAAC was justified by the threat of enemy attacks and a sense that the task of spotting enemy planes and supporting the larger purposes of the army could no longer be left to volunteers. Despite the creation of the new military units, women could not serve in the infantry or in other combat roles. By summer, 25,000 WAAC recruits were training at Fort Des Moines for noncombat roles such as switchboard operators and mechanics. Eventually, 150,000 women served in the WAAC in World War II, and 350,000 in all served in uniform.[18]

The sudden changes the war made upon family life naturally affected children. Michael G. Appel, president of the Jewish Family Welfare Society, claimed that two of every five new cases of juvenile delinquency arose from dislocations caused by the demands of the war. Appel listed five "tension points" confronting families since Pearl Harbor: job dislocation, family separations, emotional breakdowns, a son or husband in the military, and "working mothers" employed in the defense industries who could not properly care for their children. Appel believed the nation would be better served if mothers were able "to remain at home and keep the family together." The term "latchkey children" was used to describe those who waited at home unsupervised until their parents returned from work. If the mother had to work, Appel suggested, "day nurseries" should be established within factories. Sociologists in Philadelphia had a different take on the war's effects on family life, especially for teenagers. Gas rationing, for example, was seen as a benefit since "mother and dad are going to get to know one another much better by being forced to spend more evenings at home together, while daughter and son, unable to use the family car for dates, will have to devote more of their evenings with their friends in their respective homes."[19]

A series of polls taken in May revealed some of the underlying dynamics of the public response to war. A *Fortune* magazine poll showed that 67.8 percent of respondents thought the war would last more than one and a half years. Even though the news from the fronts was discouraging, 80.6 percent were confident of winning the war. Seventy percent were willing to have the government register all male civilians to work in defense industries "wherever they are needed." FDR's popularity remained as high as ever—86 percent felt he was "best man to have as president." Of a list of prominent figures that Americans hoped could join Roosevelt's administration, Douglas MacArthur beat his nearest rival (Wendell Willkie) by over twenty points.

In another poll, conducted by the Office of Facts and Figures (OFF), a majority of Americans hoped the war could be used as a way to guarantee freedom of speech and religion for people all over the world, but they were also concerned that peace would bring "economic disaster," along with fewer jobs and lower pay. OFF director Archibald MacLeish told FDR that the poll gave the president "a golden opportunity" to assure the American people "that their ideals are practical, that they can be attained when we win. . . . A full knowledge of what we are fighting for, coupled with assurance that we can win our goals, can be a positive measure in winning the war." This was no small challenge given that in early 1942 nine out of ten Americans could not name a single provision of the Atlantic Charter. In a troubling Gallup poll, only half of respondents could even name their member of Congress. The paradox of the responses suggested that in the November elections, voters might take out their frustrations on Congress while still supporting the president and the overall course of the war.[20]

Public anxieties over the war's progress produced more concerns about a postwar society. Maxwell S. Stewart, a former editor with the *Nation*, published a pamphlet that highlighted many Americans' latent fears about what would happen when G.I.s returned from the war and the nation dialed down its massive war spending. "If you are working in a war plant," Stewart asked, "do you know what is in store for you when the war ends?" In order to stave off a new and more menacing depression, Stewart suggested, the federal government should adopt policies put forward by economist Mordecai Ezekiel, who proposed that factories continue to produce at maximum levels, and pay wages sufficient to allow workers to buy those goods. If firms made goods that went unsold, Ezekiel wanted the government to buy them in order to maintain adequate employment. Stewart also called for renewed public works programs and expanded health benefits and Social Security.[21]

Any move to enact those plans would have to wait until after the war. In the meantime, the economy was booming. In the first four months of 1942,

Americans had $6.5 billion more cash to spend than they had the year before. What they did with it was revealing. They put $1.8 billion into war bonds; paid out $3.6 billion in higher prices and taxes; and paid off $1.1 billion in old debts. With fewer consumer items to purchase, Americans saved more of their incomes, another consequence of a controlled economy that helped contain inflation. The pent-up savings had another by-product that would be seen once war ended, when consumers once again had money to spend.[22]

Even if the Roosevelt administration's moves to raise taxes and persuade more Americans to buy war bonds were wholly successful, those efforts would still fall well short of actually paying for the war. The Treasury Department tried new ways to find additional revenue. On May 7, Morgenthau sent the House Ways and Means Committee another tax proposal, which lowered exemptions for married persons from $1,500 to $1,200, for single persons from $750 to $600, and for dependents from $400 to $300. He was confident that these measures would raise an extra $1.1 billion in taxes and bring nearly 7 million more new taxpayers to the rolls. His proposals, in the words of Henry Dorris of the *New York Times*, "struck the committee like a bombshell." Members complained they had had no advance word of the new taxes, and even experts within the Treasury said they had not been consulted. For a single person making $2,000 a year, the proposal would more than double the federal tax bill, from $117 to $263, a fact that did not go unnoticed by worried members of Congress facing reelection in November. Whatever committee members felt about the necessity of higher taxes or what their constituents might say, they were unified in the stipulation that "a considerable breathing spell would be taken after the enactment of the revenue bill before anything else was attempted."

Leon Henderson went even further. Just days after Morgenthau made his proposals, Henderson told the House Ways and Means Committee that the struggle against inflation was at a crucial point, and suggested lowering exemptions to even lower levels than what the Treasury secretary had proposed. Henderson also claimed that wages would have to be frozen in order to fully ensure that inflation could be curbed. For good measure, he advocated some form of compulsory savings rather than a federal sales tax to keep consumers from spending additional money. The OPA chief thought such moves would generate revenue from "low income groups" more fairly than sales taxes would. If nothing were done, Henderson again warned, the country would face "the greatest inflation in history."[23]

Henderson's actions produced a range of reactions. "As a free born American citizen," commented David J. Evans of Cleveland, he remembered the sacrifices earlier generations had experienced. "The men of Valley Forge didn't have the personal convenience of a pair of shoes in the dead of winter, but they fought and died with smiles on their faces." In that same selfless spirit, Evans felt, "the bulk of America is firmly behind Mr. Leon Henderson in everything he says and does" and, considering what was at stake, "we certainly can do without tires, gasoline, and a lot of other things." One political observer noted that Henderson's "wild man aspects" were no longer "dwelt upon on Capitol Hill," and most members of Congress were "beginning to like this cigar-chewing, blunt-talking buckaroo and to accept him as a vital ally." Yet Eugene McCoy, a member of the United Rubber Workers of America, thought Henderson had "overstepped his bounds when he proposed the freezing of wages and the lowering of the income tax exemption." McCoy believed that Henderson "has failed completely in the execution of his office" and should be removed.[24]

If wage freezes and compulsory savings were not drastic enough, Randolph Paul, an advisor to Morgenthau, suggested two additional ways to raise revenue that Arthur Krock termed "revolutionary." One was to tax the income derived from trade or businesses owned by charitable or educational units; the other was to tax money bequeathed in estates to educational institutions or charities, including churches. Krock thought these measures would have a "calamitous" impact on colleges and charities, and he called Paul's plans little more than "a New Deal social reform." Groups like the National Catholic Welfare Conference and the Presbyterian Board of Missions also protested against Paul's ideas. Taxing charities and churches, even in the crisis of war, according to the Presbyterian Board, "would be a distortion of a long-established American rule" and would amount to "state control of churches, education, research, and philanthropy." The Rev. Harold C. Gardiner wrote that while Catholic laymen supported "unity in wartime," such ideas constituted "a definite threat to the freedom of the Catholic school system."[25]

The New York East Methodist Conference was outraged, saying, "The Christian Church is vitally concerned with what kind of victory this shall be." In addition to criticizing any taxation of church property, the conference called for greater corporate taxes and opposed any type of sales tax. "Shall the National Association of Manufacturers and other special interest groups with powerful voices be permitted to foist a general sales tax on the American people," the conference asked, "while keeping unconscionable profits for themselves?" In a Gallup poll released the next week, 57 percent favored reducing the exemptions and broadening the tax base, and respondents said the median income on which a family of four ("a married man with two children") should start paying taxes was $1,800. In 1940, the median income for a single person was $956.[26]

To see the wider context of the tax fairness issue, it is helpful to have an accurate portrait of how Americans actually lived just before Pearl Harbor. The lifestyle of most Americans in the early 1940s was, in some ways, a revolutionary improvement over how their forebears had lived a century earlier. Economist Robert J. Gordon notes that from 1870 to 1940, "no other era in human history, either before or since, combined so many elements in which the standard of living increased as quickly and in which the human condition was transformed so completely." By 1940, 78.7 percent of U.S. households had electric lights, 44 percent had mechanical refrigerators, 69.9 percent had indoor running water, and 41.8 percent had central heating. But these figures concealed great geographic disparities. While 95.8 percent of urban households had electric lighting, barely one-third of farm households did, and only 16.4 percent of farm households in the South had it. The South also trailed in many other modern conveniences. Nearly 71 percent of southern households had no form of refrigeration, and only 4.7 percent had indoor flush toilets. And while 57.9 percent of U.S. urban houses had central heating, only 1.3 percent of southern rural houses did. Such regional disparities complicated the task of writing tax legislation that was fair to all Americans.[27]

Determining how gas should be rationed was just as complicated. Few regulations angered more people than gas rationing, which began on May 15 in seventeen eastern states and the District of Columbia. The primary purpose was, after all, to reduce rubber usage, not to curtail fuel consumption. Many drivers who relied on automobiles for their jobs and other daily activities could not get past the idea that gasoline was actually not in short supply; they felt the OPA was unnecessarily creating a crisis. On May 10, the OPA announced that the maximum weekly allotment of gasoline for motorists on the East Coast (for nonessential tasks) would be just three gallons. Most drivers would receive the standard A designation (shown by a sticker inside their front windshield), but ambulances, taxis, and automobiles used by physicians, war workers, or ministers would receive B or C cards. The most prized card was the X, which authorized unlimited gasoline purchases but was reserved for workers for whom it was truly necessary, such as traveling salesmen. The penalty for violating the rations was a fine of up to $10,000 and a jail sentence of up to ten years, although in reality the system relied on motorists' truthfulness. "It is the honor system," declared Henderson, "and its success must depend on the patriotic desire of those affected to help win the war."[28]

On May 13, registration began for New York City's nearly 1 million drivers, and throughout the East Coast, another 7.6 million drivers stood in long lines in school gyms to get their official cards. Tempers flared when drivers expecting exemptions were refused, as well as when some "chiselers" received X cards that some onlookers felt were unwarranted. Leslie V. Bateman, a New York rationing supervisor, was outraged when a volunteer fireman received an X card even though "he lives only two doors from the firehouse." Bateman promised that "tomorrow, that man is either going to surrender his card or is going to jail." In Boston, some drivers who had obtained X cards due to errors or indifference returned them. When over two hundred members of Congress received an X card, there was a large public outcry.[29]

Gas rationing meant different things to different people. For urban dwellers, it could mean simply having to use the subway or a bus to get to work or school. For rural people, things were very different. The suggestion of extending the rationing program nationwide worried many in the West. Perry Wright, who owned a hundred-acre ranch in Oregon, knew that the three-gallon limit meant he would have to do his daily work on horseback. For some truck drivers, the limits were devastating. The rural/urban divide was fully apparent in a Gallup poll that showed that 63 percent of people living in communities of more than ten thousand people felt they could do without their cars; in areas of fewer than ten thousand, only 32 percent felt that way.

A cattle rancher in the West noted, "We've become dependent on cars," while another said that once the rations were in effect, "we'll just get to town a lot less and ride horseback a lot more." By summer, 70 percent of those who drove less than two miles to work said they were willing to walk if necessary.[30]

People from all walks of life pleaded with the president for exemptions. The Reverend Dallas Billington of Akron, who described himself as a "soul winner for Jesus," wrote to President Roosevelt that while he was "a Baptist preacher borned in a democrat home and rocked in a democrat cradle," he had listened intently to the president's pronouncements since Pearl Harbor but had heard of no gas rationing exemptions for clergy. "I am wondering, will we be permitted our cars and gasoline to serve the people in our capacity? Please do not let it come from Washington and our Chief Executive as it has been announced from Berlin, Moscow, Tokyo, and other governments that we as a nation do not put God first!"[31] Many other complaints about gas rationing would be heard throughout the year, and government officials understood they were touching a vital part of the American economy. They knew the wrath would only intensify until the rubber crisis abated.

One administration figure who had been largely invisible since Pearl Harbor was Vice President Henry Wallace. Roosevelt had kept his previous vice president, John Nance Garner, at arm's length during his first two terms, and had followed the same path with Wallace, who had been nominated to the ticket in 1940. A progressive Iowan who was convinced the war offered an opportunity to remake the world along democratic lines, Wallace gave a speech on May 8 entitled "The Price of Free World Victory" in which he labeled the twentieth century the "Century of the Common Man." Borrowing the phrase from Henry Luce's pronouncement of "The American Century," Wallace claimed that through the Nazis, "Satan now is trying to lead the common man of the whole world into slavery and darkness. . . . Just as the United States in 1862 could not remain half slave and half free, so in 1942 the world must make its decision for a complete victory one way or another." Taking a page from Woodrow Wilson, he said that after the war, "those who write the peace must think of the whole world." While some progressives likened the speech to the Gettysburg Address, it had little impact on the public, the president, or Wallace's presidential ambitions. The *Economist* editorialized that Americans "may find the building of a better order more costly and more controversial than they realize." But Wallace's speech inspired something else. Later in the summer, composer Aaron Copland wrote a stirring piece for the Cincinnati Symphony Orchestra that became one of the most recognized American musical expressions of the twentieth century, "Fanfare for the Common Man."[32]

One WPB order had little effect in May 1942 but concerned an aspect of American life that would later be ubiquitous. Ten months earlier, after receiving approval from the Federal Communications Commission, WNBT of New York went on the air as the world's first commercial television station. The Philco Radio and Television Corporation of Philadelphia received the second license, and by February 1942, there were ten commercial television stations in the United States: three in New York City, two in Los Angeles, and one each in Philadelphia, Chicago, Washington, D.C., Milwaukee, and Schenectady, New York. Another forty-four applications were pending. But the television revolution would have to wait. In May, the WPB prohibited the further building of new stations, and many existing stations cut their hours significantly until the end of the war.[33]

An even more personal order concerned lingerie. In language that only added to the public perception of meddlesome Washington bureaucrats, the WPB set forth strict limitations: "no nightgown, slip, petticoat or pajamas may have double material yokes; balloon, dolman, or leg-of-mutton sleeves; all-over tucking, shirring, or pleating; more than one pocket; a hem wider than an inch, or a ruffle bottom." These regulations, which reduced the linen used in women's underwear by 15 percent, made more fabric available for war purposes. Yet American consumers found the intrusions irritating, and some resented that men with white shirts and dark ties, working behind metal desks, now had the power to issue unchallenged edicts about the smallest details of daily life. One of the most memorable agencies created during the war was the Biscuit, Cracker and Pretzel Subcommittee of the Baking Industry of the Division of Industry Operations of the War Production Board. While it may seem ridiculous to modern observers, this small office was suddenly a major concern to bakers throughout the country. It controlled their livelihoods.[34]

The Selective Service became an important part of the lives of young American men, and older ones as well. By late spring, some 13 million men aged forty-five to sixty-four had added their names to the swelling lists of available manpower. These men were not subject to military service but could, if the need arose, provide a pool of workers for war industries or other types of government service. The very act of registering for the draft was a public demonstration of support for the war effort, and it gave men who could not serve in the military a way to support the cause. In Tennessee, fifty-two-year-old Alvin C. York, a World War I Medal of Honor winner, went to the same crossroads store in Pall Mall in which he had registered for the draft in 1917 to sign up again. York quietly filled out his occupational questionnaire, listing the skills and experience he possessed that could be used in mobilizing manpower. When sixty-four-year-old Senate majority leader Alben Barkley failed to return his Selective Service occupational questionnaire to the local draft board #110 in McCracken County, Kentucky, he received a terse letter informing him he was delinquent in his duties. Barkley was warned that if he did not submit the form in a timely manner he would be subject to a fine or imprisonment. At the White House, James D. Hayes, chairman of local draft board #9 in Duchess County, New York, personally attended to the registration of sixty-year-old Franklin Delano Roosevelt.[35]

Who was drafted and who received deferments were as intensely contested as who would receive what gas ration card. The specific power of determining one's fitness for military service fell to four thousand local draft boards throughout the country. A lottery system was initiated that would make the operation run more smoothly, but some still felt they merited special consideration. When C. H. Cain, a Nebraska farmer, heard that the army might soon begin drafting men as young as eighteen, he wrote to Senator George W. Norris to say, "We farmers are short of help now. All we can get are older men and the boys." Cain hoped Norris would vote against lowering the draft age so that farmers could rely on young men for labor. If the draft took the area's younger men, he asked, "how are we going to harvest our crops without help?" Cain was not alone in hoping teenagers could avoid the draft. In midsummer, fewer than half of those polled thought eighteen- and nineteen-year-olds should be drafted.[36]

Within the African American community, the draft was unpopular for other reasons. At the Allah Temple of Islam in Washington, D.C., worshippers were told not to register with the Selective Service since they had already registered "in Mecca," and the racism African Americans experienced at home freed them from the responsibility of serving in the military. Nation of Islam leaders such as Gulan Bogans, also known as Elijah Muhammad, preached that the war was nothing more than a "white man's war." He quickly fell under the watchful eye of the FBI. On May 8, Bogans and other leaders of the temple were arrested for violating the Selective Service Act and charged with sedition. He would eventually be convicted and sentenced to four years in prison.[37]

The nation's bitter racial divide was not lost on foreign observers. A British journalist, William Hickey, after visiting and talking with many people in the U.S., commented that even discussing the issues of "Negroes" was "practically taboo among many of my white American friends," who tended to "dispose of it with a few stock phrases which comfortably justify discrimination." In Hickey's judgment, white Americans needed to extend "at least a sincere gesture or at best a radical, nationwide, change of heart" in order "to ensure total Negro co-operation in the war effort."[38]

While war factories did not welcome African Americans, there was at least one exception to the blatant discrimination in defense hiring. John G. Pew, president of the Sun Shipping and Dry Dock Company of Chester, Pennsylvania, announced on May 26 that all nine thousand workers at a new shipbuilding yard would be African American. If welders, pipe fitters, and other specialized workers needed supervision by whites at first, the black workers would be trained to take on the supervisory roles. "It is our intention to make the shipyard . . . an all-Negro project," Pew said, adding that preference in hiring would be given to "Negroes from Philadelphia, Chester, and other nearby areas." He also announced that the shipyard's personnel director would be Dr. Emmett J. Scott, an associate of Booker T. Washington. A local newspaper hailed the announcement as promising a new racial "utopia," but whether the all-black yard would live up to its advertising would not be known until well into the war.[39]

In early May, events in the Pacific hinted at a changing military tide. Alerted by deciphered coded messages of Japanese plans to capture Port Moresby in New Guinea and Tulagi in the Solomon Islands, American aircraft carriers intercepted enemy carriers in the Coral Sea off the northeast coast of

Australia. It was the first naval battle in history in which the warring ships never actually saw each other: all the fighting was conducted by aircraft. Both sides took major casualties. The U.S. lost several ships, the carrier *Yorktown* suffered significant damage, and 656 Americans died in the battle. The Japanese losses were even greater, with two carriers suffering extensive damage and losses of nearly a thousand men. The Japanese fleet never reached its destination. Senator Walter George of Georgia called it a "very heartening victory," and Senator Carl Hatch of New Mexico said, "We need more news of this kind." The navy cautioned against making too much of the battle of the Coral Sea and warned against the idea that Japanese sea power had been "crushed."[40]

The news from the Coral Sea, coupled with Jimmy Doolittle's raid on Tokyo, produced another reaction on the West Coast. In San Francisco, Lawrence Davies of the *New York Times* reported: "Never has the west coast felt more certain than it does today" that some type of "face saving" attack by the Japanese was coming. After the Doolittle raid, the general feeling was that "Tokyo never will lift its head quite so high again until the military has been able to announce truthfully, 'San Francisco has been bombed.'" Meanwhile, the evacuation of Japanese Americans into internment camps relieved worried whites along the coast. White residents who lived near one of the centers in Santa Anita remarked: "Most of them [Japanese Americans] may be loyal to the United States; we can't tell," and they weren't willing to risk it. "We do know we would rather have them here than unguarded and unprotected in places where, if they felt like it, they could damage defense plants or, by means of signals, guide enemy craft attacking our coast." In the Salinas Valley, a resident was angry after seeing a local rodeo grounds transformed into an "assembly center": "Why do they have to put the Japs right here? We thought we were going to be rid of them for good." *Newsweek*'s Periscope column noted, "Air-raid talk emanating from Washington is not idle chatter. Best authorities believe there'll be raids on the U.S. soon." Some in Washington actually worried that Japan would respond to the Doolittle raid by attacking the East Coast. Meanwhile, the president basked in Doolittle's glory, and on May 19 he pinned the Medal of Honor on the aviator in the Oval Office. Within a month of his daring raid on Japan, Doolittle had become a brigadier general and one of the war's best-known heroes. "Jimmy Doolittle is a man whose exploits utterly belie his name," gushed the *Baltimore Sun*.[41]

Fears of the war coming to areas other than the coasts were not fanciful. In mid-May, a German submarine sank an American cargo ship near New Orleans, killing twenty-seven people. One of the survivors, Herbert Dann, was in his bunk when the first torpedo hit. He went out on deck when more torpedoes struck and found the ship engulfed in flames. "I knew I was a goner till I prayed to the Lord and he answered the prayer immediately." Dann was able to jump overboard and was saved by a Coast Guard cutter. Yet the attack in the Gulf of Mexico proved that German subs controlled a vast area of open sea. Before military leaders could think of launching a "second front" in western Europe, they had to win control of the Atlantic, where the news was no better than that from the Pacific.[42]

On May 18, General Max officially became operational, and Henderson's control of the economy was amplified. Every large retail store posted the General Maximum Price Regulation for all items, and the owners of smaller stores scrambled to adhere to the latest regulations. Merchants wondered if the system would even work or simply break down, like the New Deal experiment a decade earlier with the National Recovery Administration and its famed blue eagle, a symbol that store owners and businesses displayed to show they were compliant with the NRA's "codes of fair competition." OPA-designed posters read: "United States Controlled Prices— Rising Prices are America's Enemy on the Home Front. They Destroy the value of your dollar. To halt further increases in the cost of living, our government has put a top limit on almost all prices." At the end of May, Henderson also ordered that rents be cut to July 1941 levels in twenty war production areas, affecting 9 million people in thirteen states. He appointed nineteen rent directors to administer the new regulations.[43]

By late spring, the public could only guess whether the nation's factories were on a pace to reach the president's goals. Within the administration, the staggering shortfalls underscored how Roosevelt's initial goals had been overly ambitious. Over four thousand planes and fifteen hundred tanks came off the assembly lines in May, along with fifty thousand machine guns—yet it was not enough. The change under way in America's factories was staggering, but the May rate of production put the nation even further behind the president's sixty-thousand-plane goal. Undeterred, Roosevelt ignored the numbers and said merely, "This is no time for the American people to get overconfident." The president resorted to vague cheerleading: "We need more and more, and we will make more and more."[44]

Roosevelt was careful not to give the nation any more bad news, an approach that seemed to be working. A Gallup poll in mid-May showed that 78 percent of respondents approved of his handling of the war, down from a high of 84 percent in January. The criticisms against FDR in the poll were that he favored labor unions too much and that he was a poor administrator because he tried "to do too much himself" and refused "to fire the dead-heads." Yet a vast majority were comfortable with the three-term president in 1942, but whether they would still feel that way when the next presidential election arrived remained to be seen. When another poll asked respondents to name the men other than FDR whom they would favor in 1944, the two people with the most support were Douglas MacArthur and 1940 Republican nominee Wendell Willkie, followed by Thomas Dewey, Vice President Wallace, and Donald Nelson.[45]

No one had ever served as president as long as Franklin Roosevelt had by 1942, and because of the Twenty-Second Amendment, ratified in 1951, no one ever will. Many young Americans had never known any other president, and despite its overwhelming challenges, he thoroughly enjoyed the job. It has often been said of FDR that his notion of the presidency was himself in it. Yet a decade of leading the nation through depression and now war had taken its toll. While reports of the president's health were couched in the most glowing of terms, insiders could already see the decline that would bring the end three years later. One insider, Ferdinand Eberstadt, submitted an unanswered memo to Donald Nelson that asked, "What would be the political and administrative constellation in case of disability of the President?"[46] The scenarios that arose worried many within the administration, who could not imagine anyone else in the Oval Office during such perilous times.

Thousands of sites across the country were dedicated to war production, but one that became the symbolic center of the American war effort seemed

larger than anything comparable. On May 21, a group of reporters and photographers on the "Production for Victory" tour visited the new Ford plant
in Willow Run, Michigan, as it was about to begin producing B-24 bombers. The colossal building was designed by Albert Kahn, who had also designed Ford's River Rouge complex in Dearborn and was known as the
"architect of Detroit." The enormous structure, more than a half-mile long
and nearly a quarter-mile wide, lit by one hundred thousand fluorescent
lights and containing over a mile of service tunnels, was designed to bring
the mass-production methods Ford had developed in the automobile industry to the construction of long-range bombers. The process required
massive coordination of sub-assembly units, since each plane required
seven hundred thousand rivets and contained over a half million individual
parts. At its peak in April 1944, the factory produced one B-24 every hour.[47]

When he saw the 3.5-million-square-foot plant for the first time, Sidney M.
Shalett wrote, it "was one of the seven wonders of the world of war—vast
enough to swallow up an entire city." Edsel Ford and Charles Sorenson led
the tour, with Sorenson bragging that he wished he could "bring the Germans and the Japs in to see it," adding, "Hell, they'd blow their brains out."
Reporters learned that the building could eventually contain over one hundred thousand workers. After touring the plant, reporters and photographers
were taken to a nearby GM plant that had once made spark plugs and auto
bodies but had been converted to producing tanks, machine guns, and jeeps.

The images of endless bombers being produced in such incomprehensi-
bly large facilities told one side of the story. The housing shortage those
workers faced after their shift told another. When Agnes Meyer, wife of
Washington Post owner Eugene Meyer, visited the area, she was struck by
the living conditions workers endured in nearby Ypsilanti, where a two-
hundred-house community called Lay Garden struggled to maintain adequate conditions. "I saw one house in which the original family of five
lived on the first floor, five men sleep in the basement, four on the second
floor, nine in the garage, with four crowded trailers in the back yard." Yet
when she asked one worker if people were angry with Henry Ford over the
housing conditions, he said, "Nope, we ain't mad at Henry for this mess."
After Pearl Harbor, the man explained, "none of us could see what was
going to happen."[48]

Journalist Anne O'Hare McCormick noted that a distinct change was under way: "people living in communal quarters in a hundred lesser Detroits and Norfolks, jammed beyond their housing capacity," yet somehow revitalized by the larger context of what they were doing and how they were respected. "Many workers are feeling 'essential' for the first time," she wrote, "and the lift it gives them underlines the failure of modern industry to offer the ordinary man his greatest compensation, a sense of importance." Even though the current picture was "too fluid and confused" to make any predictions of what might come after war, she wondered if the war had produced a fundamental change that would eventually " 'proletarianize' the nation."[49]

If Willow Run signified war manufacturing's future, the reality of rubber production was far different. Despite confident statements made earlier in the spring by Commerce secretary Jesse Jones and others, by late May the reality of the nation's rubber supply had hit home. Donald R. Longman, an economist with the Civilian Supply Division (CSD) of the WPB, wrote that the "shortage of rubber appears so acute that further drastic reductions on the part of all nations and on the part of civilians and military services must be effected at the earliest possible moment." Another CSD economist advised Henderson that the public should be immediately informed of the "gravity" of the crisis. The amount of rubber available for civilians in 1942 was already down nearly 80 percent from 1941, and soon not a single pound of rubber would be available for any nonmilitary use until the end of 1943. In the Boston area, one reporter noted that residents understood "as never before that our entire social and business fabric is founded on gasoline and rubber."[50]

Roosevelt worried that alerting the public to the dire rubber situation would not only demoralize Americans but also give comfort to the enemy. Having boldly predicted sixty thousand planes in order to induce fear in the Germans and Japanese governments, he did not think a candid assessment of rubber supplies was a viable option. Instead, on May 26, he told reporters that the rubber situation should not "cause excitement," and he hoped a new type of tire was coming that would be made from some material other than rubber. Roosevelt gave no details, and reporters noted that his comments "appeared to be almost casual." A WPB official said he "was hopeful" that American ingenuity would create a rubberless tire, but it "was not in sight yet." In historian Bruce Catton's estimation, the "rubber mess" originated with the "refusal by the administration to face the facts." The "facts," in Catton's eyes, made the president and his advisors worry that if confronted with the full reality of the situation, the American people would punish the Democrats on Election Day. In the end, "the President and Congress simply got scared."[51]

The administration's baffling contradiction on rubber, and the growing anger at tire and gasoline rationing, eventually produced a reaction in Congress. Senators and House members were swamped with angry calls and letters in late May, and many on Capitol Hill called for rescinding some of the executive branch's emergency wartime powers. Speaker Rayburn, a supporter of the president, said he saw "no reason for [gas rationing] for the people in those parts of the country where they are wading knee deep in oil." Members of both parties said they were hearing from constituents of "bureaucratic abuses" by the administration. One that seemed especially galling was an order from the Office of Defense Trucking that required all trucks taking a load to a destination to add a partial load before returning. Senator Claude Pepper of Florida likened the order to a law in the Old West that directed, "When two trains shall meet, neither shall proceed until the other has passed." Roosevelt's troubles came not only from Republicans but from within his own party. Senator Ellison "Cotton Ed" Smith, Democrat from South Carolina, was indignant about all of the president's war agencies and warned, "We have come to a condition that is actually threatening the unity of the American people." Another Democratic senator, Bennett Champ Clark of Missouri, asked, "Did anybody ever have any doubt what was going to happen when the Congress abdicated its powers and turned these bureaucrats loose?" The only way to "stop clerks and bureaucrats from issuing orders for the sake of ordering," he argued, was "to rescind the powers granted."

Whenever members of Congress talked of rescinding powers, they increasingly pointed a finger at one member of the administration—Leon Henderson. Many assumed the price-control plan would be largely self-enforcing and were stunned when Henderson suggested that he might need one hundred thousand field agents to monitor compliance. C. P. Trussell, writing for the *New York Times,* found much resentment on Capitol Hill toward Henderson: "With edicts being issued under authority of powers delegated sweepingly for general prosecution of defense and war efforts, members of Congress under siege find themselves frequently able to do nothing about it." Some blamed agency officials, while others blamed the president and hoped future visits to the White House would be about congressional recommendations, not receiving "instructions" from the president or his cronies.[52]

Despite the growing backlash, by the end of May the first effects of General Max were beginning to be felt. The cost-of-living index, which had been rising at an annual rate of over 10 percent since Pearl Harbor, actually dropped 0.1 percent in May. The administration's anti-inflationary steps were beginning to take hold and promised to avert an economic crisis, but whether they would survive the summer was anyone's guess. As the OWI stated, "The extent to which prices and wages are controlled may decide whether the peace is won or lost."[53]

Although the army and navy had made little progress, Secretary of State Cordell Hull spoke of his "uneasiness" with Americans who "are inclined to anticipate an earlier victory than they had heretofore expected." Asking citizens not to be "overoptimistic," he said that victory would come only when "every man and woman in this country" understood "the extreme danger from the purposes of the worst barbarian leaders in all history who plan to conquer and brutally subjugate the world by methods of unparalleled savagery."[54]

On the next to last day of May, a twenty-three-year-old Japanese American named Fred Korematsu was arrested in San Leandro, California. Korematsu, who had tried to enlist in the U.S. Coast Guard after Pearl Harbor but was rejected, had refused General John DeWitt's order to report to an assembly center where he would be processed for internment. He later told an FBI agent he and his family hoped to move to the Midwest and "live as normal people." After his arrest, an attorney with the American Civil Liberties Union asked him if he would allow the organization to challenge the constitutionality of the internment orders in court. Later in the year, Korematsu was convicted of violating the order, and in 1944 the U.S. Supreme

Court upheld the conviction on the grounds that Korematsu's rights were secondary to the government's need to protect citizens from espionage.[55]

Korematsu's arrest and court battle displayed how, in a time of total war, the anxious nation viewed civil liberties as secondary to its larger security concerns. The Supreme Court's sanction of presidential authority to detain over one hundred thousand Americans based on blind suspicion would be seen as one of the dangerous precedents of the war, and one that revealed the paradox of using authoritarian means to ensure the survival of democracy. One justice understood that the case's underlying dynamics extended far beyond the immediate anxieties of war. In his dissent in the *Korematsu* case, Justice Robert H. Jackson warned that once "the principle of racial discrimination" was validated, it "lies about like a loaded weapon, ready for the hand of any authority that can bring forward a plausible claim of an urgent need."[56]

6

June: Rumors of War

"IN A TOTAL WAR," ARGUED THE War Department's Bureau of Public Relations, "words are weapons." Phony stories that circulated throughout communities and regions were especially dangerous. "Rumor is one of the weapons employed by the enemy against the effectiveness of the Army." Office of Facts and Figures head Archibald MacLeish warned that "Hitler thinks Americans are suckers," and an educational periodical suggested that many rumors "are Nazi-inspired."[1] While the nation's enemies might have wished to plant rumors among Americans to damage morale, they could not have invented anything better than the rumors coming from within the country itself. Modern readers concerned about the spread of misinformation may be interested to know that this is not a recent development. In 1942, people got their news primarily from newspapers, periodicals, and newsreels. But they learned at least as much from their family, neighbors, coworkers, and strangers. Some of these sources relied on information every bit as sketchy as contemporary stories on today's social media.

The impact of rumormongering on national morale was on President Roosevelt's mind just days after Pearl Harbor. In his first fireside chat after the attack, he urged Americans "to reject all rumors," noting that "these ugly little hints of complete disaster fly thick and fast in wartime." Many of the rumors flying through the nation's capital concerned the true extent of the damage done at Pearl Harbor and what city would be targeted next.[2]

To stay atop the most widespread rumors and perhaps find a way to counter them, in 1942 the Roosevelt administration began systematically monitoring Americans. The Office of War Information, created by executive order on June 13, initiated the War Rumor Project, which relied on barbers, bartenders, doctors, hairdressers, police officers, and drugstore owners to eavesdrop on their neighbors and customers and report what they heard to their local OWI office. The use of such "rumor reporters" was not new; Roman emperors had appointed "delatores" to mingle with the general population and report back any criticisms of the emperor. The OWI's army of "reporters," who surreptitiously listened to offhand remarks, conversations, and idle speculation, left us a remarkable window into the darker corners of wartime America's psyche. These rumors reveal a society often at war with itself, coming to grips with the external war but also with its own prejudices and fears.[3]

Political scientist James C. Scott notes that as a rumor spreads, "it is altered in a fashion that brings it more closely into line with the hopes, fears, and worldview of those who hear it and retell it." Rumors serve "as a vehicle for anxieties and aspirations that may not be openly expressed." During a crisis, rumors tend to proliferate at a greater pace, and the aftermath of Pearl Harbor is a unique laboratory for exploring the power of rumor to expose the underlying strata of fear and anxiety. For a nation responding to the crisis of war, rumors were especially threatening to its democratic character. Cass Sunstein writes, "If people spread false rumors . . . democracy itself will suffer. . . . Rumors impede our ability to think well, as citizens, about what to do in a crisis."[4]

The OWI set out three distinct criteria for "detecting a rumor." The statement had to be offered as a fact, not opinion; it had to originate with a private source of information not generally available to the general public; and it had to contain a specific, rather than a general, assertion. The OWI collected these rumors in order to respond in the best way. "Ineffective replies," the agency stated, could ultimately "increase anxieties to the point where rumors are generated on all sides." It was "the duty of every loyal American to enlist in the campaign to prevent the development of virulent rumors." While not every rumor could or should be answered, the OWI hoped to combat "the more prevalent" ones "by striking at their root—ignorance." The agency felt that by quickly responding to what people were telling each other, it could make people better informed and thus better able to discount the misinformation that was spreading around them. Although the OWI would focus on the "constant preparation of informational materials," it hoped to prevent "the community from feeling that a Gestapo is being organized."[5]

The OWI selected its army of reporters carefully. Since "rumor travels along social networks," a "good rumor reporter is one who has many social contacts. He should, however, be the sort of person who, either through occupation or temperament, is on the periphery rather than in the center of the group." Such people came from all walks of life. In Florida, one rumor reporter was a salesman who visited over four hundred food stores weekly, and in Louisville, Betty Cartwright, a "beauty parlor operator," paid close attention to her customers, who, according to the OWI, were "chiefly from the middle and lower classes." A San Francisco dentist, Dr. George M. Peters, found that his patients told him little in his office, but he thought he would "hear more" at the local YMCA.[6]

The more than five thousand rumors the OWI catalogued in 1942 fell into three major categories. "Anxiety" rumors were indicative of a nation worried about enemies everywhere: in Seattle, rumors spread that "the Japs are planning to blow up the water mains"; in California, rumors grew of a Japanese plot to put glass into food or to spread typhus by releasing diseased fleas into populated areas. Nazis were said to have poisoned water supplies, and there was supposedly a worker in an Illinois gasmask factory who intentionally poked holes in the masks. Barns in the Midwest were allegedly painted with identifying marks on their roofs to guide enemy bombers.[7]

"Escape" rumors reflected people's longing for an early end to the war or Hitler's death. In Massachusetts, stories spread that "there will be a negotiated peace with both sides on equal terms," and that Lloyd's of London had placed two-to-one odds on the war being over by the end of the year.

Finally, the most common type of all, "hate rumors," were mostly centered on bigotry toward African Americans, Jews, Catholics, and Japanese Americans. People were overheard lamenting that Jews were "running the war" and were avoiding the draft by taking drugs that induced high blood pressure. Some claimed that Bernard Baruch was "running the country," while others maintained that Supreme Court justice Felix Frankfurter was the secret "power behind the throne" and asked, "What right does he have to be in American politics at all? Everyone knows he's a foreigner!" Rumors about the motives and power of Jewish Americans found a receptive audience. In a poll conducted that summer, 42 percent of Americans agreed with the statement "Jews have too much power and influence in the U.S."[8]

One of the most common and virulent rumors depicted African American women organizing "Eleanor Clubs," named after the First Lady, whose attendance at the Southern Negro Youth Council Congress in Tuskegee, Alabama, and long-standing support of a federal anti-lynching law aroused the suspicion of white southerners. In an article in the *New Republic*, she argued that "we must keep moving forward steadily, removing restrictions which have no sense, and fighting prejudice." The First Lady denied that she was "agitating the race question," maintaining that "the race question is agitated because people will not act justly and fairly toward each other as human beings."[9]

White women in Virginia Beach, nervous over the supposed existence of such clubs, thought their ultimate aim was "to have all white women doing their own work by October 1." That sentiment was also heard in Pensacola, Florida, which saw the "Eleanor Society" organizing black domestic workers to decline work "in order to force white ladies into their kitchens." Allegedly, the clubs' motto was "A white woman in every kitchen by 1943."

In Texas, a white woman reported trying to hire a black domestic worker for $1 per day and claimed that the worker countered with a price of $12.50 per week, warning that "when Mr. Hitler won the war, the white people would be working for the negroes and at less wages than $12.50 per week." Another Hitler reference came from Mississippi, where a black domestic worker was rumored to have told her white employer, "I'm waiting on Mr. Hitler. When he gets here, I won't have to wash for you but you'll have to wash for me." In South Carolina, the fear of what black domestic workers might do was so pervasive that Governor Richard Jefferies ordered state police to scour every county for reports on "Eleanor Clubs." While no evidence was found, the police reported that "the white people appear to be considerably disturbed" over what they were hearing about the clubs. In Atlanta, the FBI tried without success to verify the existence of the clubs, and a housewife in Birmingham worried that if "Northern people" did not quit "overpaying" African Americans and "hiring them for work that white people could do," eventually "we're going to have a war that's worse than Hitler's right in our own backyard."[10]

Angry African Americans were also said to be supporting the enemy. According to one rumor, a black woman in Alexandria, Virginia, who refused to sit in the back of a bus told the driver, "I'll be glad when the Japs win. Maybe we Negroes will get some consideration then." Two black soldiers in Alabama, evidently confident of an imminent Nazi victory, were even said to have entered a "whites only" restroom.[11]

The OWI project was not the only rumor-collecting effort. University of North Carolina sociologist Howard W. Odum solicited rumors from his students, and the *Boston Herald,* working with Harvard psychologists Gordon Allport and Leo Postman, established a "Rumor Clinic" that worked in conjunction with the Massachusetts Committee on Public Safety. The *Herald* received numerous reports from readers, and each Sunday it refuted some of the major stories directly. The *American Mercury* and *Reader's Digest* also published accounts of the Boston clinic and asked readers to report "wild, damaging, morale-eroding stories" that they had heard. The aim was to educate readers to ask, "Where did you hear that?" If no reputable source could be provided, the article claimed, "the rumor spreader will often be silenced by his own shame." Similar clinics were formed in San Francisco, Philadelphia, New York City, and other areas throughout the United States and Canada, which used teams of "morale wardens" to collect the rumors floating around communities. The notion was that by "smothering" rumors with facts, false stories would be minimized, if not eliminated. One worker, poring over the content of the rumors, remarked that much of it originated with "loose-tongued persons who are not very bright."[12]

The rumors printed in the *Boston Herald* revealed some of Americans' underlying tensions. Many feared that the War Department was reporting only 10 percent of the real casualties in order to maintain morale, that the millions drafted into the service would never receive their full pay, and that "the Limies" (the British) were not doing their part in the war. One rumor denounced by the paper concerned a woman who worked in a bomb factory and went to her hairdresser for a permanent wave. The treatment had left an explosive residue in her hair, and when she returned to her workplace and passed near a heat source, the resulting blast had blown her head off. The rumor clinic countered by saying that all employees in the factory were given bandanas to wear and reminded all workers to bathe promptly after their shifts.[13]

One of the more telling rumors collected by the Boston rumor clinic showed that Eleanor Club stories were not relegated to the South. The clinic learned that whites were distressed that an African American woman had the audacity to offer to pay a white woman to do her laundry. Other stories also had whites soon working for their former servants. Postman described the Eleanor Club rumors as "cancerous," and thought they slandered not only "thirteen million of our most loyal citizens" but also "the first lady of the land." The vision of a world turned upside down, Allport and Postman noted, reflected a "distinct fear of inversion of status" among whites who harbored "feelings of economic and social insecurity." Allport and Postman suggested that "by pointing to Negro aggression," whites derived "a melancholy consolation from alerting one another to the menace" of racial equality. "Rumor," the researchers concluded, "rationalizes while it relieves."[14]

"At their core," writes historian Jason Morgan Ward, "wartime race rumors reflected a white fear of losing control of black workers." Once the racial hierarchy was destroyed, other threats might emerge, such as miscegenation and black voting rights. As Allport and Postman found, the Eleanor Club rumors served a central purpose: "If the Negro is overly aggressive, illegally plotting, vulgarly menacing, then he has no right to equal status." Such stories circulated "among those predisposed to hate the victim of the story," and in the process confirmed "pre-existing attitudes rather than forming new ones." Their verdict rings through the decades: "Democracy is threatened by the ease with which disinformation about civic issues is allowed to spread and flourish."[15]

The OWI's Rumor Project exposed a society deeply worried about the war's radical possibilities. Just as African Americans complained about having to fight for democracy while being denied it at home, white Americans fretted over whether the war might threaten white supremacy. The rumors resembled those that circulated at the end of the Civil War and during Reconstruction, when former slave owners warned of the violence, sexual depravity, and social revolution that was sure to follow the end of slavery. In 1942, one often heard in Alabama that "the federal government is going to try to use Negroes in the Army, . . . subdue the south and impose a second Reconstruction." In many areas of America, fear of losing the war was sometimes secondary compared to the fear launched by the frightening possibility of African American equality.[16]

Eleanor Roosevelt figured in many other wartime rumors, such as those about her alleged Jewishness and her Communist ties. Nor did they end there. Mary Tappendorf, a member of a group called We, the Mothers, was "aghast" at the idea of women serving anywhere near the front lines. "What do they want with girls on the front line," Tappendorf demanded. "I'll tell you—sex!" She said the idea came from "Mrs. Eleanor," who was leading a wider effort, encouraged by military leaders, to unleash the sexual energy of young soldiers: "They teach it to the boys in the Army. They tell them they'll go insane without it." Meanwhile, others thought they knew the real reason some women were intent on joining the military. Rumors spread that the WAAC and WAVES were havens for lesbians.[17]

A common misperception is that rumors are usually spread by uneducated and uninformed people. On the contrary, the OWI's studies in New Brunswick, New Jersey, and Portland, Maine, showed that people considered "well informed" repeated rumors 63 percent of the time, whereas those considered "poorly informed" did so just 25 percent of the time. People with college degrees were more prolific rumormongers than those with high school diplomas, and those who had "active social lives" were twice as likely to repeat rumors than those who led secluded lives. Students at Harvard and Radcliffe were polled about how they formed their opinions before and after FDR gave a speech attempting to refute the rumors about the damage inflicted at Pearl Harbor. Twenty percent responded that even after hearing the president and reading official reports, in a time long before the internet and social media, they still relied on "rumor, confidential information, and inference" as the primary basis of their opinions.[18]

Despite their best efforts to combat rumors, the OWI and local rumor clinics found that even after being presented with the facts, people who were susceptible to rumormongering often stood solidly behind those rumors. Efforts at educating large numbers of people influenced by rumor

proved futile. Odum found that in some cases, the mere existence of a rumor convinced some southerners of its veracity. "The very fact that there
are so many rumors" about African American men waiting until white
men left for the army to rape white women, said one white southerner, "is
sure evidence that the Negroes do intend to do as is reported."[19]

By 1943, once it became clear that efforts to dispel rumors were only
helping them proliferate, the rumor projects were closed. Allport and Postman commented that "since people do not ordinarily recognize a rumor
when they encounter one, and since they are seldom deterred from believing it simply because it is clearly labeled, we are forced to conclude that the
public is not adequately rumor conscious." They determined that America
in wartime "has built up little or no immunity" to rumor.[20]

The Eleanor Club rumors demonstrated that in the early months of the
war, when the massive mobilization was fundamentally changing the
southern landscape, white southerners did not see their social order threatened by Axis armies so much as by the possibility of black equality. Jason
Morgan Ward notes that "white southerners began to see signs of black
defiance at every turn" and employed racial terrorism "to prop up an order
they claimed was under unprecedented attack." *Louisville Courier-Journal*
editor Mark Ethridge, who had been appointed by FDR to chair the Committee on Fair Employment Practices, said in June, "There is no power in
the world, not even in all the mechanized armies of the earth, Allied or
Axis, which could now force the Southern white people to the abandon-
ment of the principle of social segregation." The secretary of the Birmingham Chamber of Commerce spelled out the lengths to which southerners
would go: "There's no white man here goin' to let his daughter sleep with a
nigger, or sit at the same table with a nigger, or go walkin' with a nigger. . . .
The war can go to hell, the world can go to hell, we can all be dead—but he
ain't goin' to do that."[21]

The slightest hint of racial equality produced a backlash. A June 1942 story
in *Life* magazine praising African American contributions to the war effort
produced a blistering letter to the editor from R. J. Devine of Covington, Kentucky. Of all the images depicting African Americans in the war effort, the
one he found most offensive was a photo of the Pacific Parachute factory in
San Diego showing white and black women working side by side, supervised

by an African American boss. "How in the name of God do you expect to contribute to the promotion of unity in this country when you display pictures of white women working under the supervision of Negro men?" Devine thundered. The boss, incidentally, was Eddie Anderson, widely known for playing "Rochester" on the Jack Benny radio show. Devine was further angered that the article approvingly mentioned Lincoln's use of black troops. "Why remind the Southern people of an injustice as foul as any Hitler conceived?" The whole article, he concluded, was nothing short of "treason."[22]

The running criticism from black newspapers about the lack of democratic norms at home, even as African Americans were exhorted to support the war effort, alarmed FBI director J. Edgar Hoover. One story that Hoover found especially galling involved some black soldiers in Oklahoma City who had been forced to ride on segregated trains for twenty-four hours without food, while white soldiers were fed properly. Hoover was not concerned that the racial injustice had occurred but that the news of it had been published. He instructed his agents to look carefully at the work of a black newspaper editor in Oklahoma City, Roscoe Dunjee, who supported interracial marriage and publicly opposed the segregation of blood by the Red Cross.[23]

Hoover persuaded Roosevelt that the black newspapers were skirting with sedition. The president, in turn, directed Attorney General Francis Biddle to use the power of the Justice Department, if necessary, to "prevent their subversive language." In late June, Biddle told the *Chicago Defender's* John Sengstacke that if black newspapers did not change their tone, he would "shut them all up." A furious Sengstacke responded, "You have the power to close us down, so if you want to close us, go ahead and attempt it!" Cooler heads prevailed and the two arrived at a compromise whereby Biddle announced he would not charge any black publisher with sedition and would see that more government officials would agree to be interviewed, while Sengstacke promised vaguely to be more supportive of the war effort. The FBI and the U.S. Post Office continued to monitor papers such as the *Chicago Defender, Pittsburgh Courier,* and *Baltimore Afro-American* for potentially seditious stories.[24]

Roosevelt also found himself on the receiving end of hatred. Some of the country's most vocal anti-Semites believed he was secretly Jewish and was part of an international network fomenting war. Garland Alderman of the pro-Nazi National Workers League told the Dies Committee: "The Jews control the White House, the president is a Jew, and his wife is a Jewess," and "Jews are running Washington and the nation." Elizabeth Dilling, a Chicago member of We, the Mothers, said emphatically, "This is a Jewish war," and vowed she did not care if she were sent to a concentration camp for her beliefs. A fascist newspaper in Muncie, Indiana, told its readers that the V for Victory sign was actually part of a Jewish symbol and that the Red Cross plan for blood transfusion was "a Jew scheme to mix the blood." In a California fascist paper, William Kullgren called for a "pogrom of Jews in America" who, he said, "know the seeds that they as a race have sown." He predicted that the death rate for Jews in 1942 "will surpass anything in the history of the world." In Chicago, Agnes Waters of Mothers from Washington said, "200,000 Communist Jews are at the Mexican border waiting to get into this country." If that happened, "they will rape every woman and child that is left unprotected." One anti-Semite from Chicago blamed Jews for the war and felt "Hitler was right in kicking out all the Jews." He believed that American Jews "stay home getting rich while the other boys go out and get killed. Damn them!" If there was any doubt about where these viewpoints were leading, Garland Alderman made it clear. In order "to get rid of the Jews," he had told members of Congress, "we will have to burn and kill them off."[25]

Father Charles Coughlin's anti-Semitic paper, *Social Justice,* was targeted by Attorney General Biddle in early 1942 for its seditious messages. Across the nation, as the American Jewish Committee understood, anti-Semitism had "lost the distinction of being confined to a small group of pro-fascists" and was expanding. Under a banner headline that read, "And They Killed Christ," Coughlin wrote that although Christ "had many friends, there was no one to speak in His defense, for fear of the Jews no one spoke openly of Him." Coughlin concluded, "It has always been so. It will always be thus." Coughlin had long complained that "certain Jews" had been "working to get the U.S. into a war with Germany since 1933." "Go ahead, do your worst," Coughlin cautioned Biddle, warning that if the paper were shut down, then "the pogroms which crimsoned the soil of Europe would rank a poor second to what would happen on the streets of New York." Instead of reducing anti-Semitism, Coughlin warned that the anger against American Jews in fomenting an unnecessary war against Germany would grow "into an uncontrollable holocaust!"[26]

Few anti-Semites could match the venom of Gerald L. K. Smith, a Disciples of Christ minister, who published the first edition of his book *The Cross and the Flag* that spring. Smith proclaimed that among the principles of "Christian Nationalism" were the fight against "mongrelization" and racial integration, and the need to "safeguard America's tradition in relationship to immigration." He was joined in his mission by Gerald Winrod, publisher of another anti-Semitic paper, the *Defender*, who saw the war as a Jewish conspiracy led by FDR himself. "The New Deal, with its bungling domestic policies," Winrod wrote, "is the logical effect of the moral and spiritual sag through which our country has been passing." With America's entry into the war, "Christians pray that our country will return to realities."[27]

Interior secretary Harold Ickes claimed to possess a secret list of the Rev. Smith's donors, who included Sears and Roebuck chair Robert E. Wood, R. Douglas Stuart Jr. of Quaker Oats, and Robert McCormick of the *Chicago Tribune*. Ickes thought Smith was "as blatant and discreditable a demagogue as ever existed, supported by people who have become rich and powerful under our American institutions." He considered the list to be evidence showing "that there are plenty of people like this in the United States who are fascists at heart and who, in the hope of being able to save their dirty money, would contribute to the support of a man whose life is devoted to undermining our institutions."[28]

Making its way around the nation was a song modeled after "Onward, Christian Soldiers" known as "Onward, Christian Liberals," featuring the worst anti-Semitic rantings of the time:

Onward, Christian Liberals! Give the Jew his Rights
Weep with all his wailings while you fight his fights
Let him hog our business; let him boss our schools
Give the jobs to refugees, and let them make the rules
No more native culture; give it up for good
Take it from the movie czars in good old Hollywood.

The concluding stanza ran:

> Give them all the gravy that we have in this fair land
> Give them everything we have—Supreme Court for a start
> Give them all the juicy jobs from which they'll never part
> You know they love the Gentiles—like a rattler loves a man
> It's up to you to do your part, you should, you must, you CAN![29]

The following month, Attorney General Biddle, under increasing pressure from the president, announced that twenty-six people had been arrested for violating the Espionage Act of 1917 and the Smith Act of 1940. Among those arrested were Dilling, Winrod, and Smith, who, Geoffrey R. Stone noted, "had nothing in common except a shared hatred of Jews, communism, and Roosevelt, and a general faith in the principles of fascism." The arrests provoked outcries from civil libertarians and Republicans, who worried about the administration's power to silence its critics. Senator Robert Taft called Biddle's actions "witch hunting" and reminded him of the abuses of World War I. The "Great Sedition Trial" did not get under way until 1944. It ended in a mistrial, and in 1945 the government dropped the indictments.[30]

On June 4, the House and Senate acted quickly on a presidential request to declare war on three countries under German control—Bulgaria, Hungary, and Romania. Both houses agreed on the resolution without a dissenting vote, and President Roosevelt signed it the next day. Officially, the United States was now at war with six countries.[31] While no one at the time could have known, it was the last time Congress formally declared war. Although U.S. forces would enter numerous conflicts over the next seven decades, the president's war-making powers took center stage, bypassing the constitutional requirement for a congressional declaration.

Of all the films made in 1942, none matched the impact of one that premiered on June 4 in Radio City Music Hall in New York City. A *New York Times* critic wrote: "It is hard to believe that a picture could be made within the heat of the present strife which would clearly, but without a cry for vengeance, crystallize the cruel effect of total war upon a civilized people." The film, set in the English countryside, was *Mrs. Miniver*, directed by William

Wyler and starring Greer Garson and Walter Pidgeon. The war is seen through the experiences of Mrs. Miniver and her family, and includes a terrifying scene in which a wounded Nazi soldier breaks into their house. In the Minivers' kitchen, the German warns that while he may be finished, others like him would continue to bomb cities. The film's dramatic final scene occurs in a bombed-out country church, where the community comes together to mourn its dead and the vicar implores his parishioners to fight with everything they have.

"Perhaps it is too soon to call this one of the greatest motion pictures ever made," proclaimed the *New York Times,* but "this is a film in which a flower show is as pregnant of national spirit as Dunkerque." By the end of the month, the film had been seen by a record 558,966 people at the famed music hall. When cards were placed at the theater asking patrons to list the "ten best pictures of all time," *Mrs. Miniver* topped the rankings, ahead of *Gone with the Wind, Wuthering Heights,* and *Citizen Kane.* The film became the biggest box office hit of 1942, attracting a larger audience than *Yankee Doodle Dandy* with James Cagney or *Pride of the Yankees* with Gary Cooper. "It was admirable propaganda," commented Harold Ickes, who called it "one of the best films I had ever seen" and said it "held one spellbound." It won six Academy Awards including Outstanding Motion Picture, Best Actress, and Best Director. The movie was so popular that Revlon created a new lipstick color—"Mrs. Miniver Rose"—which it described as a "small, shining tribute to gallant women the whole world over." President Roosevelt, who screened the film in the White House, was so moved that he asked MGM to distribute it immediately in order to help with wartime morale. He loved the vicar's sermon so much that he asked to have it printed and dropped in leaflets over war areas in Europe.[32]

While many were inspired by the movie, some wondered about the impact of war films on younger audiences. Quincy Howe, the president of the National Board of Review of Motion Pictures, asked whether "realistic war films [should] be shown to children." "A great many people," he wrote, felt an impulse to protect children, "particularly in such a vivid medium as the motion picture, from too much brutality and violence, and show only the finer, better things so they might be informally taught the higher value of life." He understood that the war presented a unique challenge: "Can protection from the knowledge of evil, however hideous, have any justified part in a practical education for life that must contend, physically and emotionally, all over the globe against totalitarian education for death?"[33]

Sidonie M. Gruenberg, director of the Child Study Association of America, thought that children needed to know about the larger events occurring in the world, despite their brutality. She noted that before Pearl Harbor, she had asked a senior at a prestigious prep school whether the students ever discussed the war in Europe, and learned that they seldom talked about the war and their instructors never made them do so in class. "Our students have been made to feel that going to school is their only responsibility," Gruenberg said; she hoped that realistic portrayals of war in movies might help make them "aware of the world they live in." For too long, "parents and teachers have been on the side of excluding anything that might even be called disagreeable in *all* the media."[34]

Dudley Nichols, a Hollywood screenwriter, argued that children were not equipped to watch realistic portrayals of war. "Violence, the savagery of modern war, appeals; it fascinates the childish imagination more powerfully than it does the adult mind which has by long training developed a moral conscience. . . . Hitler and the fascist world have shown us what a forcing-bed is the childish mind. . . . We should all protect that mind up to a certain age." Frank Astor, an editor with *Youth Leaders Digest*, disagreed: "For the good of the child, as well as for the American way of life, realistic pictures can and should be shown to the youngsters who are growing up in a world of war."[35]

The National Board of Review and the New York Public Library, in an effort to gauge how children responded to war movies, sponsored a symposium in which five children, all fourteen or younger, talked about the year's notable war films. Mary Anne Kennedy, age fourteen, said she liked *Mrs. Miniver* because "it just shows a clear picture of home life and what happens to it in a war." Jimmy Kelly, also fourteen, preferred movies with more action but qualified his opinion: "I like pictures that show the real war, not one where the hero kills a hundred or so enemies in a minute, or make the enemy out to be dumb." Hollywood had quit making "gangster movies," he noted, but "some of these cheap war films are just gangster pictures modernized." Another young girl said she preferred war movies "because there's no sense trying to escape the war. It's here and you have to expect facts."[36]

American youngsters in a time of global war had few ways of seeing the world besides movies, and the ones they enjoyed in 1942 reveal how they saw their lives and the war. Movie reviewers aged eight to eighteen who belonged to 4-Star Clubs around the country chose *Mrs. Miniver* as their favorite film, followed by *Pride of the Yankees, Wake Island, King's Row*, and *The Pied Piper*. The surprise selection of *King's Row*, a drama set in a small town at the turn of the century and starring Ronald Reagan, was judged by the National Board of Review to show that "youngsters are much more impressed by subjects of this kind than their parents would like to believe." Girls aged fourteen to eighteen chose *King's Row* as their third-favorite film behind *Mrs. Miniver* and *Pride of the Yankees*, whereas for boys fourteen to eighteen, their favorite film was *Wake Island*, a more conventional war movie about American soldiers fighting in the Pacific.[37]

One of the year's more popular actresses was Hedy Lamarr, known as the "most beautiful woman in the world," who graced the June 1 cover of *Life*. Lamarr's appearance on the cover highlighted her role in the upcoming movie *Tortilla Flat*. *Life* commented that starring as Dolores Resendes in a movie adapted from a John Steinbeck novel alongside Spencer Tracy and John Garfield "indicated a new phase in her career." Few knew that Lamarr was engaged in another career that had nothing to do with motion pictures. She was awaiting word from the U.S. Patent Office on a "Secret Communication System" she had invented with composer George Antheil, which was thought to provide a jam-proof radio guidance system for torpedoes. Since America's entry into the war, the Patent Office had received forty-five thousand requests for patents and would grant just 15 percent of them. The ideas floated by ambitious inventors included electromagnetic guns, lightweight armored clothing, and a portable sound detector for airplane spotters.[38]

Later in the summer, the Patent Office approved the patent for Lamarr and Antheil's device, which, the inventors claimed, "relates broadly to secret communication systems involving the use of carrier waves of different frequencies." The two were ahead of their time. The navy dismissed the invention during the war, but it would be used a quarter-century later in the Vietnam War. Although Lamarr never profited from her invention, it is today considered a foundational element in wireless communication such as Bluetooth and Wi-Fi. She and Antheil were posthumously inducted into the

National Inventors Hall of Fame in 2014. Other inductees into the hall who were awarded patents in 1942 include Chester Carlson for xerographic printing and Donald Holmes for polyurethane. Two African Americans were awarded patents in 1942 that saved the lives of countless American servicemen and servicewomen: Frederick Jones for air-conditioned vehicles to transport blood, medicine, and food supplies; and Dr. Charles Drew for a method of preserving human blood.[39]

By June, the nation had grown resigned to the daily rhythms of war, to the knowledge that it would not end anytime soon and that things would probably get worse before they got better. "It is doubtful whether most Americans are sufficiently awake to the magnitude of the war stake of 1942," wrote journalist William Henry Chamberlin, who worried that if Hitler was victorious in Russia or if the Germans routed the British in North Africa, then the issue could have already been settled before American troops were on the offensive in Europe. "It is quite within the bounds of possibility," he suggested, that by the end of 1942, "events will have predetermined victory or defeat."[40]

On June 3, the Japanese response to the Doolittle raid that military officials feared finally arrived, but not in the way many expected. Shortly after 6:00 a.m., Japanese planes bombed warehouses and a naval base in Dutch Harbor, Alaska, a remote fishing port in the Aleutian Islands. A second wave of planes came six hours later. While the attack caused minimal damage, it was the first enemy bombing of the North American continent, even if it was on an island more than eight hundred miles from Anchorage and nearly two thousand miles from Seattle. Secretary of War Henry Stimson, rejecting the notion that the attack was in retaliation for the Tokyo raid, said he assumed a larger attack on a more significant target was likely. He was right. The Alaska attack had been a diversionary exercise meant to distract American forces from the actual target.[41]

What the Japanese were really after was, in part, a direct result of the Doolittle raid in April. Japanese military leaders saw the island of Midway, some thirteen hundred miles from Oahu, as a strategic prize. By taking it, they could control the Pacific and render the American Navy incapable of launching further attacks on the Japanese home islands. In addition, they saw Midway as a potential base from which to launch more attacks against Hawaii and perhaps force the Americans to the negotiating table. An attack there also presented a chance for Admiral Isoruku Yamamoto to destroy the American Pacific Fleet once and for all. What Yamamoto and his admirals did not know, as they began moving their carriers into position, was that they were heading into a trap.

American cryptanalysts had cracked the Japanese code in May. The navy knew all along that Midway was the primary target, and Admiral Chester Nimitz, the Pacific Fleet commander, had ordered three carriers to the area. The battle of Midway began and ended on June 4. In a stunning air attack that lasted all of five minutes, American forces destroyed four of the six carriers Japan had used to attack Pearl Harbor. The U.S. lost one carrier, *Yorktown,* but there was no doubting the extent of the American victory. The war in the Pacific was turned for good.

Most Americans did not learn the details of the battle until June 6, when Admiral Nimitz reported the first results: "It appears that the enemy's damage is very heavy indeed, involving several ships in each of the carrier, battleship, cruiser, and transport classes." While the specifics were not yet clear, Nimitz was sure that "the damage is far out of proportion to that which we have received." Navy secretary Frank Knox privately confessed that after "a fearful period of anxiety for us all," news of the battle of Midway provided "a very intense relief and joy." He described the outcome in no uncertain terms—"We gave them a first class beating"—and boasted that the Japanese were "pulling out for home ports (what's left of them) and Midway is ours." Knox understood that Midway "will seriously affect the whole war situation in the Pacific."[42]

The battle of Midway finally gave Americans a much-needed military victory after the shock of Pearl Harbor, and in addition to inflicting a devastating defeat on the Japanese Navy, it showed that the overall Japanese strategy had failed. The quick victory the Japanese had gambled on had proved a disastrous miscalculation, and while the war in the Pacific was far from over, the ability of American shipyards to produce more carriers and destroyers would eventually doom the Japanese war effort.[43]

By mid-year, U.S. war spending had reached $1 billion a week. Speaking at the University of Missouri commencement ceremony, WPB head Donald

Nelson said that output was "higher than we had any reason to suppose it could be." He was vague about the actual figures and focused instead on what the enormous productive machinery could mean for Americans after the war. Instead of another depression, Nelson envisioned a future where "poverty is not inevitable anymore." He told the crowd, "For the first time in the history of the human race, there can be enough of everything to go round. . . . The sum total of the world's greatest possible output of goods, divided by the sum total of the world's inhabitants, no longer means a little less than enough for everybody." How the economy would go from producing unprecedented amounts of war goods based on unprecedented government spending to a consumer economy that would absorb millions of returning soldiers was not something for which Nelson had an answer. He only said vaguely that "the profit motive continues to exist, but it is no longer the mainspring." Yet he was clear about one thing: anyone who bought rationed items on the black market or violated price controls was guilty of nothing less than treason.[44]

The rubber situation grew increasingly desperate. On June 12, the same day that thirteen-year-old Anne Frank received a diary as a birthday present, President Roosevelt went back to the radio, beginning with his customary clarity: "I want to talk to you about rubber—about rubber and the war—about rubber and the American people." For dramatic effect, he added, "When I say rubber, I mean rubber." Since over 90 percent of the nation's supply had been cut off by the Japanese, securing rubber by any means became a national emergency. Roosevelt implored Americans to look in their attics and garages for old and used rubber, and turn in the scrap material at over four hundred thousand gas stations throughout the country, where they would be paid a penny per pound and the station owners would be reimbursed by the government. FDR would not elaborate on what might occur if the scrap rubber drive could not provide what the military needed, but he said the war effort absolutely required enough rubber "to build the planes to bomb Tokyo and Berlin . . . enough rubber to win the war." Senator Harry Truman blamed the administration for not doing enough to halt civilians' "orgy of consumption" of rubber products. The "chief cause" of the crisis, he charged, was not that the Japanese had cut off all supplies but rather the administration's lack of focus.[45]

In the first week of the scrap rubber drive, residents of New York City handed in approximately 248 tons of old tire casings, athletic equipment, hot water bottles, garden hoses, door mats, raincoats, doorstops, and other items. The exact amount collected was unknown because the scrap committee did not have time to separate and weigh each product. Instead, they paid contributors by the "sight price" method. The Equitable Building on Broadway alone contributed 425 pounds after a campaign among its tenants.[46]

Bonds were another crucial aspect of war financing. The spirit behind the war bond drive was captured in an ad by the Bayer Company, half of which was covered with an image of General MacArthur. The text purported to show a letter to the general from an anonymous citizen who wrote, "I just paid the second installment on my income tax" and "that sure took a slice out of my income." The writer then asked why, after paying taxes, he should pay still more in the form of bonds. "Then, General, I happened to see a picture of you! And I thought about the boys on Bataan." After considering the heroic part played by MacArthur and the troops in the Pacific, the writer reflected, "what kind of a guy would I be, thinking income tax is enough? Feeding myself on the hooey that I'd done my part?" In addition to having contributed to the war effort, the writer then noted the added benefit of the bonds' 2.9 percent compound interest: "Ten years from now, for every $18.75 I put in, I'm going to get twenty-five bucks of security for me and the wife and the kids."[47]

At a hearing of the Ways and Means Committee on June 15, Treasury Department official Randolph Paul testified about the president's request to confiscate all after-tax income over $25,000. He said, "There can be no 'equality of privilege' for which the President has called when some of our citizens are permitted to enjoy a luxurious standard of living while others in less fortunate circumstances are called upon to cut their living standards to a bare subsistence level." The Treasury, Paul testified, supported the idea of the "100 percent war supertax," proudly giving the measure a nickname that future generations of government officials would never dare to use.[48]

In addition to the paramount issues of war—taxes, rationing, and the military actions in Europe and the Pacific—other issues crept into the national debate that June. One involved U.S. citizens' disturbing ignorance of

American history and civics. The *New York Times* conducted a nationwide survey of colleges and universities and discovered that 82 percent did not require students to take a course in U.S. history. The *Times* concluded, "Many students complete their four years in college without taking any history courses dealing with the country." Many college presidents responded that the time had come, "because of the world crisis," for students to know something about the nation's past. In addition to making better citizens and developing leadership skills, they noted, requiring more U.S. history courses "will give the American boys fighting against Fascism a clearer insight into the democratic traditions they are defending." Some presidents, however, thought world history was preferable and that U.S. history would promote "narrow thinking and sectional attitudes." A response from a Princeton official read: "Required courses usually kill interest in the subject and cause so much resentment that requirements must be set very low." A. R. Newsome, chair of the history department at the University of North Carolina, commented that "the overloading of professional curricula with vocational courses . . . virtually prohibit[s] students from electing American history." Of 150 students graduating with a degree in commerce from his institution in 1942, he said, only 13 had taken even one course in American history.[49]

The survey drew a harsh rebuke from C. C. Williams, president of Lehigh University, who claimed, "The assumption that a course in American history confers either civic virtue or essential understanding of public questions has no supporting evidence." Additionally, he noted, "Aside from the question of relative educational significance, the administrative difficulties of grinding through numerous sections of required history for all students and the inanity of such courses when devoid of student interest amply account for the present practice among American colleges." Richard A. Newhall, a history professor at Williams College, found the call for required courses in American history "an exhibition of patriotic hysteria" and "efforts at indoctrination." "It is a basic fallacy," he said, "to assume that, in order to know about something, you must willy-nilly 'take a course in it.' . . . In order to produce 'good' men and women, do we require them to take a course in ethics?" A New York Domestic Relations Court judge, Isaac Siegel, differed. Having sat through numerous cases involving children, he found that "95 out of 100 boys and girls know very little if anything about the story of our country. . . . There is nothing more lamentable than to sit in the Children's Court and or learn from personal questioning how many of those boys and girls do not know who the first president of the United States was." He called for a renewed effort to make citizens "active, and not merely passive, Americans." Samuel McKee, a Columbia history professor, said high school graduates displayed "an incredible ignorance" of American history, and he blamed the rise of "social studies" for feeding students an "amazing hodgepodge" of misinformation.

The following week, at a joint meeting in Denver of the National Education Association and the National Association of Manufacturers (NAM), the teaching of American history was on a lot of minds, and the industrialists and the teachers found common cause. Education professor Alonzo F. Myers of New York University stressed, "With the country engaged in a defense of its democratic heritage, it is imperative that the youth of the land know American history." Howard Coonley, past president of the NAM, expressed the general view of business leaders that "every student should know something about American history," and urged that it be stressed from elementary school through college.[50]

In the *New York Times* in early June, Arthur Krock wrote of how life had changed in the six months since December 6, 1941: "The average American citizen cannot buy a new car, or a new tire, or a reconditioned old tire, or be sure of repairs of those he has. He cannot buy a bicycle, with or without a motor; he cannot build a house or revamp an old one. . . . No longer can he summon the wide variety of electrical domestic servants which for years have waited on him hand and foot; refrigerators, irons, batteries, extra telephone sets, washing machines." Also in the *New York Times,* Samuel T. Williamson described the "signs of the times": "seats out of the backs of station wagons which are ready for transformation within five minutes into civilian defense ambulances . . . placards in groceries, 'No coffee until next week' . . . bags and baskets of crumpled-up tin cans in cellars. . . . Some housewives appear to have flexible contours, wide in the morning, trim in the afternoons and evenings," which Williamson ascribed to the need to save girdles. John Western, OPA's consumer advisor, advised women to conserve old clothes. He also noted that more people were using bicycles and fewer were playing golf. "Thus far, wartime rationing and restrictions have caused more fears in advance than hardships in realization. . . . [The] biggest worry of the moment is not over present shortages but of what Winter will bring."[51]

Young Americans kept joining the military. After Pearl Harbor, sixteen-year-old Audie Murphy of Farmersville, Texas, tried to enlist but was turned away by recruiters because of his age. On June 26, days after his seventeenth birthday, his sister signed a falsified affidavit that stated he was actually eighteen, and the 112-pound Murphy joined the U.S. Army. He reported for duty on June 30 at Camp Wolters, Texas, before embarking for Europe, where he became the war's most decorated soldier. Murphy went on to become a movie star; his career included playing himself in a film of his war exploits, *To Hell and Back*. Two months after Murphy enlisted, an African American from Birmingham, Alabama, George Watson, enlisted in the army and in March 1943 was aboard a steamer near New Guinea when it was torpedoed by the Japanese. Watson saw that several of his fellow soldiers could not swim and was able to successfully rescue them, but he swam himself into exhaustion and was pulled down into the water by the sinking hull. His body was never recovered. In 1997, President Clinton posthumously awarded him the Medal of Honor, making him one of just seven African Americans to receive the medal in World War II.[52]

On June 13, Roosevelt signed an order establishing the Office of Strategic Services (OSS), a forerunner of the Central Intelligence Agency, and appointed William J. "Wild Bill" Donovan to lead it. The OSS was placed under the direction of the Joint Chiefs of Staff and given the assignment of collecting and analyzing "such strategic information as may be directed" by the Joint Chiefs, as well as planning and operating "special services." Six days after the creation of the OSS, another arm of the American war machine was born, this time in Northern Ireland. After George Marshall visited Vice-Admiral Lord Louis Mountbatten, the two agreed that specially qualified army officers should train with the elite British Commandos and form an American rapid-deployment unit. On June 19 at Carrickfergus, U.S. major William O. Darby organized three hundred select soldiers into the First Battalion of army commandos, which would be called Rangers.

Just two months later, fifty Army Rangers would see action against German troops on a raid in Dieppe, France.[53]

A sense of the transformation brought by the war was on display at a late June meeting of the Advertising Federation of America in New York. FDR had sent a letter to the meeting, saying, "It is obvious that there are many changes going on in your field," and despite the decrease in product advertising, he was confident that it "does not mean an end to advertising." One speaker, Bruce Barton, was not convinced. Barton, the creator of Betty Crocker, was one of the nation's leading advertising executives. He told the assembled advertisers, "You and I shall not make money the rest of our lives, at least not in the sense in which we used to think of making money." The enforced collaboration between government and business would outlast the war, he said, but he believed the OPA's Leon Henderson "sincerely wants to preserve, not destroy, American business." After the war, he hoped, plans should not be made to diminish free enterprise, which would amount to "the repeal of human nature."[54]

Other voices were heard pronouncing the evils of centralized government. On June 21, Alabama governor Frank M. Dixon, nephew of Thomas Dixon, whose book *The Clansman* was the basis of D. W. Griffith's 1915 film *The Birth of a Nation*, told a gathering of other governors, "It seems that the very safety of the Democratic principles requires alertness and caution on our part. To me it seems that we have developed definite tendencies in our national life which, if not restrained, will ultimately result in the loss of that Democracy we are now so anxiously striving by force of arms to make secure."[55]

Other voices expressed worry about the growing bureaucracy in Washington. James Scott Kemper, president of the Lumbermen's Mutual Casualty Company, was not impressed by federal agencies and made light of government employees and their efforts. "Part of our difficulty," he noted in a speech in Chattanooga on June 5, "lies in the fact that we have too many people on the government payroll, many of whom have nothing really important to do." Henderson's OPA was an easy target, and Kemper quoted from OPA Circular W55-37558, which discussed how American women should wear girdles: "Try the girdle on . . . the best way to test a girdle for fit is to sit down in it. The garters should fasten securely and should be comfortable. The top of the girdle should not roll. If your waist is more than nine inches smaller than your hips, the chances are you won't fit a high-waisted girdle. You will find the waist too large. In that case, buy a girdle that sits low in the hips. If your thighs are large, make sure that the girdle comes well below your hips. Don't pull or stretch them any more than you have to . . . roll an all-fabric girdle before you step into it, then unroll over your hips. If the girdle has rigid support, ease it gently into place, first on one side, then on the other." Kemper concluded, "I'll leave to you the question of its importance in the war effort."[56]

On June 19, Prime Minister Winston Churchill met with Roosevelt in Hyde Park, New York, where they discussed plans to open a second front in Europe. Back in Washington, Roosevelt and Churchill spent the next few days meeting with the president's closest war advisors, and the prime minister was careful in presenting his overall strategy. The notion of an English Channel crossing to relieve pressure on Stalin's troops was not something Churchill felt the Allies were ready for in 1942, and he worried that such an attack could have catastrophic consequences. During one of his sessions with Roosevelt, Churchill received the devastating news that British forces had surrendered at Tobruk in Libya, which made him even more certain that a cross-channel invasion would fail.

Instead, Churchill convinced FDR that the proper place to attack the Axis was in North Africa. Roosevelt's generals disagreed, believing that a North Africa invasion would be inconsequential. Churchill reiterated that by capturing Morocco, Algeria, and Tunisia, the Allies could enter Europe via the Mediterranean rather than travel thousands of miles around the Cape of Good Hope and invade through the Middle East. He further claimed that the green American troops would be better off getting their first taste of action in the African desert than in western France. With every passing day, worries grew that the Germans could soon defeat the Russians and turn all of their attention to the British and Americans. "We should not forget," said Dwight Eisenhower in the summer of 1942, "that the prize is to keep 8,000,000 Russian troops in the war." Stalin's frustrations over Allied foot-dragging on a second front were shared by his troops. One Russian soldier told an American correspondent, "The trouble with you people is that you don't hate the Germans enough."[57]

During Churchill's visit, Roosevelt signed Congressional Resolution 303, which attempted to "codify and emphasize existing rules and customs pertaining to the display and use of the flag of the United States of America." Congress had been urged by the American Legion and the Veterans of Foreign Wars to specify proper conditions for displaying and honoring the flag. The resolution also introduced a "pledge" to accompany official recognitions. The words, written in 1892 by a Christian Socialist named Francis Bellamy, were already well known to most Americans: "I pledge allegiance to the flag of the United States of America and to the republic for which it stands, one nation indivisible, with liberty and justice for all." The proper way for civilians to salute the flag involved "extending the right hand, palm upward, toward the flag." Six months later, after people complained that this gesture closely resembled the Nazi salute, Congress amended the resolution to allow civilians instead to place "the right hand over the heart."[58]

The discord brewing between the administration and Congress over the tax bill reached a new level on June 24, when the Ways and Means Committee approved a substantially lower tax than the one sought by the president or Treasury secretary Morgenthau. The new taxes promised to bring in only $5.9 billion in additional revenue, over $2.6 billion less than the Treasury had hoped for. The bill called for a 94 percent excess profits tax on corporations and lowered personal exemptions to bring more taxpayers onto the rolls. At the last minute, the committee struck out a provision for mandatory joint tax returns and rejected higher taxes on soft drinks and carbonated beverages. A disappointed Morgenthau asserted that the "tax bill now before Congress should be the start, and not the conclusion, of the wartime revenue program." Even with new taxes, he added, "it is of utmost importance that as large a proportion of this money as possible be borrowed from the current savings of the people, and that the remainder be raised with a minimum of pressure upon price ceilings and of disturbance to the credit structure."[59]

Things only grew worse for the administration later in the day, when the House Appropriations Committee slashed Henderson's OPA appropriation. He had requested $210 million to fully finance a staff of one hundred thousand employees, but the committee appropriated only $95 million, on the theory that price control should be "self-enforcing." While committee chair Clarence Cannon of Missouri denied that the appropriation signaled a lack of confidence in Henderson, most observers knew better. Henderson wrote in response, "I am convinced that I failed to bring home to the members of the committee a full realization of the enormous administrative job embodied in rationing scarce goods to 130 million people, in fixing rents for 90 million people, and holding down the cost of living by price ceilings affecting three million business enterprises."

Members of Congress understood perfectly what Henderson wanted, and their budget displayed their growing resentment toward him. Jesse P. Wolcott, the ranking Republican on the House Banking and Currency Committee, questioned whether Henderson was "temperamentally fitted for the job he holds." Charles Plumley of Vermont snapped that "there are two ways to stop this animal—starve him to death by refusing to appropriate nourishment, or hit him with a club so hard, figuratively speaking, that he will lie down and stay put." As Bruce Catton wrote, Henderson "had nothing to stand on but the force of his own personality, and the power of his own intelligence," neither of which had much force without the power that was "vested in him by law and by executive order."[60]

Henderson reacted to the congressional slight by threatening to resign. "I predicted when I took this job that I would soon become the most unpopular man in America," he said, "and I seem to be making progress." He acknowledged that some politicians did not care for him, "but I was appointed by the greatest politician of all time and I expect to stay with it until he thinks I have outlived my usefulness." Denying the "fantastic stories" about armies of bureaucrats, Henderson said his request paid for only sixty-six thousand people, of whom just six thousand would be inspection staff. Upwards of 2.5 million "volunteers" might be needed to help enforce OPA guidelines, but these were not, he reiterated, paid employees. He admitted that "all these controls are tough on people," and "they're damned inconvenient. I can't get enough gasoline to go fishing!" After listening to Henderson on the radio, one Minnesota resident wrote to Roosevelt that he believed the government "would do well to keep such bigoted, arrogant exponents of the personal pronoun 'I' off the air."[61]

Henderson's inability to placate members of Congress had many roots. One of the criticisms leveled at him concerned the way he appointed local personnel. For many members of Congress, the complaint was not that he had hired officials based on their political affiliation but that he had actually hired Republicans. One Mississippi Democrat complained of the "Philistines," or Republicans, who controlled his state's OPA personnel. Henderson also was not receptive when senators and congressmen suggested people for various posts within the OPA. His typical response was, "This is the war on the home front," and his agency could not be used as a source of patronage. "Try to get your pets made generals and colonels in the Army," he said, "and see how far you get!" By summer, it was clear that Henderson's efforts to oversee the American economy faced growing opposition: organized labor and the farm lobby fought against his wage levels; business leaders fought against his price levels; and an increasing number of representatives and senators disapproved of his performance. Henderson understood his position: "I have to make nothing but adverse decisions, and I haven't any political prize packages to hand out, and I can't soft-soap anybody." His job involved taking "from nearly everybody the things they are accustomed to having and think they have a right to procure, war or no war."[62]

Henderson could dish out criticism as well as take it. Jewel Brown, a government stenographer in Monroe, Louisiana, sent Henderson a poem expressing her frustration at not being able to buy tires and gasoline. It ended: "So Mr. Henderson says we must all learn to walk. But what does he do daily except dish out the talk?" Henderson promptly replied:

> I read your verse, believe it or not
> Some part is good, some not so hot.
> You indicate I talk all day
> But half time's spent on what other people say
> My life is changed—it's not the same
> But Hitler is the one I blame

Beneath it he added a penciled notation—"6 a.m., at the office."[63]

On June 26, the president provided the first official figures on war production since Pearl Harbor. Having said earlier that he could not divulge numbers because they could provide "aid and comfort" to the enemy, he now reversed course and claimed that the information would give the Axis powers "just the opposite of 'aid and comfort.'" In May, FDR said, the U.S. had produced 4,000 airplanes, 1,500 tanks, 2,000 artillery and anti-tank guns, and over 100,000 machine guns. Of all these numbers, the airplane production was the most impressive, considering the country had produced just over 1,300 planes the previous May, and fewer than 500 in May 1940. Yet underlying the figures was the notion that the pace of production must still increase if the nation was to reach the president's goals. Despite the good news, the president warned the American people not to "rest on our oars" and that "serious production problems" lay ahead because of shortages in raw materials. What the public did not know was that airplane production actually declined in June to 3,704 airplanes. The nation also produced 3,164 tons of mustard gas in June and 19,749 chemical mortar shells. Meanwhile, the National Industrial Conference Board reported that, counting soldiers, a record 53,376,000 Americans had jobs.[64]

Since Pearl Harbor, many Americans had feared that enemy agents would somehow land on U.S. soil and unleash a wave of devastating sabotage and terror. In May, the *New York Times* relayed a pervasive rumor that German spies had come ashore in Florida from a submarine and had spent a weekend surveying possible targets before returning to their vessel.[65] In late June it was revealed that such notions were not paranoid delusions. On June 27, the FBI announced the arrest of eight German saboteurs carrying fake birth certificates, Social Security cards, a variety of high explosives, $150,000 in cash, and specific plans to commit a wave of terrorist acts on civilian targets throughout the eastern United States. Code-named Operation Pastorius, the effort was a coordinated attempt by Berlin to bring the war to the American people. Following their arrest, the spies revealed their plans in chilling detail.

They had been trained for the project at a specially designated school located on Quentz Lake near Berlin. In the beginning, sixteen students were recruited, but over time eight dropped out (three could not speak English). They had all lived in the U.S. and spoke fluent English. (Two were even American citizens.) After weeks of intensive training in explosives, the eight Abwehr spies swam ashore from rubber boats launched from German submarines in two locations. Four landed on Long Island, New York, on June 13, and four days later, four more landed on Ponte Vedra Beach near Jacksonville, Florida. After a few weeks of blending into American life, they were to meet in Cincinnati in early July to finalize their plans. Their lists of targets included aluminum plants in Tennessee and Philadelphia, the Hell Gate Bridge in Queens, locks on the Ohio River near Louisville, water supply systems in New York City, and a dam near Niagara Falls. The agents also planned to bomb railroad bridges and Jewish department stores. The plan fell apart because the landings were detected and the FBI undertook a national manhunt, the largest in its history. Had even a small part of their plan worked, the consequences could have been catastrophic. The capture of the eight saboteurs captivated the nation, and their trial was scheduled for July. If convicted, they faced the death penalty. Members of the American Legion Post of Olyphant, Pennsylvania, volunteered to serve in the firing squad.[66]

The arrests did a great deal for the reputation of FBI director J. Edgar Hoover, and the White House received dozens of letters and telegrams urging that he be given the Medal of Honor. This was not the authentic expression of grateful citizens but a campaign orchestrated by the FBI's Crime Records Division and its director, Lou Nichols. It worked: Hoover's star rose within Washington and throughout the country as the nation's "top cop."[67]

The details of the German plot eerily resembled an Alfred Hitchcock film that had been released two months earlier, appropriately titled *Saboteur*. The film, starring Robert Cummings and Norman Lloyd, portrayed a wartime America beset with German spies intent on blowing up such targets as a California aircraft factory, the Boulder Dam, and a ship in the Brooklyn Navy Yard. Hitchcock actually filmed a scene in New York City using the overturned hull of the *Normandie*. The suggestion that the ship had somehow fallen victim to saboteurs angered the navy and gave rise to a whole new set of rumors. In New York, the stories spread that "thousands of spies" had landed in the area. "Those eight spies were nothing at all," proclaimed one New Yorker. "Any minute now there will be explosions and disorder all over the country."[68]

On June 30, the government closed its books on the fiscal year. Federal expenditures, 80 percent of them dedicated to war, totaled $32.3 billion and the government ran a deficit of $19.5 billion. The national debt stood at $76.5 billion. Those figures would be soon dwarfed by spending already under way and would reach even higher levels by the end of the next fiscal year. War spending alone was estimated at $67 billion for the next twelve months, and with receipts totaling barely $24 billion, the borrowing would continue at unprecedented levels. By the end of fiscal 1943, the U.S. national debt was expected to reach $130 billion. Of the total military spending in 1942, a third of it went toward constructing the plants whose assembly lines would turn out the unprecedented weaponry in 1943 and beyond. Some fiscal conservatives, such as Senator Harry F. Byrd of Virginia, worried that the spending and debt were so vast that Congress was losing the ability to exercise its control of the purse and had delegated that constitutional duty to the executive branch. For now, such constitutional and economic trepidations would have to wait. Unless the war brought victory, the debates over executive and legislative authority, or the levels of government spending and borrowing, would be irrelevant.[69]

December 7, 1941: the attack on Pearl Harbor. The photograph was taken from a camera inside a Japanese plane. (Courtesy: National Archives and Records Administration.)

An unidentified woman with child and dog, fleeing from the Pearl Harbor attack. (Franklin D. Roosevelt Presidential Library.)

FDR meeting with his war cabinet, December 1941. *Clockwise from nearest front:* Harry Hopkins, Lend-Lease; Frances Perkins, Labor; Colonel Philip B. Fleming; Vice President Henry Wallace; Fiorello La Guardia, Civil Defense; Paul McNutt, Federal Security; Jesse Jones, Commerce; Harold Ickes, Interior; Frank C. Walker, postmaster general; Henry Stimson, War; Cordell Hull, State; FDR; Henry Morgenthau Jr., Treasury; Francis Biddle, Justice; Frank Knox, secretary of the navy; Claude Wickard, Agriculture. (Library of Congress, Prints & Photographs Division, FSA/OWI Collection [LC-USZ62-132995].)

The Harvest by Thomas Hart Benton, 1942, one of eight paintings from his Year of Peril series. After early public viewings of Benton's apocalyptic images, federal officials thought the paintings were too graphic and stopped promoting them. (© 2019 T.H. and R.P. Benton Testamentary Trusts / UMB Bank Trustee / Licensed by VAGA at Artists Rights Society [ARS], NY.)

In February, when African Americans tried to move into the previously all-white Sojourner Truth Housing Project in Detroit, they were met by over twelve hundred angry whites, many carrying guns and clubs. Eventually forty people were injured. Here, a man armed with a wrench confronts a police officer. (Library of Congress, Prints and Photographs Division, FSA/OWI Collection [LC-DIG-fsa-8d25268].)

Office of Price Administration head Leon Henderson riding a "Victory" bicycle, made without any essential war materials, in Washington, D.C., March. Seated in the basket is stenographer Betty Barrett. (Library of Congress, Prints and Photographs Division, FSA/OWI Collection, [LC-USZ62-102599].)

After FDR signed Executive Order 9066 establishing exclusion zones along the West Coast, over one hundred thousand Japanese Americans were sent to internment camps throughout the Southwest. Here, a young girl awaits a bus to take her and her family to an assembly center in April. (Clem Albers, photographer, California, 210-G-2A-6. Courtesy: National Archives and Records Administration.)

After over seventy-five thousand American and Filipino forces surrendered on the Bataan Peninsula in April, they were forced to march eighty miles through intense heat and subjected to brutal treatment by their Japanese captors. Approximately six hundred U.S. troops died on the Bataan Death March. Here, soldiers carry their dead in makeshift litters. (Courtesy: National Archives and Records Administration.)

Admiral Chester Nimitz, Pacific Fleet commander, pinning the Navy Cross on Messman Doris "Dorie" Miller in May. Because of the segregated nature of the navy, Miller was not trained in weaponry, but during the attack on Pearl Harbor, he fired an anti-aircraft gun, likely downing at least one Japanese plane. Despite the fact that Miller became one of the first heroes of the war, he remained confined to kitchen duty. He died in 1943 aboard the carrier *Liscome Bay* when it was struck by a torpedo. (Library of Congress, Prints and Photographs Division [LC-DIG-ppms-ca-40817].)

Many cities were on alert for enemy air attacks and had local volunteers watch the skies. Here, air-raid wardens meet in the basement of an apartment building in Washington, D.C. (Gordon Parks, photographer, Library of Congress, Prints and Photographs Division, FSA/OWI Collection [LC-USF34-013391-C].)

In June, FDR signed a resolution establishing the proper way to honor the flag, including the Pledge of Allegiance. The official salute is shown here by schoolchildren in Southington, Connecticut. When its resemblance to the Nazi salute was realized later in the year, the gesture was amended to simply placing one's hand over one's heart. (Fenno Jacobs, photographer, Library of Congress, Prints and Photographs Division, FSA/OWI Collection [LC-DIG-8d34748].)

No plant symbolized the "Arsenal of Democracy" like Henry Ford's 3.5-million-square-foot B-24 "liberator" bomber plant in Willow Run, Michigan. At its height in 1944, the plant produced a B-24 every hour. (Office of War Information photo, Franklin D. Roosevelt Presidential Library.)

Workers at the Douglas Aircraft plant in Long Beach, California, participating in an outdoor assembly. By the end of 1942, over 11 million people were employed in war industries, and the unemployment rate fell to 2.88 percent. (U.S. Army Signal Corps photo, Franklin D. Roosevelt Presidential Library.)

One of the millions of women who worked in U.S. defense plants. Here, an employee of North American Aviation in Inglewood, California, assembles a cowling for a B-25 bomber motor. (Office of War Information photo, Franklin D. Roosevelt Presidential Library.)

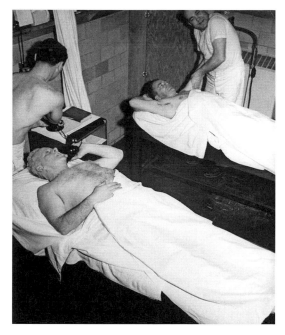

William S. Jack (*left*), owner of the Jack and Heintz Company, and son, Russ, receiving a massage, a benefit all employees enjoyed at the Bedford, Ohio, plant. "Jahco" received over $216 million in war contracts and provided "associates" with free medical and dental care, meals, and paid vacations in return for working twelve-hour shifts seven days a week. Congressional investigators criticized the company's benefits and bonuses as ways to avoid taxes. (Dmitri Kessel, photographer, The LIFE Picture Collection/Getty Images.)

NAZI SABOTEUR TRIAL, WASHINGTON, D.C.

In late June, eight German spies were captured in New York and Florida. As part of Operation Pastorius, the plan called for the agents to commit acts of sabotage throughout the U.S. After the Supreme Court ruled that they could be tried as enemy combatants, their trial took place in July in the Justice Department building. (U.S. Army Signal Corps photo, Library of Congress [LC-USE623-D-OA-000144].)

SEPTEMBER 19, 1942—P. M.

Shipyards owned by Henry Kaiser in California and Oregon utilized mass-production techniques and prefabricated parts to transform the construction of military ships. The U.S.S. *Joseph N. Teal,* a 10,500-ton liberty ship, was built in just ten and a half days. Here, it is seen on its seventh day of construction in September 1942. Shortly after this, the U.S.S. *Robert E. Peary* was completed in a record four days, fifteen hours. (Franklin D. Roosevelt Presidential Library.)

NORMA L. GREENE
Second Lieutenant

Second Lieutenant Norma L. Greene, who was stationed with the African American Army Nurse Corps in Tuskegee, Alabama. On September 12, she boarded a bus in Montgomery, Alabama, and sat in a section reserved for white passengers. Greene was arrested and suffered a broken nose from a beating by police. (Tuskegee Army Nurses Project, www.TuskegeeArmyNurses.info.)

Boston Herald assistant publisher W. G. Gavin (*seated*) at the Boston Herald War Rumor Clinic, October. The clinic collected rumors floating around the region and published a series of corrective articles. The initiative was part of a broader effort led by the Office of War Information to collect false stories and educate the public. (Bernard Hoffman, photographer, The LIFE Picture Collection/Getty Images.)

FEDERAL BUREAU OF INVESTIGATION

Form ...
This ... ... AT   MEMPHIS, TENNESSEE   7 ⊃   FILE NO. 100-1535

REPORT MADE AT	DATE WHEN MADE	PERIOD FOR WHICH MADE	REPORT MADE BY	
MEMPHIS, TENNESSEE	11-13-42	11-3,5-42	██████████	JOS

TITLE	CHARACTER OF CASE
ELEANOR ROOSEVELT CLUB OF NEGRO WOMEN, Jackson, Tennessee.	INTERNAL SECURITY - X

SYNOPSIS OF FACTS:

Investigation based upon report by confidential informant that negro women of Jackson, Tennessee were forming a club whose slogan was "not a cook in the kitchen by Christmas" results negatively. Original informant states that there was no basis for such a report.

- C -

DETAILS:

Investigation in this case is predicated upon information furnished to this office by Confidential Informant A who advised that information had been received by that informant to the effect that the negro women of Jackson, Tennessee had organized an Eleanor Roosevelt Club. Membership was reported in this club to be ten cents a week.

It was further stated by the informant that a negro cook who had worked for a ████████ or ████████ Street in Jackson, Tennessee for some time had resigned recently, stating she was a member of this club and that the slogan of this group was "not a cook in the kitchen by Christmas". The initials of the ████████ referred to and the house number were not given.

AT JACKSON, TENNESSEE

A check of the Jackson, Tennessee City Directory for 1942 lists only one family by the name of ████████ residing on ████████ Street in Jackson.

████████████████ was contacted and

APPROVED AND FORWARDED:	████ ████ SPECIAL AGENT IN CHARGE	DO NOT WRITE IN THESE SPACES	SE
COPIES DESTROYED		100-139664-1X	RECORDED & INDEXED
5 8 DEC 3 1942			
2 Bureau 0-2 (1 Atlanta; 1 Memphis) 2 Memphis		13 NOV 16 1942	

COPY IN FILE

U. S. GOVERNMENT PRINTING OFFICE—0— 7—2014

Among the leading rumors of 1942, none were as pervasive as the existence of "Eleanor Clubs," designed to organize African American domestic workers to strike, forcing white women to do their own housework. "A white woman in every kitchen by 1943" was supposedly the clubs' motto. Two southern governors ordered the state police to investigate, and the FBI also investigated in several states. (fbi.gov.)

Among the many astonishing accomplishments of the year was the building of the Alcan Highway, a fifteen-hundred-mile road from Dawson Creek, British Columbia, to Delta Junction, Alaska, carved through some of the most remote and dense environments on Earth. The U.S. Army Corps of Engineers relied heavily on African American soldiers for the road's construction. (Library of Congress, Prints and Photographs Division, FSA/OWI Collection [LC-USW33-000937].)

The *People's Voice*, an African American newspaper published in Harlem by Adam Clayton Powell, featured dramatic charcoal drawings by Ollie Harrington. This one portrays the viciousness of lynchings in Mississippi. (Courtesy of Dr. Helma Harrington.)

Henry Luce (*left*), *Life* publisher who coined the phrase "The American Century" in 1941, and his wife, Clare Boothe Luce, who won a congressional seat in 1942 campaigning on a platform that stressed focusing on a "hard war" and less on domestic issues. Her victory helped the GOP gain forty-three House seats. (Library of Congress, Photographs and Prints Division [LC-USZ62-47799].)

On November 8, American and British troops began the offensive against Hitler's forces in North Africa. Over sixty-three thousand U.S. troops were used in Operation Torch. Among the first were those landing in French Morocco and Algeria. (British government photo, Franklin D. Roosevelt Presidential Library.)

7

July: "The Principles of Democracy"

THE ARREST OF THE EIGHT GERMAN SABOTEURS set off a furious legal debate over whether they should be tried in civilian courts or some other venue. On July 2, FDR signed Executive Proclamation 2561, creating a military tribunal to try the suspects as enemy combatants. "Such persons," the order stated, "shall not be privileged to seek any remedy or maintain any proceeding . . . in the courts of the United States." The proclamation would provide the precedent for the November 2001 order by President George W. Bush to try suspected terrorists as enemy combatants in military courts.

As the trial got under way, attorneys for the defendants appealed to the U.S. Supreme Court, asking that a civilian court hear the case. Two of the defendants were American citizens who held that they were being denied their constitutional rights to a trial by jury. The justices heard the arguments just weeks later. The tenor of the case was best expressed by Justice Felix Frankfurter, who wrote a "soliloquy" to the other justices in which he pretended to be the judge presiding over the spies' trial. After reading their case, Frankfurter responded: "You damned scoundrels have a helluva cheek to ask for a writ that would take you out of the hands of the Military Commission." The eight defendants were "low-down, ordinary, enemy spies who, as enemy soldiers, have invaded our country and therefore could immediately have been shot by the military when caught."[1]

As Frankfurter's memo displayed, the court was not receptive to constitutional claims by the suspected saboteurs, and unanimously denied the defendants' appeal and ruled that they would be tried before a military tribunal: "Unlawful combatants are subject to trial and punishment by military tribunals for acts which render their belligerency unlawful." Years later, Justice Antonin Scalia admitted that the decision was "not the Court's finest hour."[2]

The trial began on July 8 in the Justice Department building, with eight generals serving as jurors and Attorney General Francis Biddle as prosecutor. Many civil libertarians were disappointed in the trial's structure, and even Secretary of War Henry Stimson questioned why the attorney general's time should be used prosecuting the case. Interior secretary Harold Ickes said of Biddle's participation in the proceedings, "It is wonderful what the itch for publicity will lead one to."

The trial ended in early August, and all eight were found guilty and sentenced to death. In exchange for their cooperation with the FBI, Roosevelt commuted two conspirators' sentences, one to life in prison and the other to thirty years of "hard labor." The remaining six were scheduled for execution. The question arose whether the convicted spies should be shot or hanged. Roosevelt hoped for the latter, but the tribunal chose a less public method, the electric chair. On August 8, the six convicted German spies were electrocuted and their bodies buried in a remote thicket in southwest Washington known as Blue Plains.

But some Americans did not want the saboteurs to be forgotten. Decades later, utility workers uncovered a small granite memorial to the executed spies on U.S. government property near the Blue Plains wastewater plant, left there by the National Socialist White People's Party, a forerunner of the American Nazi Party. Candles had been placed around the slab, which had also been regularly cleaned. The National Park Service removed the marker in 2010.[3]

As Americans celebrated the Fourth of July for the 166th time, over five hundred magazines and periodicals showed their patriotism by featuring the American flag on their covers. The "United We Stand" effort, led by the National Publishers Association, showcased the flag as a galvanizing symbol that made the war effort at home and abroad one of protecting democratic principles embodied in the Declaration of Independence. A solemn

Franklin D. Roosevelt marked the occasion by saying: "Never since it first was created in Philadelphia has this anniversary come in times so dangerous to everything for which it stands." The context of the celebration was not lost on the president, who added that the day would not be celebrated by "the fireworks of make-believe but in the death-dealing reality of tanks and planes and guns and ships." Overseas, American pilots marked the occasion by borrowing British R.A.F. planes to make the first bombing runs on German-held territory in Holland. At home, one of the consequences of the gas rationing and lower speed limits could be felt on Independence Day as seventy-eight people died in traffic-related deaths across the country, fewer than half the deaths from the same day a year earlier.[4]

Independence Day was also a time to reflect on the threat the Axis powers posed to a free society. *Time* reported that people were somber throughout the nation. "On only two occasions in the last century . . . has the Union been in more danger comparable to the danger it faces on July 4, 1942. One such day was July 4, 1863 . . . the other such day was July 4, 1918, when after three spring drives the Germans had almost broken the Allied front in France." The dark mood was not limited to Washington. In London, a shaken Churchill told the House of Commons on July 3 that since the shocking loss of Tobruk, "we are at this moment in the presence of a recession of our hopes and prospects in the Middle East and in the Mediterranean unequalled since the fall of France."[5]

July marked the first month in which the War Damage Corporation insured Americans against property loss from enemy attacks. Since the first of the year, U.S. citizens had purchased policies insuring $25 billion of property against loss from war, including a number of industrial plants well away from any coast. The service fees for agents signing up the policies totaled $1 million. The plans seemed so reasonable that the *New York Times* predicted, "Every insurable property in locations such as Hawaii and Alaska will be covered in full." For ordinary buildings, the cost was 10 cents per $100 of insurance, and for plants and manufacturing centers the cost was 30 cents per $100. The highest premiums were for vessels devoted to storage or industrial use. No protection was provided for deeds, securities, or gold bullion. The locations of the insured property provide a glimpse of how Americans felt about the prospects of attack in the summer of 1942. While the most policies were issued in New York City (232 policies valued at $464 million), 67 were purchased in Atlanta (valued at $29 million), 61 in Chicago ($60 million), 94 in Cincinnati ($76 million), and even 65 in Omaha ($22 million).[6]

Some in the financial industry thought that too many Americans were putting their assets at risk by failing to take advantage of the government-backed insurance. *Newsweek* commented, "Many large mortgage holders are almost wishing for a token air raid on this country. Having no clear legal authority to compel a mortgagor to safeguard his own property, banks and insurance companies are having a hard time persuading owners that there is sufficient danger to justify taking out war damage insurance. As a result, they find themselves forced to take out the insurance themselves—which, when many mortgages are held, becomes a considerable expense." Some New York banks, worried that the city would be the most likely targets of a German air attack, began duplicating bank records and storing them elsewhere.[7]

The fear of enemy attacks provided more opportunities for rumors to grow, and their corrosive power continued to haunt the federal government. Military and government officials worried that they could even cost lives. The danger of false information was highlighted in *Life* magazine in mid-July when, at the suggestion of presidential aide Stephen Early, it produced a "photo-dramatization" of a rumor, directed by Alfred Hitchcock. In a series of photos, a casual remark overheard in church eventually leads to a German spy alerting his superiors to American troop movements, which in turn leads to the sinking of an American ship. While no one in the fictional town realized they had played a part in the loss, the story's message to readers was clear: "Keep your mouth shut!"[8]

The need to control what was written and said about the war fell to the Office of Censorship (OC), which had come into being just days after Pearl Harbor. Led by Byron Price, the agency worried about every letter and every piece of news—no matter how apparently innocent—that could reveal information to the enemy. Weather forecasts were frowned upon as they could give enemy pilots crucial information regarding a possible bombing target. In the event of an air attack, the OC asked "stations outside the area of attack . . . to make no mention of the action unless expressly authorized

for radio by the War Department." New York papers were asked to not publish news of President Roosevelt's visits to his home in Hyde Park, and the
OC even prohibited certain quiz programs from being aired. After the
Boone (Iowa) News-Republican printed a story identifying a local soldier's
unit location, it received a letter from the OC asking that it refrain from
publishing "the identity of an U.S. military unit or ship in any combat
zone." The OC also reinstated a prohibition that had been in effect throughout World War I and has now become permanent: photographs of dead
American soldiers could not be published.[9]

The House finally passed a budget bill on July 16 and sent it to the Senate.
The details of the bill displayed Leon Henderson's weakening support on
Capitol Hill. The House budget recommendations had reduced the OPA
appropriation to $75 million, and the Senate appropriations committee ap-
proved an OPA budget of $120 million while tightening the restrictions on
Henderson's authority to hire personnel. Committee chair Kenneth McKellar of Tennessee struck essentially the same tone as his House counterparts
when he said Henderson's staff of "lawyers and snoopers," as well as the
agency's travel and printing budgets, were excessive. The bill required that
any Henderson appointee receiving over $4,500 in salary would need Sen-
ate confirmation. The Senate also gave Agriculture secretary Claude Wickard the authority to veto Henderson's directives. In response, Henderson
said, with "a deep sense of personal failure," that if the Senate budget were
approved, General Max would have to be repealed. Attacks on Henderson
as a heavy-handed and arrogant bureaucrat were getting louder, and anxious members of Congress knew that while their constituents could not
vote against him in the November elections, they might cast a vote against
their representative or senator instead.

If Henderson did not have Congress's full backing, he still had the approval of the one person in Washington whose support he needed most.
President Roosevelt still supported his OPA director and was growing frustrated with Congress over its needling of the agency and its slow progress on
the federal budget. On July 15, after returning to the White House from Hyde
Park, he had lunch with Henderson, Donald Nelson, Vice President Wallace,
Interior secretary Harold Ickes, and Labor secretary Frances Perkins.

That same day, reporters learned that FDR planned to ask Congress to pass wage and price controls in order to hold down the threat of inflation. Despite General Max, the price of foods not under federal control had risen 10 percent since May. Key to the president's thinking were Henderson's worries that the price-control program was "in danger of breaking down." Roosevelt's request that Congress forego its summer recess also had members grumbling, both because of the extreme heat in Washington and because they would not be able to do, in the words of the *New York Times,* "political fence-mending at home."[10]

Before meeting with the president, Henderson had testified before a House small business committee and reiterated his displeasure that congressional meddling was threatening the anti-inflation effort. He understood that expressing his anger at Congress could have consequences—"It means that I get my throat cut for talking plainly"—but he was unrepentant: "I would rather have it cut than to have people asking me later what the hell I was doing when I was supposed to be keeping prices down."[11]

Some members of Congress were not helping maintain public confidence. Of those who used the war for partisan advantage or said things publicly that proved embarrassing, few were more reckless than House Military Affairs Committee chairman Andrew J. May of Kentucky, who told reporters the war would be over by the end of the year or perhaps by 1943, and he saw no need to draft eighteen- and nineteen-year-olds. Columnist Ernest Lindley saw this as blatant pandering and also understood that many politicians wanted to avoid the draft age issue until after November. Lindley said: "The near-term outlook for the sound management of the war economy is getting worse. Seven months after Pearl Harbor we do not have adequate war taxation; and the probability now is that a new tax bill will not be passed until after the election. . . . Congress not only has ignored the President's request to lower the minimum price ceiling on farm products, it has proceeded to vote for still additional favors to certain farm groups. As this was written, the future of 'wage stabilization' remains thoroughly unstable." Frustration with Congress was growing in advance of the elections, which *Life* called "among the most fateful in U.S. history."[12]

The economic reality facing most Americans would have been vexing for anyone trying to formulate a proper tax and wage policy. In the thirty-three largest U.S. cities, the Bureau of Labor Statistics found, an appropriate "maintenance budget" ranged from $1,406 to $1,705 annually. Half of the nation's non-farm families lived on less than $35 per week, and one in five lived on less than $20. If farm families were included, the average incomes were even lower, but many farmers could at least raise their own food.[13] As policy makers considered how to extract more funds from taxpayers, the matter of fairness weighed heavily, yet the war's overwhelming budgetary demands required steps that would never be considered under other circumstances.

In central Appalachia, the economic reality was grim. In interviews with nearly four hundred families in seven mountain communities, the Mountain Workers' Conference found an average yearly income of just $320, with 131 of the families living on less than $200. Households spent approximately $27 per year on basic medical care, and nearly half could not obtain any kind of dental care, even though 326 replied that access to a dentist was needed "in some form." The lack of adequate health care in many parts of the country underscored how expanded medical and dental coverage would be necessary to creating a more equitable postwar society.[14]

The war had other effects on mountain communities. The promise of higher wages in war industries generated a steady migration from the mountains of Appalachia to urban areas like Detroit and Chicago. Combined with the thousands who joined the military, as much as 20 percent of eastern Kentucky's total population left the region between 1940 and 1942. In some areas, 40 percent of the men aged fifteen to thirty-four left, and one mountain teacher commented, "The young manhood of our town has moved out almost en masse. . . . Never again can this section be the same." The federal government's financing of chemical companies in the Kanawha Valley of West Virginia and the construction of TVA dams such as Fontana Dam in North Carolina and Douglas Dam in Tennessee produced an economic boom for those who stayed behind, but how they would survive after the war remained unanswered.[15]

To better understand the feelings of those working in the military industries, the OWI conducted interviews with over two hundred war workers— white males only—in Seattle, Milwaukee, and Hartford, Connecticut. Most thought the war would last two to three more years. Five percent of those interviewed thought it would be over before the end of the year. Nearly a third expected an economic depression to follow, and when asked what they would like most to see after the war, 22 percent answered "guaranteed employment." Nine percent wanted "fairer distribution of wealth." Only 6 percent listed FDR's Four Freedoms as essential, while the majority simply wanted "better economic conditions." The OWI summarized, "The expectation of a post-war depression remains one of the sources of worker anxiety—a threat to his economic security."

One worker blamed his frustrations with the current war production squarely on one new development: "They're putting in women, and that slows down production." One union member wanted the government to "take over all the shops during the war." That way, he said, "a man would feel that he was really working for the country." On the other hand, "if he thinks he is working for the company, or for Henry Ford, or J. P. Morgan, or Rockefeller, his heart isn't in it much." A Seattle shipbuilder said that after the war, he hoped "there won't be any more wars," and that "everyone has a job, and can live right and that there are no more hard times."[16]

The debates within the Treasury Department over how to manage the war's costs grew intense. One of the most thoughtful suggestions came from Morgenthau's assistant Harry Dexter White, who informed his boss, "It may reasonably be forecast that, from now on, the federal debt will increase by at least $50 billion a year as long as war lasts. . . . If the war lasts two years or more, and borrowing continues at such rates, the U.S. will have at the end of the war a public debt of over $175 billion with an annual interest burden of $4 billion." Such a debt load was a two-pronged problem: "On one hand it is the problem of withstanding inflation—of maintaining a stable price level and securing an equitable distribution of scarce supplies. On the other hand, it is the problem of financing—of getting the money needed to pay for the war in the way which will be best both for the present and the future." Under a compulsory savings plan, White argued, "some discretion must be left the executive concerning the post-war abandonment of general rationing or the rate of release on accumulated compulsory savings."[17]

The matter of compulsory savings never got beyond the memos that circulated within the Treasury Department. Yet the consequences of the federal debt and its bearing on the economy have plagued economists and pundits since the New Deal. In modern political usage, government debt is generally viewed as a universal evil, although it nevertheless manages to keep increasing whichever party is in control of Congress or the White House. Yet there are winners and losers. As economist Thomas Piketty writes, "From the standpoint of people with the means to lend to the government, it is obviously far more advantageous to lend to the state and receive interest on the loan for decades than to pay taxes without compensation." For such people, he adds, "investing in public debt can be very good business."[18]

Rather than worry about the American economy over the next century, Henderson focused on what the next eighteen months could bring. In an article he wrote for the *New York Times* magazine in mid-July, he tried to peer into the future. He began his sketch of what life in 1943 might look like by comparing himself with the prophet Jeremiah: "the gloomy fellow who went around telling everyone else how bad things were and how, before they got better, they were likely to get a lot worse." The upcoming months, he explained, would have different effects on three different income groups—"a rich man"; "another who makes and owns from about $2,500 to $3,000 a year"; and "a skilled worker."

Henderson did not define "rich" with a specific financial threshold, but he explained it in clear terms: "the pretty big fellow—the one with the town and country house, three cars and a couple of garages." The wartime controls would significantly affect his lifestyle. Instead of three cars, he would be down to one, and "no chauffeurs." His yacht would be appropriated by the government and possibly used by the navy, and "if not, it should." He might have to grow his own "victory garden" and forego lavish vacations. While this might not be "a happy picture," Henderson concluded, "I do not feel it is more than a very moderate price to pay for freedom."

For the second group, those Henderson described as "Mr. and Mrs. Middling Income," life in wartime would mean putting up with "more inconvenience" and learning "to do with less in the way of goods." The same was true of the last class, the "skilled worker," who might enjoy greater income from the various war industries. Henderson added: "I quite frankly do not believe the scaremongers who say that our programs of price, rent, and rationing will face the fate of the late and unlamented Eighteenth Amendment [Prohibition and the rise of "bootleg" alcohol]. I do not envision now—or in the future—any widespread development of so-called black markets."

He finished by saying he differed from "good, gray Jeremiah" in that he did not "expect the worst." Rather, "what worst there is we'll bear, all of us, together."[19]

Henderson's article did little to sway skeptics in Congress. On July 30, Senate minority leader Robert Taft, a Republican from Ohio, urged the president to remove Henderson's authority to set prices and instead establish a commodity control board. Taft dismissed Henderson's worries over the inflationary pressures of higher wages, saying such increases "are not likely to occur more than once a year" and were minimal compared to the pressures produced by higher prices.[20] Roosevelt refused Taft's request, but it was unclear whether he could continue to ward off congressional calls for Henderson's firing.

The news of the growing battle between the administration and Congress over inflation and taxes was rivaled by the equally gloomy news on the war front. Anxious Americans wondered when and where American forces might open a "second front" in Europe. Seven months after Pearl Harbor, the U.S. Army had still not engaged German or Italian infantry forces, yet the American military had already paid a heavy cost. On July 21, the OWI released the grim official figures of U.S. casualties since Pearl Harbor. American forces had suffered 44,143 casualties, including 4,801 dead, 3,212 wounded, and over 36,000 listed as missing. Over 1,000 additional naval officers and sailors were listed as prisoners of war. In the Atlantic, the U.S. had lost 383 sailors, including 34 in the Gulf of Mexico and 154 on the Atlantic coast. To some skeptical observers, the mounting losses on the seas contradicted the production figures that were being offered as signs of progress. Yet the tide was beginning to turn in the Atlantic. On July 19, due to better and more efficient American convoys, German admiral Dönitz withdrew his remaining U-boats from the East Coast and dispatched them to the mid-Atlantic. Although the Allies did not know it at the time, there were other turning points within Germany. In the first six months of 1942, with its forces stretched over Europe, North Africa, and Russia, Hitler ordered over two hundred thousand men to be taken from German factories and drafted into the Wehrmacht.[21]

Yet the losses inflicted on Allied shipping in the Atlantic affected the American home front. The oil tankers sunk in the first half of 1942 had reduced the amount of oil delivered to the East Coast by 173,000 barrels a day, approximately 20 percent of the amount that had been delivered before Pearl Harbor. Interior secretary Harold Ickes, who would become oil administrator in December, hoped to bring more oil to the eastern seaboard by railroads and barges, and wanted to build two large pipelines from the Southwest, but the WPB did not want to spare the steel necessary for the job. Ickes kept up his requests throughout the year, and on June 10, Donald Nelson finally agreed to build the first section of a pipeline, from Longview, Texas, to Norris City, Illinois. On June 23, construction of the pipeline began, and eight months later the first oil from Texas reached its destination in Illinois, where it was loaded onto tank cars.[22]

Meanwhile, the rubber crisis grew worse. In mid-July, Nelson issued "An Emergency Statement to the People of the United States" asking them to contribute scrap and used rubber to turn "junk" into something vitally important for the war. The rubber from six sets of passenger car tires, readers were told, would make the plugs necessary for the treads on one tank, and the rubber from thirteen thousand passenger cars would equip one battleship. Yet the vast needs of the military were far more than such makeshift plans from old tires could ever fill, and the issue of finding other sources of rubber weighed heavily on the nation's war planners.

Americans also contributed other products. When scrap hunters in Douglas County, Kansas, delivered over 158,000 pounds of scrap metal, a local newspaper declared that was enough "to build fifteen three-inch antiaircraft guns, or enough to construct ten light tanks." Four hundred boys at the Children's Village, Ferry-on-Hudson, collected waste paper and scrap metal and used the proceeds from the salvage to purchase defense bonds. Inspired by their students, the faculty at the boys' school followed suit and agreed to use part of their salaries to buy bonds. Wartime rationing also changed at least one six-year-old's dreams about what he wanted to be when he grew up. Rather than a soldier or a firefighter, the young boy said, "I'm going to be a waiter so I can swipe all the sugar I want."[23]

One child who exemplified what children were capable of, even under the toughest of circumstances, was eleven-year-old Grant Francisco of Deming Township, Washington, on the Canadian border. His father, Levi, had volunteered as a plane spotter in the Aircraft Warning Service in Bellingham,

Washington, shortly after Pearl Harbor, but had fallen ill in the spring. In July, Levi died, and in his place, Grant took over his father's post, watching the skies of western Washington for enemy aircraft. Grant soon received a letter of citation from Brigadier General William E. Kepner, commander of the Fourth Fighter Command. Grant replied to the general: "I wouldn't think that such a busy man as a general would go to the trouble of writing me a letter." Grant brushed off any claims that he was doing anything exceptional: "What I am doing is nothing out of the ordinary for a fellow of my age."[24]

When the mayor of Paducah, Kentucky, sent out a call asking all city residents to help in the war effort, he received a reply from twelve-year-old Floyd Knight, a member of a local Boy Scout troop. "I can cook, wash dishes, and help warn people of our city if attacked by the enemy. I can save paper and money and buy savings stamps." He ended his letter with a simple plea: "Can I help?" National magazines showed Notre Dame football coach Frank Leahy proclaiming, "Every Boy Can Help Win this War by Collecting Scrap Rubber and Metal," and exhorting boys to organize a "Scrap Warden Team in your community, and let's junk the Axis!"[25]

If federal rationing and price controls were proving unpopular, millions of workers found something else even more unsavory. Combating inflation meant more than freezing prices; it also involved freezing wages. Battles over pay often pitted urban workers against farm workers, organized labor against management and, ultimately, workers of all kinds against the Roosevelt administration. When employees took on new duties or longer hours and demanded a raise, it was difficult to deny them, but in the administration's eyes, they had to be denied to keep inflation in check. Yet the consequences of denying all wage increases could eventually damage the administration and its supporters on Election Day, just four months away. Consequently, the War Labor Board adopted what became known as the "Little Steel" formula, which limited wage increases to no more than 15 percent above the wage rates of January 1941. This decision was made after the board heard the cases of the United Steelworkers, who demanded a dollar a day increase for those working in the Bethlehem, Youngstown, and Republic Steel companies. The administration felt the 15 percent increase reflected the rise in the cost of living between New Year's Day 1941, and mid-1942, but it fell well short of what the unions wanted. In the end, the "Little Steel" formula pleased no one and seemed only to defer more difficult choices ahead.[26]

The racial tensions that had been building through the first part of the year exploded in July. In Virginia, a young African American sharecropper named Odell Waller was scheduled to be executed by electric chair for the murder of his former landlord. The all-white jury that found him guilty was composed exclusively of poll-tax payers, and in the ensuing months, Waller became, in the words of Pearl Buck, "a personification of all those to whom democracy is denied in this country." Many progressives, including Buck, Pauli Murray, and Eleanor Roosevelt, rallied to Waller's defense, calling on Virginia governor Colgate Darden to stay the execution on grounds that African Americans had been denied a place on the jury because of the poll tax. In June, after receiving a letter from Waller in which he wrote, "I have heard lots of people speak what a nice lady you are" and that "you believe in helping the poor," the First Lady persuaded her husband to appeal to Darden on the intrinsic injustice of the case, and the president sent the Virginia governor a private letter. "Didn't I do good?" the president asked Eleanor, who replied, "It's a grand letter." Darden, however, refused to commute Waller's sentence, saying he was not persuaded that a poll tax of $1.50 "had the effect of dividing the people of the commonwealth into economic classes." The president refused Eleanor's further requests that he intercede in the matter, and she was saddened by her husband's timidity in the face of the southern bloc. When a larger fight against the poll tax erupted later in the year, the memory of Waller was on the minds of civil rights advocates and white supremacists alike.[27]

On July 11, celebrated African American tenor Roland Hayes, who had once given a command performance at Buckingham Palace for King George V, took his family to Rome, Georgia. When Hayes's wife and daughter went shopping at Higgins Shoe Store, they sat in an area reserved for whites. The store manager promptly told them to move, and after some words were exchanged, they left, but when Roland learned of the incident, he went back to talk with the store manager, apparently thinking that a calm discussion between adults could clear up any misunderstanding. Yet to the white residents of Rome, there was no misunderstanding. Hayes's family had crossed a sacred line, and his questioning of the store manager only added to the offense. When the police arrived, they arrested Hayes and beat him in the back of their squad car, then arrested his wife and daughter. Georgia governor Eugene Talmadge predictably defended the police, saying that if "any Negro did not like the state's segregation laws," they should "stay out of Georgia." "We are going to keep the Jim Crow laws," he said. The FBI concluded that the "rough handling" of the family "seemed to be necessary in view of the refusal on the part of Hayes' wife to leave," and noted that in Rome, Georgia, "there has been in the past few months a certain atmosphere or attitude of haughtiness or superiority among the Negroes." E. M. Collins, an official with the Universal Negro Improvement Association, asked if others knew "of the insult and gross atrocity that Roland Hayes has met with in Georgia." He sarcastically described the incident as indicative of a "Great Democracy," adding, "We need some Harriet Tubmans!"[28] The "Auto Club Placard Brigade" of New York made a sign for members to display on their cars that asked: "Is There a Difference?" After noting Japanese and German acts of brutality, the sign concluded, "American Crackers Brutally Beat Roland Hayes."[29]

Two days after the Hayes beating, a twenty-five-year-old African American, Willie Vinson, was arrested in Texarkana, Texas, for the attempted rape of a local white woman. She told police that Vinson "resembled" the man who had taken her from her home. When the sheriff came to arrest Vinson, a scuffle ensued, and Vinson was shot in the stomach and taken to a local hospital. Shortly thereafter, he was removed from his infirmary bed by a mob of over a dozen men, who chained him to the back of a truck and dragged him for miles on asphalt and rocky roads before hanging his bloody and mutilated body from a cotton gin winch. The sheriff said he had made no arrests in the case because "nobody seems to know who they were." Texas governor Coke Stevenson took no action, commenting that "even a white man would have been lynched for [Vinson's] crime." A devoted white supremacist, Stevenson had once stated that "certain members of the Negro race from time to time furnish the setting for mob violence." One local African American, in considering the state of racial conditions in East Texas in 1942 and Vinson's brutal murder, told a reporter: "America needs to make democracy and justice work at home before presuming to extend and enforce them abroad."[30]

When a minister from the Truth Seekers Temple Liberal Church of Chicago sent a "respectfully submitted" resolution to William V. Brown, the mayor of Texarkana, condemning the lynching and urging that the authorities "use the power of their office to see that the perpetrators of this act are apprehended," he received this response: "While you deplore and condemn lynching, you do not in your resolution condemn or deplore the cause of the same. If the criminal, Willie Vinson, had not violated the law in the first place (the cause), there would not have been (the effect) the lynching." Brown found it hypocritical that the minister did not emphatically express "any sympathy for the innocent victim of this would-be rapist lust." Rather, the resolution "is taken up trying to make a martyr out of a criminal, which is damned hard to do." While he "hated" lynchings, such "necktie parties" were like "removing a cancer"—"it is painful to have the cancer (rape) and it is painful to cut it out (lynching)."[31]

The torture and execution of Willie Vinson were part of an American tradition of vigilante justice. Lynchings were a central component of a culture grounded in a system of racial subjugation that had not left southern life with the formal end of slavery. The full extent of the terror will probably never be known, but the Equal Justice Initiative has documented 4,084 "racial terror lynchings" in twelve southern states from 1870 to 1950. As Bryan Stevenson of the organization writes, "Racial terror lynching was a tool used to enforce Jim Crow laws and racial segregation" and "a tactic for maintaining racial control by victimizing the entire African American community, not merely punishment of an alleged perpetrator for a crime."[32]

Not all murders of African Americans by lawless mobs fell under the category "lynching." Weeks before Willie Vinson was murdered, a black man named Howard Wilpitz of Brookshire, Texas, was approached by a local constable for being drunk and disorderly. When the constable tried to place Wilpitz under arrest, he said, Wilpitz resisted and the two exchanged gunfire. When Wilpitz hid in a nearby outhouse, a "posse" of thirty men came to the scene and riddled the shack with bullets. Wilpitz was secretly buried, and armed white men went door to door to intimidate local blacks into silence. No local papers reported the incident, and Wilpitz's common-law wife, fearing for her own life, refused to comment on the shooting. After examining the case, the NAACP's Thurgood Marshall concluded that since Wilpitz had fired his weapon, "it could not be classed as a lynching." The reign of terror in Texarkana and Brookshire was part of a larger context of racial violence. The number of deaths will never be known, nor the extent to which white supremacists beat, raped, and intimidated black citizens into submission and silence.[33]

In the same month that Vinson was murdered, civil rights activist Jessie Daniel Ames published a review of the last decade of southern lynchings in which she concluded, "The white South still believes in the inherent right of the white race to rule supreme over Negroes." At the heart of southern culture, she wrote, was the core belief "that the rights and privileges of democracy can be limited by force." The end of the war promised a dark future: if "these same people, perhaps more of them, come back to a jobless, poverty-stricken existence, . . . the passions and hatreds which have characterized their lives in the past will be aroused." Ames hoped that "sane white Southerners" would begin working toward "the principles of democracy." But in 1942, many whites believed that defending white supremacy was no less essential to preserving "the principles of democracy" than defeating the Axis powers.[34]

One observer of race relations, Swedish economist and sociologist Gunnar Myrdal, finished his fifteen-hundred-page study, *An American Dilemma: The Negro Problem and Modern Democracy*, in 1942, although it would not be published until 1944. As an outsider observing the state of American race relations with the eye of a social scientist, Myrdal wrote that the "Negro problem" represented "a moral lag in the development of the nation and a study of it must record nearly everything which is bad and wrong in America." He was struck by the dual nature of American whites, who were devoted to the "American Creed" of "high national and Christian precepts" but were also tied to a system of racial repression. "Now and then," Myrdal wrote, "even the least sophisticated individual becomes aware of his own confusion and contradictions," and may even have his or her "moral precepts" shaken to the core. "But most people suppress such threats to their moral integrity together with all the confusion, the ambiguity, and inconsistency which lurks in the basement of Man's soul."[35]

The war crisis and the sheer need for manpower opened new possibilities for the disabled. In late July, the War Manpower Commission found that "physically handicapped men and women," estimated at some 4 million people, constituted a reservoir of "unused man power" that was desperately needed in the war effort. One of the first breakthroughs occurred in the diamond cutting industry, where an agreement between labor and management called for disabled veterans to "receive special preferences" in hiring. Most of this work was done in New York City and produced diamonds for industrial production. After proper training, a disability was found "to be no handicap at all." The commission noted that elsewhere, blind persons were being employed as stenographers and that the "prejudice against hiring 'handicapped' workers breaks down before proof and example."[36]

For many Americans, the home front in the first six months of 1942 had provided opportunities they had never seen before. Michael Griffin, a *Time* correspondent based in Louisville, Kentucky, observed an explosion that was happening in many urban areas: "There is no question about the booming aspects of the U.S. You see it everywhere, especially in Louisville. If the war ended today with a victory for us, the mass of folks here could truthfully say that the war was the best thing to happen in their lives." Residents of Louisville enjoyed "more of everything and they are getting more each day. The store windows are full of bargains, and all day radio announcers chant of good buys. Bars are booming. Streets are literally packed with women who have seen much worse times."[37]

While many Americans looked warily upon their socialist allies in the Soviet Union, who were bearing the full brunt of Hitler's armies, they eagerly embraced some aspects of Russian culture. In late July, national radio audiences heard Arturo Toscanini conduct the NBC Symphony Orchestra in a rousing premiere of Shostakovich's Seventh Symphony, performed at an army base in Los Angeles. The Russian composer had written the dramatic piece during the previous year's siege of Leningrad, and he said it represented the "victory of light over darkness, of humanity over barbarism." Soldiers listened to the concert with rapt attention, and one even climbed up a flagpole for a better view. No one could know that the barbarism seen at Leningrad would soon be far surpassed in the battle of Stalingrad—the largest battle in human history, and the one that would shatter the myth of the German Army's invincibility.[38]

Many Americans entertained and informed themselves through books. Two of that year's best-selling novels were John Steinbeck's *The Moon Is*

Down and Lloyd Douglas's *The Robe*. In November, Harvard economist Joseph Schumpeter published one of the century's most influential works of
social theory, *Capitalism, Socialism, and Democracy*. Franz Werfel's *The Song
of Bernadette* topped the *New York Times* best-seller list for the first time
in mid-July and held that spot for fifteen weeks, making it the top-selling
book of the year. The novel told the story of St. Bernadette Soubirous, a
nineteenth-century woman who lived in Lourdes, France, and had multiple
visions of the Virgin Mary. She was canonized by Pope Pius XI in 1933.
Werfel, a Jew, learned of the revered saint while hiding in Lourdes after the
Nazis occupied France. After escaping the German troops, he had written
the book to fulfill a promise he made to God. The book transcended Juda-
ism and Catholicism and was widely popular among readers living, in Werfel's words, in "a time of great dread." The following year it was made into
a popular movie starring Jennifer Jones.

One book that stood out for its harsh criticism of America's popular
culture and public education system was Philip Wylie's *Generation of
Vipers*. American high schools, Wylie charged, "teach nothing but gibber-
ish," due to the "pee wee caliber of teachers as a class" within an educational system that he termed "a public swindle, an assassination of sanity."
In response to polls showing that nearly 60 percent of Americans could
not locate China on a map, Wylie directed his ire at teenagers who had
"no aptitude for learning, make no use of what they do manage to be taught,
and are a waste of money." Instead of making a futile attempt to teach them
English or history, he felt, "most should be prepared for the sedentary
handicrafts," working in a factory, on a farm, or "at the pump handles of
filling stations."[39]

Franklin Roosevelt's detractors knew that the approaching elections presented an opportunity for his opponents to change the nation's political
direction and reverse the New Deal. One of the president's most vocal critics was New York City parks commissioner Robert Moses, whose relationship with FDR was described by biographer Robert Caro as grounded in
"hate." The two men had fought since Roosevelt's days as governor of New
York, and even in the White House, FDR was subject to Moses's wrath.
Moses wrote in the *Reader's Digest* in July that "ability, not politics, will win

the war!" a not-so-subtle criticism of the administration. While pretending to take the high road, Moses did not resist the temptation to enumerate the president's flaws: "partisanship, personal government, narrowness toward opponents, unwillingness to establish a truly national government, which will unify the people in war, and reluctance to select the best assistants and delegate authority to them." He also pointed fingers at others in the administration, saying of Leon Henderson and the OPA, "If we must get along with less sugar, tires, gasoline or razor blades, so be it, but let us get the word from someone who has studied the problem of rationing." Around the nation, he claimed, "contempt for amateur rationers is rampant."[40]

Given the growing dissatisfaction with the pace of war, many within Roosevelt's war cabinet hoped their boss would ignore Churchill's pleas for a North African invasion and opt instead for a major attack across the English Channel. Army Chief of Staff George Marshall told the president that if he would not authorize a channel attack, the U.S. should focus on the Pacific theater first. The commander in chief, refusing to be intimidated by his generals, told them that the suggestion was similar to "taking up your dishes and going away." He was adamant that engaging Germany first was the proper strategy, arguing that "defeat of Japan does not defeat Germany, but defeat of Germany means defeat of Japan." On July 22, after three days at Shangri-La, the new presidential retreat in Maryland's Catoctin Mountain Park (Eisenhower later renamed it Camp David after his grandson), the president made his decision and the issue was settled. The North Africa invasion, code-named Torch, was set for late October. Finally, American troops would fight against Nazis. But the decision was not without its risks. Secretary of War Henry Stimson wrote in his diary of "the evil of the President's decision," which he worried would bring a disaster like what happened to "the British at Gallipoli in 1915." In the words of author Rick Atkinson, Roosevelt's decision "repudiated an American military tradition of annihilation, choosing to encircle the enemy and hack at his limbs rather than thrust directly at his heart." Besides the military challenges, the president also understood the domestic political realities behind the invasion's timing. If a dramatic landing occurred before the November election, voters might give the president's party more leeway. If there was any doubt that the commander in chief was letting domestic politics influence Allied war strategy, his appeal to Marshall as to the timing of the invasion made it clear: "Please make it before election day!"[41]

Even though the war had not really started in earnest for the U.S., Americans in the summer of 1942 were seeing dramatic change everywhere and thinking about what sort of country should emerge from the war. It was a singular period in American history. A traumatized nation that had come through a decade of economic disaster was now fighting formidable enemies abroad, while at home, the rules that governed the economy were being rewritten. Since the beginning of the year, the government had committed to over $100 billion in new contracts.

A summer poll taken by *Fortune* magazine offered a revealing and surprising snapshot of the economic steps Americans were willing to take after the war:

- 74.3 percent thought the government should collect enough taxes after the war to provide medical care for everyone who needed it.
- 67.7 percent wanted the government to provide jobs for everyone able and willing to work.
- 31.9 percent believed that after the war there should be a law limiting the amount of money any individual could earn.

When asked, "Do you think some form of socialism would be a good thing or a bad thing for our country as a whole?," 25.4 percent said it would be "good," and 34.2 percent did not know.[42] For a brief moment, as they worried about further attacks at home and how the war would proceed abroad, Americans from all walks of life allowed themselves to consider the kind of society they wanted in peacetime. Many were thinking in unprecedented ways that would soon be considered heresy to voice out loud.

8

August: "Insuperable Difficulties"

THE ASTRONOMICAL NUMBER THAT ACCURATELY represented the nation's spending for war in 1942 wasn't the $59 billion President Roosevelt had mentioned in his State of the Union address. Rather, it was the sum of all government outlays for the war, including contracts on which payment had not yet been made, authorized between June 1940 and the fiscal year ending on June 30, 1943. That figure, as of August 1942, came to $205,514,657,286. Relative to the total output of the economy, it is equivalent to $25.5 trillion in 2018 dollars, or roughly six times the 2018 federal budget. The *New York Times* put the figure in context: "This amount is larger than all the money spent by the United States Government from the inauguration of George Washington as President until the attack on Pearl Harbor."[1]

Those responsible for fighting inflation found these spending levels truly frightening. Yet other fears kept officials up at night. The full extent of the rubber crisis led Leon Henderson, at a WPB meeting on August 4, to make some shocking recommendations. In order to save more rubber, he suggested that individual car mileage might have to be reduced from seventy-five hundred miles per year to forty-two hundred. If that did not work, he proposed that the government might have to nationalize all private automobiles within the United States. He understood that such a step "would be accompanied by political, economic, and financial problems whose solution would raise well-nigh insuperable difficulties." Not surprisingly, the idea of nationalizing private automobiles was not mentioned outside of closed Washington meetings, especially with the election just three months away.[2]

On August 6, Roosevelt appointed a special committee to investigate the rubber situation. He asked Bernard Baruch, Harvard president James B. Conant, and MIT president Karl T. Compton to recommend how to conserve existing supplies and to suggest the best method of producing synthetic rubber. The committee was given just weeks to produce its findings. While the Manhattan Project would later be seen as the war's greatest scientific accomplishment, in the fall of 1942, the production of rubber was more urgent, and possibly more crucial to victory.[3]

The public reaction to the staggering changes in the nation's economic life were noted by the OWI's Rumor Project. In Arizona and Tennessee, rumors spread that because of the enormous debts the nation was incurring, the war bonds would never be repaid. Some in Arizona fretted that FDR's real aim was "to ruin small business and to subsidize the big ones to the extent that the government can take them over later." In Kansas, his critics believed that the mobilization efforts were a "Communistic brain trust scheme to Sovietize American industry." An Alabama industrialist, lamenting that "everything I have learned in 27 years of business has been thrown out of the window," predicted that after the war, "it will be socialism and the country our forefathers built is gone forever." An unemployed man in Iowa said of postwar economic challenges, "We will run into a worse depression than we ran into in 1929." The problem would be aggravated by the number of women in the workforce: "We will have all these women in these jobs and they won't give up the jobs, and the men who come back and the men who are here won't have a chance to work." There were continuing stories that Roosevelt was intent on becoming a dictator, and intensified concerns that he would cancel the November elections.[4]

A New York banker repeated the suspicion that war bonds were a government ruse and would be devalued when holders tried to redeem them, speculating that "maybe your grandchildren will get twenty cents on the dollar." Worries about inflation echoed the challenge facing the OPA. One New York City resident heard that inflation would reduce the dollar to half its value by 1943. Another, however, saw only a shrewd government plot. "All the inflation talk is nonsense," because "with all the careful planning and bond buying, we won't have any inflation at all, and I think Henderson knows it." Henderson's subterfuge, the man claimed, was a way "to keep us in line."[5]

Wartime developments in August would have profound consequences. In Russia, German divisions began their assault on Stalingrad, six hundred miles southeast of Moscow. The bloodiest battle in human history, in a place that held such symbolic power for the Russian leader and his people, it would not end until the following March, when the last remnants of Germany's Sixth Army were rooted out of tunnels and cellars in the ruined city. In the Pacific, eleven thousand U.S. Marines landed on Guadalcanal in the Solomon Islands, the first major offensive against Japanese land forces. That battle would have lasting strategic consequences in the fight against the Japanese, who had hoped to use the island as an airstrip for bombers. Shortly after the fighting began on August 7, Allied forces began building their own runway. But it was not entirely a clear-cut American triumph in the region. At Savo Island, the Japanese sank four American ships and inflicted a twenty-to-one casualty ratio.[6]

When American soldiers went into battle, they used a weapon that had far greater firepower than their predecessors had in World War I, when a Springfield bolt-action rifle was the primary weapon in the American arsenal. By 1942, the M1 Garand .30-caliber semi-automatic rifle with an eight-bullet clip had become the infantry's weapon of choice, and it proved an especially lethal instrument. By not requiring its user to move a bolt after every round, the M1 allowed soldiers to fire rounds in a more sustained fashion, in ways that presaged the Russian-made AK-47. General George Patton called the M-1 "the greatest battle implement ever devised."[7]

Even while moving ahead with Torch, the plan to attack North Africa, the president's Joint Chiefs remained skeptical. Army Air Corps head Henry "Hap" Arnold worried about "a growing tendency in all quarters" to reduce the plans for the North Africa invasion and instead focus on the Pacific. Army Chief of Staff General George C. Marshall, perhaps the military figure closest to the president, was convinced the plan was doomed. The tension within the Joint Chiefs grew to the point that Arnold believed Marshall and others were not inclined to "think in terms of winning the war." Instead, he thought, "all seemed to think in terms of meeting the easiest enemy first."[8]

Secretary of War Henry Stimson also disagreed with the decision to invade North Africa. After failing to persuade the president to alter his plans, Stimson met with Marshall on August 9 and asked him directly: if he were "President or Dictator," would he support the North Africa strategy? Marshall replied he would not, and the two discussed ways to change the president's mind. Stimson drafted a letter to the president warning that Torch would "involve serious danger of our troops meeting an initial defeat" and urging him to reconsider. When Marshall read the letter and considered his options, he told Stimson he wanted no part in the protest. Ultimately, Stimson decided against sending it. Yet the letter shows how divided the highest echelon of the American military leadership had become, and if the invasion failed, Roosevelt would face recriminations from both the public and his own advisors.[9]

The fear of an enemy assault on the United States had not subsided. In Chicago, word spread that the city would soon be attacked, and the city leaders ordered a blackout drill on August 12, with over six thousand volunteer auxiliaries patrolling the city's mostly empty streets. While the lights were out, no crimes were reported and power usage decreased 54 percent. In New York City, the Department of Welfare got ready to help find people who went missing in an attack. In addition to preparing to coordinate the process by which sixty-three other centers would send information to its central registration bureau, the department distributed over forty thousand posters: "If the blitz comes, and you lose your child, family or friends, or change your address, report to your nearest emergency welfare center or your nearest red cross center or police station." The "system" was little more than a telephone switchboard that would forward to the police, hospitals, schools, and welfare centers any information about missing people.[10]

With so much of the federal budget now devoted to war, other areas of government suffered deep cuts, including many New Deal programs. The budget for fiscal 1943 cut funding for the Works Progress Administration by nearly $600 million, the Civilian Conservation Corps by $246 million, and the Tennessee Valley Authority by $60 million. For many Republicans and conservative Democrats, any additional spending on programs that had been designed to ease the worst effects of the Great Depression was wasteful and unnecessary. As Republicans throughout the country antici-pated running against the administration during the war, many began to see focusing exclusively on winning the war, rather than enhancing social programs, as a winning tactic.[11]

As Congress delayed action on the tax bill, discussion over the fairest way to raise more revenue turned heated. J. Cheever Cowdin, an official with the National Association of Manufacturers, urged Congress to adopt an 8 per-cent "consumption" or sales tax. While this was 2 percent below the Cham-ber of Commerce's preferred 10 percent tax, Cowdin told lawmakers it would still raise $4.8 billion. He felt that "lack of political courage" would be the only thing keeping such a tax from becoming law. On the other hand, he warned, "businessmen throughout the country" were worried over the Trea-sury's tax plan, which introduced "restrictions on business which would change the free system we have here in this country." Additional corporate taxes would "bring catastrophe to business." Corporate leaders, meanwhile, informed Congress that their companies were already being taxed to death. H. E. Bowman, treasurer of the Boeing Corporation, told the Senate Finance Committee that unless the excess profits tax were lowered, the bill's passage "would probably end the existence" of Boeing. He added that he had come to Washington "to plead with you for the life of this company." A thoroughly disgusted Henderson responded that any kind of sales tax would be "noth-ing short of butchery as far as the poor people are concerned."[12]

The Chamber of Commerce had grown weary of the OPA and its brash director, and of the administration's war agencies generally. The Los Ange-les chamber was typical in hoping Congress would reassert its control over the delegation of authority to units such as the OPA. While war was "a nec-essary evil," the chamber warned, "collectivism is not." The "collectivist" tendency was a "social cancer" that "spreads insidiously and unceasingly, destroying liberty and efficiency, devitalizing leadership and corrupting the people." Despite the billions of dollars that were being made by the largest of companies through "cost plus" government contracts, Americans, the chamber told its members, must stop asking for "collectivist handouts, subsidies, price protections and special favors that lead to extensions of government bureaucracy at the expense of free enterprise." The war had unleashed the contagion of government control, the chamber warned, and "bureaucracy is on the rampage."[13]

Many Americans were beginning to find "bureaucrats" like Henderson intrusive and inefficient, if not incompetent. A hog farmer from South Carolina noted that he had earned $9.50 per hundred pounds for his hogs in 1937, but "today they are selling for $14.50 per hundred," yet his payroll "has tripled." Representative Hampton Fulmer of South Carolina, also a farmer, told Henderson he had been offered $2.25 per bushel for his crop of sweet potatoes, while consumers were paying over $5 per bushel at market for the same potatoes. According to Fulmer, the blame lay with "thousands of useless middlemen" who "are nothing but real parasites sapping the very life blood out of farmers and consumers."[14]

What all the federal spending was buying was beginning to be realized by late summer. In Richmond City, California, the Kaiser shipyards drew national publicity when the company launched a ten-thousand-ton liberty ship just twenty-four days after its keel was laid. Industrialist Henry Kaiser boasted that his shipyards would soon reduce that time to just eighteen days. In 1941, building a ship from keel to launching had generally taken one hundred days, but the war crisis had transformed the production of such ships through round-the-clock shifts and assembly-line methods. In an attempt to bypass the damage inflicted on American ships by German U-boats, Kaiser was also preparing to present plans for building large cargo air carriers with his partner, Howard Hughes. More than any other industrialist, Kaiser was viewed by the public as the person who could make the impossible happen in producing America's war machine. Interior secretary Harold Ickes believed "Kaiser may be the miracle man to turn the war for us." Some Republicans within Washington openly talked about nominating him as their presidential candidate in 1944. A Virginia resident described him as "the one man who is capable of bringing order out of chaos in Washington and of completely restoring the damaged foundation and framework of the government structure." A Missourian noted, "I venture he could be equally efficient as a tearer-downer. One might well imagine what a perfect job he could do of demolishing that monstrous bureaucracy in Washington and building on the wreckage a safe and sound democratic structure."[15]

In addition to changing how ships were built, Kaiser transformed the workplace in other ways that would have profound consequences. He pioneered the use of on-site daycare centers, and launched the nation's first health maintenance organization (HMO) in the summer of 1942, the Kaiser Permanente Health Plan. Led by Dr. Sidney R. Garfield of Oakland, it was a comprehensive medical program for Kaiser's twenty thousand shipyard workers, who paid $3 a month for health coverage that included 111 days of hospital care for each illness and free prescriptions. Whole families, including children, could be insured for $5.65 a month. For house calls, patients paid $2 for the first visit, and all subsequent visits were free. Before being enrolled, all applicants had to take a physical exam since some preexisting conditions were excluded or treated differently, including pregnancy. Women subscribers who gave birth ten months after signing on to the plan paid $60 for all maternity care costs, while women who gave birth less than ten months after joining paid $140. There were on-site clinics to treat worker injuries, and the plan emphasized preventive care.[16]

From the outset, the Kaiser medical plan was opposed by physicians, who were threatened by the idea of pre-paid insurance. Morris Fishbein, editor of the *Journal of the American Medical Association,* had warned three years earlier that such company-sponsored insurance was "the first insidious approach to the breakdown of the democratic system of government." Like so many in the AMA, Fishbein worried that such insurance plans interfered with the doctor-patient relationship. "Give anybody the right to interfere this intimately with the lives of the people," he stated, "and you have the first step toward totalitarianism." One angry New York doctor wrote Kaiser a stinging rebuke, asking, "What was your class in medical college and what state gave you a medical license? Seems to me you are wandering far from the ship construction field!"[17]

A few other large companies offered medical insurance in 1942, many of them in the South. At the Tennessee Coal and Iron Company in Birmingham, over seventy-five thousand employees bought health insurance through payroll deduction plans, as did workers at Standard Oil of Louisiana and in textile mills in Roanoke Rapids, North Carolina. In the North, some companies understood that with wages frozen indefinitely, medical coverage was the best way to attract and keep a stable workforce. The most generous plan was provided by the Endicott-Johnson Shoe Company of New York, which paid all of the medical insurance costs for the twenty-four thousand employees who made shoes for the military. Despite the medical profession's opposition, the insurance plans were popular among workers, who began to see access to health care as a benefit just as important as wages.[18]

If "miracles" were occurring in shipbuilding and plane production, they were also occurring far out of sight, in the Alaskan and Canadian wilderness. Since spring, the Army Corps of Engineers had been carving out a fifteen-hundred-mile road from Dawson Creek, British Columbia, to Delta Junction, Alaska, that came to be known as the Alcan Highway. A route connecting the Alaska Territory to the forty-eight states had become a military necessity, especially in light of the Japanese attack at Dutch Harbor earlier in the summer. On February 11, Roosevelt had approved the project as a military emergency, and the Canadian government agreed to allow construction through its forests provided the U.S. paid for the project. Construction began in early March, and workers understood they had just a few months to get the road built before the weather turned cold again. The corps relied on African American troops to accomplish much of the job, even though many within the military hierarchy remained opposed to using African Americans in any capacity. The general in charge of the defense of Alaska claimed that if black soldiers fraternized with Eskimo women, they would produce an "astonishingly objectionable race of mongrels." Yet the need for quick completion took precedence over bigotry, and four regiments of black troops were sent to help complete the mammoth undertaking. Working through dense forests, endless swarms of mosquitoes, and thick permafrost, eleven thousand soldiers toiled in areas far removed from Europe and the Pacific under the deadline of the approaching winter freeze.[19]

By midsummer the exhausting project was at fever pitch. In the words of a *Time* correspondent, army engineers "had one of the biggest and toughest jobs since they built the Panama Canal. They were both surviving and thriving on it. There was no fanfare. Almost no outsiders had penetrated the vast, still, endless wilderness where the engineers are wrenching and hacking a great military road 1,500 miles long." One Bronx private admitted that in early spring, "it was so cold that every time we had hot stew for chow, the goddamn stuff froze before we could eat." Logs were used to cover muskeg,

a heavy, spongy layer of decomposing plants and moss that posed a nightmare for anything traveling on its surface. Engineers and troops grew accustomed to building wooden bridges in just two days. "Not many soldiers
have fewer comforts, less to do on Saturday night, less discipline from
above," commented *Time*'s reporter.[20]

Some companies tried to get in on the remarkable undertaking. An ad for
B. F. Goodrich read: "Slashing through forests and underbrush, pulling
stumps by the thousands, ploughing hub-deep in mud, they're pushing the
Alaska Highway through . . . mile after mile . . . a titanic task being rushed
to completion at incredible speed. During the war the Alaska highway may
prove to be America's lifeline." Then, in a quick segue, Goodrich brought
the point home: "After the war it may be your family's vacation boulevard.
To build this highway through bleak Canadian wilderness men must fight
swamps and marshes, swarming insects, cold that last winter averaged 30
to 50 below zero. It's a job for real men—and a job for real tires on the hundreds of trucks." The Caterpillar Tractor Company also exploited the "tough-
ness" of the Alcan's builders: "Up in the heart of the Northwest wilderness
Army engineers and contractors are making history. Through vast reaches
of desolate bush, towering mountains, and frozen muskeg, they're pushing
an overland road, 1,450 miles long. And they're doing it faster than any en-
gineering feat of such size was ever done before." The ad noted, "This is a
job for tough men and tough machines. Smashing steadily northward, powerful Caterpillar diesel tractors and motor graders clear the brush."

On September 24, teams of workers met in the shallow waters of Contact
Creek in the Yukon Territory. Like the gathering in 1869 at Promontory
Point, Utah, where the two segments of the Transcontinental Railroad were
joined, the meeting at Contact Creek brought together the two arms of the
Alcan Highway. The fifteen-hundred-mile road, built on some of the remot-
est land on Earth, had taken just six months to build from scratch. In November, at a point somewhere between the 62nd and 63rd parallels of north
latitude, the highway was officially opened. Though it had little strategic importance during the war, the highway proved another of the remarkable construction projects of 1942, alongside the Pentagon, the factories in Detroit,
and the shipyards of San Francisco. In 1942, it seemed, no job was too big
and no schedule too short.[21]

If construction efforts like the Alcan Highway in 1942 could be described as "miraculous," what was occurring in the U.S.S.R. might approach "biblical." As Russian troops in and around Stalingrad were engaged in some of the most brutal combat of the war, another undertaking was equally crucial to the Soviet Union's defense against German troops and, ultimately, the winning of the war. After the German invasion in the summer of 1941, Joseph Stalin ordered an "industrial evacuation" of western Russia. Those two words described nothing less than the actual removal and relocation of much of Russia's industrial base eastward, out of the way of Hitler's invaders, including not only the workers but the factories. In one case, a heavy machinery plant containing the only ten-thousand-ton press in the country was stripped down and placed in wagons in only five days, all while under German bombardment. By the summer of 1942, over twelve hundred factories had been restored to full production, and by fall, some 16 million people had been relocated hundreds of miles to the east. The journalist C. L. Sulzberger, calling this colossal undertaking "one of the great sagas in history," wrote that it was as if "the principal factories of New England were suddenly picked up, lock, stock, and barrel, and shifted to the slopes of the Rocky Mountains." The evacuation took a staggering human toll. Every Soviet citizen over fourteen was eligible for industrial labor, and many worked in appalling conditions on starvation diets.[22]

The penalty for failure to carry out Stalin's orders was death. No matter how extreme the circumstances, Soviet citizens had no choice but to comply. Whether citizens in a democracy like the United States could approach such feats was a question on many minds in the summer of 1942. While some in the U.S. compared Roosevelt to a dictator, the president operated under constraints that never concerned Stalin. He faced an increasingly frustrated Congress that would soon have to stand for election, and public opinion held great power to affect American foreign and domestic policy. The United States worked to produce its war machinery with existing companies and labor unions, within the confines of the Constitution and the desires of the electorate. Additionally, no one could predict the political and military consequences if the North Africa invasion failed.

Although the armament output of America's factories by late summer was astounding, the actual production figures only proved that the president's

January production goals were beyond even the most optimistic forecast. Despite the massive spending and the enormous effort to retool, the realization that America's factories would fall well short of the sixty thousand planes and forty-five thousand tanks FDR had demanded was beginning to set in among many of Roosevelt's advisors. A frustrated Harold Ickes complained, "We are not turning out supplies" to the president's satisfaction. Despite what they might be reading or hearing, Ickes thought Americans had grown too comfortable and confident. The ultimate problem was simple: "There is still too much American individualism."[23]

It fell to Donald Nelson to deliver news of the shortfall to the president. In a confidential letter, Nelson noted that Roosevelt's production goals had "served as our objective . . . toward the attainment of which every effort has been made." Then he came to the crucial part: "Although many of our associates have from the first indicated that they considered it unlikely that we could reach this figure, I have, nevertheless, felt it would be unwise to advise you of their doubts until the time had arrived when we could give you convincing evidence of what within closer limits the final figure would be. That time has now arrived. . . . It is probable that our 1942 deliveries will not exceed 48,000 planes." The actual total would be 47,694. The news got worse: if the nation had fallen some 20 percent short of Roosevelt's clearly stated objective for 1942, it would do even worse in 1943. Against the president's goal of 125,000 planes, Nelson wrote, the actual number would likely be closer to 92,000—a shortfall of over 25 percent. Despite this failure, American factories were churning out war materials at a furious pace, and more workers were needed every month. By August, the national unemployment rate had fallen to 3.74 percent, just over half of the 7 percent rate in January. Every month had seen sharp declines in the unemployed rate, and the ever-growing war machine promised to absorb even more workers by year's end.[24]

Few of the people engaged in war production doubted what was at stake. Navy secretary Frank Knox visited a New Jersey naval yard in August and told sixty-five hundred workers, "There never was a moment from Valley Forge on, when this country of ours stood in as grave danger as it does this moment. . . . There never was a moment in American history when everything we hold precious and hold dear was in graver peril than right now."

Perhaps sensing the public's waning confidence in the administration, Knox pleaded "that partisanship must take a back seat to patriotism, and must measure the accomplishments of those to whom we entrust public office on the manner in which they are supporting this country in this hour of great peril." While "we have Valley Forges ahead of us," he said, no one should forget that "behind them lies victory." He hoped to "show the Japs that they took on something when they started a war with the U.S." In private, he was not as confident, writing to his wife: "Things are not going well in the southwest Pacific." After the victory at Midway in June, Allied forces had made little headway against the Japanese elsewhere in the region, and Knox was baffled that "MacArthur does not seem to be able to stop them." Although MacArthur was not in the navy, Knox certainly knew of the general's growing reputation but, he confided, "the more I see of MacArthur, the less I like him."[25]

Although the number of African Americans working in manufacturing went from 500,000 to 1.2 million during the war, and over 2 million left the South to seek opportunities in the North and West, in many plants and factories, the promises of equal employment opportunities were fleeting or nonexistent. Executives with the Briggs Manufacturing plant in Detroit, a company that employed over thirty-one thousand people and manufactured a variety of airplane parts and truck bodies for the military, refused even to meet with local civil rights leaders, who wanted the company to employ African American women. The FBI noted that "it has been confidentially reported that the company deems itself quite liberal regarding the employment of Negro men," but that it "absolutely drew the line when colored women were involved."[26]

If one image of the war years endures, it is of millions of women joining the workforce and—at least temporarily—transforming the nation's gender roles. If people know little else about the war, they likely are familiar with the image of Rosie the Riveter and how she helped produce the material necessary for victory. During the war years, 7 million women went to work. Yet not all women found that a new day had dawned for them. The war "did not mark a drastic break with traditional working patterns or sex roles," writes historian D'Ann Campbell. "For the majority of employed women, the war brought no revolutions." Women still faced discrimination and unequal pay, and there was considerable doubt whether the jobs would last after the war.

Yet the iconic image of Rosie the Riveter originated in a poster that few actually saw at the time. Pittsburgh freelance artist J. Howard Miller was commissioned by Westinghouse in 1942 to create a poster that would lift worker morale and help lower absenteeism. He depicted a woman in a red bandana rolling up her sleeve (her hand displaying painted fingernails) to expose her arm and fist in a defiant pose with the words "We Can Do It!" across the top. The first print run was just eighteen hundred copies, and the only people who saw it were employees in Westinghouse plants. The woman depicted in Miller's poster was likely Naomi Parker Fraley, who worked as a lathe operator at the Naval Air Station in Alameda, California. She died in January 2018.[27]

Rosie's feminism threatened the manhood of some female factory workers' husbands and boyfriends. While Leonard Larsen trained at an army base in Virginia, his wife, Helen, worked the second shift at the Curtiss-Wright Aircraft factory in Buffalo, New York, helping make C-46 cargo planes for the U.S. Army Air Force. Even though Helen's work not only generated income for the young couple but also contributed to an aircraft that might be used to transport Larsen and his fellow soldiers, Leonard hoped his pregnant wife would soon resign her job. He wrote her that he was especially embarrassed after he let one of the men at his base know that his wife worked in a defense plant: "You should have seen the look on his face!" Many men frowned upon their wives working in defense plants because they could be subject to the sexual advances of other men, and many more were threatened by the way in which women were challenging traditional gender roles by earning a wage outside of the home.[28]

Some built-in structural issues also prevented more women from joining the war effort. At a number of war plants, restroom facilities for women workers were rapidly becoming an issue. The Women's Bureau of the Labor Department campaigned for better facilities, especially in plants that were built without restrooms for women, simply because no man connected with their design or construction thought that women might one day be employed there. Fixing plumbing issues proved harder than it seemed.

One employer complained that war shortages prevented him from getting the needed plumbing supplies, so he couldn't hire more women.[29]

On August 24, the War Labor Board made an announcement regarding an issue that would reverberate for decades. It set out a new wage policy that resulted from a dispute at the Norma Hoffman Bearings Corporation in Stamford, Connecticut. The new policy, which was to apply at once to all workers, was termed "equal pay for equal work to women employees." Mary Anderson, head of the Women's Bureau, commented that "in our fight for democracy we cannot permit such an undemocratic and unsound method as underpayment of women who take the place on production lines of men called to the front." The new policy did not have overnight results, and the fight for women's wage equality continues into the twenty-first century. In 2016, the U.S. Department of Labor found that American women earned 82 cents for each $1 earned by men doing the same job.[30]

Just as in many New Deal agencies, racial and gender discrimination occurred within wartime agencies. African Americans were underrepresented on OPA review boards, and price-control enforcement lagged in black neighborhoods. In St. Louis, not a single African American sat on the city's review board. When the white chairman of the city's price board was asked why the board was all white in a city with over 108,000 African Americans, he responded, "I never thought of it."[31]

If Jim Crow remained alive and well in wartime industries, it thrived in the military. Continuing calls to desegregate the army fell on deaf ears. Presidential secretary Marvin MacIntyre said, "The War Department informs me that it has taken every measure to assure proper treatment of Negro troops in the Army." Despite the segregation, he believed, "housing, feeding, clothing, and training for Negro troops should be exactly the same as those for white troops." Furthermore, he was satisfied with the racial climate in the military, especially after the War Department's directive "requiring that all commanders avoid practices tending to give Negro soldiers cause to feel that the Army makes any differentiation between them and other soldiers." A black New Jersey truck driver, Edward Lockett, related the inequality he faced on the job to his decision to refuse induction into the army. "I must have written twenty letters to the Labor Relations Board" complaining about discriminatory pay practices, but he received no response. "If it wasn't important to them to protect my rights as a citizen and give me a little democracy right here at home, then it is just as unimportant for me to protect their country and to fight for what they call democracy abroad."[32]

Ultimately, the reason the military remained segregated did not rest with review boards, cabinet officials, or military leaders, but with the commander in chief. President Roosevelt not only failed to integrate the armed forces but, fearful of angering southern Democrats in Congress, refused to support federal anti-lynching legislation. Yet it is helpful to keep in mind what Roosevelt was up against. The fragility of the Roosevelt coalition, the importance of the Deep South within that coalition, and southerners' unwavering need to protect white supremacy were all apparent in an appeal from Uniontown, Alabama, mayor J. H. Bradford, a stalwart Democrat, Roosevelt supporter, and self-described "friend of the Negro." Bradford wrote, "My dear Mr. President what our country wants now is sure enough HE men to run our fighting forces and not women and men with back bones of a jelly fish." He concluded: "We will never allow Negroes to sit with and mix with our white people and there is no use of anybody trying to force us to allow them to do so. . . . The Negro is not our equal, God did not make him so," and while decency dictated that whites should treat "the Negro right," at the end of the day "he must be held in his place."[33]

By the summer of 1942, the continuing plight of African Americans at home and in the army led writer C. L. R. James to ask, "Why should I shed my blood for Roosevelt's America" when there was so little reward except "the few dollars of relief and insults, discrimination, police brutality, and perpetual poverty?" One offshoot of the fight against Jim Crow had been the formation of the Congress of Racial Equality (CORE) in Chicago that spring. Among those at the founding meeting were nonviolent protestors whose names would become well known in the 1960s, such as James Farmer and Bayard Rustin. Farmer later wrote that as he traveled around the country in 1942, he hoped to use Gandhian nonviolence to bring racial equality to the forefront of American political discourse. The tactic promised to give "birth to a revolution in race relations with a technique new to America that would change the face of this nation."[34]

While some wanted the president to use the leverage of the federal government to confront Jim Crow, others urged him to leave things alone. In

August, Roosevelt received a letter from the commissioner of public safety in Birmingham, Alabama, Eugene "Bull" Connor, who would gain national notoriety two decades later as the nemesis of Martin Luther King Jr. Connor was worried that the federal government was trying to "break down and destroy the segregation laws of the entire South," and he told the president, "Unless something is done by you, we are going to witness the annihilation of the Democratic Party in this section of the Nation." The overriding problem of racial integration, in Connor's view, was not "social equality" but "venereal disease." Playing the role of the loyal party member, he emphasized that he had voted for Roosevelt but wondered if "one war in the South is enough."[35] Roosevelt, in characteristic fashion, did not respond privately or publicly, instead maintaining the delicate public posture of seeking some elements of social progress while trying to keep southern whites within his coalition. In essence, Bull Connor was right in 1942—the administration wanted to fight only one fight.

Sometimes, something as simple as casting a Broadway play could reveal the racism that permeated all walks of life. In August, actor Paul Robeson became the first African American to play Othello on Broadway when he took the title role in the production at the Shubert Theater. Robeson's spellbinding performance led to the play, which also featured José Ferrer and Uta Hagen, running for 296 shows, the longest-running Shakespeare play on Broadway ever. *Life* magazine published some photographs of Robeson's triumph, including one where he appeared onstage with a white actress. The mere suggestion of sexual tension between the two produced an immediate backlash. W. Ira Lane of Houston, Texas, wrote, "The article where the Negro and whites act in the same play is more than I can stomach." He closed with a familiar refrain: "What in the hell is the country coming to?" B. D. Tomlinson of Georgetown, South Carolina, was only slightly more tolerant: "There is a large group of people in this country, including myself, who believe that a better deal is due to [the] Negro," but "we also believe that the time is not ripe, if ever, for the actual social mingling of the two races." Showing the two races on the same stage might "have a tendency to create in some Negroes a longing for something that cannot be theirs." A white New Yorker was overheard declaring, "When this war is over the Negroes will be set back where they belong." The war had already led to blacks "getting entirely too 'uppity,'" In a poll, six of ten whites said that African Americans were "comfortable with the way things were and deserved no further opportunities."[36]

The racial antipathies swirling through the nation were not confined to African Americans. While Allied soldiers fought against the anti-Semitic rule of Nazi Germany, anti-Jewish feeling made itself felt throughout the United States. In New York, rumors spread of American soldiers vowing, "After we finish cleaning up the Japs and the Germans we're coming home to clean up the Jews." Such sentiments were neatly captured in a widely distributed compendium of "firsts." Titled "It's Great to Be an American," the list used noteworthy moments in the war to suggest that Jewish Americans were not doing their part:

> The First American to kill a Jap was—MIKE MURPHY.
> The First American soldier to sink a Jap battleship was—COLIN KELLY.
> The First American flyer to bag a Jap plane was—EDWARD O'HARE.
> The First American Coast Guardsman to detect German spies was—JOHN CULLEN.
> The First American to be eulogized by the President for bravery was—JOHN PATRICK POWERS.
> The First American to be granted four new tires from the Tire Rationing Board was—NATHAN GOLDSTEIN.[37]

On July 21, over twenty thousand people attended a meeting at Madison Square Garden held by the American Jewish Congress, B'nai B'rith, and the Jewish Labor Committee to "condemn the barbarous mass murders of civilian populations by the Nazis." Supporting messages were read from Churchill, La Guardia, and FDR. The president promised that the Nazis would face "strict accountability" for their actions. In their 2013 book *FDR and the Jews*, Richard Breitman and Allan J. Lichtman conclude that despite such rhetoric, Roosevelt was too concerned with the war effort to "risk political capital on Jewish priorities." Even though he "had no easy remedies for a specific Jewish tragedy in Europe," FDR "was politically and emotionally stingy when it came to the plight of the Jews."[38]

Roosevelt's need to tamp down racial anger extended to other matters involving "aliens," specifically Mexican immigrants. After hearing a number of complaints, the Fair Employment Practices Committee scheduled public hearings on discriminatory practices against Mexicans. The State Department grew worried and Undersecretary of State Sumner Welles wrote to the president that the hearings posed a threat to America's international reputation and, possibly, the war effort. If details of how Mexicans were treated in the United States were publicized, German agents might use the information to "discredit this country in Mexico." Roosevelt agreed and ordered the hearings halted. More "discreet" investigations against the offending employers were undertaken, but little was done to prevent the discriminatory pay scales and treatment that Mexican workers received.[39]

In Los Angeles, a murder near a bar named Sleepy Lagoon brought the divisions between young Mexican Americans and the Los Angeles police to the fore. After the body of twenty-two-year-old José Díaz was discovered, the LAPD rounded up more than six hundred young Mexican Americans whom the police suspected of belonging to gangs. Despite little or no evidence, twenty-two people were arrested and charged with Díaz's murder. In the ensuing trial, the judge allowed the prosecutor to tell the jury that there was "a smidgen of truth" in the notion that Mexicans were intrinsically "cowards." Nineteen were convicted in a trial that only stoked the anger of young people in Southern California. One sign of protest was the popularity of "zoot suits" worn by young Mexican Americans in California and New York as a subversive gesture given the wartime need for cloth. Describing the baggy clothing as unpatriotic, *Life* offered a series of photos of the "zoot suiters" as "solid arguments for lowering the Army draft age to include eighteen-year olds."[40]

The possibility that Russia could fall to Hitler was a reality few within the administration dared to contemplate. One who did was the economist Harry Dexter White, who drafted a long, anguished letter to the president on August 28 that he gave to Treasury secretary Morgenthau to deliver to FDR. His letter, White explained, was "written out of the knowledge that you are faced with the making of the most fateful decision a President of the U.S. has ever had to make. It is your grave responsibility as Commander in Chief to say whether or not we shall undertake a major diversion now while the bulk of German forces are engaged on the Russian front. . . . Unless you determine on such action quickly, our position will be immeasurably worsened and the winning of the war jeopardized, or at least postponed to a far distant future, involving casualties not in the thousands but in the millions. It is daily becoming more apparent that we cannot expect that Russian resistance will continue to tie up the bulk of Germany's military force until we are fully prepared to strike." Like many others, including Stalin, White called for a second front before Stalingrad was lost, a calamity that would give the German Army either total victory or a stalemate that would result in a treaty giving Hitler vast conquered areas. "When the British and American peoples are confronted with a long war, with untold losses of life and property, and with doubtful prospects of victory, they will be easy prey for the forces of appeasement, which will seize their opportunity to lead the people to a negotiated peace." On the other hand, White argued, "the opening of a second front will have an electrifying effect not only on the American and British peoples, but on the whole world." He ended: "There is a tide in the affairs of men. We believe that history will record this summer as the hour for Allied offensive action. If we fail to strike now, Germany's success in Russia will not mean just another battle loss; it will mean the turning point in the war."[41]

Morgenthau read White's letter and quietly placed it in his safe. He never showed it to the president. Years later, the motivation for White's urgent plea was revealed. After the war, he was accused by Elizabeth Bentley of being a Soviet spy, a charge he denied in testimony before the House Un-American Activities Committee in 1948. He died soon after. Years later, released Soviet archives provided evidence that White was, indeed, working for the Soviet government, along with Roosevelt's administrative assistant Lauchlin Currie.[42]

For anyone hoping to send classified information to the Soviets, nothing would have been more sensitive than the top-secret project to build an atomic bomb. In January 1942, the president had approved the plan to conduct scientific research, and in March had told Vannevar Bush, the director of the Office of Scientific Research and Development, that the project was "very much of the essence." He directed the army to oversee it, provided it "made all adequate provisions for absolute secrecy."[43] On June 17, FDR had signed a secret order directing the Army Corps of Engineers to take responsibility for the atomic bomb project. On August 13, that project took a formative step when the "Manhattan Engineer District" officially began in New York City. The Army Corps of Engineers opened offices at 270 Broadway, and while it did little actual work in the building, the project's title, first shortened to Manhattan District, soon became Manhattan Project.

Despite the subsequent looming historical presence of FDR and Churchill, in August 1942, many Americans doubted their ability to adequately lead the war effort. Eight months after Pearl Harbor, with no major offensive action yet taken against the Nazis and with growing dissatisfaction at home with wage and price controls, a Gallup poll asked respondents, "Do you think that President Roosevelt and Prime Minister Churchill should have the final decision on the military and naval plans of the war?" Only 21 percent said yes. Sixty-four percent said they preferred that ultimate authority be given to the "military and naval leaders of the United Nations." The poll concluded that the public did not necessarily lack confidence in Roosevelt's and Churchill's judgment but thought "they are too busy to devote necessary time" to complicated military matters. A majority also favored the establishment of a United Nations War Council, composed of American, British, and Russian leaders, that would have "full power" to direct the war effort, including the use of American personnel.[44]

Some Boston residents had misgivings about opening a second front. Pharmacist Joseph Burkinshaw was "very anxious" about it. William Whelan, who worked on telephone cables, added, "Sure, I think a second front should be opened," since "it doesn't look like Russia could hold out much longer. . . . If we don't do something and the Germans beat the Russians, first thing you know they'll be fighting along with Germany." He worried about fighting the Red Army because "Russia's always been our enemy." Paul Fougre also thought the Russians "might do what the French did, cooperate with the Germans." He feared that "a second front would be the end of this thing." A Boston policeman wished the offensive campaign could begin soon but hoped U.S. forces did not "get the stuffing knocked out of them."[45]

By the end of August, millions of draftees and volunteers had reported for duty and were undergoing basic training. In addition to learning how to use weapons and machinery, some draftees endured training in aspects of war that veterans of the previous world war knew all too well. "We just got our gas masks today," wrote Leonard Larsen at Camp Pickett, Virginia. "We learned of some gases and precautionary measures for those who get a dose of it." To test the masks, Larsen and other draftees went into sealed chambers filled with tear gas. Then they were ordered to remove them so they could understand for themselves the damaging effects of gas. Larsen commented, "Boy! Did my eyes water." He also wrote his wife about "Axis Day," when new recruits to the camp were fed rice, bread, and water and subjected to a long, forced march so they could learn "how the conquered people of Europe live."[46]

Reviewing the state of the incoming conscripts, some military leaders began to question the overall fitness of American soldiers. Lieutenant Colonel Frederick E. Swanson, executive officer of internal security in the Illinois area, told a gathering of teachers in Gary, Indiana, that many recruits were appallingly deficient in basic math skills. Swanson averred, "Our nation is too soft" and suggested that the teachers should focus on "running schools on a sane basis." The "only mission in life" that teachers should heed "is to do a good job teaching," and "not be influenced by every incident that is prone to distract attention from the job at hand." Major General Lewis Hershey, the director of the Selective Service, warned that the military "needs men at a rate which would have been considered superhuman a year ago," and advised young men who had received draft deferments to expect to be called up. "If I were a man with a wife only and not engaged in important war work," he suggested, "I would begin now to make arrangements to enter the Army." To meet its manpower needs, the army was accepting "illiterates and men with curable diseases or correctable defects."[47]

Recruits were quickly informed of the dangers of venereal diseases that lurked when they went off base or to foreign destinations. One recruit wrote his wife that after seeing a film about the ravaging effects of "illicit sexual intercourse," he was convinced. "Gosh! It really doesn't pay and that's another reason why I don't even think about it." To drive the point home to recruits, pharmaceutical maker John Wyeth and Brother of Philadelphia commissioned artist Arthur Szyk to draw a poster of the three Axis leaders representing syphilis, gonorrhea, and chancroid, over the slogan "Fool the Axis—Use Prophylaxis!"[48]

One would-be volunteer made an interesting case for military service. Lewis Wilder, an inmate at Eastern State Penitentiary in Philadelphia who had been convicted of armed robbery, wrote to the U.S. Supreme Court in hopes of being released from prison so he could join the military. He promised that after the war he would serve out the remainder of his sentence. "I have never been of any use to my country or my fellow man," he admitted, and was "most certainly a liability to the country while being held here." He did not want "to convey the impression that I am doing this as a means of securing any form of clemency."[49] For the time being, the nation would not open its prisons to fill the ranks of soldiers and sailors.

As autumn approached, there was the unmistakable feeling in many areas of the country that little progress had been made since Pearl Harbor. Much of this dissatisfaction was directed toward Washington. The growing frustration that many felt about the administration and the progress of war was expressed in an open letter to the president by Edwin J. Paxton Jr., an editor with the *Paducah (Ky.) Sun-Democrat:* "Eight months after we entered the war, the victory program still isn't shaping up." There was much to criticize about Congress, Paxton noted, but he admonished the president, "Congress has voted you every appropriation and every executive authority demanded of it. . . . It is not Congress which must lead us in war, Mr. President. It is yourself." He called for "drastic action" against inflation and strikes, and for raw materials, but did not specifically call for a second front. Yet his underlying message of urgent action was not lost on FDR, who kept hoping that the North African invasion could begin by late October—in time to save the election.[50]

9

September: "Threat of Economic Chaos"

BY EARLY SEPTEMBER, FRANKLIN ROOSEVELT's frustration over congressional delays on anti-inflation and revenue bills reached new levels, and he told reporters that he would deliver a major policy announcement on Labor Day. What he might announce was anyone's guess, but many assumed he would name a new domestic consumption administrator with broad authority over the wartime economy. Rumors flew that it could be Supreme Court justice William O. Douglas or New York governor Herbert Lehman, or maybe another member of the court, James F. Byrnes. Trying to anticipate what Roosevelt might say, many looked to the ominous joint statement made by Navy secretary Frank Knox and Undersecretary of War Robert Patterson: "The time has come when we must begin to win this war, or go down to shameful slavery and defeat."[1]

In an address to the American Bankers Association on September 1, Treasury secretary Morgenthau highlighted the $36 billion that had poured into the Treasury in the fiscal year just ended, saying, "There is no parallel in our history for this money-raising achievement." Against the projected costs of the war, however, these revenue-raising efforts were a drop in the bucket. "We are surrounded at this moment," Morgenthau noted, "by economic as well as military dangers, yet it is a cause for some satisfaction that inflation has been more effectively controlled to date in this war" than in World War I. Even if the tax bill passed, he estimated the government would have to borrow an additional $50 billion in the present fiscal year. "None of us can see more than a few months ahead through the murk of this most unpredictable of wars," and no one could know what the future held, but he warned the audience to "be prepared for new controls and new sacrifices as the war moves into a new and more intense phase."[2]

For Roosevelt and his Democratic allies in Congress, the complex economic challenges of raising taxes and fighting inflation were loaded with potential problems. People faced mounting scarcity as war production replaced consumer items. Workers were consequently saving more money, which presented its own challenges. *Newsweek* described FDR's essential task: "how to keep consumers from unleashing that terrific purchasing power against dwindling supplies of consumer goods and diminishing services." One "extreme" solution would be to tax it away. Another would combine taxes with some form of compulsory savings. At the other end were a set of controls as "comprehensive as the world has ever seen: . . . rigidly regulating wages and prices and rationing supplies down to the last toothpick." The OWI tried to make clear the overriding concern of inflation: "When prices skyrocket, the burdens of war fall unevenly and unfairly, morale is drained and the nation divided against itself." If government did not control the entire economy, free markets would spiral out of control. "Without proper control over prices and wages, civilian producers compete against war producers for materials and manpower. . . . The extent to which prices and wages are controlled may decide whether the peace is won or lost." Many Americans were willing to do their part, whatever that meant. Some enterprising people went to extraordinary lengths to help with the war effort. In a New York beauty parlor, Honey Girl, a dachshund, had a magnet dangling from her collar to collect hairpins dropped on the floor. Her owner estimated that over the past year, Honey Girl had collected enough metal "to make 700 hand grenades."[3]

Before his Labor Day speech, Roosevelt addressed a student assembly in Washington about the international picture. While the Nazis and the militarists of Japan offered young people nothing more than death, he said, "the United Nations is the cause of youth itself," built on the notion that life can be lived "in freedom, in justice, and in dignity." In Germany, the president noted, the young were little more than "cannon fodder" for Hitler. "We exult in the thought that it is the young, free men and women of the United

Nations and not the wound-up robots of the slave states who will mold the shape of the new world." One teenager who heard the president was thirteen-year-old Betty Jean Schwaeber of Queens, New York, who listened to him on the radio along with her ten-year-old brother and ten other children ranging in age from ten to thirteen. Betty Jean told a reporter for the *New York Times* that she "was impressed by what the President said about Hitler's doings to the people of France. . . . Just think what the Nazis are doing to children." When asked what she intended to do in response to the president's address, she said that upon turning fourteen, she would join the American Women's Voluntary Service. Another student, David Freeman, said he had lived in England for a year and was fascinated by Roosevelt's description of the brave exploits of the French underground. Freeman had even visited wounded soldiers in a hospital in England during the evacuation of Dunkirk and had heard firsthand how the French resisters had helped them.[4]

Not all young Americans were as enthusiastic. Over the summer, Dr. Mandel Sherman, an educational psychologist at the University of Chicago, studied the attitudes toward war of seven thousand local high school students who had been asked to write essays under the title "How the War Affects Me." Sherman reported that a majority of the adolescents displayed "the most dangerous attitudes to American morale," ranging from bland indifference to the war to outright hostility. He concluded, as adults in every generation seem to do about teenagers, that the majority of Chicago-area youths were more "concerned with their personal problems . . . than winning the war." Yet studies such as Sherman's failed to penetrate the world of America's teens, who had few outlets for their sense of anxiety until they reached draft age. One Indianapolis teen who wanted to contribute in some manner wrote of his frustrations. "Being 16 or 17, we're considered too young for the armed forces" or for "work in the factories." Another said that although "our elders do not seem to realize it," teenagers were especially "feeling part of the burden of this war."[5]

More babies were born in the United States in September and October 1942 than any other month of the year (the lowest birth rate occurred in May). Infant mortality rates differed starkly according to race: the rate for white children was 37.3 deaths per 1,000 live births, and 64.2 for African

Americans. The major causes of infant deaths were complications from premature birth, pneumonia, congenital malformations, injuries at birth, and diarrhea. The leading causes of death for adults in 1942 were heart disease, cancer, stroke, nephritis, and pneumonia. Among adults, the death rate from cirrhosis of the liver reached levels not seen since the end of Prohibition. There was at least one beneficial by-product of gas rationing and lower speed limits: deaths from automobile accidents fell to their lowest level since 1926.[6]

The increase in the birth rate prompted the *Catholic Telegraph-Register,* published by the Archdiocese of Cincinnati, to warn that "the advocates of birth control, which now masquerade as Planned Parenthood," would need "to change their tactics." By encouraging contraception, the paper suggested, the supporters of family planning "seek to yoke together family welfare and family destruction." More was at stake than met the eye: "National salvation is insured only if birth control is unequivocally condemned morally wrong under all circumstances."[7]

When President Roosevelt addressed the nation on September 7, he began with a theme he had stressed throughout the year: "We are fighting a war of survival," and without higher taxes and price ceilings on farm products, "the whole objective must fail." He acknowledged that ceilings on prices and rents were "one of the most far-reaching economic steps that this Nation has ever taken—in time of peace or war." Protecting the nation against both foreign enemies and domestic economic calamity, he said, was the paramount concern, and "nothing can yield to the overall necessity of winning this war, and the winning of the war will be imperiled by a runaway domestic economy." After months of congressional inaction, the president's patience was at an end and he issued a blunt ultimatum. If lawmakers did not produce an anti-inflation bill by October 1, he would do so under his wartime powers: "I shall accept the responsibility, and I will act." He claimed the power to "take measures necessary to avert a disaster which would interfere with the winning of the war" but would wait until October 1 because of his "unalterable devotion to the processes of democracy. . . . Inaction on your part," he told Congress, "will leave me with an inescapable responsibility to see to it that the war effort is no longer imperiled by threat of economic chaos."[8]

After the war, Roosevelt reassured Congress, all emergency powers would "automatically revert to the people—to whom they belong." But during the crisis, "the responsibilities of the President in wartime to protect the nation are very grave. This total war, with our fighting fronts all over the world, makes the use of executive power far more essential than in any previous war. I cannot tell what powers may have to be exercised in order to win this war." With the congressional elections just weeks away, the president's words were a lightning rod to those already worried about executive overreach. Senator Robert La Follette, a Republican from Wisconsin, said that Roosevelt had "placed a pistol at the head of Congress." The sentiment was shared by Thomas Parkinson, president of the Equitable Life Assurance Society of New York, who believed that FDR's threatened actions constituted "probably the most serious assault upon the Constitution under which this country lives than has been made since the Civil War." Parkinson asked: "Is this what the American People want? Do they want an executive with the power to levy taxes without the approval of Congress? Why, the shades of the Boston Tea Party come to mind."[9]

In issuing his ultimatum, Roosevelt followed the advice of Supreme Court justice Jimmy Byrnes. Even though Byrnes did not believe that the chief executive possessed the power to circumvent Congress, he told Harold Ickes that he advised FDR to give Congress until October 1 to produce the necessary legislation. Responding to Roosevelt's speech, Ickes found the president "pretty rough in his language," even "dictatorial." Ickes understood what might happen if Congress refused to budge: the president would "have to exercise unconstitutional power or back down completely."[10]

Roosevelt's loyalists considered the speech a necessary assertion of executive authority in the face of a Congress too timid to act on taxes and farm prices before the election. His opponents considered it a brazen usurpation of power far worse than Lincoln's suspension of habeas corpus. Senator Robert Taft was outraged that the president's ultimatum "raises a question so revolutionary and so dangerous to the American form of government. If the president can change the price law by Executive order, he can draft men in violation of the Selective Service Act by Executive order and impose taxes by Executive order." Taft warned that rumors of suspended congressional elections in November might be true, and unless

Congress challenged Roosevelt's actions, "we could have a complete one-man dictatorship." Despite such statements, members grumbled that the president would nonetheless have his bill before the October deadline. Navy secretary Frank Knox confided to his wife that "the reaction to the President's message is about what I expected. Congress will growl and grouch but they haven't the courage to either fight the President or propose some course of action of their own. FDR will get what he wants and on or before the date fixed."[11]

Roosevelt's use of executive power in war displayed the uneasy tension such crises present to the business of lawmaking within the Constitution. Historian William E. Leuchtenburg concludes, "Unhappily, of FDR's many legacies, one is a certain lack of appropriate restraint with respect to the exercise of executive power." In fact, his use of executive orders has never been approached by any other president. In 1942 alone, he signed 289, compared to the 380 signed by Ronald Reagan in his eight years in office, and Barack Obama's 277. In his first full year in the White House, Donald Trump signed 58 orders. In his twelve years in power, Roosevelt signed a total of 3,466 executive orders.[12]

If members of Congress were growing frustrated with the administration, so were their constituents. A grocer in New Bern, North Carolina, wrote to Leon Henderson, imploring the OPA to allow his suppliers more gas and warning that if they did "not get relief on the gas situation, it will demoralize the entire business structure." A *New Yorker* cartoon showed two young women in a convertible being eyed by a male driver. "Don't be a goon," says one, "probably all he's after is your tires."[13]

On September 10, the Baruch Rubber Committee submitted its findings, warning in the gravest terms that the rubber shortage threatened the nation's ability to win the war. Unless drastic steps were taken immediately to save every spare ounce of rubber and to manufacture synthetic rubber in significant amounts, the nation faced "both a military and civilian collapse." The final phrase had been revised from an earlier draft written by Harvard president James Conant, which contained an assessment that may have seemed too bleak for the American public to bear: without new supplies of rubber, "we will lose this war."[14]

The committee report stressed that time was running out before an even greater crisis occurred that would harm the nation's ability to wage war. The nation had on hand 578,000 tons of rubber as of July 1942, with estimated imports for the year totaling just 53,000 tons, for a total of 631,000 tons available through the rest of the year. By the end of 1943, the armed forces would require 842,000 tons a year. In other words, at the current rate of usage, the time was fast approaching when rubber supplies "with which to equip a modern mechanized army" would be exhausted. By 1944, if the situation did not improve, there would be "an almost complete collapse of the 27,000,000 passenger cars in America." This was one of two important places in the report where the committee used the alarming term *collapse*. In its conclusion, the report recommended that the nation extend the gasoline rationing program nationwide to hold average mileage per car to five thousand miles annually and increase synthetic rubber production to 1.1 million tons. The president, it said, should appoint a rubber administrator to oversee the process.[15]

The report did not blame any person for the crisis, but noted that early in the year, American officials had missed an opportunity to approach Soviet government officials, who possessed the technical capacity to produce synthetic rubber. The "failure of responsible officials to request the aid of Russia in setting up our synthetic system," the authors commented, "is a neglect for which we have not had a satisfactory explanation." A massive synthetic rubber program was needed immediately, an effort that would constitute "one of the most complicated technical projects ever undertaken in this country."[16]

The industry magazine *Rubber Age* praised the Baruch report, saying that it "pulled no punches," and "put the issue squarely up to the American public—Discomfort or Defeat!" The oil industry was less enthusiastic. An editorial in the *Houston Post* captured the brewing hostility to "rigid nationwide gasoline rationing": "It will deal a crippling economic blow to Texas and other oil producing states. . . . Universal rationing would be disastrous [and] would put many enterprises out of business, and tens of thousands of people out of work. . . . If it is just to save rubber, what is the rubber being saved for? Does the government require the tires from the people's cars? If so, why not take them? If not, what difference does it make to the government whether the people's tires wear out six months from now or a year from now?"[17]

The *New York Post* thought that "a number of people ought to be fired as a result of the Baruch committee's report," and that FDR was "under a single duty to find out who turned down Russia's offer of last February to supply us with synthetic rubber experts." Columnist Drew Pearson dug into the story to discover that Russian officials had offered patents, information, and technical expertise to Will Clayton, assistant secretary of commerce and Jesse Jones's "right hand man," but they did not even receive a reply. Pearson speculated if the reason could have been that the Russians used alcohol as a base for synthetic rubber, and Jones favored "the big oil companies of Texas" who wanted to use petroleum. One Detroit citizen, after reading the Pearson column, responded that "one cannot help but wonder what sinister influence has stalled our rubber production," and that whoever was responsible for the rubber crisis "should be shot at sunrise." Roosevelt, meanwhile, approved Nelson's naming of William Jeffers, the president of the Union Pacific Railroad, as the nation's rubber administrator.[18]

Not everyone was impressed with the Baruch report. Gerald L. K. Smith, for instance, said it was "common knowledge among all experts, scientists, and industrialists" that the entire rubber shortage was phony. Smith said there were rubber substitutes "available right now" that could "recap 100 million new tires without using one ounce of new rubber." The report was the product of "Wall Street monopolies and bureaucratic politicians." Smith claimed that after the war, the United States would join "an Imperialistic World Empire" without "tariff walls" that would compel American workers "to compete with the Chinese coolie, and the American farmer would have to compete with the Russian peasant and the Egyptian slave." This world government already had a name—"Federal Union." Smith also advocated a unique plan to keep America safe from any further foreign invaders—"a hoop of military steel" to be constructed all around the perimeter of the country. Such a barrier "guaranteed protection" and would "make it unnecessary to wage future foreign wars."[19]

One city that stood to benefit from the Baruch report was Louisville, Kentucky, which called itself the "synthetic rubber capital of the world." Shortly after the release of the report, the Carbide Chemical Corporation came to west Louisville to look for land on which to build a synthetic rubber plant that would manufacture a product called "Buna S." Carbide was joined by other companies, including Goodrich, DuPont, and the National Synthetic Rubber Company. Once they were up and running, the various plants would employ over four thousand workers and, at their peak in 1944, produce nearly two hundred thousand tons of Buna S, butadiene, copolymer, and neoprene rubber. The west end of Louisville, where the companies were located, came to be known as Rubbertown and has remained a center of chemical production, as well as environmental hazards, ever since.[20]

New Jersey governor Charles Edison was among the first state executives to take action to reduce rubber consumption after the Baruch report's release. Edison ordered a statewide speed limit of thirty-five miles per hour and urged all citizens to reduce their automobile usage to matters of urgent necessity. Drivers on the state's freeways were soon greeted with new signs: "War Speed—35 miles per hour."[21]

The rubber crisis made the news from the Maritime Commission even more worrisome. The commission reported that in August, 56 liberty ships had been built, bringing the total for the year to 259 ships. Every month more ships had been built in fewer days, yet shipyards would soon need more rubber if they hoped to continue their hectic pace. While the 3 ships constructed in January had taken an average of 235 days from keel to delivery, the 56 ships in August had required just 82.9 days. The Kaiser shipyards were even faster, producing 9 ships in an average of 50.2 days. While those figures were good news for the navy, without more rubber the shipbuilding program would come to a standstill. In addition to prefabricated methods, another reason shipyards were so productive was wage stabilization and the benefits many yards provided to workers. In World War I, the labor turnover rate in American shipyards exceeded 25 percent a month, and in some areas it reached 300 percent. In 1942, U.S. shipyards averaged turnovers of less than 4 percent.[22]

As the nation dealt with gas rationing and the rubber shortage, at least one member of Congress was thinking about future automobile travel. Representative Elmer Wene of New Jersey introduced a bill in September 1942 that had little hope of passing but that presented a new concept of highway travel. He wanted to commit $10 billion to build a twenty-five-thousand-mile nationwide network of "military superhighways" once the war was over. Besides providing thousands of jobs that would "eliminate all need of a dole, relief, or charity to any able-bodied citizen," Wene saw the highway system as a defense program that would "make the United States impregnable to any possible invasion from any border line by providing the swiftest means of transportation for mechanized units of the Army."[23] Fourteen years later, Wene's vision began to be realized with the passage of the Federal Interstate Highway Act.

The backlash against the rubber shortage and gasoline rationing, as well as the continuing standoff between Roosevelt and Congress, led some to consider the opportunities presented by the November election. Republicans residing in congressional districts where Democrats had won narrowly saw a chance to forge a new political era. While criticizing the president might have seemed out of the question immediately after Pearl Harbor, recent months had shown that there was plenty of room to criticize both FDR and his party, if it was done carefully. Republican leaders began looking for new candidates with fresh messages who could begin building the GOP into a party that could hold majorities in the House and Senate, and even perhaps win the White House for the first time since 1928.

One such possibility was someone whose last name was as powerful as any in the country. The fact that the potential candidate was a woman and a celebrity who had never run for any office made it all the more intriguing. In early 1942, Clare Boothe Luce was a recognized playwright and magazine writer married to Henry Luce, the publisher of *Life* and *Time*. By the end of the year, she was the representative-elect from Connecticut's Fourth District and epitomized a turn in American politics that would transform the nation for the rest of the century.

Clare Boothe was born in 1903 in New York City and was, in the phrase of the day, "illegitimate." Her parents were musicians and actors who never married, and after they separated her mother became, in Clare's words, "a call girl." Clare attended schools in New York and hoped to become an actress, and at ten years old was an understudy of Mary Pickford on Broadway. In 1919, her mother married Albert E. Austin, a Connecticut surgeon and active Republican. Four years later, Clare married millionaire George

Tuttle Brokaw, giving birth to a daughter in 1924. The marriage to Brokaw ended in 1929. In the early 1930s she began a long-term affair with Bernard Baruch. By the time FDR went to the White House, she had emerged as a noted author and the managing editor of *Vanity Fair*, and she soon met Henry Luce, the powerful publisher of the most widely read magazines in the nation. After they married in 1935, she focused on her career as a playwright. Two of her best efforts eventually became movies: *The Women*, starring Norma Shearer and Joan Crawford, and *Margin for Error*, which starred Joan Bennett. She also began writing for *Life*, and when the war broke out in Europe, she became a war correspondent and visited the Maginot Line just days before Hitler's troops crossed it. Her profile of Douglas MacArthur was the *Life* cover story in its issue of December 8, 1941. In February 1942, *Vogue* featured an article of the Luce home in Greenwich, complete with a glamorous photo of Clare in black gloves lounging on a sofa.[24]

Although she was an early supporter of FDR, Clare broke with him during the 1940 campaign. It was not that she had become an isolationist: she gave impassioned speeches supporting Republican Wendell Willkie, and the fall of France had convinced her of the danger of the "moral cowardice" that she thought infused both the administration and "America Firsters" like Charles Lindbergh. If anything, she thought the U.S. should intervene in the war right away. But she thought Roosevelt had led a reckless increase in the government's size and reach. In the weeks before the 1940 election, she warned of "the corrupting evils of bloated state sovereignty" and stressed that the choices confronting the nation were "never between the desirable and the undesirable, but between the more or less undesirable." Much as campaigning for Barry Goldwater in 1964 turned Ronald Reagan from a Hollywood figure into a bona fide politician, Clare's forceful speeches for Willkie in 1940 made many within the Republican Party see her as a rising star. In 1941, traveling in China and witnessing Axis savagery, she concluded that Roosevelt's continued trade with Japan while allied with China was a "piece of gigantic stupidity" that would "stand unchallenged in the annals of Democratic Foreign Policy." The president's weak-kneed approach to the threat of Germany and Japan would lead "into a two-ocean multiple front war, with a one-ocean navy and no armies to put into the

field." The administration's policy was "a monstrosity, which if not traitor-
ous, is surely imbecile."[25]

In 1938, her stepfather, Dr. Albert Austin, was elected to Congress from
Connecticut's Fourth District, a wealthy area that contained the town of
Greenwich, where Henry and Clare resided. He was defeated for reelection
in 1940 by Democrat LeRoy Downs. When Austin died in January 1942,
some members of the state Republican Party encouraged Clare to run for his
old seat. At first she thought she was not well suited for politics, and without
any prior experience would not be able to mount a successful campaign. She
wrote a letter to the state chairman in late August withdrawing her name
from consideration, claiming she was not well enough acquainted with the
people of the district and their specific problems. Another reason was personal: "Political rivals have already shown that they will not be content to
attack me but will also seek to attack my husband." Given that "his publica-
tions are giving leadership to the nation and the world, it would not be an act
of patriotism to drag him through the mud of an absurdly provincial election."[26] Yet within days she was rethinking her decision. The state party
knew Luce had advantages more seasoned politicians did not—she was rich,
smart, beautiful, and famous, and she had the ability to criticize the administration's war efforts in ways that did not call her patriotism into question.

Running for Congress presented its share of challenges. Although Roosevelt was not on the ballot, the off-year election, like many midterms, would
be a referendum on the president's performance. Criticizing the president
during war had its risks, but millions of Americans, including many in the
Fourth District of Connecticut, were increasingly discouraged by the administration's handling of the war and worried that its officials were more
concerned with extending the New Deal than with victory. In words that
would later be appropriated by Douglas MacArthur, Clare claimed in the
summer of 1942, "Too many men in Washington do not yet realize that,
whereas there are substitutes for rubber, there is no substitute for victory."[27]

In addition to many leading Republicans in the Fourth District who
hoped she would change her mind, a few friends who were Democrats
urged her to run. Former ambassador Joseph P. Kennedy wrote her, "I seriously believe that the country will be the loser if you don't make the try."
Clare responded that she was maintaining the "rather ignominious and

highly acrobatic position habitual to politicians: sitting on the fence." Another Kennedy offering encouragement to her candidacy was Ambassador Kennedy's son, twenty-five-year-old John Fitzgerald Kennedy, who was at the U.S. Naval Training Station in Newport.[28]

Unlike the endless campaigns that mark modern elections, a successful campaign for Congress in the 1940s could be only weeks long. On September 11, less than two months before the election, Clare was still not an official candidate, but when she delivered the keynote address to the Connecticut Republican convention in Hartford, she sounded ready to throw her hat in the ring. Calling Washington "a madhouse run by its inmates," she said the administration talked a "tough war" but was fighting a "soft one." Republicans stood for those who had died at Pearl Harbor, she declared, and differed from the New Dealers in wanting "total victory, which is not only the military defeat of their enemies, but a just and fruitful peace and a better world for their children."

Clare managed to criticize the Roosevelt administration without sounding like an isolationist. The administration, she said, played "politics as usual with the selfish elements in labor unions" and was too ready "to extend vote-getting special privileges and exonerations to unpatriotic labor leaders and to war profiteers and employers who try to protect their machinery and plants for profitable post-war use." It was using the New Deal to "raise false political issues such as pre-Pearl Harbor isolationism" and "prevent minority groups, such as Negroes, from playing the full part their patriotism warrants." She ended the speech with a clear announcement of how the minority party could counter the three-term president and his congressional majority: "We have to remain free men and women, though our very souls sweat for it. We have promised that we shall live and die, not in the darkness of defeat but in the light of victory. We have promised the living and dead a hard war but a happy peace."

Some items that were removed from her speech at the last minute—obtained and published by the *New York Times*—reveal that she was no longer a writer looking to address readers on both sides, but a partisan interested in winning a nomination. She had written that "internationalism" required abandoning "absolute national sovereignty" and the establishment of an international authority after the war "to maintain world peace and order. If bigger and better wars are not to be the rule for the next one hundred years, each nation, big and little, must yield some of its power to an international authority with power to enforce the basic minimum worldwide law for peace." But she took that out, along with the comment that if "the stupid barriers of excessive nationalism" had been broken down earlier, "we would have gone a long way toward solving the world's economic problem."[29]

After the speech, other candidates for the Fourth District seat cried foul, claiming she was the party leaders' "hand-picked candidate." One accused the party of the same tactics "that destroyed France," while another, Vivien Kellems, charged that the Luce nomination would be "a victory for those who wish to nullify our constitution and substitute an evil internationalism for our true democracy." The party leaders, however, knew the power of a Luce candidacy. By a vote of 84–2, she became the Republican candidate for the Fourth District congressional seat. In accepting the nomination, she stated three major goals: win the war; prosecute the war as loyally and effectively as possible; and bring about a better world and a durable peace, with special attention to postwar security and employment at home. Sounding like FDR, she added, "Never again here in Fairfield County shall there be the terrors and humiliation of post war unemployment and insecurity." She hoped that the election of a woman to Congress might "interest more women to help maintain our kind of government," adding, "I have seen minority groups pushed around in many foreign countries" and she was "determined that it shall not happen here."[30]

Like many across the political spectrum, Clare Boothe Luce endorsed the concept of full employment but left unclear what that meant in terms of policy or legislation. Should the government provide guaranteed jobs to stimulate a flagging economy? Or should it simply endorse general programs of tax incentives and economic growth, of which jobs would presumably be a by-product? "Full employment" meant different things to different people, and Luce was ready to defend it without going into specifics about how she would obtain it. She supported raising taxes, claiming, "The burdens of total war must be assumed, according to the ability of each, by the total population. . . . In the past, the attempt to distribute the existing wealth merely by punishing or confiscatory taxation had only succeeded in distributing depression and poverty."[31]

It helped Luce's chances that a Stamford architect, David Mansell, decided to enter the race on the Socialist ticket. Observers thought Mansell would draw votes away from Downs, which might provide the margin of victory Luce needed. Outside the district, few paid much attention to the two men running for the seat. The focus was on the "smart-looking" and "fast-talking" Luce.[32]

The Fourth District of Connecticut had supported Democrats in previous elections, but only narrowly. Luce's opponent, LeRoy Downs, had defeated her stepfather by a mere half percentage point two years earlier. While President Roosevelt had carried Connecticut with 53.4 percent of the vote in 1940, his share in the Fourth District was just 50.7 percent. And a lot had happened since that election. Luce called Downs a "rubber stamp" for the Roosevelt administration. In response, the town of Monroe formed the Rubber Stamp Club, claiming that if "supporting your Commander-in-Chief and supporting labor makes you a rubber stamp, then you gladly accept the designation." While the district, like the nation, was frustrated with the course of the war, Downs still had the backing of local labor unions and stood proudly with the president. If any district might prove a bellwether for the political direction of the country, the Fourth District could be it.[33]

At 6:24 a.m. on September 9, a forestry service observer noticed a small plane circling near Mt. Emily, Oregon, in the southwestern corner of the state. Not long after, there were two bright flashes followed by plumes of smoke. The plane, a Yokosuka E14Y floatplane that had been launched by a nearby Japanese submarine, was fitted with collapsible wings for storage inside the sub and was armed with incendiary bombs. Later that day, a forestry crew found remnants of a bomb at Wheeler Ridge, near a scorched crater approximately three feet wide and twelve inches deep. Wet conditions kept the fire from spreading and no one was injured, but it was the only enemy bombing of the continental United States during the war. Despite blackouts, war insurance, saboteurs, and the internment of over one hundred thousand people throughout the Southwest, the Japanese never inflicted any more harm on the mainland than a crater the size of a toddler's wading pool.[34]

The Mt. Emily bombing did nothing to ease the fear of future attacks. An ad from the Hartford Insurance Company noted that "it is a shorter distance by air from Tokio to Salt Lake City than from Tokio to San Diego" and warned readers that it wasn't "a question of whether or not there is going to be a bombing or an invasion." The only question was "How you would be fixed without any insurance protection if there were one?"[35]

On September 17, Colonel Leslie Groves was appointed head of the Manhattan Engineer District. A stern, results-minded leader who had directed the construction of the Pentagon, Groves would influence the course of the war and the subsequent decades every bit as much as Eisenhower or Patton did. Two days after his appointment, he selected a fifty-two-thousand-acre site in eastern Tennessee called the Clinton Engineer Works, or Oak Ridge, as it would become known, as the site for a vast factory to produce the atomic material necessary for a bomb. Four days after that, Groves was promoted to brigadier general and given the highest priority in procuring material, and the Army Corps of Engineers began the process of buying the land through eminent domain—or, as the locals called it, "The Taking." The following month, Groves selected physicist J. Robert Oppenheimer to lead the scientific effort to create a fission bomb. The scientists Oppenheimer assembled in Los Alamos, New Mexico, began an undertaking that would change the nature of warfare.[36]

As it struggled to raise taxes and pass an anti-inflation bill that September, Congress also took up an issue that seemed, on its face, a straightforward matter with no political overtones or need for prolonged debate. It considered a bill to allow soldiers serving far from home to vote via absentee ballot. At a time when democracy was at risk, what better way to display its enduring character than by allowing the men putting themselves in harm's way to exercise their democratic rights? The measure had the support of veterans groups and families of soldiers serving abroad. Legislators facing reelection were eager to vote for it.

Yet when Representative Estes Kefauver of Tennessee proposed amending the House bill to waive the poll-tax requirement for white soldiers, he exposed one of the fault lines of American politics. If the poll tax were waived in this circumstance, it might serve as a wedge to make the tax illegal in all elections, and that was unacceptable to southern conservatives. The poll tax was one of the crucial instruments by which African Americans were kept from voting. Since elections were administered locally, many southern members of Congress considered Kefauver's amendment a direct threat to state sovereignty and, more directly, their hold on power. Representative Sam Hobbs of Alabama described the soldier voting bill as "an attack on our Southern way of life and on white supremacy," and an attempt "to cater to the soldier vote at the expense of the very foundation of our democracy."[37] Not even the crisis of war would persuade southern Democrats to shrink from their sacred duty to defend white supremacy at all costs.

No one in Washington was more opposed to the Soldier Voting Act than Mississippi's John Rankin. In the plot to waive the poll tax, the eleven-term representative saw dangerous elements everywhere. The effort, he thundered, was "part of a long-range communistic program to change our form of government." On the House floor, he railed that the bill would take control of elections "out of the hands of white Americans" and give it to "certain irresponsible elements that are constantly trying to destroy private enterprise and to stir up trouble, especially in the Southern states." Rankin's condemnation of the bill failed to win over the majority of House members, who passed it on September 9 by a vote of 247–53. An outraged Rankin called the final bill "a scheme to abolish State governments," adding that "the next step will be to abolish Congress."[38]

The Senate passed the bill on a voice vote, although Senators Tom Connelly of Texas and Lister Hill of Alabama said that in the process of approving the measure, the Senate had "ruptured Constitutional processes." Roosevelt signed it into law on September 16, too late to be fully operational for an election just forty-eight days away. Southern members of the Senate, who had kept quiet about the soldier voting bill, were ready when a more direct assault on the poll tax came just weeks later.[39]

The southern wartime spirit was displayed in the Democratic primary for the Louisiana Senate seat, where E. A. Stephens challenged incumbent Allen Ellender. Rather than focus on issues such as the course of the war or the fight against inflation, Stephens warned that "social equality" was being "forced down the throats of white people." In fact, he told voters, African Americans in Louisiana were "sitting around midnight candles" plotting against whites. He saw a conspiracy whenever local draft boards gave deferments to African Americans while placing local whites in the military. So many white men leaving home created disturbing possibilities. Stephens knew the rumors swirling through the South that once white men all left to fight the war, African American men were planning a coordinated campaign of rape. Ellender answered Stephens by reminding voters of his long, unblemished record on race, noting his twenty-seven-hour filibuster against a federal anti-lynching law in 1938. "I invite the unknown critic who is asking how I stand on the negro issue," he said, "to read some of my speeches." Louisiana voters did not need to read those speeches to be reminded of Ellender's racial policies. He easily defeated Stephens with 72 percent of the vote, ensuring his victory in the general election in November.[40]

In Louisiana, as was the case throughout the South, elections reinforced a system of Jim Crow segregation that touched every aspect of daily life. The structure of public education, for example, was divided along lines of color. Whereas the state expended $60.37 per white student in its schools each year, it spent just $12.62 per black student. Yet these racial disparities were eclipsed by neighboring Mississippi, which spent $38.96 on white students and $4.97 per black student. In Georgia, which managed to spend less on black students than Louisiana did, the State Board of Education banned several books from its public schools because they did not accurately reflect "Southern views on the Negro question." Two of the banned books were *Education for Democracy in Our Time* and a biography of Ulysses S. Grant.[41]

While the war abroad continued, and as the nation's government argued into the night, life went on in mundane but important ways. In St. Louis, the first game of the 1942 World Series was played between the National League champion, the Cardinals, and the American League champs, the New York Yankees. The Yankees won the game 7–4 in front of thirty-four thousand fans in Sportsman's Park. The Cardinals, led by Stan Musial and Enos Slaughter, swept the next four games to win the series. For Joe DiMaggio, who had hit .305 with twenty-one home runs in the 1942 season after starting spring training by holding out for a higher salary, these were the last major league games until the war ended. In February 1943, he enlisted in the Army Air Force.

In August, the War Production Board reported that 4,282 planes had been produced in August, 12 percent short of its original forecast. WPB economist

Robert R. Nathan had been convinced for months that the president's goals were beyond reach, and he relied on Simon Kuznets's study of probabilities to make his case. Kuznets, an economist working in the Bureau of Planning and Statistics of the WPB, had proposed that the production objectives be adjusted downward to meet the realities of the situation. Nathan was convinced that a production goal that could not possibly be reached would, in the end, hurt production. "If you can only do 40,000 airplanes and try to build eighty," Nathan remarked, "you're gonna have pieces and parts and things laying all over the field." When the estimates reached Army Service Forces commander General Brehon Somervell, some of the tensions of the war came to light. A decorated soldier from the battle of the Meuse-Argonne in 1918, Somervell had little use for any of the civilian war agencies and thought their real effort was to allow "Henry Wallace and the leftists to take over the country." Somervell dismissed the report entirely and questioned the value of experts such as Kuznets. He preferred to hear from the president, Nelson, and "military personnel knowing something of the problem of production," rather than a "board of 'economists and statisticians.' I am not impressed with either the character or basis of judgments expressed in the reports and recommend they be carefully hidden from the eyes of thoughtful men."[42]

Nathan, who considered Somervell "a real bastard," replied that he regretted that the report, "which spells out the significant problems in relation to objectives and production planning," had not been "phrased so as to be comprehensible to you." He accused the general of "an ostrich-like attitude when goals are established that are above probability of achievement" and was furious that Kuznets, "one of the ablest and soundest authorities on our national economy and upon its ability to produce for war," was not considered worth listening to.[43] After the war, Kuznets had a distinguished career at the University of Pennsylvania and Harvard and received the 1971 Nobel Prize in economics.

The New Deal agencies that still managed to survive had to struggle to adapt to changing domestic and international developments. One such survivor was the Tennessee Valley Authority, created in 1933 to provide power to the South through a series of hydroelectric dams. Its director, David Lilienthal, became convinced that after the war, the TVA should be used to plan the reconstruction of China, India, Africa, Latin America, and the Danube River valley. Such ideas were considered ludicrous by William P. Witherow, the former president of the National Association of Manufacturers, who asserted that the U.S. was not fighting in Europe and the Pacific in order "to provide a quart of milk for every Hottentot baby or to build a TVA dam on the Danube." Progressive New Dealers like George W. Norris were incensed. "How blind!" cried Norris, asserting that Witherow "wants to fight the war where he will make more money. If that be the result, we will have fought this war in vain. If we can't get men of extremes to combine their interest in a common effort, then we'd better surrender tonight to Hitler and Japan."

Such squabbles irritated Ralph Bard, the assistant secretary of the Navy for labor relations, who told a gathering of union workers in late September that the U.S. was "losing the war," a sobering reality that "we should damn well understand." Americans, he told the workers, embraced "an insufferable and materialistic pride," and "we are whistling in the graveyard to keep from facing reality."[44]

On Monday, September 21, at his headquarters in London, General Eisenhower made a decision that would change the course of the war—and, possibly, American politics. Despite Roosevelt's urging that the Torch invasion of North Africa begin sometime before the November election, Eisenhower chose Sunday, November 8—five days after the election—as the day the attack would begin. While the president stressed the political importance of some major military action against Hitler before voters went to the polls, Eisenhower believed he must ignore domestic politics and concentrate on the complex details of the attack. In addition to needing more time to prepare the ships and train the troops, he also wanted the darkness provided by the new moon that would begin on the eighth of November.[45]

If the hostility between Roosevelt and Congress were not already at a rapid boil by late September, Representative Martin Dies managed to get it there. Dies, the chairman of the Special House Committee on Un-American Activities, placed nineteen names in the *Congressional Record* of people he said belonged to groups affiliated and controlled by the Communist Party. Among the names were Mary McLeod Bethune, director of the Division of Negro Affairs of the National Youth Administration, E. Franklin Frazier, who taught sociology at Howard University, and Gardner Jackson, an economist in the Department of Agriculture. Dies was outraged that the nineteen were still employed with the federal government, especially after Attorney General Francis Biddle could find only two "subversives" in a list of over a thousand federal employees the committee had sent him. The administration well knew that Dies was a bigot who, in the words of journalist John Egerton, "harbored a deep admiration for Hitler that was in large measure tied to the German dictator's philosophy of Aryan racial purity."

In a letter to Dies, Walter White of the NAACP called the charges against Bethune "utterly fantastic and vicious." White wrote that "impugning the loyalty and integrity of the most beloved and best-known Negro woman in America would be an infinite service to the Axis, if your statements were believed, in destroying the faith of Negroes and of colored people in other parts of the world in their belief that the U.S. is in truth fighting a war for democracy. . . . Segregation in the armed forces, discrimination in the industrial phases of the war program, disfranchisement and lynching in your state of Texas, vicious assaults upon Negro soldiers and civilians," White went on, only highlighted the "obvious hypocrisy of many of the Americans who talk glibly about democracy, while they have not the slightest intention of extending the benefits of that democracy to other peoples in the US, India, and other parts of the world, [and] have already dropped the morale of Negroes to a tragic and dangerous low." Bethune herself later issued a statement that "if Rep. Dies sees fit to name me a Communist as a result of my outspoken belief in a true democracy, then the names Mr. Dies chooses to apply are to me but tinkling cymbals and sounding brass."[46]

While Dies was seen by many as a right-wing demagogue, in his home district in Texas he was considered a hero. Since winning his seat in 1930, he had run unopposed in every general election except 1932, when he won 95 percent of the vote. In 1942 the GOP would again offer no opposition. At a gathering of fifteen hundred worshippers at the Sabine Tabernacle Church, Pastor Harry Hodge thanked Dies "for bringing the truth to the American people for exposing subversive forces now at work in this nation to overthrow our God-given heritage. . . . In every crisis, God has always raised up a man to sound the alarm," Hodge told parishioners, and in 1942, "Martin Dies is the man of the hour." Like so many others throughout the district, Hodge was devoted to winning the war but also committed to the wider struggle at home. The struggle, led by Dies, to defend the nation from Communists and those bent on racial equality had even greater import. "Actually, our greatest battle is being fought here at home," Hodge said. "The enemy within the camp is doing his dirty work." "These so-called American liberals" were more concerned with "setting up their godless dictatorship than they are [with] winning the war."[47]

The reactions to Congressman Dies underscored how race remained the essential dividing line in the United States. The Southern Conference for Human Welfare sponsored a full-page ad addressed to "Our Commander-In-Chief," lamenting that in a time of universal sacrifice, "there has been artificially created in the South grave racial tension. . . . Violent speeches filled with Nazi ideas and phrases are inciting race hatred and conflict," and unnamed "politicians are aiding Hitler by their efforts to provoke racial strife." Unhelpfully, the ad did little more than pledge support for the president and for the preservation of "Southern unity, free from race conflict."[48]

Racist assumptions were taught early to children and permeated the wider culture. In addition to segregated schools and "whites only" counters and restrooms, even the way children played was often grounded in racial stereotypes. At Abercrombie and Fitch in New York City, shoppers could pay $6.50 to purchase a "Darkie Target Game," which included six balls and a painted target consisting of a large black face with an open mouth. "Every boy who likes to throw," the store assured parents, "will improve his accuracy with this game."[49]

On September 12, an African American woman wearing the uniform of the U.S. Army, Norma Greene, anticipated Rosa Parks by more than a decade and was lucky she was not killed. Second Lieutenant Greene was stationed at the Tuskegee Veterans Administration Hospital and was attached to the Ninety-Ninth Pursuit Squadron, an African American unit of the Army Air Force better known as the Tuskegee Airmen. She had volunteered for overseas duty and was preparing to go abroad when she boarded a public bus in Montgomery, Alabama. When she refused the driver's order to board through the rear door, the Montgomery police were called. That Greene was wearing an army uniform did not give her special privileges or respect. Instead, it was possibly a trigger to white supremacists. She was arrested and thrown into a police van, where four officers beat her, broke her nose, robbed her, and then arrested her for disorderly conduct. The incident provoked A. Philip Randolph to write to Senator John H. Bankhead of Alabama about the "brutal assault" against Greene; he hoped the senator would work to bring "the culprit to justice." Bankhead, who had urged George Marshall not to bring African American servicemen and women to the South in any capacity, ignored Randolph's letter. Despite being up for reelection in just a few weeks, he was not worried about offending Randolph, Lieutenant Greene, or the state's nearly 1 million African Americans, because they had been effectively disenfranchised through devices such as the poll tax. Besides, he had no opposition in the contest. No one was arrested, no apology was forthcoming from any local or state authority, and Greene's stand against Jim Crow was quickly forgotten.[50]

On September 30, just hours before the president's deadline, the Senate passed its anti-inflation legislation without a dissenting vote. Majority leader Alben Barkley of Kentucky rejoiced, "I almost want to sing that old hymn, 'This is the Hour I Have Long Sought.'" House and Senate conferees met to iron out differences while the White House waited.[51]

On that same day, Adolf Hitler gave a major speech on the course of the war in which he expressed his contempt for "the string pullers of the psychopath of the White House." The German military, he warned, was prepared for an offensive from the Allied forces anywhere. "It may be the craziest sort of undertaking," but such was to be expected from "these mentally sick and perpetually drunk persons" leading the Allies. Throughout the world, he added, "anti-Semitism is growing, and every nation that enters this war will come out of it an anti-Semitic state." The German leader also ridiculed FDR's Four Freedoms, especially the freedom from want: "It would have been much more simple" if Roosevelt "had used the whole working strength of his country to build up the useful production and to care for his own people."[52]

Roosevelt gave no response. As the day approached when the president had warned he would assume new powers against a lethargic Congress, there was no word from the president or his aides about how he intended to use them. FDR had made no public statements of any kind for two weeks, nor had he appeared publicly at the White House. Considering all that was happening, the unusual silence emanating from the White House seemed odd.

10

October: "Pay As You Go"

ON OCTOBER 1, THE DEADLINE PRESIDENT Roosevelt had set weeks earlier, the anti-inflation bill was in its final stages. While the House and Senate scrambled to reach a deal, most members of Congress and the American public were unaware that Roosevelt had not even been in Washington since September 17. He had embarked on a twenty-four-state, eighty-seven-hundred-mile tour of the nation's military and defense installations. Although thousands of workers and soldiers had seen the president at his many stops, the press had been ordered not to report his whereabouts. Once he was safely back in Washington, the secrecy was lifted and he gave a press conference to relate what he had observed. One senator said after hearing the news, "All this time there has been an impression in this country that there has been a life and death struggle on between the President and the Congress, and he has not even been here."

Roosevelt told reporters that after visiting various defense plants throughout the country, he was pleased with what he saw and thought that neither Congress nor the press really understood the American people's fierce determination. The trip seemed to have lifted his spirits after months of waiting for Congress to approve new economic rules. In response to a question concerning the anti-inflation battle, the president casually replied that he had not even had time to consider the bill emerging from Congress.[1]

Then he offered reporters a thoroughly confusing summary of where American war production stood in respect to the goals he had stated so forcefully in early January. "When I talked about the objective in the message to Congress," he said, "there were a great many 'doubting Thomases.'" Now, with three months to go, he let slip the puzzling statement that even if his original goals were not reached, "I think 94 to 95 percent is an objective that covers the working out of a great war." Overall, he added, "it's a pretty darn good record." The reporters tried to get him to clarify—did that mean the actual number of planes and tanks produced would reach 95 percent of his goals? "No, no, it's impossible," he answered, but added, "I hope that we will get it by the time set, which is December." The reporters tried again—had the president not asked for sixty thousand planes in 1942? FDR's answer was befuddling—"No, rate of. That was perfectly clearly understood." Except by his listeners, who asked yet again, "Mr. President, of the January objectives, planes, tanks, guns, can you say now what percentage you expect to be attained?" "About 94 or 95 percent." Those who had followed the monthly production figures released by various arms of government knew that the president's numbers simply did not add up.[2]

On October 2, a day after Roosevelt's deadline, the House finally passed the anti-inflation bill, known as the Stabilization Act, by a vote of 257–22, and the Senate quickly passed it, 80–0. The White House received the legislation at 9:00 p.m. After conferring with a number of advisors, including Majority leader Alben Barkley, budget director Harold Smith, Leon Henderson, and, significantly, Justice James F. Byrnes, the president signed the bill at 10:15, avoiding what could have been a major confrontation with Congress had he vetoed it and assumed new wartime powers. Roosevelt said the bill provided the necessary language "to do the job," and he immediately used its authority to order price ceilings on a variety of foods, including poultry, butter, cheese, eggs, onions, navy beans, and oranges. In all, the bill was a major victory for the president.[3]

Deep within the language of the Stabilization Act was a parenthetical exception that permanently changed the workplace and the lives of Americans. To its definition of the ways in which "wages" and "salaries" could not be raised, Congress had added the line "excluding insurance and pension benefits in a reasonable amount." Unable to compete for workers by increasing wages, employers took advantage of the exclusion and began attracting them in another way: through employee-sponsored health insurance policies. By the end of 1942, approximately 11 million people were enrolled in the new insurance plans, typically paying between 50 and 85 cents per month for individuals and up to $2 per month for a family. After the War Labor Board decided that health insurance should not be considered wages, the Internal Revenue Service ruled the next year that health insurance benefits were a deductible expense for employers and employees, and so not liable for taxes, and the American system of employee-sponsored health insurance began in earnest.[4]

On October 3, Roosevelt signed Executive Order 9250, creating the Office of Economic Stabilization (OES) and giving it sweeping authority to control prices, wages, and fight inflation. To head it, he selected Justice Byrnes.[5] Byrnes had come from humble beginnings in South Carolina, where his mother had once told him to learn shorthand in order to escape poverty. Instead he chose politics, was elected to the House and Senate, and became the president's ally in passing a variety of New Deal bills. He also enjoyed the financial backing of Bernard Baruch. He was rewarded for his years of loyalty to the administration in June 1941, when Roosevelt nominated him to the nation's highest court. Carter Glass, a conservative Virginian, moved to approve the nomination before it was even read, and the popular Byrnes was confirmed the same day.

But Byrnes did not enjoy his time at the court. When the president asked him to return to the political front, he immediately resigned from the bench and moved to an office in the White House, becoming one of the few people ever to serve in all three branches of the government. For Byrnes's new role in overseeing the nation's economy, the president conferred on him sweeping powers "relating to the control of civilian purchasing power, prices, rents, wages, salaries, profits, subsidies, and all related matters." Byrnes gave up his lifetime judicial appointment and took a pay cut of $5,000, but he also made himself a contender for a future Democratic nomination for president. Interior secretary Harold Ickes considered him "conservative, but not a reactionary" and thought the president viewed him as a possible successor. Members of Congress hailed his appointment. In an administration plagued with chronic fights over resources, Byrnes would have the final say over all other previous appointees, including Nelson and Henderson. "My duty," he said, "would be to hear the differences, resolve the conflicts and relieve the President of that determination." In time he became known as the nation's second-most powerful figure, the "assistant president." Some even called him "the vicar of the president."[6]

Although Byrnes was popular among his Senate colleagues and within the administration, African Americans worried about his southern background. Alfred Lewis Baker of the NAACP wrote to Roosevelt, "It is a question whether Justice Byrnes, who comes from the state of South Carolina where discrimination against Negroes is the usual practice of whites, and who originally opposed the Wage and Hour Law, might not use his broad powers to refuse to permit the War Labor Board to raise the wages of Negroes to the level of white workers doing the same work." Baker asked the president to issue an executive order to "make sure that Senator Byrnes' power is not used to prevent the equalization of the Negro."[7]

If anyone saw in Byrnes's selection the death of the New Deal and the birth of a new conservative tone from FDR, another section of the executive order showed that the president who had thundered against the "economic royalists" in 1936 was alive and well. FDR used the order to once again take up the cause of a maximum wage or "supertax" on incomes over $25,000. To address "gross inequities and to provide for greater equality in contributing to the war effort," the order authorized the OES director "to take the necessary action, and to issue the appropriate regulations, so that, in so far as practicable, no salary shall be authorized to the extent that it exceeds $25,000 after the payment of taxes allocable to the sum in excess of $25,000." The total income, one Treasury expert figured, actually amounted to a gross salary of $67,200, which left approximately $25,000 in after-tax income. Any money above this would be taxed fully. Roosevelt had ordered the IRS to find out how many taxpayers reported salaries over $67,000 in 1941 (the income equivalent in 2018 would be $3.4 million). The agency found that only 2,090 people reached that level, or .000015 percent of the population. While it affected very few taxpayers, the philosophy behind the supertax immediately brought to the surface some of the divisions that would dominate American politics for the next seven decades.

Roosevelt had first proposed a maximum wage six months earlier, but it was rejected by both the House Ways and Means Committee and the

Senate Finance Committee. That original plan would have limited all net income, including investment income, but Byrnes's controls could affect only salaries, bonuses, gifts, loans, and fees. While no one had calculated how much money the tax would actually generate for the Treasury, a previous estimate found that the new tax would yield about $180 million annually. Opponents such as Republican senator Arthur Vandenberg of Michigan calculated the yield would pay the federal government's war bill for a total of four days and ten hours. Senator Walter George, a Democrat from Georgia, said the tax would "work a terrific disadvantage on the fellow who is working for something as against the fellow who is just sitting and cutting coupons." George thought the tax would actually reduce revenue. In order to avoid the tax and pay executives high salaries, he speculated, corporations would begin to compensate their officers with stocks and other benefits. Moreover, the "night-club type of spender" who inherited his income would spend far more than someone who worked for a large salary. Although his $75,000 presidential salary was not covered in the executive order, Roosevelt instructed Secretary Morgenthau to adjust his salary to comply with the new order.[8]

While some found the "supertax" inherently unfair, others saw it as a way to enhance economic and racial equality. In a poll conducted in September, 70 percent of respondents agreed that high wages and salaries should be regulated by the federal government. Conductor Eva Jessye, an African American woman who had been selected by George Gershwin as the first musical director of *Porgy and Bess*, argued that the tax "should be of particular interest to the Negro people because it is directly tied to the problem of discrimination." Racial segregation, in her view, was "the child of the system that divides the country into rich and poor." Jessye claimed that by limiting incomes, the nation would be able to "win the struggle for a decent standard of living for all people" and "abolish race prejudice for all time."[9]

The *Wall Street Journal* was appalled at the idea of a supertax and viewed the administration's desire to confiscate all incomes above a certain level as "a device capable of being used to liquidate—economically, not physically—a group of citizens." If the tax were adopted, "no one should fool himself that it will stop with the small group who are the initial victims." When rich people canceled golf club memberships, for example, "the poor people working as caddies or gardeners would be hardest hit." The thinking behind the tax was part of the "demagogic philosophy that hitting people with large incomes would please the great mass who do not have large incomes." It was perhaps even "a bit of sadistic practice."[10]

How the provisions would actually be enforced "in so far as practicable" was difficult to say. Byrnes said that while the tax would impact fewer than three thousand taxpayers, "from the fury of the protests one would think it affected three million." In a nationwide radio address, he tried to reassure critics that he, too, opposed continuing the tax after the war, and that only Congress could sustain the tax afterward by legislation. "If a man fears Congress," he said, "he fears the people."[11]

The political drama that had occurred throughout the year and culminated in the Stabilization Act displayed how Congress was relegated to a secondary role in the country's governance. Treasury secretary Morgenthau provided a vivid indication of this status on October 5, just three days after Congress passed the anti-inflation bill. Morgenthau announced that the administration would be seeking newer taxes that would yield an additional $6 billion. Representative Robert L. Doughton, chair of the House Ways and Means Committee, called the new tax figures "astounding," and an indignant Senate Finance Committee chair, Walter George, protested that the American taxpayer could not possibly absorb any more increases. On the same day, the WPB reported that the nation was spending $227 million a day on the war. The labor force had grown to over 56 million workers, who earned an average of 85 cents an hour, up from 54 million and 75 cents per hour in August 1941. Morgenthau considered even higher taxes essential for other reasons than revenue. Higher taxes meant less disposable income for everyone and thus less consumer spending, which had the effects of keeping prices down, decreasing hoarding, and allowing rationed commodities to be more widely and fairly distributed. The Treasury Department claimed that higher taxes would also reduce the danger of a postwar inflation that could occur with the sudden spending of so much accumulated capital.[12]

Consumers received another tough bit of unwelcome news when rubber administrator William M. Jeffers announced that nationwide gasoline rationing would begin in November. It was not a popular decision. A confidential assessment by the Office of War Information remarked that "a majority of Americans throughout the great non-rationed areas of the country were not convinced of the necessity for this measure" and that the "lack of centralized authority for handling the problem has led to conflicting statements." The OWI urged that after the release of the Baruch committee report, "there should be a corollary information program aimed at selling and selling again the reasons why it is incumbent upon every car driver in every part of the land to recognize the intimate relationship between gasoline rationing and winning the war." Committee member and Harvard president James Conant understood that the U.S. would have to make up for lost time: "Our past sins are going to pursue us for some time."[13]

In the places where gasoline rationing was already in force, few items caused as much complaint. Many found the restrictions personally unsettling. Louise Ames of Massachusetts wrote to Harold Ickes that she had a special need for an exemption: "I am appealing for help in getting gas to visit my only daughter, a former teacher and beautiful girl who following a severe nervous breakdown has had to be placed in the Danvers State Hospital." Ames saw her daughter once a week, and these visits provided the only "cheer in her life." Calling herself a "loyal citizen" and a "sorrowing mother" who would not ask for "one gallon of gas for pleasure," Ames pleaded with Ickes for "any consideration." She received a cold reply from the chief of the Gasoline Rationing Division of the OPA: "Under section 1394.801 (b) (1) of the Gasoline Rationing Regulations, a special gasoline ration may not be granted for the purpose of visiting a patient in a mental hospital."[14]

Mrs. Jack Adams of Hawthorne, California, wrote to Eleanor Roosevelt: "I hope you will pardon my bothering you, but I don't know who else to write to who would bother with us." Claiming that she and her husband were "invalids," Adams said she depended on her car ("a Bantam Coupe") for her livelihood, which involved selling novelties and household items. Without more fuel, she told the First Lady, she would have to rely on "county relief, which means we will lose our little home which I've worked and struggled to buy, and in this state the county workers are most anxious to have the invalids go to the County Poor Farm, rather than give direct aid." Burdette Marvin from Riverside, California, wrote Bernard Baruch that the directives from Washington were "tensing the people's nerves." He hoped administration officials would stop acting in such a heavy-handed manner and understand that "power calls for consideration, sympathy," and "the human decencies in its exercise."[15]

The brewing irritation from so many motorists came just at the time when Republican candidates were exploiting widespread anger and frustration with the war agencies and Congress. Conservatives saw the OPA's growing power over prices and wages as indeed a violation of "human decencies" and worried that Roosevelt was using the war as an excuse to establish a command economy. W. G. Curtis, chair of the Insurance Economics Society of America, warned that the administration's economic politics were a direct assault on the Constitution: "When the government enters any field now run by private endeavor, it introduces socialism." Rather than interfere in the economy, Curtis hoped, the administration would focus exclusively on winning the war and not social reform—the same theme being pushed by candidates such as Clare Boothe Luce.

Other business leaders worried about the future of capitalism. Speaking before the National Association of Credit Men, Robert R. Mason, a member of the "postwar problems committee" of the National Association of Manufacturers, said that if the free enterprise system was not allowed to operate and create jobs, "then our economy will be socialized and we will all work for the government." On the other hand, Charles Watts, president of the Beneficial Industrial Loan Corporation, foresaw a business boom "such as the world has never known." Watts advised his colleagues not to be afraid of generously extending credit in the postwar era. "It is entirely possible," he told a meeting of bankers, "that men and women of the future will live by credit and upon credit." High wartime wages and the resulting high savings rate, he thought, were "the chief deterrent in the unlimited extension of credit."[16]

Some aspects of the new economy were as worrisome to workers as to the nation's business elite. In October, a dramatic moment arrived that underlined the challenges facing the labor movement. For millions of union members, the war had brought many challenges, including the no-strike pledge and the various price and wage ceilings. Additionally, some unions were bitterly divided by leadership struggles and fights over tactics. Few groups felt as alienated as coal miners, whose union head, John L. Lewis, had parted ways with FDR in 1940 and was engaged in a running feud with CIO president Philip Murray. On October 7, at their convention in Cincinnati, the United Mine Workers (UMW) voted to formally withdraw from the CIO. The miners charged that the CIO owed them over $1.6 million in loans and that Murray was trying to undermine Lewis and the miners' union. The miners saw a pattern emerging that would debilitate their union and their workforce. From 1935 to 1941, bituminous coal production had increased from 372 million tons a year to 514 million tons, yet because of mechanization, the number of miners working in the industry had actually declined. Like many others, the miners were frustrated with wage freezes, "unfair rationing," and other wartime controls. Attempts to merge major unions such as the American Federation of Labor and the CIO had failed earlier in the year, and the October 7 announcement only contributed to the increasing divisions with the labor movement as well as the UMW's decreasing economic and political clout.[17]

Autumn brought the annual harvest season, but the manpower shortages meant that some crops would never reach market. To fill the gap, the U.S. State Department asked the Mexican government to supply thousands of agricultural workers to cross the border to save crops in the Southwest. "These Mexican workers have crossed the border with great enthusiasm," commented Roosevelt. Farms from Virginia to Nebraska used German POWs to gather the harvest.[18]

On October 7, Roosevelt dealt with another issue that would have far-reaching implications. "This government," he noted, "is constantly receiving information concerning the barbaric crimes being committed by the enemy against civilian populations in occupied countries, particularly on the continent of Europe." He promised that when the war was successfully concluded, the "war criminals" responsible for the "organized murder of thousands of innocent persons" would face a "just and sure punishment." Acting Secretary of State Sumner Welles would not say whether Adolf Hitler himself would be tried for his crimes. At the end of the year, Roosevelt's acknowledgment of "thousands" of Holocaust victims would be a gross underestimate.[19]

"Barbaric crimes" were not limited to war zones. In late October, three more lynchings occurred in Mississippi. One involved fourteen-year-old Charlie Lang and fifteen-year-old Ernest Green, who according to local authorities had "confessed" to the attempted rape of a thirteen-year-old white girl. After their arrest, a white mob descended on the Quitman, Mississippi jail where the boys were being held, took them away, castrated them, and gouged out chunks of their flesh with pliers. Lang and Green were found hanging from a railroad bridge in Shubuta, Mississippi, that was known locally as the Hanging Bridge. A local white farmer told an undercover investigator that the structure was "not in use anymore as a bridge, we just keep it for stringing up niggers."[20]

Roy Wilkins, who later headed the NAACP, read the news from Mississippi and compared it to the call for Americans to serve abroad. "Why, indeed fight? For the Four Freedoms? For China? For Greece?" Wilkins concluded, "OK, but, hell, how about us?" His frustration was tempered by the reality that the nation had to fight and "our side has got to win," but he could not reconcile a nation fighting for freedom overseas with one that brutally tortured and murdered two teenagers. He wanted the nation to remember a haunting image: "Two kids, swinging from a bridge! Terror in the night. Dragged from jail. Two kids against a mob of grown men. Two nooses at midnight on a lonely country road near a stream. Dawn and the dangling bodies of two youngsters of fourteen swinging in the morning light."[21]

In another case, a forty-five-year-old man, Howard Wash, was taken from the county jail in Jones County, Mississippi, after he had been convicted of murdering his employer. The jury had failed to agree on an appropriate sentence. State law mandated that when a jury could not agree on whether to order the death penalty, the defendant was to receive a life sentence. The idea of Wash avoiding death was too much for many of the local whites to accept. A mob of one hundred armed men took Wash from the county jail early on the morning of October 17 and hanged him from a bridge over the Tallahoma Creek. Federal agents eventually arrested five men for Wash's murder, but an all-white jury acquitted them. During the trial, a lawyer for the defense declared: "We intend to have in the South white supremacy until Gabriel blows his horn."[22]

In response to the "reign of terror," the National Negro Council asked FDR to declare martial law in Mississippi. The *New York Times* editorialized that while Hitler's agents may not have been active in Mississippi, "Hitler's work is being done there." John H. Sengstacke, the general manager of the *Chicago Defender,* wrote to the president that the Mississippi lynchings were "a national calamity comparable to a disastrous rout on the battlefield. Negroes are incensed, shocked, and grieved that such a revolting act could be committed against children, regardless of race, by any group of citizens in this country." A. Philip Randolph wrote, "It appears that race prejudice and hate are beginning to ride the storm of mob violence and terror." He called the Mississippi lynchings "a threat to American democracy which the war now waged by the United Nations is professed to preserve." *Raleigh News and Observer* publisher Jonathan Daniels commented, "Sometimes it's easier to ask people to give their lives than to give up their prejudices."[23]

Another lynching occurred in October, but few knew about it until the summer of 1943. A thirty-three-year-old African American soldier, Private James E. Person, who had been honorably discharged by the army, was traveling through Vigo County, Indiana, on October 12, 1942. According to Attorney General Francis Biddle, Person was "peacefully making his way" through the county and had committed no crime, and no warrants had been issued for him. Yet after Vigo County sheriff John Trierweiler's office received reports of a man begging for food, he, along with three deputies and at least nine other men, picked up Person, killed him, and took his body into Illinois. In November it was discovered in Edgar County, Illinois, where the coroner ruled that Person had died of "exposure after numerous gunshots." Biddle charged the men with violating Person's civil rights. In 1946, a jury acquitted the sheriff and his deputies but found the nine others guilty of civil rights violations. For the murder of James Person, they each paid a fine of $200.[24]

On October 20, at a remarkable meeting in Durham, North Carolina, fifty-seven African American leaders led by P. B. Young and Gordon Blaine Hancock discussed the situation facing blacks in the wartime South. The gathering produced a report that came to be known as the Durham Manifesto. "In an hour of national peril," the document read, "efforts are being made to defeat the Negro first and the Axis powers later." While declaring themselves "fundamentally opposed to the principle of compulsory segregation," the authors steered clear of calling for "social equality." Instead, they advocated a variety of reforms, such as voting rights, the elimination of the poll tax, a federal anti-lynching law, an end to all-white juries, and the inclusion of domestic service and farm workers in Social Security benefits. Though quickly dismissed, the document laid the foundation for a variety of civil rights programs that would begin after the war. "The correction of these problems," the manifesto read, "is not only a moral matter, but a practical necessity in winning the war." An example of the discrimination faced by African Americans was on display two days later, when the Undergraduate Council of Princeton University voted against a motion to allow African Americans into the undergraduate college. The student newspaper editorialized that "Princeton continues its principles of white supremacy and, in an institution devoted to the free pursuit of truth, implicitly perpetuates a racial theory more characteristic of our enemies."[25]

Attorney General Biddle used the occasion of Columbus Day to announce that the federal government was lifting the "enemy alien" stigma from the nearly 700,000 Italian Americans who had not yet obtained American citizenship. Biddle claimed that since Pearl Harbor, only 228 Italian Americans had been interned in camps on the West Coast, not mentioning that over 10,000 had actually been removed from their homes and forced to restrictive zones fifty miles inland, and over a half million were under humiliating curfews. Sociologist Constantine Panunzio was convinced that Italian Americans were no threats: "Now that the test of war has come, there is no question as to where almost one hundred percent of our Italian immigrant population stands." The timing of the announcement may have also had to do with the upcoming elections. One Republican congressman had boasted that Italians in America "will all be Republicans . . . when they find out what is going on." Roosevelt, who had said that he was not so much concerned with the threat of Italian Americans ("They are a lot of opera singers"), approved of Biddle's announcement, calling it "a masterly stroke of international statesmanship and good politics."[26]

By October, the implications of "total war" were affecting almost every American. In just one year, war production employment increased by

54 percent, and 5 million citizens had joined the armed forces. Twelve percent of all American men aged eighteen to sixty-four were in the military, and 61 percent of men and 11 percent of women worked in some form of war industry. Over 60 percent of the American working population had been "mobilized" in one form or another, while countless children collected scrap steel or rubber, and other citizens bought war bonds or watched the skies for enemy bombers.[27]

As General Eisenhower planned the Torch invasion for early November, the Axis forces in Europe seemed as strong as ever. Author Jay Winik writes that Hitler "commanded more of Europe than any leader since Napoleon."[28] Not only did Stalin continue to plead for a second front in western Europe to relieve the pressure on his troops, the American public demanded some offensive action that could turn the tide of war. Every day brought the chance that German forces might break through at Stalingrad, with grave consequences for the United States and Great Britain. For those needing some form of escapism that brought military victory, they could see Errol Flynn and Ronald Reagan in *Desperate Journey*, a film (said its advertisement) about "five commandoes who asked no quarter and gave none," who would "blast their way to Berlin and back." For exotic locales, they could see the film adaptation of W. Somerset Maugham's *The Moon and Sixpence* starring George Sanders. The film's ad claimed that "Women are Strange Little Beasts," elaborating: "You can treat them like dogs (he did!), beat them till your arm aches (he did!) and they still love you (they did!)." Those wanting a complete escape from the war could enjoy a breezy new Fred Astaire and Rita Hayworth movie, *You Were Never Lovelier*.

On October 20, a goal that Roosevelt, Morgenthau, and Congress had worked toward all year came to a climax when Congress approved the largest tax bill in American history. The Senate passed the Revenue Act on a voice vote "that sounded unanimous," according to the *New York Times,* and the bill then passed the House with only two dissenting votes (by Republicans John Hinshaw of California and John M. Robsion of Kentucky). The final bill contained 181 sections and weighed over nine pounds. The act brought millions of new taxpayers onto the rolls and made more changes from the tax tables laid out by Morgenthau earlier in the year. In 1939, approximately 4 million people had paid federal income taxes; after the 1942 legislation, that figure was 27 million. On top of the basic income tax, a "victory tax" levied another 5 percent on all incomes above $624. This was expected to affect 90 percent of all workers, or approximately 46 million people. One part of the bill specified that taxpayers were no longer required to have their returns sworn before a notary. Said one Treasury official, after adding up what they owed, Americans would do enough swearing on their own.[29]

The new tax law lowered personal exemptions, resulting in a rate of 19 percent on the first dollar a person earned, then rising as income increased. Corporate taxes were raised from 31 to 40 percent, and excess profits were taxed at 90 percent. Deductions were included for alimony but not for charitable gifts. Representative John McCormack of Massachusetts said that high-income earners would lament not having been born thirty years earlier, "for what the Lord giveth, the government in this period of war taxation promptly proceeds to take away." The top tax bracket, which had been raised from 25 percent to 81 percent since World War I, was increased to 88 percent. The general feeling was expressed by a *New Yorker* cartoon in which a man robs another man at gunpoint. "I wouldn't feel too bad about this, Mac," says the gunman. "It all goes to the government eventually anyhow."[30]

Despite the lower exemptions, the new brackets displayed the progressive quality of taxation during World War II and would persist with only minor changes for the next two generations. A single taxpayer earning $1,500 would have a new tax bill of $220, a rate of 14.6 percent. A married couple with no dependents at the same income level paid just over 5 percent, and if they had two dependents, they would pay less than 2 percent. At an income of $5,000, the rates increased to 22, 17, and 14 percent in the three categories. A single person earning $10,000 still paid just 27 percent in income taxes. The passage of such a mammoth tax bill just two weeks before the election was not the timing the administration or nervous legislators had hoped for, and the $7 to $8 billion in proposed new revenue was still a fraction of the war's total cost.

One aspect of the Revenue Bill would have lasting effects on the way Americans viewed payday and taxes. Since 1913, Americans had waited

Table 2. Federal income tax rates approved by Congress, October 1942

Income ($)	Single (no dependents)			Married (no dependents)			Married (2 dependents)		
	Tax	Victory tax	Total	Tax	Victory tax	Total	Tax	Victory Tax	Total
500	0	0	0	0	0	0	0	0	0
600	15	2	17	0	1	1	0	1	1
1,000	89	18	107	0	15	15	0	14	14
1,500	181	39	220	48	31	79	0	29	29
2,000	273	60	333	140	48	188	13	45	58
3,000	472	102	574	324	81	405	191	76	267
5,000	920	185	1,105	746	148	894	592	138	730
10,000	2,390	393	2,783	2,152	315	2,467	1,914	294	2,208
20,000	6,816	810	7,626	6,452	648	7,100	6,088	605	6,693
50,000	25,811	2,247	28,058	25,328	1,747	27,075	24,845	1,547	26,392
100,000	64,641	5,024	69,665	64,060	4,524	68,584	63,479	4,324	67,803
500,000	414,616	27,247	441,863	414,000	26,747	440,747	413,384	26,547	439,931
1,000,000	854,616	44,884	899,500	854,000	45,000	899,000	853,384	45,413	898,[797]

Source: New York Times, October 21, 1942.

until early in the next year to pay their taxes for a given year. The income citizens earned in, say, 1939 would be totaled and they would "settle up" with the government in early 1940. The Revenue Act doubled the burdens on taxpayers in 1943, because they would have to pay their 1942 taxes at the same time that their employers were deducting their 1943 taxes from their paychecks. A nation at war needed a completely new way of paying taxes.

The idea of tax withholding came from Beardsley Ruml, the director of the New York Federal Reserve Bank and the treasurer of Macy's, who called it "Pay As You Go." A system of payroll deductions, in Ruml's estimation, gave "relief to the taxpayer and yet does not embarrass the revenues." The benefits were obvious: the government would not have to wait months for the revenue, and with less cash in their pockets, consumer spending would add less inflationary pressure. Ruml had originally proposed giving taxpayers a one-time pass on their 1942 taxes, but Randolph Paul, general counsel to the Treasury Department, called this forgiveness policy a "giveaway" to the wealthy. President Roosevelt agreed with Paul: he was not inclined to forgive the highest wage earners part of their tax debts while others were giving their lives abroad. A congressional compromise was a one-time forgiveness in early 1943 of 1942 taxes below $50 and on 75 percent of bills higher than $50. Modern wage earners can thank Ruml for the deductions they see in their pay stubs, and for being free from what he termed the "vicious practice of paying out of one year's income a tax on the year that had gone." Ironically, another Treasury Department economist who helped design the withholding tax plan was Milton Friedman, a future Nobel laureate who became a hero to libertarians for his opposition to Keynesian economics and government intrusion.[31]

The reaction to the new tax law was swift. The *Wall Street Journal* condemned it as "inadequate in the total amount of revenue it would raise" and criticized the notion that "a few—rich individuals and rich corporations—could by themselves pay for this war." The administration and Congress, according to the paper, ignored the fact that most Americans understood "that they must pay and pay and pay, and are ready to do so." Basil Brewer, publisher of the *New Bedford (Mass.) Standard-Times,* called the law "dishonest and disastrous" and a "hydra-headed monster" that "impinges on initiative and the freedoms for which we fight this war." Brewer saw the bill's underlying motive as "class warfare and not war revenue." A fairer way to pay for the war, he thought, would be a federal sales tax. Taxing "the big union war chests" would also bring in more revenue.[32]

If new taxes, price and wage freezes, and gas rationing did not sufficiently test the American consumer's patience, an OPA announcement on October 26 may have been the final straw. Starting on November 28, citizens over fifteen years old would be allowed a ration of one pound of coffee every five weeks, which equaled approximately one cup per day. In anticipation of an outcry, Henderson urged Americans not to "run to the corner grocer, put the 'squeeze' on him to help a hoarder." To make matters worse, the OPA added there was little possibility of finding substitutes. Black tea consumption had been cut to 50 percent of its 1941 usage, and green tea was virtually unobtainable. Robert F. Whitney of the *New York Times* complained that the OPA's announcements came "in a series of waves like those measured by a seismograph."[33]

The uproar over coffee did not prevent Henderson from continuing to direct the economy's tiniest details. In late October, he announced he would soon establish price ceilings for rates charged in pool halls and bowling alleys. He published articles in magazines and gave numerous speeches about the urgent need for price and wage controls, and he never minced words: "The world we live in today is grim and bloody," and "it will grow grimmer and more bloody." He likened inflation to "a disease that must be fought with bitter, ill-tasting medicines," or else the result could prove "fatal" to the nation.[34]

By the autumn of 1942, many Americans had grown tired of Henderson's edicts as well as his exhortations. In October, agriculture commissioners from twenty-eight states came to Washington demanding Henderson's "impeachment." Within the administration, his star was beginning to fade. "More and more people are saying Henderson is an active candidate for president," said Harold Ickes, while noting that recent *Life* photos showing Henderson in shorts "were pretty gross." As for Henderson's public posturing, "I don't happen to believe that people like their public officials to be totally lacking in dignity and self-restraint." When Henderson gave a speech at Hunter College in New York City, a student asked him if people's fundamental freedoms would be gutted by the war, leading to a dictatorship. "Not at all," Henderson casually replied. "You need never worry about me interfering with the four freedoms if you people buckle down and beat Hitler. . . . This thing we call government, if it really is a democracy, is not apart from yourself. It is an instrumentality for getting things done that you want done." Then he added, in a line that did little to calm nerves, "If you are scared of government, you will be scared of the post-war period."[35]

The increasing pressure on Henderson had predictable outcomes. He grew petulant and irritable in meetings. The arrogant and inflexible General Somervell, who continued to dispute the projections of economists and government officials over procurement and production levels, became a particular target. At one meeting, in a tirade that one observer described as "the most violent personal attack ever heard in a meeting of the War Production Board," Henderson openly accused Somervell of padding requirement figures and not understanding the consequences of unreachable goals. An enraged Somervell sat silently as others in the room squirmed.[36]

Adding to the administration's stress were the agonizing wait for Torch and the continuing struggles in the Pacific. Despite the victory at Midway, the Japanese Navy was still a formidable enemy, and in the battle of Santa Cruz Islands in late October, Japanese torpedoes sank the American carrier *Hornet*, the ship from which Jimmy Doolittle had launched his raid on Tokyo six months earlier. The loss of the *Hornet* left the damaged *Enterprise* as the only American carrier in the Pacific, while the Japanese had eight. The crew of the *Enterprise* posted a sign on the ship's deck that expressed their pride but also their vulnerability: "Enterprise vs. Japan."[37]

The president's public statements notwithstanding, it was clear the nation would not meet the ambitious production goals he had set in January. In an October 29 memo to Donald Nelson, Roosevelt expressed his frustration with the pace of production. After Nelson reduced the targets for 1943 from 125,000 planes to 107,000, the president wrote: "For the sake of the record, I want to make it clear that the above figure was the figure which you and the Army and Navy agreed could be produced within the calendar year 1943." In case this did not effectively convey his displeasure with Nelson and the military, the president ended the memo: "It is really essential that in one way or another this program be carried out in toto." But even though the president's lofty goals were out of reach, there was no question that the nation was undergoing an epic transformation. In 1938, the American economy produced 1 percent of the world's armaments. In 1942 it produced 35 percent and was expected to reach 50 percent in 1943. The United States now accounted for a quarter of the entire world's real national income, and it would soon be producing more armaments than the rest of the world's economies combined.[38]

In the final days of her campaign for a congressional seat, Clare Boothe Luce proved she was not easy to categorize. She had no voting record to criticize, and journalist Dorothy Thompson, whom *Time* described as the "second most popular and influential woman in the country behind Eleanor Roosevelt" endorsed Luce, calling her a "modern" politician who had broken with "Toryism and nineteenth century concepts." When Luce appeared at a campaign event with the Daughters of the American Revolution, she was asked whether she supported the idea of limiting incomes to

$25,000. She replied: "I say here, unequivocally, in the sight of the good Lord and you patriotic ladies, that if it is necessary that they should pass a tax and legislation which would cut down my income and the income of my fellow citizens not only to $25,000, but to $20,000, or $10,000, or $5,000, or even $2,000, I wish they would do it and do it quickly, so we can get on with the war." Yet in an address to Catholic clergymen, she turned vitriolic when asked about her suspicions of the Roosevelt administration: "Too many economists and sociologists employed by the present administration have a distinct dedication to Marxist principles. I shall resist to the last spark of life this mad, undercover drive to transform our nation into soul-crushing collectivism."[39]

Luce learned quickly on the stump. To illustrate the administration's waste and corruption, she liked to tell her audiences that the WPA had spent $100,000 on "bull fiddles" in West Virginia. "Nero had only one fiddle while Rome burned." After several repetitions, the "bull fiddle" spending had grown to over $400,000. When she went to one high school auditorium and found too many empty seats, she grew angry over the apathy she saw throughout the district. "If you had seen soldiers without guns, as I have in the Philippines," she claimed, "you would be mad, too!" In another speech, when a drunken heckler refused to be silent, she told the crowd, "See how generous the Republican Party is? We provide speakers for both ends of the hall."[40]

Her campaign drew support from well beyond the Fourth District. In addition to nearly $2,000 given by her husband, she received a $500 donation from Hollywood film producer David O. Selznick and $750 from tobacco heiress Doris Duke. And although African Americans composed just 2.4 percent of the population of Fairfield County, Luce went to a "colored rally" in Bridgeport where she noted how blacks usually received the worst defense jobs and said she favored "equal pay for equal work." John E. Pringle, a black voter in Fairfield County, vowed to support her because she "has upheld the torch of Lincoln." Luce urged African Americans to vote for the party that "had done the most for them."

She experienced a dismaying visit to the Bridgeport Brass Company. Four workers told her that the nation should "kill all the Jews and we won't have any more wars." Another way to end all wars, they thought, was if all the money were taken from the rich and given to the poor. "I tried to reason with them," she said, reminding them that "Jews bled like Christians," but the workers "would have none of it."[41]

Luce and many other Republicans did not have to say much. Voters were not in good spirits, and the administration and Congress had given them little to feel good about. The year had seen an unending series of bureaucratic restrictions, taxes, pay freezes, and little progress on the war front. Despite unprecedented production of planes and tanks, the president's ambitious goals would not be reached. The previous midterm election had not gone well for Democrats. In 1938, they had lost seventy-two House seats and seven in the Senate. In 1940, although FDR had won a third term in the White House, his party gained only seven seats in the House and actually lost three more in the Senate. LBJ biographer Robert Caro argues that Democrats could very likely have lost their House majority in 1940 had it not been for Representative Lyndon Johnson funneling Texas oil money to selected Democrats throughout the nation.[42] Democrats maintained working majorities in both houses, but they were nowhere near the level the president enjoyed when he first took office in 1933.

The president himself had grown tired of Luce's demands for a "hard war" and tried to persuade congressional allies to enter into the *Congressional Record* a satirical poem he had read about Luce by lyricist Howard Dietz, who was MGM's vice president of publicity. Part of it read:

O lovely Luce—o lovely Clare
Do you remember—way back there
Holding your lacquered nails aloft
"The war we fight," you said, "is soft."

No one took up the president's request, but it displayed his growing frustration with Luce and the other GOP candidates for exploiting the public dissatisfaction with the war and the lack of a major ground offensive against the enemy.[43]

In the last weeks leading up to the election, *Newsweek* magazine polled fifty political correspondents for their election forecasts. Most expected slight to moderate Republican gains in both houses, the average being a net GOP gain of twenty-nine seats in the House and five in the Senate, leaving

Democrats in firm control of both houses. One correspondent boldly predicted a Republican gain of forty-nine House seats while another went the
other way, predicting the GOP would actually lose three seats.[44]

Behind the various predictions was a brewing anger among voters, who
were increasingly disenchanted with the administration and the Democrats. G. E. Stearnes of Buffalo wrote, "In running this country during the
past years, this administration has shown more inane experimentation,
more extravagant blunders, than any other." Consequently, many had "lost
faith in this administration." Another sign that the Democrats faced an
uphill battle came from a poll indicating that 52 percent of Americans felt
"President Roosevelt should be a tougher boss in dealing with the heads of
government departments concerned with the war." What the respondents
did not know, of course, was that the invasion of North Africa was almost
ready to commence and that the long-awaited ground assault against Hitler's troops would finally begin. But news of the invasion would not arrive
until after the election. When voters went to the polls on Tuesday, November 3, heroic images of Allied troops storming beachheads would not be on
their minds. Rather, they were thinking about higher taxes, gas rationing,
coffee restrictions, and the army's inability to take the battle to the Germans after having been at war for almost eleven months.[45]

For the millions of Americans who had been drafted or volunteered for
military service, the fall of 1942 was a difficult time. They were in the process of leaving their homes and families, and reporting for basic training,
where they would be taught to wage battle against the German Wehrmacht,
the Royal Italian Army, and the Imperial Japanese forces. On October 23,
my father, Alexander Brown Campbell, reported for duty at Fort Benjamin
Harrison in Indianapolis. He was twenty-one years old, which made him
prime material for the draft. The draft board in Boyle County, Kentucky,
concluded that neither his lack of a high school diploma nor his small
frame (he was listed at five feet six and 121 pounds) would prevent him
from serving for the "duration of the War and other emergency, plus six
months," subject to "the discretion of the President."[46] On the rare occasions he later spoke about the war years, which was usually while watching
a John Wayne movie, he made it clear he never had any intention of being

a "hero." He simply hoped to survive. Like millions of other young Americans—but unlike John Wayne—he answered his neighbors' and the president's call to defend the nation against its seasoned and deadly adversaries. The unspoken anxiety that had gripped the country since Pearl Harbor weighed heavily on countless young Americans like my father. Where he would go and what he would experience after his training in Indiana was as unknown and frightening as the fate of the nation itself.

November: Second Fronts

ON SUNDAY, NOVEMBER I, READERS OPENING the morning papers learned of the chilling details of a Japanese attack in September on American Marines in the Solomon Islands. One Marine spoke of a night of relentless assaults by enemy troops against a fortified machine-gun nest manned by twenty-five-year-old Sergeant Keith Perkins of Knott County, Kentucky. As he fired his weapon, Perkins yelled, "This is the way to fight a war!" Moments later, a Japanese grenade landed in his lap, killing him. Seeing the ferocity of the enemy up close, one American soldier commented, "Those Japs have got more guts than I have."

In New York City, the Sunday *Times* reported on Navy secretary Frank Knox awarding the Distinguished Service Medal to Rear Admiral John Mc-Cain for "exceptionally meritorious services" in the South Pacific. Representative Melvin J. Mass of Minnesota, a Marine Corps colonel who had recently returned from the Pacific, told an Armistice Day rally in Richmond, Virginia, that despite what the public might have heard about "victories" over the Japanese, the U.S. was losing the war in the Pacific.

Since citizens were told to keep their indoor temperatures at sixty-five degrees to conserve fuel, New York City department stores held Election Day sales on furs. Some draft boards that could not fill their quotas began taking married men with no children. Presidential aide Harry Hopkins gave a speech in which he described a "dire, dismal future for the U. S." In Chicago, police were called to restore order at a grocery store when the coffee truck arrived. The *Chicago Tribune* reported that "housewives fought like a football team trailing in the fourth quarter" for the precious beans. Those attending morning services at North Presbyterian Church in New York City heard the Rev. Paul Floyd Jones's sermon, "The Christian Voter," and at the First Baptist Church on Broadway, the Rev. Arthur Franklin Williams preached "The Ministry of Christ to the Jew."[1] So began a week that would transform American politics at home and the war in Europe.

In two previous congressional elections during wartime, 1862 and 1918, the parties opposing the president had scored major gains. In 1862, many Americans in the states still in the Union were frustrated with the course of the war, the economy, and President Lincoln's management of both. Like their descendants in 1942, they debated whether soldiers should be allowed to vote away from home. Lincoln's Republican Party bore the brunt of the widespread frustration, and Democrats won twenty-eight House seats.[2] Fifty-six years later, as Democrat Woodrow Wilson led the nation in World War I after having campaigned for reelection on the slogan "He Kept Us Out of War," Republicans won five Senate seats and twenty-five House seats to take control of both houses of Congress. Wilson's grand vision of American leadership in a postwar League of Nations changed dramatically with his opponents in charge of Capitol Hill. Those contests haunted Franklin Roosevelt and his loyalists in November 1942.

Democrats had to face discouraged constituents who were weary of gas and food rationing, price ceilings, wage freezes, and higher taxes. Voters were frustrated because unelected bureaucrats were determining the tiniest details of their lives, and because elected officials had started the year with the disastrous pension bill and then stalled the anti-inflation bill until the president threatened to assume new powers if he didn't get some action. Voters would also go to the polls disappointed over the lack of U.S. ground forces to engage the enemy in Europe.

Despite conspiracy theories warning that Roosevelt might cancel the elections, the contest proceeded as in peacetime. Experts predicted that the GOP would score some gains but leave the Democrats in firm control of Congress. A Gallup poll taken on the eve of the election showed that Americans favored Democrats 52 to 48 percent; Gallup concluded that the GOP "has failed to convince the majority of the public that the war effort would proceed faster if the Republicans had more power in Washington." The *New York Times* predicted Republicans would add three to six seats in the Senate and perhaps as many as thirty in the House of Representatives. The anti-Roosevelt *Chicago Tribune* forecast a Republican gain of five to ten Senate seats and forty in the House. More than anything else, the polls indicated that turnout would be light given the number of voters who had moved in the last few months and had not changed their registration, and of course the induction of 5 million men into the military (of whom less than 2 percent were considered likely to vote).[3]

One race that drew wide attention was the campaign for New York governor, an office once held by FDR and occupied by Democrat Herbert Lehman ever since Roosevelt resigned in 1933 to assume the presidency. The race came down to Democratic attorney general John J. Bennett against New York county district attorney Thomas E. Dewey. If Dewey could wrest control of the coveted governorship from the Democrats, some observers thought he would become the front-runner for the Republican presidential nomination in 1944. Arthur Krock wrote that a Dewey victory would "be viewed as the emergence of popular dissatisfaction with the present conduct of the war" and a "setback to those who intend to urge the Democratic Party to nominate the president for a fourth term."

Battling a cold and "admittedly tired from the campaign pace she has set," Clare Boothe Luce spent the last days before the election giving radio speeches and appearing before voters in Stamford and Norwalk. She said in her final appearance, "There has never been so shocking and tragic a contest as the heroism of the men on the battlefronts, and the cowardice of so many politicians on the home front." Luce said she felt confident of victory. So did her opponent, LeRoy Downs, who spent the final hours of the campaign appealing to the "wives, mothers, and sweethearts" of servicemen, often highlighting his own experiences in World War I. When one supporter told Luce not to feel "too badly" if she lost, she replied that if she did lose, "Praise the Lord and pass the cyanide."[4]

On election night, November 3, Democrats across the nation were stunned by the results. Republicans picked up forty-three seats in the House and nine in the Senate, the greatest gain by an opposition party in midterm elections since 1918. The results, according to the *New York Times,* "surprised even [the GOP's] own chieftains and prophets." Krock saw the result as a clear referendum on Roosevelt's management of the war: "Republican candidates in general were critical of the president's administration for the clearly demonstrated delays in preparation, failures, errors and compromises in performance, group favoritisms, partisan political approaches, and tolerated incompetence." Republican candidates who campaigned on a "strong war" platform found receptive audiences, and of thirty-four House Democrats who voted for the price-control bill, twenty-eight were defeated. Republicans also won two high-profile gubernatorial races: Thomas Dewey easily won in New York, with a 590,000-vote majority, and Earl Warren, the California attorney general who had overseen the establishment of the Japanese American internment camps, won his state with 57 percent of the vote. Throughout his campaign, Warren had vowed to keep California's public schools open regardless of wartime budget cuts. "A people without the education that will give them a knowledge of the world in which they live," he said, "cannot function efficiently as citizens." Six years later, Dewey and Warren became the GOP presidential ticket. Perhaps most humiliating to the president was the victory by isolationist Republican representative Hamilton Fish in Roosevelt's home congressional district.[5]

In Connecticut, Clare Boothe Luce won with 46.2 percent of the vote, while LeRoy Downs managed just 41.9 percent. Socialist David Mansell won over 11 percent, likely taking most of his votes from Downs. Following a nationwide pattern, Luce's 63,719 votes were far behind the 91,192 Downs had received in defeating Austin two years earlier. Luce was one of six Republican women running for Congress (five won). Despite the low turnout, she interpreted her victory in the widest way: "This election proves how the American people want to fight this war." Her supporter Robert McCormick wrote her, "If it had not been for the courage and energy of you and the other Republican candidates in this election, it would have gone by default, and with it our form of government."[6]

In the Senate, a 65–29 Democratic majority shrank to 57–38, and in the House, a 267–165 spread became 222–209. The Democrats held their slimmest majority since Roosevelt took office in 1933, and Republicans needed to sway just seven Democrats in the House to defeat any administration measure. The power of the Democrats' reactionary southern bloc increased accordingly. Martin Dies and John Rankin were reelected to their House seats without opposition. Among the newly elected senators was Mississippi's James O. Eastland, who over the next thirty years would become one of the leading opponents of civil rights. Eastland was one of eight southern Democrats in the Senate who won their seats without Republican opposition. Progressive New Dealers like Republican George Norris of Nebraska and Prentiss Brown of Michigan, on the other hand, were defeated. Norris, one of the New Deal's most loyal allies and a driving force behind the Tennessee Valley Authority, said before the election that if he lost, he would consider it a "repudiation of forty years of service." On election night, teary-eyed, he asked, "Why should people be so mad at me?" *Newsweek* interpreted the overall results as "the revolt of the middle classes, including the farmers, against the New Deal." The *Wall Street Journal*'s editors wrote that "the voters of any successful democratic or republican form of government possess the instinct, if not the actual knowledge, that the continued success of that government depends on the change and progress which can only come from an infusion of new blood." The frustratingly slow pace of the war effort, they added, played a part in the results—"People in war are not patient people." The voter turnout, 33.9 percent, had been the lowest for a congressional race since 1926, and has remained the lowest ever since.[7]

Despite the low turnout, the results were interpreted in sweeping terms. The anti-Roosevelt *Chicago Daily Tribune* concluded that "the long night has ended and from millions of hearts a prayer of Thanksgiving has arisen. . . . The people of this land have turned back the most terrible threat which has confronted them in their national history"—by which the paper meant not Hitler but the New Dealers. In the *Nation*, Robert Bandiner called it the "Dunderhead Election." "Taken as a whole," he wrote, "the election showed the same shortsightedness throughout the county, the same preoccupation with the petty, the local, and the immediate" that accounted for the country's "failure to rise to the greatness of the times." Vice President Henry Wallace, however, was not wholly disappointed. Considering the millions who were serving overseas or had moved to take war jobs and did not cast a vote, Wallace interpreted the election as "a miracle and a godsend" because Democrats retained majorities in both houses. He believed the results ultimately proved the enduring popularity of President Roosevelt and the New Deal. Krock responded that "this fantastic flight into the stellar spaces of nonlogic must quickly come to ground," and that the election was in fact "a protest by the civilian population." House Democrat Hatton Sumners of Texas saw a meaning that reached the heavens: "God Almighty has intended that people shall be free to run their own business and be the masters of their own government. In the goodness of God Almighty, He has put somewhere in the nature of people a sort of instinct, that seems to warn them when they are in danger of losing their ability to govern, to get down and stand on their own feet, and exercise their capacity to govern before they lose it by its nonuse. That is what happened in America."[8]

Time magazine was blunt in its appraisal: "No man can say, even in the retrospect of history, exactly when one political movement dies and another is born. But anyone who looked last week could see that Franklin Roosevelt's New Deal was sick, with ailments that could not lightly be thrown off. Democratic leaders privately admitted that great blocks of labor, farm and independent votes—once the keystone of the peculiar New Deal alliance—had gone Republican." The GOP's success in twenty-three states with a combined total of 321 electoral votes spelled disaster for FDR and the Democrats in the 1944 presidential election. It would be tough, the magazine suggested, for Democrats to retain the White House, but Supreme Court justice William O. Douglas "may be the man to bring off the final cure." In a Gallup poll only 38 percent of respondents said they would vote for FDR in 1944 if he ran for a fourth term.[9]

Democratic National Committee secretary Edwin Pauley concluded that one person was to blame for the party's poor showing. Among voters, he told Roosevelt, "the most universal and serious complaint of all" concerned Leon Henderson, whose "attitude and methods" came under fire from people in every region of the country. He was widely criticized for saying that the troops in North Africa must be supplied with petroleum even if it meant people in New England would get pneumonia. "It was a brutal way to put it," said Harold Ickes. Looking at the options, Pauley counseled the president that the situation with Henderson was "correctible," meaning that Henderson's days in the administration were numbered. A few weeks later, former DNC chair and Postmaster General James A. Farley offered a simple explanation for the election results: "The American people just got a little tired of being pushed around." Roosevelt had little comment other than "I assume that the Congress of the United States is in favor of winning the war, just as the President is."[10]

While partisans interpreted the results to fit their own narratives, a more reserved interpretation came from E. E. McClain, a high school principal in Miami, Arizona, who claimed that the results came down to the fact that "the people were disgusted with Congress and they know but one way to express themselves and that is by voting against its members." He cautioned against seeing the results as "a rebuke for the New Deal, the management of the war, or approving Republican policies as such." Instead, the best way to "be sure of the will of the people is to have an election in which the issues are defined beforehand in terms of the whole nation. That will come in 1944."[11]

The election also had more immediate consequences. The chairs of five Senate and House committees called for legislation to create a single agency with power over all nonmilitary economic and manpower issues. This new agency, the Office of War Mobilization (OWM), would absorb the many agencies now competing with each other, including the WPB and the OES. Claude Pepper of Florida, chair of the Senate Education and Labor Committee, said he hoped the legislation would be ready before the first anniversary of Pearl Harbor. The committee chairs said the proposal was a response to voters' frustration with Congress and the administration. "The people," said Pepper, "have expressed dissatisfaction with loose organization."[12]

A poll taken by the Princeton University Office of Public Opinion examined how voters in the election had interpreted a number of issues. Most partisans voted for their party, seeing it as the one that would best advance their own economic situation. Sixty-seven percent of Democrats approved of Roosevelt's handling of the war, while only 35 percent of Republicans approved. The most striking difference came on the issue of race. When asked if they agreed with the assertion "Negroes are getting all the opportunities they deserve," 90 percent of those who answered yes voted for Democrats; when asked if they thought "Negroes are not being treated fairly," 53 percent of those who agreed voted Republican. In all, the poll suggested that the primary reason the GOP won was simply that more Republicans went to the polls, perhaps because they were more interested in the election than Democrats. Although the Soldier Voting Act of 1942, passed in September, allowed soldiers to vote by absentee ballot, the law came too late to make a difference that year. Only twenty-eight thousand soldiers, less than 1 percent of those overseas, voted in 1942. In addition to the millions of Africans Americans who were disenfranchised, millions of others who had joined the armed services or had moved to take a defense job were left out of the election. Throughout the year, polls showed that a majority of Americans wanted universal health care and federal job programs after the war, and the president's plans for limiting incomes remained popular. Those issues, however, would be soon forgotten, and for the rest of the war and afterward, the election would be seen as proof of a new conservatism. American electoral history has often demonstrated that there is little correlation between the policies Americans want and the politicians they put in office.[13]

For Americans, the war had begun on a Sunday morning with the attack on Pearl Harbor eleven months earlier. Now, on Sunday, November 8, another major attack occurred, but this time Americans were uplifted by the news. Some seventy-three thousand Allied troops (including sixty-three thousand Americans) in over seven hundred ships and a thousand aircraft, led by Generals George Patton, Lloyd Fredendall, and Charles Ryder, landed in North Africa and soon took Algeria and French Morocco. While the 1944 D-Day invasion of France is well known as the largest amphibious assault in history, the 1942 Torch invasion of Algiers, Oran, and Casablanca was the largest assault the U.S. had undertaken in forty-five years. According to author Rick Atkinson, some "believed it to be the greatest amphibious gamble since Xerxes crossed the Hellespoint in the fifth century B.C." In announcing the offensive, the White House said, "In order to forestall an invasion of Africa by Germany and Italy, which if successful, would constitute a direct threat to America across the comparatively narrow sea from Western Africa, a powerful American force equipped with adequate weapons of modern warfare and under American Command is today landing on the Mediterranean and Atlantic Coasts of the French Colonies in Africa."[14]

Yet Eisenhower's carefully planned invasion was not the offensive action many had expected when the nation entered the war. At first, rather than engaging directly with German troops, Americans found themselves under fire from French forces led by Marshal Philippe Pétain. Eisenhower, searching for a French collaborationist leader who would cooperate with him, settled on Admiral Jean Darlan, a Nazi sympathizer, who agreed on November 10 to the cease-fire in exchange for the Allies' recognizing him as the high commissioner of French North Africa. The agreement was met with outrage in the United States. What were Americans fighting for, many asked, if they made deals with men like Darlan? When Allied forces did engage German troops, the results were also disappointing. German general Erwin Rommel's tank divisions at first overran the Allies, beginning a prolonged battle that would last into May 1943.[15]

The landings in North Africa finally gave Americans something they had yearned for since Pearl Harbor. *Life* editorialized that the invasion produced an "electric current" that was more than mere "optimism" and " was generated by something far more profound. . . . Since the collapse of 1929 the U.S. has seemed trapped in a deep, dark valley of frustration." Through the Depression and the rise of Hitler to Pearl Harbor and Bataan, the frustration had only intensified. But the invasion of North Africa was an assault on that frustration, and the editors thought the country was now feeling "what it was like to be American again—to do things in a big, imaginative way, to act with efficiency that left observers breathless."[16] Even without a quick victory, Roosevelt and dozens of defeated members of Congress were left to wonder how the election might have gone if the invasion had taken place just a few days earlier.

Meanwhile, the vicious fighting at Stalingrad continued. "We have fought for fifteen days for a single house," a German soldier reported, "with mortars, grenades, machine-guns and bayonets." Soviet troops managed to encircle the German Sixth Army just as bitter winter weather set in, causing the German commander at Stalingrad, Friedrich Paulus, to lament that his troops were engaged in *rattenkrieg*—a "rat's war." The Russians were partly aided by American machinery. By the end of the year, the U.S. had sent Russia eleven thousand jeeps, sixty thousand trucks, and 2 million pairs of boots.[17]

In the Pacific, the war also took a significant turn. On November 12, the Japanese tried to retake Henderson Field on Guadalcanal. American forces sank most of the incoming Japanese transport ships, and only 2,000 of the 13,500 Japanese troops ever reached the island. In fierce fighting on land and sea, led by the First Marine division under the command of General Alexander Vandegrift, the Americans successfully defended the airfield and the island. The months-long battle on Guadalcanal cost the Allied forces over 7,000 men and twenty-nine ships, yet the Japanese suffered far worse. By losing Guadalcanal, the badly damaged Japanese naval fleet lost the ability to cut off supply lines to Australia.[18]

That battle also produced a profoundly tragic outcome for one American family. Weeks after Pearl Harbor, the five Sullivan brothers of Waterloo, Iowa, decided to enlist in the U.S. Navy. The brothers—George, Francis, Joseph, Madison, and Albert—insisted they be allowed to serve on the same ship and were assigned to the U.S.S. *Juneau*. On November 13, their ship was hit by a Japanese torpedo, killing 687 sailors including all five brothers. Pope Pius XII sent the parents a rosary, and President Roosevelt informed them, "As one of your sons wrote, 'we will make a team together than can't be licked.' It is this spirit which in the end must triumph." The five brothers' deaths caused the navy to change its policy and prohibit family members from serving together on the same ship. Their story resulted in a 1944 film, *The Fighting Sullivans*, and was mentioned in the 1998 blockbuster *Saving Private Ryan*.[19]

Although 5 million Americans were serving in the military by late fall, millions more were needed. On November 13, Roosevelt signed a bill reducing the draft age from twenty to eighteen. Much like the president, the American public had been torn on this question for most of the year, but by October, 69 percent agreed that eighteen-year-olds should be eligible for the draft. In the fall of 1942, the average soldier in the army's combat divisions was over twenty-five years old. Yet as he signed the bill, the president was already thinking ahead to what should be done for the millions of servicemen after the war was over. He asked the War and Navy Departments to study returning veterans' educational needs and report on how the federal government could encourage veterans to seek higher education. This early discussion became the seed of one of the most important laws of the twentieth century, the G.I. Bill, which Roosevelt signed in June 1944 and which eventually educated millions of American servicemen who otherwise would never have gone to college.[20]

The draft caused resentment among some Americans, who felt it treated certain people or groups unfairly. In a Gallup poll, 28 percent felt that the draft was corrupted by "favoritism" and agreed with the statement "Poor boys were taken and big fellows deferred." Eighteen percent felt too many "farm boys" were selected, and 17 percent thought local draft boards were taking too many married men and overlooking single men. Only 2 percent of the respondents felt the draft was "not taking enough Negroes."[21]

As the meeting in Durham, North Carolina, had displayed weeks earlier, African Americans were redefining their roles in war and society. The very idea of assigning racial hierarchies within science or the humanities, which was widely accepted in the early twentieth century, was beginning to crumble. Scholars at the November meeting of the American Ethnological Society agreed that it was "a distortion of anthropology" to assume that one race of people was superior to another. The group stated, moreover, that it was "impossible" to assert that civilization depended upon the enslavement of any race. The resolution that was approved read: "Racial persecution and discrimination cannot be scientifically justified," and "We protest the distortion of anthropology which falsely assigns inborn superiority to some one 'race' and assigns others to inborn inferiority." One of the attendees, Ruth Benedict of Columbia University, discussed how even after centuries of tyranny, the people subjected to peonage still hope to achieve "a more general distribution of opportunity."[22]

In the wake of the election and the invasion of North Africa, the debate over the supertax on incomes over $25,000 reached fever pitch. Complications arose: did companies that were obliged by contract to pay net salaries above $25,000 continue to pay those salaries for the rest of 1942? For the first time, the Treasury Department revealed that the original intent of the proposal was to keep large corporations, which operated on cost-plus contracts, from swelling their government contracts by paying exorbitant salaries to their executives. FDR had hoped the matter could be addressed by legislation, but after Congress balked, the administration dealt with it through an OES directive. Despite its early popularity, backlash over the supertax grew.

The *New York Times* claimed that the philosophy underlying the tax was that "in the eyes of the New Deal it was a criminal offense, and therefore morally wrong, to earn more than $25,000." The Treasury countered by saying it was more interested in "morale, not morals," and that if large salaries were paid to executives working for corporations making millions off the war, "it would be difficult to put a ceiling over the wages of those who perhaps for the first time in their lives are holding good jobs."[23]

Despite the intent of the regulations, many opponents were horrified at the supertax's larger consequences—none more so than Arthur Krock, who saw confiscatory taxation as "one of those 'social gains' which the President has steadily said must not be lost or even laid aside for purposes of carrying on and pressing the war effort." Krock worried that such regulations, which smacked of "de-Stateism and collectivism," would prove so confusing "that many an honest salary-earner and salary-payer will stand in peril of prison." The outcome of this policy, he warned, would be "unemployment, default of fixed family and personal obligations, dried-up charity and educational gifts and a brake on personal incentive." Noting that the $25,000 limit on salaries was first proposed in the Communist Party platform of 1928, Krock saw a "collectivist," anti-capitalist line that went straight from Marx and Lenin to Franklin Roosevelt. Another critic, Percy H. Johnston, the president of the Chemical Bank and Trust Company of New York, said that while he was now well compensated, he had grown up in Kentucky as "a poor country boy" and had risen to his present position only through years of "hard work and frugality." His salary was approximately $150,000, but he had voluntarily reduced it to $75,000 in order to distribute the remainder to other officers of the bank. "I am not a Wall Street banker or a plutocrat," he insisted, but a "plain, everyday citizen who has risen from the ranks." What "gravely" concerned him was that the supertax would help "socialism creep into our government and into our nation."[24]

Another protest came from Utah governor Herbert Maw, a Democrat worried about the general direction of the federal government since Pearl Harbor. If the "scores of Federal bureaus now in existence are permitted by Congress to expand and to continue arbitrarily to dominate the activities of American life," he warned, "the future of American democracy will be a sorry one." The administration's wartime bureaus were populated by those "who honestly believe that local self-government has failed, that the free enterprise system of the past is antiquated, and we would all be better off if our welfare was placed in the hands of trained experts who have authority to work out our destinies for us."[25]

Equally outraged over the administration's tax policy was another organization, the Committee for Constitutional Government, which had formed in 1937 in opposition to FDR's court-packing plan, and among its members were author Booth Tarkington and Norman Vincent Peale, the New York minister who served as the organization's chairman and later wrote *The Power of Positive Thinking*. On November 13, Peale testified about the supertax before the Senate Finance Committee. "Let us be direct," he said: the purpose of the tax was "not to raise revenue or curb inflation by taxation, but to win and uphold support of radical labor organizers and to further a program to redistribute the wealth of America by executive decree." Peale felt the supertax was an assault on the free enterprise system that would inhibit the nation's natural economic growth by a dangerous philosophy that stressed "pushing [down] all those who stick their heads economically above an arbitrary level."[26]

A few businessmen saw Roosevelt's plan as a step in the right direction. John B. Hawley Jr., president of the Northern Pump Company of Minnesota, wrote to the president that he was voluntarily reducing his salary from $448,000 to a net of $25,000 retroactively to December 7, 1941. (In 1943, the Treasury Department reported that despite his claims, Hawley still earned $400,000 in 1942.) Some business leaders even wanted the threshold lowered from $25,000 to $10,000. Edward J. Smith published a pamphlet titled *The $10,000 Issue* that described the current state of affairs as the "natural consequences of the maldistribution of wealth." By limiting all family incomes to $10,000, Smith argued, the nation would "retain our democratic form of government and economic system of free enterprise" as well as the "practicing of Christianity." He estimated that $10,000 was more than 99 percent of American families earned and asked, "Is it this excess of income which we have been allowing this one percent of our families to have which has been causing the greater portion of our poverty and our slums?" Smith then addressed those who earned more:

Shame! Shame on all of you people receiving those big net incomes of over $10,000. Think of it—while our boys are marching off to war—to save our country, our freedom, and our families and even our own lives from being enslaved—taking chances of being slaughtered upon the battlefields, of losing a leg, an arm, or an eye, of being permanently injured—yes, think of it! And while they receive between $40 and $50 a month for doing this, you sit here drawing down incomes of from $10,000 to $50,000 and upward per year—living in supreme comfort and lavishness and taking no chances whatsoever of losing your lives on account of the horrors of war. Yes, again, Shame!"[27]

British journalist Alistair Cooke found Hollywood's reaction to the $25,000 limit somewhat more "realistic." "In the commissary of a famous studio," he observed, "you could hear conversations between male and female stars oddly like the lamentations that sounded through the more exclusive London clubs in the 1920s after the Socialist government had stepped up death duties and estate taxes." Some of the stars, Cooke wrote, were worried "how they were going to live."[28]

For consumers, the impact of the 1942 Revenue Act would be felt at year's end, when they began filling out their new tax forms. In selling *Your Income Tax* by J. K. Lasser, publisher Simon and Schuster warned readers that "the new income tax rates will upset the entire household budget and scale of living of millions of families," and that most individuals would find themselves paying two to seven times the amount they had paid in 1941. While "each of us wants to do his full share," the company noted that the government did not expect anyone to pay more than legally required. To avoid overpaying, Simon and Schuster encouraged Americans to buy "America's most widely used tax guide" for $1.[29]

For women, the opportunity to work for the first time presented a host of changes, but disparity in wages did not disappear. According to the 1940 census, a woman in the United States made 62 cents for each $1 earned by a man in the same job. The National War Labor Board had made a ruling in August mandating pay equality in a bearings factory in Connecticut, but it had not yet issued a larger policy directive. The struggle for equality hit a turning point in November when the NWLB ruled against General Motors in a series of pay disputes concerning discriminatory wage levels for women workers. Late in the month, the NWLB's General Order 16 established the principle that in cases where women performed the same duties as men, female employees "must be allowed equal pay for equal work." The order was voluntary and the war ended before it was widely enforced, yet its significance extended far into the future. Some companies did not need federal orders to democratize their workforces and pay scales. At the Todd Erie Basin Dry Docks in Brooklyn, women were hired as welders and machine shop workers at the same rate as men—82 cents an hour.[30]

The complex relationship between production, sacrifice, and profit was caught perfectly in an ad for Warner and Swasey Turret Lathes of Cleveland: "There are thousands of Americans in foul Japanese prisons—farmers, businessmen, workmen, as well as professional soldiers. Beaten, starved, scorned by their captors, is this what they're thinking? 'I'm here, and these Japs have won so far, because their people were willing to make more sacrifices than we were at home.'" The ad depicted the thoughts of one such prisoner: "I used to think pleasure, time off, my rights were all that mattered. They don't seem very important now. Ten more planes might have saved us in that last fight. I wonder, if I had worked harder and longer back in the shop—I wonder if those planes might have been there. I used to squawk about paying taxes. I wish I had the chance to do it right now. I wonder how the folks back home are doing. If they think rationing is bad, they ought to try living on rice and fish heads. Wonder if the boys left in the shop are turning it out faster than I did? If they're not, I'll be here till I die." The ad asked readers: "Will you pledge yourself to use this equipment to turn out enough planes, ships, tanks, and guns in time to rescue Americans from Jap-German prisons, and to keep yourself and all Americans out of them?"[31]

The darker aspects of war were also captured in an ad for the Carrier Corporation in which the company displayed a letter from Arthur Hocking, a worker in its factory in Syracuse, New York, whose son had recently died in the war. Hocking's letter connected the pain of losing a son in war to the shop floor. He noted that he was hearing a lot about "the war lasting for years" and worried "that sort of thinking might keep anyone from hurrying." Instead, he hoped workers would ignore "talk about a 5 or 10-year war" and do things such as "finish our refrigeration machines for the synthetic rubber program this month—not next. . . . It's not easy to put 10% of your pay into War Bonds. None of us go for gas and fuel and food rationing," but "these are nothing compared to losing someone you love. I know."[32]

Despite the production triumphs, by late November it was apparent that Roosevelt's production goals would not be achieved. Rather than increasing in the final months, the numbers revealed that the rate of production had actually fallen. When the official figures for October came in, WPB economist Stacy May found them "disappointing in almost every category." Airplane production had fallen from September levels, and ship tonnage was down 19 percent. Economist Robert Nathan reiterated that the president's objectives had been too high from the beginning and that "the present objectives for 1942 munitions are approximately 25 percent above what the actual performance would be." Meanwhile, news came from the Kaiser shipyards in Richmond, California, that the 10,500-ton freighter *Robert E. Peary* went from keel to completion in just four days, fifteen and a half hours, breaking the previous record by almost six days.[33]

After the anti-inflation and tax bills were signed, Treasury secretary Morgenthau knew that the overwhelming challenges of fighting inflation and raising revenue were not over. As difficult as achieving the legislation had been in 1942, Morgenthau understood that even more drastic measures would be needed. He told Byrnes, "An effective and equitable solution of the problem of inflation will require measures more fundamental than any yet adopted. The more taxes we obtain, the less net savings do we have to induce." In considering where to turn for revenue in 1943, he thought "our first recourse should be additional taxation." Taxes avoided further ceilings and controls, helped lower the federal debt, and reduced "the danger of post-war spending from pent-up savings." Unless more significant ways were found to withdraw nearly $40 billion of purchasing power from consumers, "price ceilings will be broken through on a broad front, causing empty shelves, large-scale black markets, widespread evasion and dealer favoritism, and illegitimate profits."[34]

Actions on the floor of the U.S. Senate in late November displayed how nothing—not war or economic crises—could challenge the structure of white supremacy. Since Reconstruction, poll taxes had been one of the most effective ways—along with violence and the "white primary"—to keep African Americans from voting. They also disfranchised poor whites. While 66 percent of adults in non-poll-tax states voted in 1940, only 24 percent voted in the eight poll-tax states. Of the 11 million people kept from voting because of the tax, 60 percent were white. But the taxes were essential in keeping southern Democrats in power. Through their iron grip on elections, Democrats were reelected time and again, and their resulting seniority meant chairmanships on crucial committees. In 1942, southerners chaired seven of the ten most powerful Senate committees, including Agriculture (Ellison "Cotton Ed" Smith of South Carolina); Appropriations (Carter Glass of Virginia); Commerce (Josiah Bailey of North Carolina); Finance (Walter George of Georgia); Foreign Relations (Tom Connally of Texas); and Rules (Harry Byrd of Virginia).[35]

In the eight states where poll taxes were in effect—Virginia, Tennessee, South Carolina, Georgia, Alabama, Mississippi, Arkansas, and Texas—the usual tax, $1 or $2, hit poor whites and African Americans especially hard. From an outsider's viewpoint, poll taxes seemed out of step with a time in which Americans were paying with their lives to try to defeat fascism and Japanese imperialism. In October, the House passed a bill to end the taxes, originally sponsored by Representative Lee Geyer, a California Democrat who died in October 1941. The Senate Judiciary Committee favorably reported a bill sponsored by Senator Claude Pepper of Florida that outlawed all poll taxes. When the Senate took up the measures, southern Democrats, who had agreed to suspend poll taxes on members of the armed forces in the soldier voting bill, were now poised to fight those who waged "war against the white people of the southern states."[36]

The filibuster was led by Theodore Bilbo of Mississippi and Richard Russell of Georgia. Together with other southerners, they brought the Senate to a standstill for seven days in November, amid endless quorum calls and demands for complete readings of the Senate *Journal*. Bilbo thundered that "if this poll tax bill passes, the next step will be an effort to remove the registration qualifications, and the education qualifications," at which point "we will have no way of preventing Negroes from voting." If progressives succeeded in this plan, he warned, they would provoke a white backlash against the "Hitler domination" of the South. Tom Connally of Texas went even further, saying that the bill would mean "federal bayonets at the voting places." "Cotton Ed" Smith of South Carolina worried that "we will wake up some morning and find that the power of the states has gone, and that their affairs are being conducted by bureaucrats in Washington."

The impasse reached a dramatic moment on Saturday, November 14, when majority leader Alben Barkley called for a quorum and ordered the "arrest" of eight southern senators who were not present. One of the lawmakers brought to the chamber by this maneuver was Tennessee's Kenneth McKellar, who then took to the floor to proclaim that "being called a filibusterer holds no terror for me" and that he would fight to his last breath to "defeat this iniquitous measure." In response to Barkley's assertion that the southerners' flight from the chamber resembled "the exodus from Egypt," McKellar charged that "our so-called leader is leading us straight into the Republican Party." Barkley attempted to take race out of the issue by saying that "this bill's passage would enfranchise 200,000 white people—poor tenant farmers who may want to vote but will think a long time before paying $1.50 for that right when the money might be needed to put shoes on their barefoot children."[37]

Barkley's stance caused McKellar to withdraw his name from a letter, signed by several senators, urging President Roosevelt to name Barkley to the Supreme Court seat vacated by Justice Byrnes's resignation. That Barkley was considered at all shows how attitudes have changed toward Supreme Court appointments. He was a lifelong politician, and except for one year at Emory College (now Emory University) and a two-month law course at the University of Virginia, his only formal higher education had been at Marvin College, a school in Clinton, Kentucky, that boasted one building and a dormitory. His graduating class in 1897 included four other students; the school closed in 1922. Barkley had never served as a judge, but no one doubted his intelligence, integrity, and fairness. Although Washington insiders such as Tommy Corcoran thought Barkley wanted the post, Roosevelt was reluctant to nominate him and even suggested to Francis Biddle that he might hold the position open until after the war, when Byrnes might return to his old seat. Biddle considered this a "shabby" thing to do to the Supreme Court.

Whether southern opposition cost Barkley a spot on the Supreme Court is unknown. When Roosevelt nominated Wiley Rutledge for the job in January 1943, he told Barkley he had "really thought a lot" about nominating him, but "I had come to the conclusion that there are nine Justices, but only one Majority Leader in the Senate—and I can't part with him in that capacity."[38]

While thousands of American troops fought in North Africa and the Pacific, the Senate ground to a halt as one southerner after another took to the floor to read irrelevant documents so as to thwart any movement on the poll-tax bill. The filibusterers knew they might be seen as obstructionists, but not by the constituents who elected them. When Senator George W. Norris of Nebraska spoke out against the filibuster, Charles E. Simons of Austin, Texas, sent him an angry response. "You must not have very much to do," wrote Simons, except "to be sticking your nose into the home affairs of states which have proven just about as capable of running their own business as your home state." He urged Norris to stop expending "energies on things that do not affect you or your state." Texans, he said, had proven that they "can get along without the help of your gratuitous reform."[39]

If there was any doubt that the southern bloc's power rested on white supremacy and voter suppression, the filibuster of 1942 should have erased it. The reason for opposing the Geyer and Pepper measures was made abundantly clear by Mississippi's Wall Doxey: "We intend to keep control of our state and see that it always remains under the domination of Anglo-Saxon supremacy." On November 23, the Senate failed to invoke cloture on a 41–37 vote and the poll-tax bill was shelved. While Barkley called the tax "a hangover from feudalism, a survivor of bourbonism," the cloture failed because too many southern senators opposed the bill and too many of their colleagues were reluctant to limit Senate debate. Walter White of the NAACP made his outrage clear: "America today is tasting the bitter fruits of a new secession, a rebellion against constitutional government by a handful of outlaws who have successfully defied the will of the people and a majority of the United States Senate." An unrepentant Bilbo vowed he would always fight the "enemies who would destroy our scheme of government from the inside" and boasted that his efforts to save the poll tax made him "as much a soldier in the preservation of the American way and American scheme of government as the boys who are fighting and dying on Guadalcanal."[40]

In Phoenix, racial discrimination in the military generated yet another bloody riot. Nearly 300 African American soldiers and 100 military police fought a three-hour gun battle that left three dead and twelve injured. The violence began when a military police officer shot a soldier for resisting arrest. To quell the riot, local police and the MPs cordoned off twenty-eight blocks and used mounted armored personnel carriers to find rioters hiding in houses. At times, when suspects refused to come out, .50-caliber machine guns filled the houses with bullet holes. The police rounded up over 150 African American soldiers and civilians, some of whom were court-martialed.[41]

Not everyone was absorbed in the grim realities of war or domestic division. In its November issue, *Popular Science Monthly* published "War's End Will Bring a Better Life," which outlined a breathtaking future in which Americans would "travel faster and live better than ever before." The breezy article highlighted that "new skills not only make new industries possible," they "make them inevitable." Americans would ride in new, lighter cars that would go thirty miles on a gallon of gasoline on "superspeed highways," and for longer trips would board "giant passenger planes." "Flivver planes," two-engine personal craft that could seat a small family, would fly to and from thousands of small landing strips. It was a wonderful vision that anticipated vast peacetime benefits from the pent-up industrial and scientific know-how the war had unleashed.[42]

On Thanksgiving Day, Americans found that many of the old routines had changed. Millions of families had empty seats at their tables, and rationing curtailed the feast. The Macy's Thanksgiving Day Parade was canceled because the rubber balloons and floats had been sent to the New York Salvage Committee. Edna St. Vincent Millay marked the occasion with a poem, "Thanksgiving, 1942," in which she paid tribute to "a dark and hungry year":

Give thanks: that men well-clothed, men
    well commanded.
Well fed—and knowing what it is to be
United—having all their lives been free
Now take the avenging path;

That they are well armed, and well—and not
    against the wrath
Of Anti-Christ they march forth empty-handed!

Push back your chairs, and rise.
And Stand.
Stern vision bright in dedicated eyes,
And glass held high in steady hand.
Pledging that by our courage and our skill
And by most bold sacrifice
(For this is what we fear the most:
Self-sacrifice, without whose rigid, scrupulous routine
We have no hope at all to win!)
Pledging, by these and with the aid of our
    robust allies,
And with God's will,
That vulture shall be driven from the skies .
For ever, whose dark shadow now across
    All Freedom lives.[43]

Still smarting from the results of the election, President Roosevelt ignored the pleas of western and rural legislators and announced that nationwide gas rationing would begin on December 1. The Baruch rubber report was obviously on the president's mind, and he could no longer afford to waste time simply conserving available supplies of rubber. "With every day that passes," Roosevelt said, "our need for [a] rubber conservation measure grows more acute." William Jeffers, the rubber director, was clear: "The limitation of the use of gasoline is not due to shortage of that commodity—it is wholly a measure of rubber saving." Rationing gasoline was "the only way" to save rubber. Henderson was even clearer, claiming that critics of gas rationing who maintained that the new lower speed limits were enough to save rubber were simply wrong. Those "powerful and self-serving groups, working through whispering campaigns," he said, "would gamble America's future, not for a mess of pottage, but for a gallon of gasoline."[44]

Before Americans could grasp the reality of full gas rationing, on November 28 they faced a more pervasive anxiety. As Lucy Greenbaum wrote, it was a "drab and gloomy day" on which nationwide coffee rationing began. Consumers used to unlimited cups of "joe" throughout the day were now limited to one cup. Robert F. Woodworth, a Columbia psychologist, warned that coffee drinkers could soon fall into depression: "If you're determined to lay off drinking coffee, just like smoking, then it's easier," Woodworth said, "but if you're made to stop, you think: 'this is terrible. How can I stand it?'" Years later, an OPA staff economist, John Kenneth Galbraith, admitted that "we perhaps shouldn't have done it." In retrospect, he thought, "we should have left coffee to the market" and simply allowed the tightening supplies to set the price.[45]

In a year of endless crises and tragedies, the night of Saturday, November 28, produced one of the saddest incidents. When a fire suddenly erupted shortly after 10:00 p.m. at the Cocoanut Grove Night Club in Boston, the entire structure was soon engulfed in flames. Over eight hundred people scrambled for an exit but found themselves trapped with no way out. "One moment they were seated at their tables or at the bar or were slowly moving across the dance floor," one observer noted, "the next second, almost, they were on the ground with the fire's hot breath reaching for them." In no time, the flames and toxic smoke spread, and panicked patrons climbed over layers of bodies in the pitch dark, trying to find an exit. Some tried to smash through tiny windows but were impaled by the glass. Others pushed toward exit doors that were either bolted shut or opened inward. The club's revolving front door could not function in such a crush with panicked customers pushing against both sides. When rescuers later pried the front doors open, they found "charred forms six and eight deep reaching back twelve to fourteen feet."

The *Boston Globe* noted that the area was "unparalleled in scenes of frightfulness." As he walked among the bodies littered along the sidewalk, one reporter observed, "Many of the bodies were mere blackened trucks, without arms and legs, unrecognizable." In all, 492 people perished, making it the worst nightclub fire in American history. Many of the dead were soldiers and sailors; others had come from a local college football game. In time, the events at Cocoanut Grove led to a series of safety reforms for crowded buildings, such as independently lit "Exit" signs and outward-swinging doors next to revolving doors, as well as new techniques for treating burn victims. As psychiatrists coped with the anguish that overwhelmed survivors and the loved ones of the dead, the fire had another long-term outcome: some of the first systematic studies of long-term grief and post-traumatic stress disorder came from those who experienced it.[46]

The Cocoanut Grove fire occurred at a time when many Americans were concerned with wider disasters. Arthur Upham Pope, chair of the Committee for National Morale and the founder of the American Institute for Persian Art and Archaeology, noted that Cocoanut Grove was a fair warning that "Americans are by no means panic-proof." He wondered if "such panics then mean that there are defects in the American national temperament." Pope and his fellow committee members had few suggestions for dealing with such instances of panic other than to propose that every large gathering have someone trained in "emergency leadership" on hand with a loudspeaker to direct people in an emergency. "We may yet have urgent need of such services," they wrote, "for the danger of token bombing is not wholly past, and a defeated and desperate enemy may have recourse to shrewdly engineered catastrophes which may threaten whole groups with panic conditions."[47]

Nearly a year after Pearl Harbor, the sense of panic and the possibility of imminent catastrophe dominated every aspect of American life, with no sense of an end in sight. Rather, the events of November demonstrated that the nation was in the battle of its life, and the sacrifices and disappointment so many had experienced were no longer seen as temporary exceptions but as the new rule.

December: A New Democratic Capitalism

IN DECEMBER, SEVENTY-FIVE HUNDRED AIR-RAID wardens in the nation's eighth-largest city went door to door over several weeks to prepare residents for a blackout on Monday, the 14th. At 10:00 p.m., the lights went off throughout the city, and the wardens considered the exercise a success. The area had gone almost completely dark except for a stuck stage door and the neon lights of a fur company. In a nearby suburb, the mayor spotted only one violation, a man walking with a lit cigarette. In the main post office, workers crowded into the basement, which served as a makeshift bomb shelter, and Mrs. Spencer Dors gave birth in a shrouded delivery room in a local hospital. The city that conducted this blackout in preparation for possible air attacks was St. Louis, Missouri, located over eight hundred miles from the nearest ocean.

St. Louis's citywide shutdown was part of the largest planned blackout of the year, one that spanned nine states: Missouri, Colorado, Kansas, Nebraska, the Dakotas, Iowa, Minnesota, and Wyoming. Altogether, the blackout covered one-fourth of the continental United States and affected nearly 10 million citizens. In the last month of 1942, a year since Pearl Harbor, no area in the nation felt safe from enemy bombers. Even in the most remote regions of the country, local and state officials were not about to be caught unprepared.[1]

While some nervous Americans participated in blackouts, an experiment in Illinois would soon take worries of enemy attacks to a new level.

On December 2, Enrico Fermi, winner of the 1938 Nobel Prize in physics, directed the world's first controlled nuclear chain reaction under the stands of the University of Chicago football stadium. An encoded message soon reached Roosevelt: "The Italian navigator has landed in the new world." In the same year as the last American mounted cavalry charge, scientists were beginning to unleash the enormous power of the atom. One of the scientists who witnessed the event, Eugene Wigner, wrote, "For some time, we had known that we were about to unlock a giant; still, we could not escape an eerie feeling when we knew we had actually done it." Wigner said that afterward he felt "as, I presume, everyone feels who had done something he knows will have very far-reaching consequences which he cannot foresee."[2]

As American and British troops fought against Erwin Rommel's armored divisions in North Africa, they found the task of taking Tunisia and Algeria more difficult than imagined. Military leaders such as Eisenhower, George Patton, Mark Clark, and Omar Bradley learned much from their experience in Africa, and all began to fear that the war against the Nazis might turn into another World War I: a long, bloody battle of attrition. A War Department report from North Africa commented that "the German army makes war better than we are now making it," and that among the American forces, "both officers and men are psychologically unprepared for war." If the war in Algeria took much longer than planned, invading Italy and then opening a second front in France would be delayed, at a cost of time and blood. Meanwhile, at Stalingrad, German and Soviet troops continued their nightmarish siege, in which nearly 2 million soldiers would perish by January 1943. In the Pacific, the Japanese were finally on the defensive but were nowhere near defeated. In the last weeks of 1942, the only certain future was a long, protracted battle in Europe and Asia with no end in sight. Admiral Jean Darlan, the French Nazi sympathizer turned Allied collaborator, was assassinated. Freda Kirchwey of the *Nation* wrote of Darlan's death: "Prostitutes are used; they are seldom loved."[3]

As Democratic Party officials brooded over the dismal November elections, a December Gallup poll showed that the results might not have been as definitive as some feared. Among possible presidential candidates in 1944, Roosevelt had the highest favorability rating (73 percent), while

New York governor-elect Thomas Dewey's rating stood at 46 percent, one point higher than the 1940 Republican nominee, Wendell Willkie.[4] The GOP's November triumphs, meanwhile, gave its party members hope that the political winds were shifting. The new Republican Party chair, Harrison Spangler, understood that the southern bloc constituted a formidable slice of Roosevelt's coalition, and the poll-tax filibuster told him that for these crucial players, race trumped party loyalties. Even if they did not immediately bolt the Democratic Party for the GOP, Spangler hoped that southern conservatives might form "a new party" or would be content with simply "defeating the New Deal." Southern Democrats, meeting in Atlanta, refuted Spangler's claims but admitted that the "Solid South" was "splitting at the seams."

Alabama governor Frank M. Dixon, one of those Democrats, was one of the administration's most outspoken critics. He hated the Washington "bureaucracy" and the increasing "centralization" of the Roosevelt administration, saying that if the president "gives us a few more years of the political pap-sucking which has bought us and paid for us in the past . . . we will be fair spoil for the two-penny American Hitler." No one, in his view, deserved more scorn than Leon Henderson, who "plans our democratic privileges into oblivion." Yet there was more to Dixon's resentment than frustration with unelected federal officials. The newspaper *Afro-American* noted that for Dixon, segregation was dearer than the Four Freedoms the president had placed at the heart of the war effort. Where those ideals threatened the Jim Crow system, Dixon believed that "the federal government is now tampering with the one thing that we cannot permit, will not permit, whatever the price to ourselves." He accused the administration of "dynamiting the social structure of the South."[5]

For Clare Boothe Luce, the election produced a flood of congratulatory telegrams along with another perk of being a newly elected member of Congress. A news syndicate had offered her $13,000 a year, "with the possibility of making a lot more," if she agreed to write a weekly column. Considering that the congressional salary at the time was $10,000, the offer might have turned some heads, but not Luce's. At the end of 1942, her stock holdings alone were valued at more than $521,000. She would wait until after she left Congress to become a syndicated columnist.[6]

As polls showed most Americans to be more progressive than the election results indicated, the growing disenchantment with the administration played into conservative hands. Polls or the historically low turnout in the elections did not matter—election results did. In the first year after the new Congress was sworn in, conservatives succeeded in thwarting most of the New Dealers' initiatives concerning health care and employment. While the full implications of the election would not be felt for months or years, it was clear that any efforts to use the war to advance New Deal liberalism at home would no longer have congressional support.[7]

No one understood better than Henderson that the election results would bring changes in the administration. His congressional opponents wasted no time nominating him as the sacrificial lamb. On December 1, the Joint Committee on Reduction of Non-Essential Federal Expenditures, which was headed by Senator Harry Byrd of Virginia and included Walter George, Gerald Nye, and Clarence Cannon, as well as Secretary Morgenthau and budget director Harold Smith, issued a scathing report on Henderson's OPA. The committee heard scores of witnesses recount how wartime agencies overwhelmed them with official questionnaires and other burdensome requirements. The report concluded that the OPA was strangling legitimate business and hampering war production. By the end of 1942, the entire country had lost patience with the endless "nonessential" OPA requirements. The committee called for swift legislative remedies.

Democratic representative Thomas Ford of California called one of the OPA's questionnaires, designed to protect the taxpayer from waste and fraud, the "kind of thing that disgusts and alienates the American people." One group of managers at a manufacturing facility allegedly spent nearly half a million man-hours in a three-month stretch of 1942 filling out complicated OPA questionnaires. A drug manufacturer estimated that the endless sea of paperwork demanded by the OPA cost his firm $100,000 in employee time. Federal contractors reported they were required to respond to fifty-two questionnaires each month, and the National Association of Manufacturers noted that eighty-nine of its members had had to file nearly 3,500 reports in 1942, an average of 164 for each company. One OPA critic was an attorney who had been employed by the agency from January to August. Richard Nixon left the OPA to join the navy, but the experience had left a lasting impression. "I became greatly disillusioned about bureaucracy and about what the government could do," Nixon later recalled, "because I saw the terrible paperwork that people had to go through."

Senator Arthur Vandenberg, outraged at "the burden of paper work, the enervating enmeshments of red tape which has descended upon American business," testified that the OPA and other administration agencies were "a deadly menace to national morale and a serious threat to the war itself." He quoted fellow senator Harry Truman of Missouri: "Washington has become a city where the large portion of the population makes its living not by taking one another's washing, but by unreeling one another's red tape." Others pointed the finger directly at Henderson. Representative Ford said House Democrats distrusted Henderson "because he is dictatorial and lacking in common sense." Harold Ickes wrote in his diary that Henderson had become "the most hated figure in the country."[8]

The coffee-rationing program did not aid the OPA's cause. Consumers struggled with their meager limits, and restaurants were often tempted to hoard precious coffee beans for their loyal customers. At the country's first rationing trials, held in the Empire State Building, six restaurant owners were charged with understating their inventories by 2,000 pounds. Other New York City eateries cited for coffee hoarding included Joe's Diner in Queens, which reported 100 pounds of coffee on hand while actually having 225 pounds, and Vic's Lunch on Broad Street, which declared only 4 pounds but had over 1,000 pounds in its stock. The possible penalties for these restaurants ranged from a cut in the defendant's ration to a ban on buying any coffee at all.

Henderson concluded that the general public was more indifferent to conserving fuel than to anything else: "My guess is that the full seriousness of it never has permeated," he remarked, adding that the nationwide limits struck at the "freedom that people attach to their movements." "Some advise you to tell the people what is needed and they will do it," he complained, but when it came to gasoline rationing, "that just ain't so." Comparing gasoline "bootlegging" to liquor bootleggers during Prohibition, he admitted that "we will have this winter people who scrupulously observed the rationing laws who will be inconvenienced." He was particularly frustrated with Louisiana governor Sam Jones's claims that "Eastern interests" had imperiously imposed rationing and that people in his state must "make the best of a bad situation until the bureaucrats see fit to relax." Henderson replied that the "bureaucrats" responsible for rationing worked in Tokyo, and that "if I ever had it to do over again, which God forbid, I'd be harder and tougher 'til they cut me down."[9]

Yet amid the endless criticism, the OPA's assault on inflation was working. OPA general counsel David Ginsburg projected that OPA price controls had saved the American taxpayer close to $58 billion and noted that the cost of living had risen only 4 percent since May. Rent controls had saved American tenants an additional $1 billion. He estimated overall savings of about $170 for every American citizen. The OPA, Ginsburg concluded, had done "an extraordinary job" in controlling inflation, even if "it isn't perfect." Another OPA staff member, director of research Richard V. Gilbert, boasted, "Ninety percent of the cost of living and virtually all prices except for furnished combat items have been brought under price control. . . . We have stopped inflation in its tracks."[10]

On December 2, shortly after Congressman Lyndon B. Johnson of Texas concluded a fifteen-minute appointment with the president, Henderson arrived at the White House for a meeting with FDR. What they discussed is unknown, but it likely centered around Henderson's future in the administration. Nearly twenty members of Congress had telephoned the White House in December to complain about "the Henderson arrogance" and ask if he was staying on. They received no reply, but there was no doubt he had become a major liability.[11]

Despite knowing his time was short, Henderson kept up appearances. On December 10 he took part in a national radio show, *100 Million Questions*, in which he responded to concerns submitted by listeners. Henderson answered all queries in his usual gruff manner. One outraged tenant wrote to say that his landlord had raised his rent because of improvements he had made to a rented garage, a move the tenant thought was illegal due to OPA rent freezes. "Who is right?" the letter demanded. Henderson answered directly: "The landlord is right" as long as he could prove he had made a substantial alteration. "That tenant is being unreasonable and from the tone of that letter he's got the wrong bull by the horns." He added that "rent control isn't a device to crack down on landlords, it's meant to correct abuses and inequities," and the program would not be successful unless "it works both ways."[12]

By Tuesday, December 15, the rumor throughout Washington was that Henderson had resigned and that the president had already appointed Senator Prentiss Brown of Michigan to succeed him. Brown, who had been defeated for reelection a few weeks before, seemed a nonthreatening choice to mollify Congress. Though the president denied he had received Henderson's resignation, Brown lunched with FDR and Jimmy Byrnes that day and later admitted he had been offered a post in the administration.[13]

That afternoon, Henderson informed Roosevelt of his intention to cut his "connection with government completely," saying that this "stubborn decision" was based on his health as well as "political liabilities." Two days later, he submitted his official resignation to the president, claiming that his departure was due to "a recurrent physical difficulty." The president, hoping to avoid a difficult farewell, did not call Henderson personally to accept the resignation but had Jimmy Byrnes do it. Harold Ickes, no fan of Henderson's, thought, "It was characteristic of the President to do it this way, but it is a rotten way to treat such a man." Roosevelt later sent Henderson an official response, accepting the resignation "with great reluctance," and noting that "the duty of placing a ceiling on the prices of commodities and when a shortage exists, rationing the available supply among the civilian population is an exceedingly difficult and thankless task. . . . You have performed this service with energy and unexampled courage."[14]

While the ostensible reason for the resignation was a bad back, the *New York Times* understood that Henderson's "relations with Congress were so estranged that the OPA would have difficulty in obtaining enough funds to administer price control and increasing rationing problems so long as he remained head of the agency." Many within the Democratic Party saw his departure as a necessary "sacrifice" if the administration hoped to deal successfully with the new Congress in January. Republicans had made it abundantly clear they wanted Henderson out. When Representative Carl T. Curtis, a Nebraska Republican, said, "America must destroy the OPA or the OPA will destroy America," a *Times* editorial noted, "He meant Mr. Henderson."[15]

The *Charlotte Observer* concluded Henderson had been "catty with the public" and was seen as a "swashbuckling, buccaneering type of official who hasn't been able to get along with people." Yet while deploring Henderson's management style—"brusque in his mannerisms, officious, imperious, and dictatorial"—the *Observer* suggested that the real issue lay elsewhere: "It would be fairer to say that Mr. Henderson has been run out of his job, he has been chastened by Congress rather than by the unorganized American masses, a majority of whom have never heard of him but who, one way or another, have only had contacts with local or state authorities working under his central Washington administration. . . . This is hard, bitter, grim business—making the pampered and spoiled American people toe the mark in respect to governmental control of prices and goods and markets." Even the *Wall Street Journal* confessed to "a definite liking and respect for the qualities that [Henderson] has displayed," and hoped that eventually "those qualities can be made most useful to his country in more ways than one." The paper expressed sympathy for the difficulty of Henderson's position, which compelled him "to reach into the intimate recesses of the citizen's daily routine."[16]

When word of Henderson's resignation reached the public, Minnie Morgan Webster of Baltimore was heartened by the "very welcome" news, which she thought "most acceptable to Real American People." She concluded that Henderson had "done more to hamper the war effort and cause more disunity than any other one person." California fire marshal Lydell Peck hailed the resignation and told FDR that "unless complete house cleaning" was undertaken immediately within a number of wartime agencies, "you may be sure that the democratic party and your administration is in for certain defeat."[17]

Not everyone was so happy to see Henderson go. Dabney Yarbrough, a banker in Columbia, South Carolina, wrote to Henderson that in his travels throughout the state, he encountered many people who saw the inconvenience of gas rationing as one of the necessities of waging war. "You are the only man in Washington with any 'guts.' . . . I am sorry to see the ONE REAL MAN in Washington quitting, and want you to know that lots of the citizens of this section feel as I do. I don't see how you can be replaced."

I. F. Stone wrote in the *Nation* that Henderson's "fate deserves a place in the meditation of philosophers" and that his ouster meant a declining role for liberalism in the war. While several reasons had been given for his resignation, "none of them would have mattered had it not been for the last election and the next Congress." Author Eliot Janeway concluded that Henderson was "the key figure in the war economy."[18]

The defeated Henderson understood the political transformation that had taken place, and said in June 1943 that "liberal ideas, liberal leaders, liberal movements, and liberal gains . . . have all been slaughtered by combinations of their opponents." He never returned to government service, but he met with Roosevelt in the White House one more time, on March 13, 1945, a month before FDR's death. Though the details of that final meeting are unknown, it likely had to do with Henderson's invitation from Chiang Kai-Shek to visit China and advise the government on how to initiate a price-control program to combat rising inflation. As a co-chair of the liberal Americans for Democratic Action, Henderson led an anti-Truman movement in 1948 in the hope of persuading General Dwight Eisenhower to seek the Democratic nomination for president. On one occasion he bitterly criticized his former boss. In a speech at Carnegie Hall in November 1943, he accused the Allied governments, and Roosevelt and Churchill in particular, of "moral cowardice" for failing to address "the major political weapon of Nazi bestiality," the extermination of the Jews. With his usual candor, he declared that "this war issue has been avoided, submerged, postponed, played down, and resisted with all the forms of political force available to powerful governments."[19]

One of Henderson's former staffers fondly remembered his accomplishments. John Kenneth Galbraith, an OPA economist who would become a Harvard professor and one of the nation's most popular writers on economics, viewed Henderson as "one of the unsung heroes of World War II," and compared him favorably with another administrator: "There has been an enormous amount of literature on Albert Speer and the way he was presumed to have organized German production," yet Henderson "organized the United States far more effectively than Germany had ever been. . . . The man whose organization failed is celebrated, while the man who had in mind the successful national venture is lost to history."[20]

The saga of Henderson's rise and fall in 1942 proved that government controls on prices, rents, and wages could actually halt inflation. In the twelve months before the adoption of General Max in late April, wholesale prices had risen 1 1/3 percent each month. After May, the increase for the remainder of 1942 was only 1/4 percent each month. For the year, the national inflation rate was under 11 percent and would fall to just 1.6 percent within two years. In a candid and revealing reflection about his role in combating inflation, Henderson concluded: "I'd rather be remembered for that than for the people who love me."[21]

The political winds seemed to herald the end of the New Deal. The president himself said in 1943 that he was no longer "Dr. New Deal" but "Dr. Win the War"—a phrase that could have been taken straight from Clare Boothe Luce's congressional campaign. Yet FDR was not ready to yield to his opponents, even if Democratic leaders informed him that "social reform is out." Although the supertax on incomes above $25,000 affected fewer than three thousand taxpayers, Roosevelt found such large salaries hard to accept in a time of war and widespread sacrifice. "There's an awful lot of kick going around the country," he told reporters, "about the fellow who has got his income more or less fixed because he is getting a salary and the fellow who is getting a much larger income just out of invested securities not being held down at all." He reminded his listeners that the salaries of railroad executives had been cut to $60,000 in 1933 when they faced bankruptcy. In 1942, the nation faced bankruptcy and far worse if it lost the war. Noting that the issue of large incomes produced "a very widespread complaint around the country," he added, "I am very curious to know what the Congress is going to do about it."[22]

Roosevelt's challenge to Congress to include more categories within the supertax infuriated his opponents. Columnist Godfrey Nelson was among many conservatives who found the president's suggestions "un-American" and "an absurdity." The "leveling" principle, he argued, would do widespread harm to industries and initiative. "Would an investor in real estate refrain from collecting rents when he has attained collections of an amount yielding $25,000? If his income is from stock equities, would he reject and return dividends when he has received the amount limited by executive order?" Should bondholders refuse to clip coupons "under penalty for going to prison?" While a year-end Gallup Poll showed that 65 percent of those surveyed supported limiting incomes after taxes to $30,000 or less, the nation's financial sector was united in fighting the tax, which it viewed as a political stunt that could establish dangerous precedents.[23]

While many uncertainties remained about the wartime economy, one thing was certain: the Great Depression was over. By the end of 1942, desperate people waiting in breadlines, nervous depositors hoping to withdraw their savings from banks, and shuttered factories seemed like relics of a distant age. With the massive wartime spending and millions having left the workforce to join the military, the national unemployment rate had fallen to just 2.88 percent, over four points lower than when the year began. "We are closer to a full employment economy and the full use of our productive facilities than ever before" claimed a year-end review from the Twentieth Century Fund. "Never have more of us had jobs; never has the total of our income been so great."[24]

With the economic crisis of the 1930s in the past, several New Deal work programs came on the chopping block. With the Civilian Conservation Corps having ended on June 30, one of the few holdovers from the New Deal was the Works Progress Administration. In the seven years since its creation in 1935, the WPA had created much of America's infrastructure: 651,000 miles of highways, over 77,000 new bridges, 38,000 schools and libraries either built or improved, and over 4.7 million feet of airport runways. It had employed 8.5 million people and planted 176 million trees. It enrolled over 100,000 people in vocational training schools and supported nearly 6,000 concerts attended by 2.5 million people. Its artists had completed 108,000 paintings, 17,000 sculptures, and over 2,500 murals. WPA

Table 3. **National unemployment rates by month, 1942 (%)**

January—7.0	July—4.33
February—6.71	August—3.74
March—6.34	September—3.26
April—5.75	October—3.23
May—4.94	November—3.12
June—4.57	December—2.88

Source: National Bureau of Economic Research, Federal Reserve Bank of St. Louis, fredstlouis.org.

clinics provided immunizations and had served over 1.2 billion school lunches. Since March 1942, the agency had also spent $4.47 million building Japanese American internment camps in the western U.S. Roosevelt noted the WPA had "added to the national wealth, repaired the wastage of depression, and strengthened the country to bear the burden of war." On December 4, the president announced that it was time to issue the WPA an "honorable discharge." One of the first casualties was the WPA Symphony Orchestra in New York City, which on December 27 played for the final time at Carnegie Hall before 2,400 people. The musicians, who made less than $25 a week, refused to rise at the end of the concert but sat and applauded the young conductor, twenty-six-year-old Emerson Buckley, who had served in that post throughout 1942.[25]

The transformations in American life for teenagers worried Buffalo, New York, probation officer Timothy W. Regan, who felt that too many young people were leaving high school for high-paying jobs in defense plants and that "transient girls" attracted to war industries were falling into "bad company." Milton E. Praker, clerk of the Niagara Falls Children's Court, believed that increased employment opportunities for women had been "a minor factor" in the 50 percent increase in juvenile delinquency in his court. Others saw changing parental roles generated by the demands of war and longed for a return to prewar society. Captain Raymond J. Smith, a Buffalo police officer, hoped mothers of young children would not work outside the home "until all other sources are exhausted." More than ever, he thought, "the mother's place is with her children." Katharine F. Lenroot, chief of the Children's Bureau in the Labor Department, agreed: "Mothers who had a job to do at home should not be made to feel it is their patriotic duty to go out and work." Doing so, she felt, increased the "day care problem" and thus juvenile delinquency. Even J. Edgar Hoover was compelled to join the argument, fearing the "drift of normal youth toward immorality and crime" that had been produced by women leaving home to work. Hoover implored women to reject war work if it meant "the hiring of another woman to come in and take care of [their] children."[26]

Finding adequate childcare became a paramount issue for women trying to join the workforce. In Baltimore, over five hundred women could not find care centers for their children in December and as a result had not taken defense jobs. The dissolution of the WPA and its nursery schools and childcare facilities only made matters worse. Without the WPA, the only remaining federal funds for childcare came from a Federal Works Agency grant that distributed a little over $200,000 for eight childcare projects throughout the nation. The vacuum would soon be filled under the auspices of the 1940 Lanham Act, which provided federal funds to assist communities contributing to defense industries with water, sewage, schools, and housing. Emergency nursery schools began to open; at their peak in 1944, they served over thirty-one hundred communities and 130,000 children. Yet federally sponsored childcare remained fleeting. For too many Americans, the notion of the government somehow replacing mothers as daytime caregivers was too dangerous to consider after the war emergency.[27]

Within the administration, Assistant Solicitor General Oscar Cox wrote to Harry Hopkins that aside from winning the war, "the outstanding want of the American people is doubtless for some assurance that reasonable plans are being made and steps are being taken now to see that they have jobs after the war." Cox listed some causes the administration might advance to help assure Americans of "productive and full employment" after the war, including planning ways for private industry to absorb returning soldiers and war workers, building new hospitals and adequate housing, and enlarging unemployment insurance and Social Security.[28]

Others hoped that the United States would follow Great Britain's example and think boldly of a postwar government that promised "cradle to grave" assistance to all. In November, a report from Sir William Beveridge helped pave the way for the modern British welfare state. Citing five threats to postwar England (want, ignorance, disease, squalor, and idleness), Beveridge argued that the crisis of war offered a chance that might never come again. He termed 1942 "a revolutionary moment in the world's history" that provided the opportunity for something bold, "not patching." His report resulted in the implementation of the National Health Service, the publicly funded, single-payer health care program for all citizens in the United Kingdom, as well as many other reforms designed to eliminate the same scourge that worried FDR—"want." Whether the same could be achieved in the United States remained to be seen. By the end of the year, I. F. Stone was trying not to be discouraged by the political landscape: "The immediate outlook for progressivism is dark, but it has been dark before, and it is some comfort to know that its future is nowhere near as bleak as Adolf Hitler's."[29]

The American reaction to the Beveridge report seemed to acknowledge the revolutionary impulse behind it. Agnes Meyer, the wife of *Washington Post* owner Eugene Meyer, told Beveridge that the report's effect in America had been "electrifying." The *Atlanta Constitution* found it "an idealistic yet probably practical framework for what is really a new social order." Commentator Raymond Clapper thought Beveridge's plans represented "a determination to make England a better place to live in after the war." Like many other New Dealers, WPB economist Robert Nathan believed that "as our economy becomes more complex and more interdependent, it appears inevitable that the responsibility of government must grow." Yet by mid-December, reports from the British Ministry of Information revealed that many Americans considered the plan "more evolutionary than revolutionary," and the notion of "cradle to grave" government support "more Utopian than practical." Dorothy Thompson saw "nothing of the agitator or the demagogue in the report" and contrasted its levelheaded approach with Roosevelt's "demagogic proposal of placing a ceiling on salaries," which she thought would only "bring economic and social disorder." In the view of William Randolph Hearst's *New York Journal-American,* the report revealed "the dangerous tendencies which might lead to the demoralization of society and thus prepare the way for some form of socialism." Some of the harshest criticism came from Seattle, where the *Times* found Beveridge's plan "leaves out nothing that the most indolent and thriftless person might think the government should do for him." The British ministry astutely predicted that "Socialist aspects of the report would meet with the stiffest opposition" in the U.S.[30]

Some in the federal government clung to the idea that the war could be an opportunity to provide a new structure of government support for the needy, sick, unemployed, and aged. Ralph J. Watkins, the assistant director of the National Resources Planning Board, prepared a confidential report, "The Framework of an Economy of Plenty," outlining how the administration should focus on building a new economy. Still referring to the "War of Survival," Watkins wrote, "Profound changes are inevitable, changes that

will alter the political, economic, and social structure throughout the earth."
While he viewed all of FDR's Four Freedoms as essential, Watkins highlighted two—freedom from want and freedom from fear—as "guidelines
for the future." The U.S. might emerge from war as the world's leading
military power, but its armed strength could also serve as "an invitation to
imperialism." Watkins argued that in the past, imperialistic ambitions had
always been "found to be wanting" and that the nation should instead focus
on the domestic situation, especially a "New Social Security" that would
expand on the guarantees embedded in the 1935 act and include the "assurance to all workers of the right to work." Watkins believed Social Security
benefits should be extended to include "continuity of income" if someone
was unemployed, sick, or disabled, as well as "assurance of mothers' assistance, paid vacations, minimum nutrition, and housing." The large federal debt that would result should be seen as "a device whereby wealth is
transferred from those who at any given time do not need it or do not want
to use it to those who do."[31] Terms such as "transferring wealth," and "cradle to grave," which seemed natural to discuss in 1942, would soon fall out
of favor when the nation was no longer in peril.

On the one-year anniversary of Pearl Harbor, the United States found itself
fundamentally transformed. The U.S. Armed Forces had grown from a total of 2.1 million personnel in January 1942 to over 7 million by year's end,
with 5.3 million in the army and 1.6 million in the navy. Thirty-nine thousand of this total were women. Over 11 million civilians were employed in
war industries, and millions more lived with rations, shortages, and higher
taxes. War employment accounted for 29 percent of all jobs in the nation,
up from 13.4 percent the year before. A December Gallup poll found that
76 percent of Americans felt the U.S. was finally winning the war. While
the nation's factories were pumping out war machinery, with just weeks
remaining in the year, it was clear that the "Arsenal of Democracy" would
fall far short of Roosevelt's overwhelming production goals. The OWI gave
the year's output as 49,000 planes, 32,000 tanks, 17,000 anti-aircraft
guns, and 8.2 million tons of merchant shipping, versus FDR's goals of
60,000 planes, 45,000 tanks, 20,000 anti-aircraft guns, and 8 million
tons of shipping. The OWI's numbers, however, were somewhat inflated.

The War Production Board later adjusted the figure to 47,694 planes. The president's original number of 60,000 had included 45,000 combat planes, but the nation produced only 24,864. Donald Nelson blamed the shortfall on a lack of machine tools and skilled labor. But to call the year's production a failure would be absurd. The United States' productive output dwarfed that of the other warring countries. Germany, for instance, produced just 15,400 planes and 9,200 tanks in the entire year. Robert Nathan recalled that although Roosevelt's goals had not been achieved, by the end of 1942 the production levels were "skyrocketing" and the idea of building 100,000 planes was no longer a dream. "In the final enumeration of Hitler's mistakes in waging the Second World War," wrote John Keegan, "his decision to contest the issue with the power of the American economy may well come to stand first."[32]

The nation's shipyards were producing warships at a furious pace. By the end of 1942, three aircraft carriers had been launched and construction was under way on six more. The U.S.S. *Essex,* launched in July 1942, was the first of a new type of large carrier that weighed twenty-seven thousand tons, was nearly one-sixth of a mile long, and could hold up to one hundred airplanes. By the end of the war, the U.S. had produced twenty-four *Essex*-class carriers. The navy commissioned thirty-two submarines and sixty-two destroyers, along with four thirty-five-thousand-ton *South Dakota*–class battleships and two forty-five-thousand-ton *Iowa*-class battleships. The Brooklyn Navy Yard was constructing the U.S.S. *Missouri*, which after it was launched in 1944 would become the site of the formal Japanese surrender in Tokyo Bay.[33]

The U.S. economy's year-end figures also revealed the enormous changes under way: the gross domestic product, which had been $126.7 billion in 1941, was $161.9 billion in 1942. The GDP's nearly 28 percent increase remains the largest single-year leap in American history. The amount of the economy devoted to war, which was 1.5 percent in 1939 and 9 percent in 1941, had reached 31.3 percent. For the last quarter of 1942 it was nearly 40 percent. By the time the war ended in 1945, the nation's GDP would reach $223 billion, almost 250 percent more than when the war in Europe began in 1939. The unemployment rate, nearly 16 percent in April 1940, reached 0.91 percent in October 1944, the lowest ever recorded.[34]

In December, the Treasury Department announced that since May 1941, the U.S. had sold $6.8 billion in war bonds, but denied rumors that holders were cashing them in by "leaps and bounds." While 3 percent of the holders had redeemed their bonds, for a total of $211 million, 97 percent of the E War Bonds sold remained with their buyers. The Treasury called it "a great tribute to the common sense of the American people that they are holding bonds which increase in value after being held one year." Yet the new taxes and the bonds could not begin to offset the amount of money being spent on the war. By year's end, the national debt exceeded $100 billion, and most observers knew these numbers were likely to multiply as the war intensified. By the time the war ended in 1945, the national debt stood at $260 billion. The debt incurred by four years of war was not paid off until 1970.[35]

Consumer spending fell to 55.8 percent of GDP, a sixteen-point drop since 1939. The nation's largest mail-order chain, Sears and Roebuck, saw its sales fall from $906 million in 1941 to $848 million in 1942. Yet the WPB noted that the change was "not due to a decline in consumption itself." In fact, consumption was actually 15 percent higher in 1942 than three years earlier. The Safeway grocery chain, for example, generated over $100 million more in sales than in 1941. The difference was due "to a more rapid growth of output for war." At the height of war spending in 1944, the nation spent a record 35.8 percent of its GDP on war. Although American forces had only limited involvement in major military campaigns in the first year after Pearl Harbor, as of December 20 they suffered over 61,000 casualties, including 8,531 dead and 7,389 wounded, and nearly 43,000 were listed as "missing." The navy and Marines reported 1,344 POWs.[36]

It is helpful to recall how America's efforts in 1942 to gear up for war compare to those of its chief adversary. The War Department, using information obtained from confidential Swiss reports, analyzed the ways in which Germany and the U.S. mobilized their economies and industries. The essential difference in the "Controlled Materials Plan" of the two belligerents was succinctly stated: "The American system relies on centralized control by government agencies loosely aided by industry advisory committees whereas the German system relies on industrial self-government, i.e. the rule of industry over itself; subject to the guidance, planning, and strict control of performance by government agencies." In 1942, unlike the U.S., Germany no longer used cost-plus contracts for military work but instead adopted a stricter fixed-price system.[37]

The necessities of total war afforded a rare economic experiment in the life of the United States. With its very existence on the line, and with unprecedented spending for the war effort, the U.S. resorted to a mostly centralized planned economy that may have proved unpopular and heavy-handed at times, but saved the nation from ruinous inflation and financial catastrophe. Coming off a decade of the Great Depression, which brought home some of capitalism's jarring inadequacies—unemployment, inequality, and years of grinding poverty—the war offered the capitalist system an opportunity to showcase some of its strengths: innovation, vast and rapid mobilization of resources, and entrepreneurial advances. These qualities could be harnessed to serve the war effort, but only with careful supervision over prices, wages, and rents. We give little praise to the bureaucrats who performed such thankless tasks, either then or now, and unelected officials such as Leon Henderson and agencies such as the OPA are mostly invisible in the narrative of the war years. But their efforts were essential to the war effort and, as economist Thomas Piketty notes, "It was the chaos of war, with its attendant economic and political shocks, that reduced inequality in the twentieth century. . . . There was no gradual, consensual, conflict-free evolution toward greater equality," only the policies and plans formulated from war "that erased the past and enabled society to begin anew with a clean slate." The share of national income enjoyed by the top 10 percent of earners reached a high of 49.3 percent in 1929, right before the stock market crash and the onset of the Great Depression. It stood at 41.9 percent in 1941 and then dropped to 36.1 percent in 1942, the largest single-year decline of the twentieth century.[38]

Although the year had provided few nuggets of good news from the war front, there was reason for some relief with the invasion of North Africa. Yet the brutality of the Axis nations toward civilians and surrendered enemies was not lost on worried Americans. "Nazis and Japs have made 1942 the most shameful year since the Dark Ages," claimed one Pennsylvania newspaper. The country was not yet seeing the light at the end of the tunnel, but it had avoided further catastrophe. Or, as Churchill famously said, 1942 was not "the end. It is not even the beginning of the end. But it is, perhaps, the end of the beginning."[39]

In a choice that drew little applause, Henry Luce and his editors chose Joseph Stalin as *Time*'s "Man of the Year" for 1942; in a year of "blood and strength," Stalin had halted Hitler's armies at Stalingrad. The magazine stated, "The man whose name means steel in Russia, whose few words of English include the American expression 'tough guy,' was the man of 1942." Finishing second was William Temple, the archbishop of Canterbury, who was recognized for challenging "all Britain's well-established institutions of economic privilege." Third place went to Henry Kaiser, whose "gospel challenged U.S. industry to lead the postwar world out of depression." No American military leader made the shortlist. Eisenhower's "able occupation of North Africa," the magazine suggested, "only placed him on the threshold of his real test." While MacArthur and Admiral William "Bull" Halsey were acknowledged for their roles in the Pacific, *Time* found no military figure on either side worthy of its highest acclaim because "there was no military victory of the year which showed signs of being conclusive."[40]

Even if victory came (and in January 1943, Roosevelt raised the bar by defining victory as "unconditional surrender"), there remained the overwhelming fear among both economists and the general public that reduced government spending and millions of returning G.I.s would plunge the nation back into a major recession or depression. Vice President Henry Wallace, in a December radio address, asked, "If everybody can be given a job in war work now, why can't everybody have a job in peacetime later?"[41]

One source that suggested a different future was Henry Luce's *Fortune* magazine. In February 1941, Luce had coined the term "The American Century" to describe an era in which the United States would be the world's dominant economic, social, and cultural power. Like *Time* and *Life*, Luce's business magazine was widely successful, and he envisioned *Fortune* as a forum to "assist in the successful development of American Business Enterprise at home and abroad." In December 1942, *Fortune*'s editors spelled out how the nation's industrial base, having been brought to life by war, could continue in peacetime. The editors hoped that at war's end the nation would redefine its economic policies and pursue "permanent prosperity," centered in the broad concept of "full employment." They argued for an expanded Social Security program that included generous health, education, and housing benefits, as well as a flexible program of public works planned in advance and put into motion when private employment fell off. In many ways this vision mirrored the New Dealers' grandest dreams, in which the federal government would guarantee against devastating health care costs or the loss of a job. By promising a social safety net that went beyond even the Beveridge report, this ambitious agenda demonstrated a sense of economic possibilities that the November election had failed to capture. "This program is not socialism, nor fascism, nor a return to laissez faire," *Fortune*'s editors argued. "It is, we believe, a synthesis of the conflicting elements in our recent past." They called their concept "a new democratic capitalism, which will allow production and consumption to keep on expanding as fast as science and human ingenuity point the way."[42]

Yet some considered such prospects an ominous threat. On December 11, Governor Dixon of Alabama warned of the dangers of centralized government led by bureaucratic "planners," whom he labeled "crackpots playing with the dangerous weapons of federal control." Such "crackpots," he said, had more on their minds than universal health care. Their "control" was meant to chip away at white supremacy, and for evidence, Dixon felt he needed look no farther than the recent poll-tax fight. "Never in the history of this country until then had there been any question but that the qualification of voters was a matter of state concern, . . . yet in time of war, when the very life of this nation is at stake, there was an insistence on the passage of this type of legislation changing our constitutional form of government, slapping in the face the people of eight sovereign states of this Union." Dixon believed that the bill interfered in the internal affairs of sovereign states, "holding them up to the enemies of our country as if they were representatives of a democracy which was no democracy, and this under the pretense that it is essential to the war effort."

Far from denying that Jim Crow existed in the Deep South, Dixon embraced it. "The social structure of the South has been built, and can endure, only on the principle of segregation," which "implies separation of the races, not mistreatment of anyone. . . . Segregation itself is a ruling, a basic principle, without which there can be no orderly society below the Mason-Dixon line." In Alabama, he explained, "Our problem is different from the problem in any other section of the world. Our Negro population approaches forty percent of the total. This percentage means the balance of power. In many Alabama counties there are four and five to one. Either white men control them, or there will be a repetition of the venality of reconstruction, the ruin of the South. Either there is segregation, or no white man can live there unless he is willing to abandon all of that personal and racial pride which has made the Anglo-Saxon great. . . . The situation is delicate, difficult, fraught with danger for the Southern people."

Six years later, Dixon gave the keynote address at the States' Rights Party ("Dixiecrat") convention, a bloc of former southern Democrats who had bolted from the party over civil rights and nominated South Carolina governor Strom Thurmond for president. Dixon thundered that the Democratic Party's civil rights policies were an attempt "to reduce us to the status of a mongrel, inferior race." Thurmond won four states and thirty-nine electoral votes, and his rise foreshadowed a partisan transformation that did not occur suddenly but took place over several decades. The origins of that transformation, however, were plainly visible in 1942.[43]

As the holidays approached, the usual gifts of toys and clothing were either scarce or nonexistent. Some manufacturers worked to remind consumers why their products were not readily available and promised better days ahead. An ad for the Hamilton Watch Company of Lancaster, Pennsylvania, told shoppers, "You can't make this a normal Christmas," but promised "America will live to know a day when boys and girls can love and marry and not be torn apart" and "mothers can tuck their children into bed without an anxious look to the sky." While they may "have to hunt a little harder to find the Hamilton Watch you want to give the one you like best," the ad reminded readers that the company was "busy today making wartime precision instruments."[44]

The Jack and Heintz Company in Ohio basked in the glow of its larger than expected profits, and rewarded over twelve hundred employees at its holiday banquet with a turkey dinner, a Waltham eighteen-jewel wristwatch, a "swell automatic pencil," and a bonus that averaged $300. The company's newsletter even offered its own version of a popular Christmas poem:

'Twas the night before Christmas, and all through the shops,
No man was idle, not even the cops;
Fill up the socks with starters galore,
Pilots and instruments, Uncle Sammy wants more![45]

Children's concepts of holiday gifts had changed with the war. Shortly before the holiday, U.S. postmaster Albert Goldman displayed letters sent to Santa Claus. Many asked Santa for guns, especially machine guns, and some even specified the precise caliber of the firearm they wanted. One girl said she knew Santa "won't be able to have enough to put in everyone's stockings and bring them enough toys," but she hoped "you can remember me with a dress or something to wear." Another wrote: "My dad is in the Army and my mom has to work. I have been a good girl. Will you please bring me some books and dishes?"

Others saw the holidays as a chance to spread the wartime message of sacrifice. Children in New York participated in the Neediest Cases Fund drive. The 9BR class of Seth Low Junior High School in Brooklyn donated $1.50 to the fund, writing, "We realize that it is a very small sum, but we feel that the few pennies given by each student will help make someone's Christmas a happier one." Twelve-year-old Howard Levison gave $2 and said, "I recall that President Roosevelt has said that the home front is just as important as the war front." He made his donation, he explained, in the hope that "when this war is over, the people here at home and abroad will live in happiness. That is the kind of world I want to live in when I grow up."

On Christmas Eve, FDR reminded Americans that "there is no better way of fostering good will toward man than by first fostering good will toward God." Accordingly, he declared, the next day would be the only day of the year when the plants and factories of the nation would be idle. "So Christmas becomes the only holiday in all the year." Soldiers abroad enjoyed chicken and turkey flown in from the U.S. Writer Katherine Anne Porter captured the holiday mood: "The men are simply off to the army and navy without a backward look, the women are taking hold at whatever they have to do. . . . The capacity of human beings to rise to an emergency is always astonishing and admirable."[46]

On the final weekend of the year, worshippers went to synagogues and churches around the country to pray for distant loved ones as the nation entered both a new year and a new phase of the war. At the Temple Rodeph Sholom in New York, Rabbi Louis Newman spoke on a subject that would grow increasingly relevant: "Exact Justice and Retribution for the Nazis: Is This Religious?" At St. John's Cathedral, Bishop William T. Manning declared, "May this Christmas bring to our allies and to all who are bearing their part in this struggle, new strength and courage" so that "darkness and evil shall not dominate this world." At the Riverside Baptist Church, the Rev. Henry Emerson Fosdick closed the year with a sermon fittingly entitled "A New Year When Almost Anything Can Happen."[47]

At the Paramount Theater in Times Square on December 30, bandleader Benny Goodman introduced singer Frank Sinatra for his first solo performance in front of four thousand eager young fans, who would soon be known as "bobbysoxers" and were ready to think about something other than war. The twenty-seven-year-old Hoboken native was already well known as a crooner for Tommy Dorsey's band and had just embarked on his own career. The deafening roar that came after Goodman's introduction led the startled bandleader to ask, "What the hell was that?"[48]

On New Year's Eve, President Roosevelt celebrated with a few close friends at the White House. After dinner, settling in to watch a movie that would not be released nationally until January, they became one of the first audiences to view *Casablanca*, starring Humphrey Bogart and Ingrid Bergman. Perhaps only the president appreciated the irony of the movie's setting. Within two weeks, he would travel to Casablanca for a meeting with Winston Churchill, becoming the first president to leave the country in wartime.

Throughout the nation, anxious citizens celebrated New Year's Eve with muted enthusiasm. As nearly four hundred thousand revelers gathered in Times Square, one observer thought the crowd brought in the New Year "in melancholy fashion." Considering all they had been through and the prospects that lay ahead, the *New York Times* detected "a sluggishness" about the celebration, "an absence of real gayety." After midnight came, a sound truck asked for ten seconds of silence in honor of those serving overseas. "Men removed their hats," and "women's laughter suddenly stopped." Observers noted that draft-age men seemed in short supply, while teenagers were present in large numbers. Police reported less drunkenness than in previous years, and overall it was an eerily solemn occasion.

An American soldier serving overseas wondered, "Does it seem kind of out of place to be talking about a 'Happy New Year?'" While 1942 had been a year "which brought us the bitterness and humiliation of defeat after defeat," he also thought it was "the turning point of the war." In all, he felt that "the spark of culture has survived the dark ages again." In Chicago, revelers toasted the troops and one resident, Lloyd Hall, marked the occasion by saying, "Here's to the time when we'll triumph and when democracy will be more than just a word."[49]

Epilogue

AS 1943 DAWNED, the relentless fear that had gripped the nation since Pearl Harbor had somewhat lessened, and although most understood that the most difficult days of the war still lay ahead, many worst-case scenarios had been avoided. There were no additional Pearl Harbors, economic chaos was averted, and democratic forms of constitutional government managed to endure. The year also displayed how a planned economy saved the nation from ruinous inflation and that government could work effectively to confront a grave crisis. In all, the nation had utilized vast economic and human resources and had made a national commitment to sacrifice life and treasure in what Franklin Roosevelt had termed "the most tremendous undertaking of our American history."

After the searing heat of a crisis passes, often the original feelings of impending doom can be almost forgotten. The pervasive national anxiety of early 1942 would gradually be replaced by nostalgic and comforting memories of Americans confidently coming together, bound by their "righteous might" to build a vast arsenal that triumphed over enemies on two fronts.

That reassuring saga hides a more complicated story. Democracy had survived its most stringent test since the Civil War, but that outcome was far from assured. The nation's fate would have been very different if Congress had challenged the president for ultimate war-making or budgetary authority. If attempts to control inflation or raise taxes had been crushed, the resulting economic disaster might have made the "Arsenal of Democracy" little more than a rhetorical flourish. If more attacks had occurred in the U.S., civil liberties might have eroded even further. If the Germans had been victorious at Stalingrad, the resulting military and diplomatic scenarios would have been harrowing. Observers who warned of dire consequences did so for good reason.

If an inept politician or demagogue had been in the White House, constitutional government would have been in jeopardy. Not that FDR was always fastidious about preserving constitutional norms. He was sometimes accused of using the crisis to seize dictatorial control, and he threatened Congress that he might assume new authority if he did not get his way on the anti-inflation impasse. His administration established internment camps for Japanese Americans, maintained strict segregation in the armed forces, and intruded into the economic affairs of citizens more than any other president before or since. Yet Roosevelt did not use his popularity or three-term status to suspend the Constitution or impose martial law. He did not imprison his political opponents, and the election of 1942 went on as usual, with the president's party losing many seats.

Democracy is essentially an act of faith, and national leaders mostly acted in good faith and did not exploit the war crisis for personal or partisan reasons. Leon Henderson and Donald Nelson were more focused on keeping inflation contained than concerned with their own careers. Many in Congress and the administration understood the peril that the nation faced and rose to the occasion. FDR was more interested in ensuring economic fairness and in making "Freedom from Want" an essential American principle than in becoming an autocrat. Still, if bigots such as Theodore Bilbo or Martin Dies had held more power, or if isolationists or opponents of government had won the day, the survival of democracy at home and abroad would not have been certain. The political and economic experience of America in 1942 demonstrates the fragile nature of self-government in times of national stress. As Steven Levitsky and Daniel Ziblatt write in *How Democracies Die*, "Would-be autocrats often use economic crises, natural disasters, and especially security threats—wars, armed insurgencies, or terrorist attacks—to justify antidemocratic measures."[1] Fortunately, that did not happen after Pearl Harbor, but not because it was somehow foreordained.

Despite the fact that the nation endured with its institutions and values intact, for millions of Americans in 1942 democracy was in short supply and the Constitution provided no safe haven. The treatment of Japanese Americans, the white supremacist efforts against African American equality in employment and housing, the racial riots at numerous military bases, the rising tide of anti-Semitism, the daily humiliations of Jim Crow policies in communities across the country, and the horrific episodes of lynchings all demonstrated that in times of national anxiety, we do not necessarily come together as one. Deep-seated hatreds are not put aside. They grow.

The trauma of Pearl Harbor and the fear that the nation might be invaded and conquered exposed America's domestic paradoxes as nothing else could. They provided a rare opportunity to see what was possible when many economic and social structures were suspended and new ideas were debated. Some used the chance to dream of a more democratic society while others clung to old hatreds and suspicions. Historian John Hope Franklin, writing in the midst of the war, noted that two competing concepts deep within American life had long battled each other: "One tradition—that of democracy and liberalism—has built American civilization, while the other—that of narrowness and bigotry—has threatened to transform the great American dream into a nightmare." "It is indeed a matter of survival," he warned, "to see to it that the best of American traditions are not overwhelmed by the worst."[2] That war still rages.

NOTES

Preface

1. http://books.google.com/ngrams. Jean-Baptiste Michel, Yuan Kui Shen, Aviva Presser Aiden, Adrian Veres, Matthew K. Gray, William Brockman, the Google Books Team, Joseph P. Pickett, Dale Hoiberg, Dan Clancy, Peter Norvig, Jon Orwant, Steven Pinker, Martin A. Nowak, and Erez Lieberman Aiden, "Quantitative Analysis of Culture Using Millions of Digitized Books," *Science*, January 14, 2011, 176–82.
2. Samuel P. Huntington, "Democracy's Third Wave," *Journal of Democracy* 2 (spring 1991): 12.
3. *New York Times*, September 21, October 2, 2008; Ben S. Bernanke, *The Courage to Act: A Memoir of a Crisis and Its Aftermath* (New York: Norton, 2015), 336, 386; Adam Tooze, *Crashed: How a Decade of Financial Crises Changed the World* (New York: Viking, 2018), 143–65.
4. Tom Brokaw, *The Greatest Generation* (New York: Random House, 1998); "National Survey Finds Just 1 in 3 Americans Would Pass Citizenship Test," Woodrow Wilson National Fellowship Foundation, October 3, 2018.
5. Jack Saul, *Collective Trauma, Collective Healing: Promoting Community Resilience in the Aftermath of Disaster* (New York: Routledge, 2014), 1–17; Arlene Audergon, "Collective Trauma: The Nightmare of History," *Psychotherapy and Politics International* 2 (February 2004): 16–31; Arthur Neal, *National Trauma and Collective Memory: Extraordinary Events in the American Experience* (Armonk: M. E. Sharpe, 2005), 56–70; *New York Times*, December 17, 2016.
6. John Keane, *The Life and Death of Democracy* (London: Simon and Schuster, 2009), xiv–xv.

December 1941

1. *New York Times*, December 10, 1941. Engelson's background was found in ancestry.com.

2. Gallup poll, December 1941, at ropercenter.cornell.edu; John Keegan, *The Second World War* (New York: Penguin, 1989), 255–56.

3. Harold L. Ickes Diary, December 14, 1941, Library of Congress, Washington, D.C.; Steven M. Gillon, *Pearl Harbor: FDR Leads the Nation into War* (New York: Basic Books, 2011), 145–62. Shortly after Pearl Harbor, FDR appointed a commission led by Supreme Court justice Owen Roberts to investigate the attack and assign responsibility. In late January, the commission released its findings, which laid the blame on two military officials—U.S. Pacific Fleet commander Husband E. Kimmel and army general Walter Short.

4. *Pittsburgh Courier*, May 9, 1942; *New York Times*, May 11, June 29, 1942. Miller died in action in November 1943.

5. *Time*, February 16, 1942; R. W. Goldsmith to Robert Nathan, October 26, 1942, Leon Henderson Papers, Franklin D. Roosevelt Presidential Library, Hyde Park, N.Y.; Henry L. Stimson Diary, December 7, 1941, Henry L. Stimson Papers, Manuscripts and Archives, Yale University Library, New Haven, Conn.; Ickes Diary, January 11, 1942; *New York Times*, May 24, 1942; Steven M. Gillon, *Pearl Harbor: FDR Leads the Nation into War* (New York: Basic Books, 2011), 8; George H. Roeder Jr., *The Censored War: American Visual Experience during World War II* (New Haven: Yale University Press, 1993), 4.

6. U.S. Department of Justice, *Report to the Congress of the United States: Review of Restrictions on Persons of Italian Ancestry during World War II* (Washington, D.C.: U.S. Department of Justice, November 2001), 4–5; Mary Elizabeth Basile Chopas, *Searching for Subversives: The Story of Italian Internment in Wartime America* (Chapel Hill: University of North Carolina Press, 2017), xvi, 2–9.

7. *New York Times*, December 8, 1941; Greg Robinson, *A Tragedy of Democracy: Japanese Confinement in North America* (New York: Columbia University Press, 2009), 60–61; Richard Reeves, *Infamy: The Shocking Story of the Japanese American Internment in World War II* (New York: Picador, 2015), 2–5; Matthew Dallek, *Defenseless under the Night: The Roosevelt Years and the Origins of Homeland Security* (New York: Oxford University Press, 2016), 185.

8. http://www.archives.gov/exhibits/charters/treasure/declaration_travels.html.

9. Nigel Hamilton, *The Mantle of Command: FDR at War, 1941–1942* (Boston: Houghton Mifflin Harcourt, 2014), 94–95; Adam Tooze, *The Wages of Destruction: The Making and Breaking of the Nazi Economy* (New York: Penguin, 2006), 501; George C. Herring, *From Colony to Superpower: U.S. Foreign Relations since 1776* (New York: Oxford University Press, 2008), 549; FDR fireside chat, December 9, 1941. Representative Jeannette Rankin had voted against the declaration against Japan on pacifist grounds, but after public uproar, she abstained in the vote concerning war with Germany and Italy.

10. *New York Times*, October 31, 1940.

11. Arthur Herman, *Freedom's Forge: How American Business Produced Victory in World War II* (New York: Random House, 2012), 175; P. M. H. Bell, *The Origins of the Second World War in Europe* (New York: Routledge, 1986), 41; Victor Davis Hanson, *The Second World Wars: How the First Global Conflict Was Fought and Won* (New York: Basic Books, 2017), 215, 241; Susan Dunn, *A Blueprint for War: FDR and the Hundred Days That Mobilized America* (New Haven: Yale University Press, 2018), 103–4.

12. "Report of the Commanding General of the Army Air Forces to the Secretary of War (1944)," Donald M. Nelson Papers, Huntington Library, San Marino, Calif.

13. U.S. Selective Service System, *Selective Service in Peacetime, 1940–41: First Report of the Director of Selective Service* (Washington, D.C.: U.S. Government Printing Office, 1942), 17; John R. Craf, *A Survey of the American Economy, 1940–1946* (New York: North River, 1947), 11.

14. *Chicago Daily-Tribune*, December 6, 1941; Amanda Smith, *Newspaper Titan: The Infamous Life and Monumental Times of Cissy Patterson* (New York: Knopf, 2011), 392–98; Jim Lacey, *Keep from All Thoughtful Men: How U.S. Economists Won World War II* (Annapolis: Naval Institute Press, 2011), 86–89, 146–50; Mark R. Wilson, *Destructive Creation: American Business and the Winning of World War II* (Philadelphia: University of Pennsylvania Press, 2016), 50–62.

15. *Time*, January 5, 1942; Craig Shirley, *December 1941: 31 Days That Changed America and Saved the World* (Nashville: Thomas Nelson, 2011), 281; *New York Times*, December 13, 22, 1941; Doris D. Reed and Thomas H. Reed, "Insurance for War Damage," *Survey Graphic* (February 1942).

16. Jesse Jones to FDR, March 24, 1943, President's Official Files, FDR Library; Matlaw Corporation v. War Damage Corporation, 164 F.2d 281 (1947); *New York Times*, April 27, 1942; Craf, *A Survey of the American Economy*, 47; "Commerce Secretary Press Release," June 2, 1942, "Federal Loan Agency," December 31, 1941, President's Official Files.

17. *New York Times*, December 11, 1941.

18. *New York Times*, December 11, 15, 1941; *New Yorker*, December 20, 1941.

19. Stimson Diary, December 18, 1941.

20. *Popular Science Monthly*, May 1942, 102–3; Susan L. Smith, "Mustard Gas and American Race-Based Human Experimentation in World War II," *Journal of Law, Medicine, and Ethics* (Fall 2008): 517–21; *Independent*, March 17, 1993.

21. *New York Times*, December 20, 1941.

22. *New York Times*, December 16, 1941.

23. Ira Katznelson, *Fear Itself: The New Deal and the Origins of Our Time* (New York: Norton, 2013), 118–23.

24. *Wall Street Journal*, December 20, 1941; *New York Times*, December 17, 1941; Sanford Levinson and Jack M. Balkin, "Constitutional Dictatorship: Its Dangers and Designs," *Minnesota Law Review* 94 (2010): 1789–1856; Katznelson, *Fear Itself*, 337; Richard Polenberg, ed., *America at War: The Home Front, 1941–1945* (Englewood Cliffs, N.J.: Prentice-Hall, 1968), 5–6; Thomas Fleming, *The New Dealers' War: FDR and the War within World War II* (New York: Basic Books, 2001), 1–91.

25. Lester V. Chandler, *Inflation in the United States, 1940–1948* (New York: Harper, 1951), 1; *New York Times*, December 27, 1941.

26. *New York Times*, December 28, 30, 1941; Lynne Olson, *Those Angry Days: Roosevelt, Lindbergh, and America's Fight over World War II* (New York: Random House, 2014), 276.

27. *New York Times*, December 31, 1941; Robert Dallek, *Franklin D. Roosevelt: A Political Life* (New York: Viking, 2017), 334.

28. *New York Times*, December 28, 1941; W.E.B. Du Bois, "A Chronicle of Race Relations," *Phylon* 3 (First Quarter, 1942), 66.

Chapter 1. January

1. *Duke* magazine, November–December 2011, 38–41; Brian Curtis, *Fields of Battle: Pearl Harbor, the Rose Bowl, and the Boys Who Went to War* (New York: Flatiron Books, 2016); Steven M. Gillon, *Pearl Harbor: FDR Leads the Nation into War* (New York: Basic Books, 2011), 50.

2. Marc Wortman, *1941: A Divided America in a World at War* (New York: Atlantic Monthly, 2016), 277–79.

3. *New York Times*, January 31, February 1, 21, 1942; *Nation*, January 3, 1942; *Life*, January 5, 1942; *New Yorker*, January 31, 1942.

4. Gillon, *Pearl Harbor*, 103; *New York Times*, January 4, 1942; Robert Klara, *The Hidden White House: Harry Truman and the Reconstruction of America's Most Famous Residence* (New York: St. Martin's, 2013), 157–58; Nigel Hamilton, *The Mantle of Command: FDR at War, 1941–1942* (Boston: Houghton Mifflin Harcourt, 2014), 146–49.

5. *Los Angeles Times*, January 7, 1942.

6. Samuel Rosenman, ed., *Humanity on the Defensive*, vol. 11 of *The Public Papers and Addresses of Franklin D. Roosevelt* (New York: Harper and Bros., 1950), 37; *Newsweek*, January 19, 1942; Max Hastings, *Inferno: The World at War, 1939–1945* (New York: Random House, 2011), 224–25; Robert E. Sherwood, *Roosevelt and Hopkins: An Intimate History* (New York: Harper, 1948), 444; *Life*, January 19, 1942.

7. *Budget of the United States Government for the Fiscal Year Ending June 30, 1943* (Washington, D.C.: Government Printing Office, 1942), xxi; James T. Sparrow, *Warfare State: World War II Americans and the Age of Big Government* (New York: Oxford University Press, 2011), 6; Lester V. Chandler, *Inflation in the United States, 1940–1948* (New York: Harper, 1951), 61–65, 115; Rosenman, *Humanity on the Defensive*, 6–13; *Time*, January 19, 1942; *Economist*, January 17, 1942; *New York Times*, January 8, 11, 1942.

8. *Budget of the United States Government for the Fiscal Year Ending June 30, 1943*; Rosenman, *Humanity on the Defensive*, 19–20; *New York Times*, January 8, 1942.

9. Rosenman, *Humanity on the Defensive*, 35–36, 42; Susan Dunn, *A Blueprint for War: FDR and the Hundred Days That Mobilized America* (New Haven: Yale University Press, 2018), 93–96.

10. *New York Times,* January 6, 7, 1942.

11. Archibald MacLeish Memo, "Intelligence Report No. 4," January 12, 1942, Wayne Coy Papers, Franklin D. Roosevelt Presidential Library, Hyde Park, N.Y.; *Life,* January 5, 1942.

12. Ken Silverstein, "Ford and the Führer," *Nation,* January 24, 2000; *Time,* March 23, 1942; Neil Baldwin, *Henry Ford and the Jews: The Mass Production of Hate* (New York: Public Affairs, 2001), 218–40; Steven Watts, *The People's Tycoon: Henry Ford and the American Century* (New York: Vintage, 2006), 504–10.

13. *Time,* January 19, 1942; Edwin Black, *IBM and the Holocaust: The Strategic Alliance between Nazi Germany and America's Most Powerful Corporation* (New York: Crown, 2001), 51, 105–217; *New York Times,* February 11, 2001.

14. *New York Times,* January 26, 1942.

15. Rosenman, *Humanity on the Defensive,* 14–18; *Newsweek,* January 19, 1942; Chandler, *Inflation in the United States,* 86; *New York Times,* January 12, 14, 1942.

16. Address by Joseph W. Martin Jr., of Massachusetts, to the National Radio Forum, NBC Radio, January 12, 1942, www.ibiblio.org/1942/; *Newsweek,* January 19, 1942; *New York Times,* January 8, 1942.

17. *New York Times,* January 14, 22, 1942; Donald M. Nelson, *Arsenal of Democracy: The Story of American War Production* (New York: Harcourt Brace, 1946), 3–7.

18. *Newsweek,* January 19, 1942.

19. *New York Times,* January 8, 1942; *Washington Post,* January 12, 1942.

20. FDR meeting with A. Philip Randolph and Frank Knox, September 27, 1940, at millercenter.org/fdr/audiovisual/whrecordings/corrected/fdr_09_1940_randolph.html; *Indianapolis Recorder,* January 17, 1942; Stimson Diary, January 17, 21, 24, 1942, Henry L. Stimson Papers, Manuscripts and Archives, Yale University Library, New Haven, Conn.

21. "Now Is Not the Time to Be Silent," *Crisis,* January 1942; Reginald Kearney, *African American Views of the Japanese: Solidarity or Sedition?* (Albany: State University of New York Press, 1998), 94–97; *New York Times,* January 11, 1942; John Hope Franklin, *Mirror to America: The Autobiography of John Hope Franklin* (New York: Farrar, Straus and Giroux, 2005), 104–8.

22. *PM,* January 21, 22, 1942; *Louisiana Weekly,* January 24, 1942; *New York Times,* January 11, 1942; Anonymous to Walter White, January 13, 1942, NAACP Papers, Library of Congress, Washington, D.C.; William M. Simpson, "A Tale Untold? The Alexandria, Louisiana, Lee Street Riot," *Louisiana History* 35 (Spring 1994): 133–49; Robert A. Hill, ed., *The FBI's RACON: Racial Conditions in the United States during World War II* (Boston: Northeastern University Press, 1995), 326–27.

23. Thomas A. Guglielmo, "'Red Cross, Double Cross': Race and America's World War II–Era Blood Donor Service," *Journal of American History* (June 2010): 70–74; *Journal of the American Medical Association,* July 4, 1942, 801; Spencie Love, *One Blood: The Death and Resurrection of Charles R. Drew* (Chapel Hill: University of North Carolina Press, 1996), 155–57, 195–202.

24. *People's Voice,* July 4, 1942.

25. Harold G. Vatter, *The U.S. Economy in World War II* (New York: Columbia University Press, 1985), 131; *New York Times*, January 23, 1942; Hill, *The FBI's RACON*, 689; Thomas J. Sugrue, *Sweet Land of Liberty: The Forgotten Struggle for Civil Rights in the North* (New York: Random House, 2008), 63–77.

26. A. Philip Randolph, "Why Should We March?" *Survey Graphic* 31 (November 1942): 488–89; Clarence Lang, *Grassroots at the Gateway: Class Politics and the Black Freedom Struggle in St. Louis, 1936–1975* (Ann Arbor: University of Michigan Press, 2009), 47–48; Keona K. Ervin, "We Rebel: Black Women, Worker Theater, and Critical Unionism in Wartime St. Louis," *Souls: A Critical Journal of Black Politics, Culture, and Society* 18 (June 2016): 32–58; *People's Voice*, June 6, 1942.

27. *Sikeston Herald*, January 29, 1942; *Sikeston Standard*, January 29, 30, 1942; *Labor Action*, March 23, 1942; Dominic J. Capeci Jr., *The Lynching of Cleo Wright* (Lexington: University Press of Kentucky, 1998), 14–24; *New York Times*, January 26, 1942.

28. "An Informal Report on Attitudes in Southeast Missouri Relative to the Lynching of Cleo Wright," NAACP Papers.

29. Walter White to FDR, January 26, 1942; James Rodgers to FDR, November 10, 1942, President's Official Files, FDR Library, 93, "Colored Matters," FDR Library; Hill, *The FBI's RACON*, 101; *Washington Post*, December 28, 2018.

30. *Pittsburgh Courier*, January 31, 1942.

31. U.S. Department of Justice, "Report to Congress of the United States: Review of Restrictions on Persons of Italian Ancestry during World War II" (November 2001); *New York Times*, January 11, 31, 1942; Francis Biddle, *In Brief Authority* (Garden City: Doubleday, 1962), 205–11; Stephen Fox, *The Unknown Internment: An Oral History of the Relocation of Italian Americans during World War II* (Boston: Twayne, 1990), 41–50; Stefano Lucano, "Contested Loyalties: World War II and Italian Americans' Ethnic Identity," *Italian Americana* 30 (Summer 2012): 151; David A. Taylor, "During World War II, the U.S. Saw Italian-Americans as a Threat to Homeland Security," Smithsonian.com, February 2, 2017.

32. Leni Yahil, *The Holocaust: The Fate of European Jewry* (New York: Oxford University Press, 1990), 312–16; Daniel Jonah Goldhagen, *Hitler's Willing Executioners: Ordinary Germans and the Holocaust* (New York: Random House, 1997), 157–58; *New York Times*, January 5, 1942.

33. David M. Kennedy, *Freedom from Fear: The American People in Depression and War, 1929–1945* (New York: Oxford University Press, 1999), 565–67; Ed Offley, *The Burning Shore: How Hitler's U-Boats Brought World War II to America* (New York: Basic Books, 2014), 112–13; Michael Gannon, *Operation Drumbeat: The Dramatic True Story of Germany's First U-Boat Attacks along the American East Coast in World War II* (New York: HarperCollins, 1990), 214–41; *New York Times*, June 17, 2018.

34. *New York Times*, January 20, 29, 1942; *Newsweek*, January 26, 1942; Gail Levin, "Edward Hopper's *Nighthawks*, Surrealism, and War," *Art Institute of Chicago Museum Studies* 22 (1996): 181–95; "Nighthawks, 1942," at edwardhopper.net.

35. *New York Times*, January 13, 20, 26, 1942.

36. Address by Colonel George J. B. Fisher, January 13, 1942, www.ibiblio.org/1942.

37. *Time,* January 5, 1942.

38. Alvin H. Hansen, *After the War—Full Employment* (National Resources Planning Board, January 1942); *Boston Herald,* September 20, 1942.

39. *New York Times,* January 15, February 5, 1942; National Resources Planning Board, "Security, Work, and Relief Policies, 1942," 447; John Morton Blum, *V Was for Victory: Politics and Culture during World War II* (San Diego: Harcourt Brace Jovanovich, 1976), 237–38; *Wall Street Journal,* January 5, February 18, 1943.

40. Federal Reserve Economic Data, National Bureau of Economic Research, "Unemployment Rate for the United States," Federal Reserve Bank of St. Louis, fred.stlouisfed.org; Rosenman, *Humanity on the Defensive,* 23–24, 42–48; John R. Craf, *A Survey of the American Economy, 1940–1946* (New York: North River, 1947), 160–61; Robert H. Zieger, *The CIO: 1935–1955* (Chapel Hill: University of North Carolina Press, 1997), 111–211.

41. *New York Times,* January 11, 1942.

42. Stanley Weintraub, *Pearl Harbor Christmas: A World at War, December 1941* (Cambridge, Mass.: Da Capo, 2011), 111.

43. *Newsweek,* January 12, 1942.

44. *Time,* February 2, 1942; *New York Times,* February 3, 1942.

45. *New York Times,* January 10, 1942.

46. Rosenman, *Humanity on the Defensive,* 62.

47. *New York Times,* January 17, 1942.

48. *Life,* August 17, 1942; *New York Times,* January 20, 22, 1942; Harold L. Ickes Diary, January 11, 1942, Library of Congress, Washington, D.C.; Gallup poll, February 1942, at ropercenter.cornell.edu. Congress waited until 1946 to revive the pension.

49. Rosenman, *Humanity on the Defensive,* 67–73; *New York Times,* January 28, 1942.

50. Craf, *A Survey of the American Economy,* 66, 72–73; Vatter, *The U.S. Economy in World War II,* 41; *Newsweek,* January 19, 1942.

51. *New York Times,* January 11, 1942.

52. *Life,* September 14, 1942; *New York Times,* January 16, 21, 1942.

53. *New York Times,* January 23, 24, 1942.

54. "Speech by H. W. Prentis, Jr., Before the Joint Dinner of the Association of American Colleges, Baltimore, Maryland, January 2, 1942," www.ibiblio.org.

55. *New York Times,* January 11, 1942.

56. *New York Times,* May 24, 1942.

57. *New York Times,* January 20, 21, 1942.

58. *New York Times,* January 23, 1942; Julia Felsenthal, "A Size 2 Is a Size 2 Is a Size 8," *Slate,* January 25, 2012. See *Women's Measurements for Garment and Pattern Construction,* U.S. Department of Agriculture no. 454, December 1941.

59. *New York Times,* January 29, 1942.

60. George C. Herring, *From Colony to Superpower: U.S. Foreign Relations since 1776* (New York: Oxford University Press, 2008), 544–45.

61. Robert Dallek, *Franklin D. Roosevelt: A Political Life* (New York: Viking, 2017), 620; Carlo Levi, *Christ Stopped at Eboli: The Story of a Year* (New York: Farrar,

Straus and Giroux Classics, 2006), 122; Nelson, *Arsenal of Democracy*, 14; *New York Times*, April 13, 1945.

62. *Fortune*, January, February 1942.

63. *Time*, February 9, 1942; Nelson, *Arsenal of Democracy*, 283.

Chapter 2. February

1. *The Point Log*, Gray Court, Stamford, Conn., 1933. Florence Coleman Nimick appears in census records, passenger lists, and school yearbooks in ancestry.com. *New York Times*, August 9, 1912.

2. *New York Times*, April 30, May 9, June 26, 1942; *Catholic Telegraph-Register*, September 4, 1942; *Chicago Tribune*, March 24, November 23, 1942; Leslie J. Reagan, *When Abortion Was a Crime: Women, Medicine, and Law in the United States, 1867–1973* (Berkeley: University of California Press, 1997), 163, 171.

3. *New York Times*, January 31, 1942; Alan F. Guttmacher, "The Genesis of Liberalized Abortions in New York: A Personal Insight," *Case Western Reserve Law Review* 23 (1972): 756–64.

4. Tileston v. Ullman, 129 Conn. 84 (1942); Tileston v. Ullman, 318 U.S. 44 (1943); Griswold v. Connecticut, 381 U.S. 479 (1965); David M. Kennedy, *Birth Control in America: The Career of Margaret Sanger* (New Haven: Yale University Press, 1970), 254–55.

5. *New York Times*, February 15, 16, 17, 1942; *Cleveland Plain Dealer*, February 15, 1942; *Chicago Daily Tribune*, February 15, 1942.

6. *New York Times*, January 28, 29, February 17, March 6, 1942; *Social Justice*, February 16, 1942.

7. *New York Times*, January 31, February 1, 1942.

8. *New York Times*, February 1, 1942; *Brooklyn Daily Eagle*, June 1, 1942; Leonard Larsen to Helen Larsen, November 16, 1942; Helen Larsen to Leonard Larsen, November 14, 1942, Leonard Larsen Papers, New-York Historical Society, New York. Information on Nollman and Gusko was obtained through ancestry.com.

9. *New York Times*, December 9, 1941; Wolfgang Schivelbusch, *The Culture of Defeat: On National Trauma, Mourning, and Recovery*, trans. Jefferson Chase (New York: Picador, 2004), 7–10, 22–29.

10. *Nikkei* is a word of Japanese origin for citizens and aliens living in the U.S. *Issei* refers to first-generation aliens born in Japan, and *Nisei* refers to second-generation citizens born in the U.S.

11. Telephone Conversation, Neustadt and Powell, February 1942, Japanese-American Evacuation and Resettlement Records (JERS), reel 4, Bancroft Library, University of California, Berkeley; Yuji Ichioka, ed., *Views from Within: The Japanese American Evacuation and Resettlement Study* (Los Angeles: Asian American Studies Center, 1989); Richard Reeves, *Infamy: The Shocking Story of the Japanese American Internment in World War II* (New York: Picador, 2015), 40–41.

12. Mr. and Mrs. Harden to FDR, January 12, 1942; J. Violet Sims to FDR, January 28, 1942; Luis Gonzales to FDR, January 24, 1942; Frank Harvey Miller to FDR, February 16, 1942, JERS; *Los Angeles Times*, February 17, 1942.

13. Harold L. Ickes Diary, February 15, 1942, Library of Congress, Washington, D.C.; *Life*, April 13, 1942; Greg Robinson, *A Tragedy of Democracy: Japanese Confinement in North America* (New York: Columbia University Press, 2009), 84; Reeves, *Infamy*, xxiii.

14. Samuel Rosenman, ed., *Humanity on the Defensive*, vol. 11 of *The Public Papers and Addresses of Franklin D. Roosevelt* (New York: Harper and Bros., 1950), 174–77; Reeves, *Infamy*, 32–56; Kyle Longley, *Senator Albert Gore, Sr: Tennessee Maverick* (Baton Rouge: Louisiana State University Press, 2004), 52–53; John Eric Schmitz, "Enemies among Us: The Relocation, Internment, and Repatriation of German, Italian, and Japanese Americans during the Second World War" (Ph.D. diss., American University, 2007), 5–12, 236–45.

15. *Time*, April 6, 1942; John Morton Blum, *V Was for Victory: Politics and American Culture during World War II* (San Diego: Harcourt Brace Jovanovich, 1976), 163.

16. Stephen Fox, *The Unknown Internment: An Oral History of the Relocation of Italian Americans during World War II* (Boston: Twayne, 1990), 75–76; Mary Elizabeth Basile Chopas, *Searching for Subversives: The Story of Italian Internment in Wartime America* (Chapel Hill: University of North Carolina Press, 2017), 2–30.

17. *Time*, February 9, 1942; *New York Times*, February 10, 1942.

18. John Taber to Henry Morgenthau, February 10, 1942; Morgenthau Press Conference, February 9, 1942, Henry Morgenthau Jr., Papers, Franklin D. Roosevelt Presidential Library, Hyde Park, N.Y.; Neal Gabler, *Walt Disney: The Triumph of the American Imagination* (New York: Random House, 2006), 384–86.

19. *New York Times*, February 6, 15, 1942; Donald M. Nelson, *Arsenal of Democracy: The Story of American War Production* (New York: Harcourt Brace, 1946), 269–89.

20. *New York Times*, January 25, February 20, 1942.

21. Frank Knox to Annie Knox, February 3, 1942, Frank Knox Papers, Library of Congress, Washington, D.C.; *New York Times*, February 3, 8, 11, 1942.

22. "Digest of Minutes of War Production Board, February 17, 1942," Harry L. Hopkins Papers, FDR Library.

23. Lester V. Chandler, *Inflation in the United States, 1940–1948* (New York: Harper, 1951), 208; Alan Brinkley, *The End of Reform: New Deal Liberalism in Recession and War* (New York: Knopf, 1995), 147.

24. *Life*, September 14, 1942; *Saturday Evening Post*, September 13, 1941.

25. *Life*, September 14, 1942.

26. Drew Pearson and Robert S. Allen, "Washington Merry-Go-Round," May 6, 1939; *New York Times*, October 21, 1986; *Life*, September 14, 1942; *Saturday Evening Post*, September 13, 1941; Walter Karig, "The Toughest Guy in Washington," *Liberty*, June 6, 1942; Speech by Leon Henderson before Chicago Better Business Bureau, February 20, 1942, www.ibiblio.org/1942; Eliot Janeway, *The Struggle for*

Survival: A Chronicle of Economic Mobilization in World War II (New Haven: Yale University Press, 1951), 164, 199.

27. *Saturday Evening Post,* September 13, 1941.

28. *New York Times,* May 10, 1942; Brinkley, *The End of Reform,* 84; *Saturday Evening Post,* September 13, 1941; *Philadelphia Inquirer,* October 22, 1986.

29. Leon Henderson and Donald M. Nelson, "Prices, Profits, and Government," *Harvard Business Review* (Summer 1941): 389–404; Harvey C. Mansfield and Associates, "A Short History of OPA," OPA Office of Temporary Controls, 1947, 29–30; Andrew H. Bartels, "The Politics of Price Control: The Office of Price Administration and the Dilemmas of Economic Stabilization, 1940–1946" (Ph.D. diss., Johns Hopkins University, 1980), 20–52, 66–86.

30. *Life,* January 26, September 14, 1942; *New York Times,* January 15, 1942; *New York Daily News,* January 15, 1942; George E. Shaw to FDR, January 15, 1942, President's Official Files, FDR Library; Gallup poll, March 1942, ropercenter.cornell.edu.

31. *New York Times,* February 14, 1942.

32. Speech of Leon Henderson before the Chicago Better Business Bureau, Chicago, Illinois, February 20, 1942, www.ibiblio.org/1942.

33. *New York Times,* February 22, 1942.

34. *New York Times,* February 3, April 5, 1942.

35. "War Workers Point of View," July 28, 1942, Oscar Cox Papers, FDR Library.

36. Louis P. Lochner, ed., *The Goebbels Diaries, 1942–1943* (New York: Doubleday, 1948), 88.

37. *Time,* February 23, 1942; *New York Times,* February 11, 1942; John Strausbaugh, *Victory City: A History of New York and New Yorkers during World War II* (New York: Twelve, 2018), 269–70.

38. *Time,* February 23, 1942; Committee to Defend America to Francis Biddle, February 18, 1942, JERS; George H. Roeder Jr., *The Censored War: American Visual Experience during World War II* (New Haven: Yale University Press, 1993), 8; Nigel Hamilton, *The Mantle of Command: FDR at War, 1941–1942* (Boston: Houghton Mifflin Harcourt, 2014), 202–5; *New York Times,* February 18, 1942; Alistair Cooke, *The American Home Front, 1941–1942* (New York: Grove, 2006), 55; *Nation,* February 14, 1942; *Life,* February 23, 1942.

39. *Kentucky Club Woman,* March–April 1942; Rosenman, *Humanity on the Defensive,* 103.

40. *New York Times,* January 1, 1942; Bureau of the Census, *Statistical Abstract of the United States, 1950* (Washington, D.C.: U.S. Government Printing Office, 1950), 11.

41. *New York Times,* January 8, February 15, 1942; Margaret Mead, ". . . To Keep Our Children Safe from Fear," *Guild Teacher,* February–March 1942.

42. Pauline Rush Fadiman, "Children's Attitudes in Wartime," *Barnard Alumnae* (May 1942).

43. *New York Times,* February 22, 1942.

44. Margaret Mead, "Rehearsals for No Panic," Margaret Mead Papers, Library of Congress.

45. Lester Markel to Margaret Mead, May 20, 1942, Margaret Mead Papers.

46. *New York Times*, February 13, 1942.

47. Address of Wendell Willkie before Lincoln Birthday Dinner, Middlesex Club of Boston, February 12, 1942, www.ibiblio.org/1942.

48. *Newsweek*, February 23, 1942.

49. *New York Times*, February 13, 1942.

50. George C. Herring, *From Colony to Superpower: U.S. Foreign Relations since 1776* (New York: Oxford University Press, 2008), 544; *New York Times*, February 7, 14, 21, 1942.

51. *New York Times*, February 12, 1942; Nelson Lichtenstein, *State of the Union: A Century of American Labor* (Princeton: Princeton University Press, 2002), 101–3.

52. *New York Times*, February 7, 1942; Matthew Dallek, *Defenseless under the Night: The Roosevelt Years and the Origins of Homeland Security* (New York: Oxford University Press, 2016), 213–19; Eleanor Roosevelt, *The Autobiography of Eleanor Roosevelt* (New York: Harper, 1961), 230–31.

53. *New York Times*, February 9, 10, 1942; Garry Wills, *John Wayne's America: The Politics of Celebrity* (New York: Simon and Schuster, 1997), 102–13.

54. *New York Times*, February 8, 15, 1942; Gallup poll, February 1942, ropercenter. cornell.edu.

55. *New York Times*, February 15, 24, 1942.

56. Donald R. Longman to Arthur Burns, February 2, 1942, and Leon Henderson to Ferdinand Eberstadt, February 18, 1942, Henderson Papers, FDR Library; Speech by Leon Henderson to Chicago Better Business Bureau, February 20, 1942, www. ibiblio.org/1942.

57. *New York Times*, February 21, 1942.

58. *New York Times*, February 22, 1942; Nelson Lichtenstein, *Labor's War at Home: The CIO in World War II* (Philadelphia: Temple University Press, 2008), 72–81; Nelson Lichtenstein, *The Most Dangerous Man in Detroit: Walter Reuther and the Fate of American Labor* (New York: Basic Books, 1995), 154–93; Steven Fraser, *Labor Will Rule: Sidney Hillman and the Rise of American Labor* (New York: Free Press, 1991), 452–94.

59. William S. Jack, "Jack and Heintz: Blueprint for Labor Relations," *Public Opinion Quarterly* 7 (Autumn 1943): 413–30; *Newsweek*, January 5, 1942; *JAHCO News*, August 28, 1942; Maury Klein, *A Call to Arms: Mobilizing America for World War II* (New York: Bloomsbury, 2013), 525–28.

60. *JAHCO News*, June 26, August 28, October 23, 1942, July, August, 1943; Ernst and Ernst to Board of Directors, Jack and Heintz, January 26, 1943, Jack and Heintz Company Records, Bedford Historical Society, Bedford, Ohio; *Life*, March 22, 1943; *Editor and Publisher*, November 21, 1942; *Cleveland Plain-Dealer*, February 8, 1943; Agnes E. Meyer, *Journey through Chaos* (New York: Harcourt Brace, 1944), 19–26.

61. "How JAHCO Achieves Production," Jack and Heintz Records; *JAHCO News*, February 27, March 27, June 26, 1942; U.S. Department of Labor, "Hourly Entrance Rates Paid to Common Laborers, 1942," Bulletin of the U.S. Bureau of Labor Statistics, 733 (February 1943): 1–5.

62. John A. Kouwenhoven, "Jack and Heintz: Factory or Free for All?" *Harper's*, May 1, 1943; Jack, "Jack and Heintz"; *Time*, December 12, 1942; *New York Times*, March 25, 1942; *Entrepreneur*, August 6, 2015. In 1944, the War Department ordered Jahco to pay $1.75 million in excess profits tax for 1942. *Cleveland News*, January 14, 1944.

63. *New York Times*, November 24, 1942.

64. *New York Times*, February 15, 18, 1942, February 14, 2017.

65. Rosenman, *Humanity on the Defensive*, 105–16.

66. *Newsweek*, March 2, 1942; *San Francisco Chronicle*, February 24, 1942; *Los Angeles Times*, February 24, 1942; *New York Times*, February 25, 1942; James MacGregor Burns, *Roosevelt: The Soldier of Freedom, 1940–1945* (San Diego: Harcourt Brace Jovanovich, 1970), 212–13.

67. *New York Times*, February 25, 1942; *Life*, January 12, 1942.

68. *Los Angeles Times*, February 26, 27, 1942; *New York Times*, February 25, 26, 1942; *Newsweek*, March 9, 1942.

69. *Newsweek*, March 9, 1942; *New York Times*, February 25, 26, 1942; David M. Kennedy, *Freedom from Fear: The American People in Depression and War, 1929–1945* (New York: Oxford University Press, 1999), 566.

70. *New York Times*, March 10, 1942.

71. *New York Times*, February 28, 1942; *Life*, March 16, 1942; *People's Voice*, March 7, 1942; Thomas J. Sugrue, *The Origins of the Urban Crisis: Race and Inequality in Postwar Detroit* (Princeton: Princeton University Press, 1996), 73–74.

72. Hasan Kwame Jeffries, *Bloody Lowndes: Civil Rights and Black Power in Alabama's Black Belt* (New York: New York University Press, 2009), 32; Glenn Feldman, *Politics, Society, and the Klan in Alabama, 1915–1949* (Tuscaloosa: University of Alabama Press, 1999), 286–87.

73. Mordecai W. Johnson to Alben Barkley, February 18, 1942, Alben W. Barkley Papers, box 63, Special Collections Research Center, University of Kentucky, Lexington.

Chapter 3. March

1. *New York Times*, June 9, 1999.

2. Howard Markel, "The Real Story behind Penicillin," *PBS Newshour*, September 27, 2013; Eric Oatman, "The Drug That Changed the World," *P&S*, Columbia University College of Physicians and Surgeons (Winter 2005); Keith Lowe, *The Fear and the Freedom: How the Second World War Changed Us* (New York: St. Martin's 2017), 91; *New York Times*, August 28, 1942.

3. *Life*, March 2, 1942.

4. David M. Kennedy, *Freedom from Fear: The American People in Depression and War, 1929–1945* (New York: Oxford University Press, 1999), 526–29; Ernie Santos, "Wasting Talents," ca. February 1942, James F. Byrnes Papers, Special Collections Library, Clemson University.

5. *New York Times*, April 9, October 11, 1942; *Life*, March 30, 1942.

6. *Washington Post*, January 29, 1980; Carol M. Petillo, "Douglas MacArthur and Manuel Quezon: A Note on the Imperial Bond," in William M. Leary, ed., *MacArthur and the American Century: A Reader* (Lincoln: University of Nebraska Press, 2001).

7. Address by Donald Nelson, Blue Network, Washington, D.C., March 2, 1942, www.ibiblio.org/1942.

8. *New York Times*, March 29, 1942.

9. Isaac Asimov, *I, Robot* (New York: Bantam, 2004), 25–45; "Do We Need Asimov's Laws?" *MIT Technology Review*, May 2014.

10. *New York Times*, March 1, 1942.

11. A. J. Baime, *The Arsenal of Democracy: FDR, Detroit, and an Epic Quest to Arm an America at War* (Boston: Houghton Mifflin Harcourt, 2014), 94–95, 286; Doris Kearns Goodwin, *No Ordinary Time: Franklin and Eleanor Roosevelt; The Home Front in World War II* (New York: Simon and Schuster, 1994), 56; Arthur Herman, *Freedom's Forge: How American Business Produced Victory in World War II* (New York: Random House, 2012), 354–57. During the war, the Ford Company manufactured 8,685 B-24 "Liberators." The U.S. produced 324,750 planes by 1945. "Chrysler Corporation at War," December 1942, Raymond Clapper Papers, Library of Congress, Washington, D.C.

12. *Time*, March 23, 1942.

13. *Nation*, March 7, 1942; *New York Times*, March 1, 1942; Address of John W. Boehne Jr. at the Bronx Real Estate Board, March 21, 1942, www.ibiblio.org/1942.

14. Bruce Catton, *The War Lords of Washington* (New York: Harcourt Brace, 1948), 180–81.

15. *Newsweek*, March 2, 1942.

16. *New York Times*, March 3, December 27, 1942; *Life*, March 2, 1942.

17. FDR to Churchill, March 18, 1942, Map Room Papers, Franklin D. Roosevelt Presidential Library, Hyde Park, N.Y.; James MacGregor Burns, *Roosevelt: The Soldier of Freedom, 1940–1945* (San Diego: Harcourt Brace Jovanovich, 1970), 243–44; John Keegan, *The Second World War* (New York: Penguin, 1989), 112, 118–19.

18. *New York Times*, March 1, 1942; Max Hastings, *Inferno: The World at War, 1939–1945* (New York: Random House, 2011), 502.

19. *New York Times*, March 1, 19, 20, 1942.

20. *Newsweek*, March 9, 1942; "Statement by Henry Morgenthau before House Ways and Means Committee, March 3, 1942," Henry Morgenthau Jr. Papers, FDR Library; John F. Witte, *The Politics and Development of the Federal Income Tax* (Madison: University of Wisconsin Press, 1985), 114–15.

21. W. Elliot Brownlee, "Tax Regimes, National Crisis, and State-Building in America," in W. Elliot Brownlee, ed., *Funding the Modern American State, 1941–1995: The Rise and Fall of the Era of Easy Finance* (Cambridge: Cambridge University Press, 1996), 45–54; Pollock v. Farmers Loan and Trust Company, 158 U.S. 601 (1895).

22. Brownlee, "Tax Regimes," 59–60; Michael Lind, *Land of Promise: An Economic History of the United States* (New York: Harper Collins, 2012), 138.

23. Brownlee, "Tax Regimes," 70–72; Lind, *Land of Promise*, 240–41; James T. Sparrow, *Warfare State: World War II Americans and the Age of Big Government* (New York: Oxford University Press, 2011), 124; taxfoundation.org.

24. Thomas Piketty, *Capital in the Twenty-First Century* (Cambridge, Mass.: Belknap Press of Harvard University Press, 2014), 473; Gunnar Myrdal, *An American Dilemma: The Negro Problem and Modern Democracy* (New York: Harper, 1944), 399; *Time*, March 9, 1942; *Newsweek*, March 16, 1942. The top marginal tax rate climbed to 94 percent in 1944 and remained in that range until 1963, when it was cut to 77 percent. By 1988, the rate had fallen to 28 percent before a series of increases raised the level to 40 percent by 2000. See piketty.pse.ens.fr/files/capital21c/en/pdf/sup/TS14.1.pdf. *Newsweek*, March 16, 1942.

25. *New York Times*, March 26, 1942.

26. *New York Times*, March 6, 9, 1942.

27. *Miami Daily News*, March 11, 1942.

28. Joy Bowerman to FDR, March 11, 1942, President's Official Files, FDR Library,

29. *Miami Herald*, April 3, 1942; E. L. Cline to Stephen Early, April 3, 1942, Murray S. Parker to Stephen Early, March 23, 1942, President's Official Files, FDR Library.

30. *New York Times*, February 15, 1942; *Pittsburgh Press*, August 19, 1941.

31. *New York Times*, March 19, 1942.

32. *New York Times*, March 10, 1942.

33. *New York Times*, March 11, 1942.

34. Richard V. Gilbert to Leon Henderson, March 9, 1942, Gilbert to John Kenneth Galbraith, March 7, 1942, Richard V. Gilbert Papers, FDR Library.

35. Address of Alfred M. Landon, Blue Network, Kansas City, Missouri, March 8, 1942, www.ibiblio.org/1942.

36. *Vogue*, January 15, February 1, 1942.

37. *New York Times*, March 4, 6, 26, 1942.

38. *New York Times*, March 5, 1942.

39. *New York Times*, March 28, 1942; Thomas Philippon and Ariell Reshef, "Wages and Capital in the U.S. Financial Industry, 1909–2006," *Quarterly Journal of Economics* 127 (November 2012): 1551–1609; Angus Deaton, *The Great Escape: Health, Wealth, and the Origins of Inequality* (Princeton: Princeton University Press, 2013), 167–217.

40. *New York Times*, March 24, 1942.

41. *New York Times*, March 20, 1942; Scott Donaldson, *Archibald MacLeish: An American Life* (Boston: Houghton Mifflin, 1992), 355–57; Archibald MacLeish to David Lilienthal, August 17, 1942, David E. Lilienthal Papers, Seeley G. Mudd Manuscript Library, Princeton University, Princeton, N.J.

42. Samuel Rosenman, ed., *Humanity on the Defensive*, vol. 11 of *The Public Papers and Addresses of Franklin D. Roosevelt* (New York: Harper and Bros., 1950), 181–85; *New York Times*, March 29, 1942.

43. *New York Times*, March 27, 1942.

44. *New York Times*, March 8, April 1, 6, 1942.

45. *New York Times*, March 8, 1942.

46. *New York Times*, March 7, 13, 1942; Richard Reeves, *Infamy: The Shocking Story of the Japanese American Internment in World War II* (New York: Picador, 2015), 3–5, 61; Stephen Fox, *The Unknown Internment: An Oral History of the Relocation of Italian Americans during World War II* (Boston: Twayne, 1990), 68–69.

47. *New York Times*, March 24, 1942.

48. *New York Times*, March 25, 27, 1942; Edward Warner, "What Airplanes Can Do: Present Limitations and Possible Developments," *Foreign Affairs* 20 (January 1942): 339–58.

49. *New York Times*, March 29, 1942; Matthew Dallek, *Defenseless under the Night: The Roosevelt Years and the Origins of Homeland Security* (New York: Oxford University Press, 2016), 224, 235.

50. Reeves, *Infamy*, 98–102; *San Francisco Chronicle*, February 24, 2017; W. A. Graham, "Martial Law in California," *California Law Review* 31 (December 1942): 6–15.

51. U.S. House of Representatives, *Report of the Select Committee Investigating National Defense Migration, March 19, 1942* (Washington, D.C.: Government Printing Office, 1942), 3–25; John Eric Schmitz, "Enemies among Us: The Relocation, Internment, and Repatriation of German, Italian, and Japanese Americans during the Second World War" (Ph.D. diss., American University, 2007). The FBI noted in February 1943 that since Pearl Harbor, over twelve thousand aliens had been "apprehended," including over five thousand Germans and twenty-two hundred Italians. After each case was investigated, 23 percent of the Germans detained were released without a hearing, and over 61 percent of Italians. "Custodial Detention" file, at vault.fbi.gov.

Chapter 4. April

1. Thomas Hart Benton, *Year of Peril: A Series of War Paintings* (Chicago: Abbott Laboratories, 1942); Justin Wolff, *Thomas Hart Benton: A Life* (New York: Farrar, Straus and Giroux, 2012), 308–9; *New York Times*, April 6, 7, 12, 1942, December 8, 2003.

2. *St. Louis Post-Dispatch*, April 7, 8, 1942; Matthew Avery Sutton, "Was FDR the Antichrist? The Birth of Fundamentalist Antiliberalism in a Global Age," *Journal of American History* 98 (March 2012): 1071–72; Frances Fitzgerald, *The Evangelicals: The Struggle to Shape America* (New York: Simon and Schuster, 2017), 162–65, 236–323.

3. George C. Herring, *From Colony to Superpower: U.S. Foreign Relations since 1776* (New York: Oxford University Press, 2008), 538–39.

4. *New York Times*, April 10, 1942; Max Hastings, *Inferno: The World at War, 1939–1945* (New York: Random House, 2011), 229–30; David M. Kennedy, *Freedom from Fear: The American People in Depression and War, 1929–1945* (New York: Oxford University Press, 1999), 529–31.

5. Harold L. Ickes Diary, April 11, 1942, Library of Congress, Washington, D.C.

6. *New York Times*, June 10, 1942; *Life*, July 6, 1942; Richard E. Holl, *Committed to Victory: The Kentucky Home Front during World War II* (Lexington: University Press of Kentucky, 2015), 246–49.

7. *New York Times*, April 10, 1942; John R. Craf, *A Survey of the American Economy, 1940–1946* (New York: North River, 1947), 32–34.

8. Memo, Richard V. Gilbert to Leon Henderson, April 8, 1942, Leon Henderson Papers, Franklin D. Roosevelt Presidential Library, Hyde Park, N.Y.

9. *New York Times*, April 5, 1942.

10. *New York Times*, April 10, 1942; *Newsweek*, April 13, 1942.

11. War Production Board, "Official Munitions Production, December 1, 1942," Harry L. Hopkins Papers, FDR Library; Richard V. Gilbert to Leon Henderson, April 11, 1942, Richard V. Gilbert Papers. FDR Library.

12. "FDR Day by Day, April 8, 1942," www.fdrlibrary.marist.edu; *New York Times*, April 9, 1942.

13. Memo, "The General Program," n.d.; Leon Henderson to Franklin Roosevelt, April 24, 1942, Henderson Papers.

14. Harry Dexter White to Henry Morgenthau, April 8, 1942, Harry Dexter White Papers, Seeley G. Mudd Manuscript Library, Princeton University, Princeton, N.J.; *New York Times*, April 14, 25, 1942; www.measuringworth.com is the most sophisticated tool for measuring historic currency values.

15. *Newsweek*, April 13, 1942; *Time*, April 13, 1942; *Chain Store Age*, February, May 1942.

16. Hugh Rockoff, "Price and Wage Controls in Four Wartime Periods," *Journal of Economic History* 41 (June 1981): 382; Caroline F. Ware, *The Consumer Goes to War: A Guide to Victory on the Home Front* (New York: Funk and Wagnalls, 1942), 27; Lizabeth Cohen, *A Consumers' Republic: The Politics of Mass Consumption in Postwar America* (New York: Vintage, 2003), 68–70; Milton Friedman and Anna Jacobsen Schwartz, *From New Deal Banking Reform to World War II Inflation* (Princeton: Princeton University Press, 1980), 140–41.

17. *New York Times*, April 12, 15, 1942.

18. Ickes Diary, June 14, 1942; "Miscellaneous, Salt Lake City," World War II Rumor Project Collection, Archive of Folk Culture, American Folklife Center, Library of Congress; *New York Times*, April 12, 1942.

19. *New York Times*, April 14, 15, 22, May 3, 1942.

20. "Executive Organizational Survey, War Production Board, April 1942," Donald M. Nelson Papers, Huntington Library, San Marino, Calif.

21. George H. Roeder Jr., *The Censored War: American Visual Experience during World War II* (New Haven: Yale University Press, 1993), 21; *New York Times*, April 16, 1942.

22. *Newsweek*, August 17, 1942; *Time*, August 24, 1942; Neal Gabler, *Walt Disney: The Triumph of the American Imagination* (New York: Vintage, 2006), 397–99.

23. *New York Times*, April 13, 1942.

24. *New York Times*, April 3, 4, 1942; Cohen, *A Consumers' Republic*, 90–91.

25. *New York Times*, April 18, 19, 21, 1942.

26. Samuel Rosenman, ed., *Humanity on the Defensive*, vol. 11 of *The Public Papers and Addresses of Franklin D. Roosevelt* (New York: Harper and Bros., 1950), 214–16; Stimson Diary, April 18, 1942, Henry L. Stimson Papers, Manuscripts and Archives, Yale University Library, New Haven, Conn.; James M. Scott, *Target Tokyo: Jimmy Doolittle and the Raid That Avenged Pearl Harbor* (New York: Norton, 2015), 309–21; Kennedy, *Freedom from Fear*, 532–35.

27. *New York Times*, April 24, 1942; Albert Einstein to FDR, August 2, 1939, at fdrlibrary.marist.edu.

28. Rosenman, *Humanity on the Defensive*, 216–21; www.measuringworth.com.

29. Rosenman, *Humanity on the Defensive*, 223–33.

30. *New York Times*, April 29, 1942.

31. *New York Times*, April 29, May 3, 7, 1942; Office of War Information, *Battle Stations for All: The Story of the Fight to Control Living Costs* (Washington, D.C.: Office of War Information, February 1943), 67–68; Harvey C. Mansfield and Associates, "A Short History of OPA," OPA Office of Temporary Controls, 1947, 43; *Newsweek*, April 20, 1942; Meg Jacobs, *Pocketbook Politics: Economic Citizenship in Twentieth-Century America* (Princeton: Princeton University Press, 2005), 192.

32. Office of War Information, *Battle Stations for All*, 67–68.

33. James MacGregor Burns, *Roosevelt: The Soldier of Freedom, 1940–1945* (San Diego: Harcourt Brace Jovanovich, 1970), 121; Mark Leff, *The Limits of Symbolic Reform: The New Deal and Taxation, 1933–39* (Cambridge: Cambridge University Press, 1984), 290; *Newsweek*, June 8, 1942.

34. Alan Brinkley, *Voices of Protest: Huey Long, Father Coughlin, and the Great Depression* (New York: Knopf, 1982), 72, 288; T. Harry Williams, *Huey Long* (New York: Knopf, 1969), 693–94; Sam Pizzigati, *Greed and Good: Understanding and Overcoming the Inequality That Limits Our Lives* (Lanham, Md.: Rowman and Littlefield, 2004), 481.

35. *New York Times*, April 29, 1942.

36. *New York Times*, May 29, 1942, December 1, 2010.

37. *New York Times*, April 29, 1942; Fred L. Israel, ed., *The War Diary of Breckinridge Long: Selections from the Years 1939–1944* (Lincoln: University of Nebraska Press, 1966), 263–64.

38. James T. Sparrow, *Warfare State: World War II Americans and the Age of Big Government* (New York: Oxford University Press, 2011), 176; Mark H. Leff, "The Politics of Sacrifice on the American Home Front in World War II," *Journal of American History* 77 (March 1991): 1299–1306.

39. Brehon Somervell to Leon Henderson, April 28, 1942, Henderson Papers.

40. *Newsweek*, April 20, 1942.

41. *Newsweek*, May 11, 1942.

42. Steve Vogel, *The Pentagon: A History* (New York: Random House, 2007), x, 209–17; *Life*, December 21, 1942.

43. Rosenman, *Humanity on the Defensive*, 193–95; *New York Times*, April 15, 29, 1942; Kim Phillips-Fein, *Invisible Hands: The Businessmen's Crusade against the New Deal* (New York: Norton, 2010), 31.

Chapter 5. May

1. Herbert Hoover, *The Challenge to Liberty* (New York: Charles Scribner's Sons, 1934), 111, 192–93.
2. Richard Norton Smith, *An Uncommon Man: The Triumph of Herbert Hoover* (New York: Simon and Schuster, 1984), 308–11; William E. Leuchtenburg, *Herbert Hoover* (New York: Times Books, 2009), 154–55.
3. *New York Times,* May 21, 1942; *Newsweek,* June 1, 1942.
4. *People's Voice,* June 6, 1942; Brian Dolinar, *The Black Cultural Front: Black Writers and Artists of the Depression Generation* (Jackson: University Press of Mississippi, 2012), 180–81.
5. Federal Reserve Economic Data, Bureau of Economic Research, "Unemployment Figures for the United States," Federal Reserve Bank of St. Louis, fred.stlouisfed.org.
6. *New York Times,* December 27, 1942.
7. "Rumors Collected from August 3 to 8, 1942," New York, World War II Rumor Project Collection, Archive of Folk Culture, American Folklife Center, Library of Congress, Washington, D.C.; Mrs. Georgia Schad to Frank Knox, February 18, 1942, Japanese-American Evacuation and Resettlement Records, Bancroft Library, University of California, Berkeley; *New York Times,* May 24, 1942.
8. Memo, FDR to H. H. Arnold, May 6, 1942, Henry Harley Arnold Papers, Library of Congress.
9. Robert J. Ferrell, ed., *The Eisenhower Diaries* (New York: Norton, 1981), 51, 54; David M. Kennedy, *Freedom from Fear: The American People in Depression and War, 1929–1945* (New York: Oxford University Press, 1999), 530–31; Max Hastings, *Inferno: The World at War, 1939–1945* (New York: Random House, 2011), 230.
10. Mordecai Ezekiel to Robert R. Nathan, March 28, 1942, Simon Kuznets to Planning Committee, August 31, 1942, Robert R. Nathan to William Batt, September 8, 1942, Donald M. Nelson Papers, Huntington Library, San Marino, Calif.; Gregory Hooks, *Forging the Military-Industrial Complex: World War II's Battle of the Potomac* (Urbana: University of Illinois Press, 1991), 113–18.
11. Robert R. Nathan to Donald M. Nelson, March 27, 1942, Nelson Papers; FDR to Donald Nelson, Ferdinand Eberstadt Papers, Seeley G. Mudd Library, Princeton University, Princeton, N.J.; WPB Meeting, June 16, 1942, Harry L. Hopkins Papers, Franklin D. Roosevelt Presidential Library, Hyde Park, N.Y.; U.S. Civilian Production Administration, "Industrial Mobilization for War: History of the War Production Board and Predecessor Agencies, 1940–1945" (1947), 281–82.
12. James MacGregor Burns, *Roosevelt: The Soldier of Freedom, 1940–1945* (San Diego: Harcourt Brace Jovanovich, 1970), 246–47.
13. *Life,* July 20, 1942; *New York Times,* May 4, 1942; John Morton Blum, *V Was for Victory: Politics and American Culture during World War II* (San Diego: Harcourt Brace Jovanovich, 1976), 90–116; Richard Kluger, *Ashes to Ashes: America's Hundred-Year Cigarette War, the Public Health, and the Unabashed Triumph of Philip Morris* (New York: Knopf, 1996), 113–19.

14. *Life,* January 19, May 18, 25, 1942; Martha N. Gardner and Allan M. Brandt, "The Doctors Choice Is America's Choice," *American Journal of Public Health* 96 (February 2006): 222–32.

15. *Newsweek,* May 25, 1942; Denise Scheberle, *Federalism and Environmental Policy: Trust and the Politics of Implementation* (Washington, D.C.: Georgetown University Press, 2004), 56; Jacqueline Karnell Korn and Jennifer Starr, "Historical Perspective on Asbestos and Protective Measures in World War II," *American Journal of Industrial Medicine* 11 (1987): 357–73; Kara Franke and Dennis Paustenbach, "Government and Navy Knowledge regarding Health Hazards of Asbestos: A State of the Science Evaluation, 1900–1970," *Inhalation Toxicology* 23, no. 53 (2011): 1–20.

16. Lizabeth Cohen, *A Consumers' Republic: The Politics of Mass Consumption in Postwar America* (New York: Vintage, 2003), 81–83; William H. Chafe, *The Paradox of Change: American Women in the Twentieth Century* (New York: Oxford University Press, 1991), 123.

17. *Life,* May 18, 1942.

18. Doris Weatherford, *American Women and World War II* (Edison, N.J.: Castle Books, 1990), 29–31; Judith A. Bellafaire, "The Women's Army Corps: A Commemoration of World War II Service," Center for Military History, #72-15 (1993); D'Ann Campbell, *Women at War with America: Private Lives in a Patriotic Era* (Cambridge, Mass.: Harvard University Press, 1984), 19–20.

19. *New York Times,* May 24, 1942; Richard Polenberg, *War and Society: The United States, 1941–1945* (Philadelphia: J. B. Lippincott, 1972), 147–50.

20. *Fortune* poll, May 1942, *Public Opinion Quarterly* (Summer 1942); AIPO Gallup poll, May 13, 1942, *Public Opinion Quarterly* (Fall 1942); Blum, *V Was for Victory,* 29, 46.

21. Maxwell S. Stewart, *After the War?* Public Affairs Pamphlet no. 73 (1942), 1–16.

22. *Time,* June 15, 1942; Cohen, *A Consumers' Republic,* 70.

23. *New York Times,* May 8, 12, 1942.

24. David J. Evans to FDR, May 31, 1942, Eugene McCoy to FDR, May 18, 1942, President's Official Files, FDR Library; *New York Times,* May 3, 7, 16, 1942.

25. *New York Times,* May 17, 1942; Harold C. Gardiner, "Danger to Schools in Tax Proposals," *America,* May 16, 1942.

26. *New York Times,* May 19, 23, 1942; 1940census@archives.gov.

27. Robert J. Gordon, *The Rise and Fall of American Growth: The U.S. Standard of Living since the Civil War* (Princeton: Princeton University Press, 2016), 120, 287.

28. *New York Times,* May 10, 17, 1942; Maury Klein, *A Call to Arms: Mobilizing America for World War II* (New York: Bloomsbury, 2013), 432.

29. *New York Times,* May 13, 24, 1942.

30. *New York Times,* May 31, June 26, 1942.

31. Dallas F. Billington to FDR, January 5, 1942, President's Official Files.

32. Henry A. Wallace, "Century of the Common Man," in *Prefaces to Peace* (New York: Simon and Schuster, Doubleday, Reynal and Hitchcock, Columbia University Press, 1943), 369–75; *Economist,* May 30, 1942; John C. Culver and John Hyde,

American Dreamer: A Life of Henry Wallace (New York: Norton, 2001), 271–78; Alan Brinkley, *The Publisher: Henry Luce and His American Century* (New York: Vintage, 2010), 271–73; Mike O'Connor, *A Commercial Republic: America's Enduring Debate over Democratic Capitalism* (Lawrence: University Press of Kansas, 2014), 156–57.

33. *Radio Annual, 1942,* 897–98; Gordon, *The Rise and Fall of American Growth,* 413.

34. *Time,* June 22, 1942; *New York Times,* May 10, 1942.

35. *Newsweek,* May 4, 1942, *Life,* May 11, 1942; Alben W. Barkley Papers, box 63, Special Collections Research Center, University of Kentucky, Lexington.

36. C. H. Cain to George W. Norris, May 25, 1942, George W. Norris Papers, Library of Congress; Gallup poll, June 1942, ropercenter.cornell.edu.

37. Wallace Fard Muhammad FBI File, FBI FOIA Reading Room, fbi.gov; Robert A. Hill, ed., *The FBI's RACON: Racial Conditions in the United States during World War II* (Boston: Northeastern University Press, 1995), 243.

38. *Life,* March 23, 1942.

39. *New York Times,* May 27, 1942; Merl E. Reed, "Black Workers, Defense Industries, and Federal Agencies, 1941–1945," in Joe William Trotter and Eric Ledell Smith, eds., *African Americans in Pennsylvania: Shifting Historical Perspectives* (University Park: Pennsylvania State University Press, 1997): 363–88.

40. *New York Times,* May 10, 1942; Robert Dallek, *Franklin D. Roosevelt: A Political Life* (New York: Viking, 2017), 463.

41. James M. Scott, *Target Tokyo: Jimmy Doolittle and the Raid That Avenged Pearl Harbor* (New York: Norton, 2015), 361; *Newsweek,* June 1, 1942; *New York Times,* May 10, 1942; *Baltimore Sun,* May 20, 1942.

42. *New York Times,* May 16, 1942.

43. *New York Times,* May 17, 18, 27, 1942; Ellis W. Hawley, *The New Deal and the Problem of Monopoly: A Study in Economic Ambivalence* (Princeton: Princeton University Press, 1966), 53–55.

44. Samuel Rosenman, ed., *Humanity on the Defensive,* vol. 11 of *The Public Papers and Addresses of Franklin D. Roosevelt* (New York: Harper and Bros., 1950), 292.

45. *New York Times,* May 13, 20, 1942.

46. Memo, n.d., Ferdinand Eberstadt Papers, Seeley G. Mudd Manuscript Library; Doris Kearns Goodwin, *No Ordinary Time: Franklin and Eleanor Roosevelt; The Home Front in World War II* (New York: Simon and Schuster, 1994), 606.

47. Ford News Bureau, "Summary of the Willow Run Bomber Plant," Raymond Clapper Papers, Library of Congress.

48. Agnes E. Meyer, *Journey through Chaos* (New York: Harcourt Brace, 1944), 33–34; Polenberg, *War and Society,* 140–42.

49. *New York Times,* December 6, 1942.

50. Memo, Donald R. Longman to Arthur Burns, February 2, 1942; Burns to Leon Henderson, February 2, 1942, Leon Henderson Papers, FDR Library; *New York Times,* May 22, 23, 24, 1942.

51. Bruce Catton, *The War Lords of Washington* (New York: Harcourt Brace, 1948), 155; *New York Times,* May 27, 1942.

52. *New York Times*, May 29, June 7, 1942.

53. Office of War Information, *Battle Stations for All: The Story of the Fight to Control Living Costs* (Washington, D.C.: Office of War Information, February 1943), 5, 67–68; Hugh Rockoff, "Price and Wage Controls in Four Wartime Periods," *Journal of Economic History* 41 (June 1981): 382. After controls were lifted in 1946, the inflation rate increased 28 percent.

54. *New York Times*, May 24, 1942.

55. Korematsu v. United States, 323 U.S. 214 (1944); Hirabayashi v. United States, 320 U.S. 81 (1943); Lorraine K. Bannai, *Enduring Conviction: Fred Korematsu and His Quest for Justice* (Seattle: University of Washington Press, 2015), 37–44; Peter H. Irons, *Justice at War: The Story of the Japanese American Internment Cases* (Berkeley: University of California Press, 1983), 93–99. In 1976, President Ford officially terminated Roosevelt's executive order, and, in 1988, President Reagan signed legislation giving the detainees of the camps $20,000. President Clinton awarded Korematsu the Medal of Freedom in 1998. Trump v. Hawaii, no. 17–965, 585 U.S. __ (2018).

56. In June 2018, Chief Justice John Roberts wrote that the time had arrived "to make express what is already obvious: *Korematsu* was gravely wrong the day it was decided, has been overruled in the court of history and—to be clear—'has no place in law under the Constitution.'" Trump v. Hawaii; Aziz Z. Huq and Tom Ginsburg, "How to Lose a Constitutional Democracy," *UCLA Law Review* 65 (2018): 77; Korematsu v. United States, 323 U.S. 214 (1944).

Chapter 6. June

1. "Rumor File," Bureau of Public Relations, U.S. Department of War, Margaret Mead Papers, Library of Congress, Washington, D.C.; *American Unity: A Monthly Educational Guide*, November 1942; Jill Lepore, *These Truths: A History of the United States* (New York: Norton, 2018), 489.

2. Samuel Rosenman, ed., *Humanity on the Defensive*, vol. 11 of *The Public Papers and Addresses of Franklin D. Roosevelt* (New York: Harper and Bros., 1950), 283.

3. Robert H. Knapp, "A Psychology of Rumor," *Public Opinion Quarterly* 8 (Spring 1944): 33.

4. Gordon W. Allport and Leo Postman, "An Analysis of Rumor," *Public Opinion Quarterly* 10 (Winter 1946): 501–17; Knapp, "A Psychology of Rumor," 22–37; Cass Sunstein, *On Rumors: How Falsehoods Spread, Why We Believe Them, What Can Be Done* (New York: Farrar, Straus and Giroux, 2009), 5–10; James C. Scott, *Domination and the Arts of Resistance: Hidden Transcripts* (New Haven: Yale University Press, 1990), 144–45.

5. "Rumor-Combating Projects," World War II Rumor Project Collection, Archive of Folk Culture, American Folklife Center, Library of Congress; *New York Times*, January 24, 1943.

6. World War II Rumor Project Collection.

7. "Report of Observation Post, Wichita, Kansas, January 8, 1942"; Al Grover to J. R. Fleming, March 14, 1942, World War II Rumor Project Collection; Matthew Dallek, *Defenseless under the Night: The Roosevelt Years and the Origins of Homeland Security* (New York: Oxford University Press, 2016), 230–31.

8. "Race Discrimination—Jews"; "Massachusetts, June 1942," World War II Rumor Project Collection; Office of Public Opinion Research Survey, July 1942, roper center.cornell.edu.

9. Eleanor Roosevelt, "Race, Religion, and Prejudice," *New Republic*, May 11, 1942; Doris Kearns Goodwin, *No Ordinary Time: Franklin and Eleanor Roosevelt; The Home Front in World War II* (New York: Simon and Schuster, 1994), 328.

10. Katz to Alexander, World War II Rumor Project Collection; "Report of Rumors, Alabama August 1942," World War II Rumor Project Collection; Eleanor Roosevelt FBI File, part 4, fbi.gov; Jason Morgan Ward, *"Hanging Bridge": Racial Violence and America's Civil Rights Century* (New York: Oxford University Press, 2016), 94; Robert A. Hill, ed., *The FBI's RACON: Racial Conditions in the United States during World War II* (Boston: Northeastern University Press, 1995), 259; John Morton Blum, *V Was for Victory: Politics and American Culture during World War II* (San Diego: Harcourt Brace Jovanovich, 1976), 192–93; Jason Morgan Ward, "'A War for States Rights': The White Supremacist Vision of Double Victory," in Kevin M. Kruse and Stephen Tuck, eds., *Fog of War: The Second World War and the Civil Rights Movement* (New York: Oxford University Press, 2012).

11. "Report of Observation Post, Wichita, Kansas, January 8, 1942"; Al Grover to J. R. Fleming, March 14, 1942; Dallek, *Defenseless under the Night*, 230–31.

12. *Life*, October 12, 1942; *American Mercury*, September 1942; *Reader's Digest*, September 1942; "The Boston Herald Rumor Clinics of World War II," newengland historicalsociety.com.

13. *Boston Herald*, September 6, 1942.

14. Allport and Postman, "An Analysis of Rumor," 503–8; *Boston Herald*, September 27, 1942.

15. Ward, *"Hanging Bridge,"* 93; Allport and Postman, "An Analysis of Rumor," 507–8; Gordon W. Allport and Leo Postman, *The Psychology of Rumor* (New York: Russell and Russell, 1947), 180–82.

16. See Steven Hahn, "'Extravagant Expectations of Freedom': Rumour, Political Struggle, and the Christmas Insurrection Scare of 1865 in the American South," *Past and Present* 157 (November 1997): 122–58; Steven Hahn, *A Nation under Our Feet: Black Political Struggles in the Rural South from Slavery to the Great Migration* (Cambridge, Mass.: Belknap Press of Harvard University Press, 2003), 57–60, 129–35.

17. *Life*, April 13, 1942; D'Ann Campbell, *Women at War with America: Private Lives in a Patriotic Era* (Cambridge, Mass.: Harvard University Press, 1984), 28.

18. "Rumor-Combating Projects"; Robert H. Knapp, "Serial Reproduction and Related Aspects of Rumor" (Ph.D. diss., Harvard University, 1947), 157–63; Allport and Postman, *The Psychology of Rumor*, 180–83.

19. Howard W. Odum, *Race and Rumors of Race: The American South in the Early Forties* (Chapel Hill: University of North Carolina Press, 1943), 57; Brendan Nyhan and Jason Reifler, "When Corrections Fail: The Persistence of Political Misperceptions," *Political Behavior* 32 (June 2010): 303–30; Gordon Pennycook and David Rand, "Why Do People Fall for Fake News?" *New York Times,* January 19, 2019.

20. Allport and Postman, "An Analysis of Rumor," 503–8; Allport and Postman, *The Psychology of Rumor,* 199; *Harvard Crimson,* March 13, 1942.

21. *New York Times,* July 2, 1942; John Egerton, *Speak Now against the Day: The Generation before the Civil Rights Movement in the South* (New York: Knopf, 1994), 216–17; Merl E. Reed, *Seedtime for the Modern Civil Rights Movement: The President's Committee on Fair Employment Practices, 1941–46* (Baton Rouge: Louisiana State University Press, 1991), 69–70; Ward, *"Hanging Bridge,"* 5, 92, 112.

22. *Life,* June 15, July 6, 1942; George H. Roeder Jr., *The Censored War: American Visual Experience during World War II* (New Haven: Yale University Press, 1993), 45.

23. Hill, *The FBI's RACON,* 340–41.

24. Hill, *The FBI's RACON,* 696–97; Ethan Michaeli, *"The Defender": How the Legendary Black Newspaper Changed America* (New York: Houghton Mifflin, 2016), 245–47.

25. "Chicago Rumors Area Study File," World War II Rumor Project Collection; *Life,* April 13, 1942; *Beacon Light,* January 1942.

26. *Social Justice,* March 30, 1942; American Jewish Committee, Harry Schneiderman, ed., "Review of the Year, 5702 (1941–1942)," The United States, 151–60, Lillian Goldman Reading Room, Center for Jewish History, New York, N.Y.

27. Glen Jeansonne, *Gerald L. K. Smith: Minister of Hate* (Baton Rouge: Louisiana State University Press, 1977), 138–41; *Defender,* January, February 1942.

28. Harold L. Ickes Diary, October 4, 1942, Library of Congress.

29. "Onward Christian Liberals," World War II Rumor Project Collection.

30. *New York Times,* July 24, 1942; U.S. v. McWilliams, 54 F. Supp. 791 (D.D.C., 1944); Geoffrey R. Stone, *Perilous Times: Free Speech in Wartime, from the Sedition Act of 1796 to the War on Terrorism* (New York: Norton, 2004), 272–75.

31. *New York Times,* June 5, 1942.

32. *New Yorker,* November 7, 1942; Ickes Diary, August 16, 1942; Jan Herman, *A Talent for Trouble: The Life of Hollywood's Most Acclaimed Director, William Wyler* (New York: Da Capo, 1997), 235–36; Clayton R. Koppes and Gregory D. Black, *Hollywood Goes to War: Patriotism, Movies and the Second World War from "Ninotchka" to "Mrs. Miniver"* (New York: Free Press, 1987), 222–30; *New York Times,* June 5, 30, July 2, 1942.

33. Quincy Howe to Mead, April 28, 1943, Mead Papers.

34. Sidonie M. Gruenberg to Quincy Howe, April 30, 1943, National Board of Review of Motion Pictures Records, box 19, Brooke Russell Astor Reading Room, New York Public Library.

35. Dudley Nichols to Quincy Howe, n.d.; Frank Astor to Quincy Howe, n.d., National Board of Review of Motion Pictures Records.

36. *New York Times,* November 11, 1942, January 17, 1943.

37. Press Release, December 16, 1942, National Board of Review of Motion Picture Records.

38. *Popular Science Monthly,* May 1942, 98–101; *Life,* June 1, 1942.

39. Richard Rhodes, *Hedy's Folly: The Life and Breakthrough Inventions of Hedy Lamarr, the Most Beautiful Woman in the World* (New York: Random House, 2012), 149–81; Spencie Love, *One Blood: The Death and Resurrection of Charles R. Drew* (Chapel Hill: University of North Carolina Press, 1996), 83; www.invent.org.

40. William Henry Chamberlin, "The Crisis Is Here," *Atlantic Monthly,* June 1942, 667–74.

41. *New York Times,* June 3, 4, 1942.

42. Frank Knox to Annie Knox, June 6, 1942, Frank Knox Papers, Library of Congress; *New York Times,* June 6, 1942.

43. David M. Kennedy, *Freedom from Fear: The American People in Depression and War, 1929–1945* (New York: Oxford University Press, 1999), 535–43.

44. *New York Times,* June 10, 13, 19, 1942.

45. Rosenman, *Humanity on the Defensive,* 271–73; *New York Times,* June 13, 16, 1942.

46. *New York Times,* June 19, 1942.

47. *New York Times,* June 15, 20, 1942.

48. "Statement of Randolph E. Paul to the Ways and Means Committee," June 15, 1942, James F. Byrnes Papers, Special Collections Library, Clemson University.

49. *New York Times,* June 21, 1942.

50. *New York Times,* June 24, 28, September 27, October 4, 1942.

51. *Newsweek,* June 1, 1942; *New York Times,* June 7, 28, 1942.

52. Audie Murphy's and George Watson's Medal of Honor citations can be found at valor.militarytimes.com.

53. James Holland, *The Allies Strike Back, 1941–1943: The War in the West* (New York: Atlantic Monthly, 2017), 282; www.army.mil/ranger.html.

54. *New York Times,* June 23, 1942; John W. Jeffries, *Wartime America: The World War II Home Front* (Lanham, Md.: Rowman and Littlefield, 2018), 142–43.

55. Address by Governor Frank M. Dixon, at the Governors Conference, Asheville, North Carolina, June 21, 1942, www.ibiblio.org/1942; Egerton, *Speak Now against the Day,* 499.

56. Address by James Scott Kemper, before the Bar Association of Tennessee, Chattanooga, June 5, 1942, www.ibiblio.org/1942.

57. "FDR Day by Day," June 19–25, 1942, fdrlibrary.marist.edu; *Life,* July 20, 1942; Kennedy, *Freedom from Fear,* 573–77; Rick Atkinson, *An Army at Dawn: The War in North Africa, 1942–1943* (New York: Picador, 2002), 13.

58. Richard J. Ellis, *To the Flag: The Unlikely History of the Pledge of Allegiance* (Lawrence: University Press of Kansas, 2002), 1–2, 114–16; Public Law 77-623, 56 Stat 377, HJ Res 303. Congress added the words "under God" to the Pledge of Allegiance in 1954.

59. Office of War Information, *Battle Stations for All: The Story of the Fight to Control Living Costs* (Washington, D.C.: Office of War Information, February 1943), 14–20; *New York Times,* July 1, 3, 5, 31, 1942; "Sales of US Savings Bonds, May

1941 to July 1942," Henry Morgenthau Jr. Papers, Franklin D. Roosevelt Presidential Library, Hyde Park, N.Y.

60. *New York Times*, June 22, 25, July 1, 3, 1942; *Life*, September 14, 1942; Bruce Catton, *The War Lords of Washington* (New York: Harcourt Brace, 1948), 121.

61. *New York Times*, June 21, 1942; Reynolds Guyer to FDR, n.d., President's Official Files, FDR Library.

62. Walter Karig, "The Toughest Guy in Washington," *Liberty*, June 6, 1942; *Life*, September 14, 1942; *New York Times*, June 21, 1942; Claude Ackley to Leon Henderson, June 16, 1942, Office of Price Administration Records, RG 188, National Archives, Washington, D.C.; Richard Polenberg, *War and Society: The United States, 1941–1945* (Philadelphia: J. B. Lippincott, 1972), 33–34.

63. *Newsweek*, June 15, 1942.

64. War Production Board, "Preliminary Monthly Report on Munitions Production, July 1942," Harry L. Hopkins Papers, FDR Library; *New York Times*, June 27, 1942; *Time*, June 29, 1942.

65. *New York Times*, May 24, 1942.

66. Robert E. Cushman, "The Case of the Nazi Saboteurs," *American Political Science Review* 36 (December 1942): 1082–91; *New York Times*, June 28, 1942; *Life*, July 13, 1942; "O.S.S. Memorandum on Saboteurs, July 20, 1942," CIA-RDP-13X00001R000100170004-2, FOIA Reading Room, cia.gov; Michael Dobbs, *Saboteurs: The Nazi Raid on America* (New York: Knopf, 2004), 15–53, 87–188; Gallup poll, July 1942, ropercenter.cornell.edu.

67. Curt Gentry, *J. Edgar Hoover: The Man and the Secrets* (New York: Plume, 1992), 289–91.

68. "Rumors, New York, August 1942," World War II Rumor Project Collection.

69. *New York Times*, July 1, 1942; Mark R. Wilson, *Creative Destruction: American Business and the Winning of World War II* (Philadelphia: University of Pennsylvania Press, 2016), 77–78.

Chapter 7. July

1. "F. F.'s Soliloquy," box 124, Robert H. Jackson Papers, Library of Congress, Washington, D.C.

2. Louis Fisher, "Detention and Military Trial of Suspected Terrorists: Stretching Presidential Power," *Journal of National Security Law and Policy* 2 (2006): 1–51.

3. *In the Matter of the Application of Edward John Ferling for a Writ of Habeas Corpus*, July 29, 1942, James F. Byrnes Papers, Special Collections Library, Clemson University; Harold L. Ickes Diary, Library of Congress, July 5, 1942; Robert E. Cushman, "The Case of the Nazi Saboteurs," *American Political Science Review* 36 (December 1942): 1082–91; *New York Times*, August 9, 1942; Francis Biddle, *In Brief Authority* (Garden City: Doubleday, 1962), 325–42; Curt Gentry, *J. Edgar Hoover: The Man and the Secrets* (New York: Plume, 1992), 290–93; Michael Dobbs, *Saboteurs: The Nazi Raid on America* (New York: Knopf, 2004), 207–53; Ex

parte Quirin, 317 U.S. 1. In 1948, President Truman granted clemency to the remaining two spies and ordered them returned to Germany. *Washington Post*, June 24, 2017.

4. *New York Times*, July 4, 1942; Peter Guillen Kreitler, *United We Stand: Flying the American Flag* (San Francisco: Chronicle Books, 2001).

5. *Time*, July 6, 1942; *New York Times*, July 3, 1942.

6. "Insurance in Force Statements for July 1942," War Damage Corporation Records, RFC Records, RG 234, National Archives, Washington, D.C.; *Newsweek*, September 14, 1942; *New York Times*, June 3, 1942; "Commerce Secretary Press Release, June 2, 1942," President's Official Files, 4982, Franklin D. Roosevelt Presidential Library, Hyde Park, N.Y.; *New York Times*, July 2, 1942.

7. *Newsweek*, September 14, 1942; *Banking*, May 1942.

8. *Life*, July 13, 1942.

9. W. R. Howard to the Editor, *Boone (Iowa) News-Republican*, September 22, 1942; J. H. Ryan to Broadcasters, July 6, 1942; John H. Sorrells to Editor, January 27, 1942, Office of Censorship Records, National Archives; George H. Roeder Jr., *The Censored War: American Visual Experience in World War II* (New Haven: Yale University Press, 1993), 8.

10. *New York Times*, July 16, 1942; Caroline F. Ware, *The Consumer Goes to War: A Guide to Victory on the Home Front* (New York: Funk and Wagnalls, 1948), 53–55; FDR "Day by Day," July 15, 1942, www.fdrlibrarymarist.edu.

11. *New York Times*, July 16, 1942.

12. *Life*, July 13, 1942; *Newsweek*, July 20, 1942; Keith E. Eiler, *Mobilizing America: Robert P. Patterson and the War Effort, 1940–1945* (Ithaca: Cornell University Press, 1997), 296–97. In 1943, May was accused of divulging secrets concerning submarine warfare, and he was later convicted of accepting $53,000 in bribes. He served nine months in a penitentiary, and was pardoned by President Truman in 1952.

13. *New York Times*, July 19, 1942; Ware, *The Consumer Goes to War*, 43.

14. *Mountain Life and Work* (Spring 1942), 19.

15. Ronald D Eller, *Uneven Ground: Appalachia since 1945* (Lexington: University Press of Kentucky, 2008), 11–16.

16. Office of War Information, "The War Worker's Point of View, July 28, 1942," Oscar Cox Papers, FDR Library.

17. Memo, Harry Dexter White to Henry Morgenthau, July 20, 1942, Harry Dexter White Papers, Seeley G. Mudd Manuscript Library, Princeton University, Princeton, N.J.

18. Thomas Piketty, *Capital in the Twenty-First Century* (Cambridge, Mass.: Belknap Press of Harvard University Press, 2014), 130–31.

19. *New York Times*, July 19, 1942.

20. *New York Times*, July 31, 1942.

21. *Life*, July 27, 1942; *New York Times*, July 22, 1942; Paul Kennedy, *Engineers of Victory: The Problem Solvers Who Turned the Tide in the Second World War* (New York:

Random House, 2013), 20–22; Adam Tooze, *The Wages of Destruction: The Making and Breaking of the Nazi Economy* (New York: Penguin, 2006), 513.

22. T. H. Watkins, *Righteous Pilgrim: The Life and Times of Harold L. Ickes, 1874–1952* (New York: Henry Holt, 1990), 738–41.

23. *New Yorker,* February 14, 1942; *New York Times,* January 12, February 18, 1942.

24. *New York Times,* December 6, 1942; ancestry.com.

25. *Indianapolis Recorder,* January 10, 1942; *Life,* July 20, 1942; *New York Times,* July 21, 26, 1942; *Lawrence (Kan.) Daily-Journal,* October 3, 1942.

26. John R. Craf, *A Survey of the American Economy, 1940–1946* (New York: North River, 1947), 146; Nelson Lichtenstein, *Labor's War at Home: The CIO in World War II* (Philadelphia: Temple University Press, 2008), 103–16; Paul A. C. Koistenen, "Mobilizing the World War II Economy: Labor and the Industrial-Military Alliance," *Pacific Historical Review* 42 (November 1973): 443–78.

27. *New York Times,* July 3, 1942; Richard B. Sherman, *The Case of Odell Waller and Virginia Justice, 1940–42* (Knoxville: University of Tennessee Press, 1992), 114–58; Blanche Wiesen Cook, *Eleanor Roosevelt,* vol. 3, *The War Years and After, 1939–1962* (New York: Penguin, 2016), 432–33; Doris Kearns Goodwin, *No Ordinary Time: Franklin and Eleanor Roosevelt; The Home Front in World War II* (New York: Simon and Schuster, 1994), 352–53.

28. Christopher A. Brooks and Robert Sims, *Roland Hayes: The Legacy of an American Tenor* (Bloomington: Indiana University Press, 2015), 242–47; Robert A. Hill, ed., *The FBI's RACON: Racial Conditions in the United States during World War II* (Boston: Northeastern University Press, 1995), 259–60; E. M. Collins to A. L. King, July 18, 1942, Universal Negro Improvement Association Records, Schomburg Center for Research in Black Culture, New York Public Library; *New York Times,* July 24, 1942.

29. "New York" file, World War II Rumor Project Collection, Archive of Folk Culture, American Folklife Center, Library of Congress.

30. *Texarkana Gazette,* July 13, 1942; *San Antonio Register,* July 24, 1942; *St. Petersburg (Fla.) Evening-Independent,* July 13, 1942; Robert Dallek, *Lyndon B. Johnson: Portrait of a President* (New York: Oxford University Press, 2005), 65. In 1998, three white supremacists in Jasper, Texas, dragged James Byrd Jr. by a truck. His agony ended when his body hit a culvert and he was decapitated. The bill signed by President Obama was named the Matthew Shepard and James Byrd, Jr. Hate Crimes Prevention Act. *Salon,* October 25, 1999; Pamela Colloff, "Jasper," *Texas Monthly,* December 2003; Wade Goodwyn, *Texas Funeral,* National Public Radio, June 3, 1998.

31. Ross D. Brown to William V. Brown, August 6, 1942; William V. Brown to Ross D. Brown, August 12, 1942, NAACP Papers, Library of Congress.

32. Equal Justice Initiative, *Lynching in America: Confronting the Legacy of Racial Terror,* 3rd ed. (Montgomery, Ala.: Equal Justice Initiative, 2017), 5–6.

33. "Hold Secret Burial for Mob Victim," May 29, 1942; Thurgood Marshall to Walter White, March 16, 1942, NAACP Papers; *Indianapolis Recorder,* March 14, 1942.

34. Jessie Daniel Ames, *The Changing Character of Lynching: Review of Lynching, 1931–1941* (Atlanta: Commission on Interracial Cooperation, 1942); Eugene Katz to Will Alexander, August 28, 1942, World War II Rumor Project Collection.

35. Gunnar Myrdal, *An American Dilemma: The Negro Problem and Modern Democracy* (New York: Harper, 1944), xiv–xix.

36. *New York Times*, May 31, June 28, 1942.

37. *Time*, July 20, 1942; *Louisville Courier-Journal*, November 4, 1942; *New York Times*, August 1, 1942.

38. *Life*, July 27, 1942.

39. Philip Wylie, *Generation of Vipers* (New York: Rinehart, 1942), 87–90; Michael C. C. Adams, *The Best War Ever: America and World War II* (Baltimore: Johns Hopkins University Press, 1994), 8.

40. Robert Moses, "Ability, Not Politics, Will Win the War!" *Reader's Digest*, July 1942; Robert A. Caro, *The Power Broker: Robert Moses and the Fall of New York* (New York: Knopf, 1974), 282–83, 289–93, 426–43.

41. Stimson Diary, July 24, 1942, Henry L. Stimson Papers, Manuscripts and Archives, Yale University Library, New Haven, Conn.; David M. Kennedy, *Freedom from Fear: The American People in Depression and War, 1929–1945* (New York: Oxford University Press, 1999), 576–78; Rick Atkinson, *An Army at Dawn: The War in North Africa, 1942–1943* (New York: Picador, 2002), 16; Robert Dallek, *Franklin D. Roosevelt: A Political Life* (New York: Viking, 2017), 471.

42. *Fortune* poll, July 1942, *Public Opinion Quarterly* (Fall 1942); *Time*, July 20, 1942; Bureau of the Budget, *The United States at War: Development and Administration of the War Program by the Federal Government* (Washington, D.C.: Government Printing Office, 1946), 112–14.

Chapter 8. August

1. *New York Times*, August 8, 29, 1942; www.measuringworth.com.

2. WPB Meeting, August 4, 1942, Harry L. Hopkins Papers, Franklin D. Roosevelt Presidential Library, Hyde Park, N.Y.; Bruce Catton, *The War Lords of Washington* (New York: Harcourt Brace, 1948), 151–52.

3. Samuel Rosenman, ed., *Humanity on the Defensive*, vol. 11 of *The Public Papers and Addresses of Franklin D. Roosevelt* (New York: Harper and Bros., 1950), 320–21.

4. "Rumors Sample, Arizona, August 17, October 9, 1942"; "Inflation, August 6, 1942," "Post War World," August 5, 1942, World War II Rumor Project Collection, Archive of Folk Culture, American Folklife Center, Library of Congress, Washington, D.C.

5. "New York, August 3–August 8, 1942," World War II Rumor Project Collection.

6. *New York Times*, August 10, 13, 1942; Victor Davis Hanson, *The Second World Wars: How the First Global Conflict Was Fought and Won* (New York: Basic Books, 2017), 144–45.

7. Hanson, *The Second World Wars*, 200–201.

8. H. H. Arnold, "Memorandum of Record," August 11, 1942, Henry Harley Arnold Papers, Library of Congress, Washington, D.C.

9. Nigel Hamilton, *The Mantle of Command: FDR at War, 1941–1942* (Boston: Houghton Mifflin Harcourt, 2014), 367–69.

10. *New York Times*, August 2, 1942; *Chicago Daily Tribune*, August 13, 1942.

11. *New York Times*, August 8, 1942.

12. *New York Times*, August 14, 15, 1942.

13. "Congress—Bulwark of Freedom," *Southern California Business*, August 3, 1942.

14. *New York Times*, August 29, 1942.

15. W. G. Welbourne to Henry Kaiser, November 6, 1942, Henry J. Kaiser Papers, Bancroft Library, University of California, Berkeley; Harold Ickes Diary, August 8, 1942, Library of Congress; *New York Times*, August 29, 1942; *Newsweek*, August 17, 1942; *National Geographic*, May 1942; Stephen B. Adams, *Mr. Kaiser Goes to Washington: The Rise of a Government Entrepreneur* (Chapel Hill: University of North Carolina Press, 1997), 43, 65, 131–43.

16. "The Permanente Health Plan," Henry J. Kaiser Papers, Bancroft Library; Donald M. Nelson, *Arsenal of Democracy: The Story of American War Production* (New York: Harcourt Brace, 1946), 249–52.

17. Elliott C. Burrows to Henry Kaiser, November 24, 1942, Kaiser Papers; Rickey Hendricks, *A Model for National Health Care: The History of Kaiser Permanente* (New Brunswick: Rutgers University Press, 1993), 40–48.

18. Michael M. Davis to Henry Kaiser, November 25, 1942, Kaiser Papers; National Public Radio, *All Things Considered*, December 1, 2010.

19. John Virtue, *The Black Soldiers Who Built the Alaska Highway: A History of Four U.S. Army Regiments in the North, 1942–1943* (Jefferson, N.C.: McFarland, 2013), 6–8.

20. *Time*, August 31, 1942; Virtue, *The Black Soldiers Who Built the Alaska Highway*, 15–22.

21. *Time*, October 12, 26, 1942.

22. Max Hastings, *Inferno: The World at War, 1939–1945* (New York: Random House, 2011), 150; Martin Malia, *The Soviet Tragedy: A History of Socialism in Russia, 1917–1991* (New York: Free Press, 1994), 289; Rebecca Manley, *To The Tashkent Station: Evacuation and Survival in the Soviet Union at War* (Ithaca: Cornell University Press, 2009); Sanford R. Lieberman, "The Evacuation of Industry in the Soviet Union during World War II," *Soviet Studies* 35 (January 1983): 90–102; John Keegan, *The Second World War* (New York: Penguin, 1989), 209–10; *Life*, July 20, 1942.

23. Ickes Diary, July 26, 1942.

24. Donald Nelson to FDR, August 1942, Henry Harley Arnold Papers; Federal Reserve Economic Data, National Bureau of Economic Research, "Unemployment Rate for the United States," Federal Reserve Bank of St. Louis, fred.stlouisfed.org.

25. Frank Knox to Annie Knox, August 12, 30, 1942, Frank Knox Papers, Library of Congress; *New York Times*, August 11, 1942.

26. William H. Chafe, "Race in America: The Ultimate Test of Liberalism," in *The Achievement of American Liberalism: The New Deal and Its Legacies* (New York: Columbia University Press, 2003), 163; Clarence Lang, *Grassroots at the Gateway: Class Politics and the Black Freedom Struggle in St. Louis, 1936–1975* (Ann Arbor: University of Michigan Press, 2009), 47–48; Robert A. Hill, ed., *The FBI's RA-CON: Racial Conditions in the United States during World War II* (Boston: Northeastern University Press, 1995), 123.

27. D'Ann Campbell, *Women at War with America: Private Lives in a Patriotic Era* (Cambridge, Mass.: Harvard University Press, 1984), 83; James J. Kimble and Lester C. Olson, "Visual Rhetoric Representing Rosie the Riveter: Myth and Misconception in J. Howard Miller's 'We Can Do It' Poster," *Rhetoric and Public Affairs* 9 (Winter 2006): 533–70; *New York Times*, January 22, 2018.

28. Leonard Larsen to Helen Larsen, December 1, 1942, Leonard Larsen Papers, New-York Historical Society, New York; Michael C. C. Adams, *The Best War Ever: America and World War II* (Baltimore: Johns Hopkins University Press, 1994), 70.

29. *Newsweek*, September 7, 1942.

30. *New York Times*, August 25, 1942; U.S. Department of Labor, Bureau of Labor Statistics, "Household Data Annual Averages" (2017), 39.

31. Lizabeth Cohen, *A Consumers' Republic: The Politics of Mass Consumption in Postwar America* (New York: Vintage, 2003), 86–87.

32. Marvin MacIntyre to James A. Bray, October 8, 1942, President's Official Files 93, "Colored Matters," FDR Library; *People's Voice*, May 16, 1942.

33. J. H. Bradford to FDR, November 6, 1942, President's Official Files 93, "Colored Matters."

34. Neil A. Wynn, *The African American Experience during World War II* (Lanham, Md.: Rowman and Littlefield, 2010), xi–xii, 42–80; James Farmer and Don E. Carleton, *Lay Bare the Heart: An Autobiography of the Civil Rights Movement* (New York: Arbor House, 1985), 101–2.

35. John Morton Blum, *V Was for Victory: Politics and American Culture during World War II* (San Diego: Harcourt Brace Jovanovich, 1976), 193–94; Glenn Feldman, *The Irony of the Solid South: Democrats, Republicans, and Race, 1865–1944* (Tuscaloosa: University of Alabama Press, 2013), 192–93.

36. *Life*, August 31, September 21, 1942; "Negroes, August 10–15, 1942," World War II Rumor Project Collection; Allan M. Winkler, *Home Front U.S.A.: America during World War II* (Arlington Heights: Harlan Davidson, 1986), 58.

37. "It's Great to Be an American," "Wedge-Driving Rumors," World War II Rumor Project Collection; Deborah Dash Moore, *GI Jews: How World War II Changed a Generation* (Cambridge, Mass.: Belknap Press of Harvard University Press, 2004), 27–34.

38. Richard Breitman and Allan J. Lichtman, *FDR and the Jews* (Cambridge, Mass.: Belknap Press of Harvard University Press, 2013), 198–99, 210; *New York Times*, July 22, 1942.

39. Blum, *V Was for Victory*, 198–99.

40. Luis Alvarez, *The Power of the Zoot: Youth Culture and Resistance during World War II* (Berkeley: University of California Press, 2008), 45–46; Robin D. G. Kelley, *Race Rebels: Culture, Politics, and the Black Working Class* (New York: Free Press, 1994), 161–80; *Life*, September 21, 1942.

41. Draft, Harry Dexter White to FDR, August 28, 1942, Harry Dexter White Papers, Seeley G. Mudd Manuscript Library, Princeton University, Princeton, N.J.

42. John Earl Haynes and Harvey Kiehr, *Venona: Decoding Soviet Espionage in America* (New Haven: Yale University Press, 1999), 138–42, 145–50.

43. FDR to Vannevar Bush, March 11, 1942, President's Secretary's File, FDR Library.

44. *New York Times*, August 7, 1942.

45. *Boston Herald*, August 30, 1942.

46. Leonard Larsen to Helen Larsen, November 30, December 1, 1942, Larsen Papers.

47. *New York Times*, August 19, 22, 1942.

48. Leonard Larsen to Helen Larsen, November 25, 1942, Larsen Papers. The Szyk poster was featured in a 2018 exhibition at the New-York Historical Society, *Arthur Szyk: Soldier in Art*. Steven Heller, "The Almost-Forgotten Jewish Artist Who Propagandized against Hitler," *Atlantic*, May 29, 2014.

49. Lewis Wilder to James F. Byrnes, December 31, 1941, James F. Byrnes Papers, Special Collections Library, Clemson University.

50. *Life*, August 17, 1942.

Chapter 9. September

1. *New York Times*, September 7, 1942.

2. "Remarks by Secretary Morgenthau Before the American Bankers Association, September 1, 1942," Henry Morgenthau Jr. Papers, Franklin D. Roosevelt Presidential Library, Hyde Park, N.Y.

3. Office of War Information, *Battle Stations for All: The Story of the Fight to Control Living Costs* (Washington, D.C.: Office of War Information, February 1943); *Newsweek*, September 7, 14, 1942.

4. *New York Times*, September 4, 1942.

5. *New York Times*, December 8, 1942; Richard M. Ugland, "Viewpoints and Morale of Urban High School Students during World War II: Indianapolis as a Case Study," *Indiana Magazine of History* 77 (June 1981): 150–78.

6. *Vital Statistics of the United States, 1942*, part 1 (Washington, D.C.: U.S. Government Printing Office, 1944), 12–15; AIPO poll, September 1942, ropercenter.cornell.edu.

7. *Catholic Telegraph-Register*, September 4, 1942.

8. Samuel Rosenman, ed., *Humanity on the Defensive*, vol. 11 of *The Public Papers and Addresses of Franklin D. Roosevelt* (New York: Harper and Bros., 1950), 356–64.

9. Rosenman, *Humanity on the Defensive*, 364–65; *New York Times*, September 8, October 2, 1942.

10. Harold Ickes Diary, September 12, 1942, Library of Congress, Washington, D.C.

11. Frank Knox to Annie Knox, September 9, 1942, Frank Knox Papers, Library of Congress; *New York Times*, September 8, 1942.

12. archives.gov/federal-register/executive-orders/1942.html; William E. Leuchtenburg, *The FDR Years: On Roosevelt and His Legacy* (New York: Columbia University Press, 1995), 32.

13. *Houston Post*, September 11, 1942; *New Yorker*, June 27, 1942; J. H. Sawyer to Leon Henderson, July 22, 1942, Office of Price Administration Records, RG 188, National Archives, Washington, D.C.

14. "Third Draft of Dr. Conant's Draft," Records of the President's Rubber Survey Committee, FDR Library.

15. *New York Times*, September 11, 1942; "Full Report of the Rubber Committee," September 10, 1942, Records of the President's Rubber Survey Committee; Bureau of the Budget, *The United States at War: Development and Administration of the War Program by the Federal Government* (Washington, D.C.: Government Printing Office, 1946), 293–97.

16. "Full Report of the Rubber Committee."

17. *Rubber Age*, September 1942; *Houston Post*, September 11, 1942; "Full Report of the Rubber Committee"; Jennet Conant, *Man of the Hour: James B. Conant, Warrior Scientist* (New York: Simon and Schuster, 2017), 246–49; Maury Klein, *A Call to Arms: Mobilizing America for World War II* (New York: Bloomsbury, 2013), 509.

18. Drew Pearson syndicated column, August 12, 1942; *Chicago Daily Tribune*, September 16, 1942; Mark Wells to Rubber Survey Committee, August 1942, Records of the President's Rubber Survey Committee.

19. *The Cross and the Flag*, September 1942.

20. *Louisville Courier-Journal*, August 27, October 20, 21, 24, 1942; "Full Report of the Rubber Committee"; *Leo Weekly*, March 17, 2010.

21. *New York Times*, September 18, 1942.

22. *New York Times*, September 12, 1942; Paul R. Porter to Wendell Lund, n.d., Donald M. Nelson Papers, Huntington Library, San Marino, Calif.

23. *New York Times*, October 1, 1942.

24. Sylvia Jukes Morris, *Rage for Fame: The Ascent of Clare Boothe Luce* (New York: Random House, 1997), 44–48, 161–206; *Vogue*, February 15, 1942.

25. Morris, *Rage for Fame*, 407–45.

26. Statement by Clare Boothe Luce, August 22, 1942, Clare Boothe Luce Papers, Library of Congress; *New York Times*, September 1, 1942.

27. Clare Boothe Luce to J. K. Bradley, July 31, 1942, Luce Papers.

28. Joseph P. Kennedy to Clare Boothe Luce, August 4, 1942; Clare Boothe Luce to Joseph P. Kennedy, June 9, 1942; John F. Kennedy to Clare Boothe Luce, November 4, 1942, Luce Papers.

29. *New York Times*, September 11, 15, 1942.

30. *New York Times*, September 1, 13, 15, 1942. "Notes on the Congressional Campaign of Mrs. Clare Boothe Luce," Luce Papers.

31. Interview with Clare Boothe Luce by League of Women Voters, August 18, 1942, Luce Papers; Alan Brinkley, *The End of Reform: New Deal Liberalism in Recession and War* (New York: Knopf, 1995), 228–35. See also Stephen Kemp Bailey, *Congress Makes a Law: The Story behind the Employment Act of 1946* (New York: Columbia University Press, 1957).

32. *New York Times*, September 25, 1942; *St. Petersburg Times*, September 20, 1942.

33. State of Connecticut, Public Document 26, "Statement of the Vote, General Election, November 5, 1940," Hartford, 1940, portal.ct.gov; *New York Times*, October 12, 1942.

34. *Newsweek*, September 21, 1942.

35. *Newsweek*, October 19, 1942.

36. General Leslie Groves, *Now It Can Be Told: The Story of the Manhattan Project* (New York: Da Capo, 1983), 19–25; Richard Rhodes, *The Making of the Atomic Bomb* (New York: Simon and Schuster, 1987), 426–27; Kai Bird and Martin J. Sherwin, *American Prometheus: The Triumph and Tragedy of J. Robert Oppenheimer* (New York: Vintage, 2005), 183–87; Denise Kiernan, *The Girls of Atomic City: The Untold Story of the Women Who Helped Win World War II* (New York: Simon and Schuster, 2013), 20–27.

37. Jason Morgan Ward, "'A War for States Rights': The White Supremacist Vision of Double Victory," in Kevin M. Kruse and Stephen Tuck, eds., *Fog of War: The Second World War and the Civil Rights Movement* (New York: Oxford University Press, 2012); Molly Guptill Manning, "Fighting to Lose the Vote: How the Soldier Voting Acts of 1942 and 1944 Disenfranchised America's Armed Forces," *New York University Journal of Legislation and Public Policy* 19 (2016): 349–51.

38. *New York Times*, September 2, 9, 1942.

39. *New York Times*, September 11, 1942; *Chicago Daily Tribune*, September 17, 1942; Alexander Keyssar, *The Right to Vote: The Contested History of Democracy in the United States* (New York: Basic Books, 2000), 246–47; Manning, "Fighting to Lose the Vote."

40. Thomas A. Becnel, *Senator Allen Ellender of Louisiana: A Biography* (Baton Rouge: Louisiana State University Press, 1995), 119–20; Adam Fairclough, *Race and Democracy: The Civil Rights Struggle in Louisiana, 1915–1972* (Athens: University of Georgia Press, 1995), 80, 168.

41. W. E. B. Du Bois, "A Chronicle of Race Relations," *Phylon* 3 (First Quarter, 1942): 84.

42. Brehon Somervell to Robert Nathan, September 12, 1942, Hopkins Papers; War Production Board, "Preliminary Monthly Report on Munitions Production, August 1942," Hopkins Papers; Interview with Robert Nathan by Tracy Campbell, June 9, 1995, Arlington, Va., Edward Prichard Oral History Collection, Special Collections, University of Kentucky, Lexington; David M. Kennedy, *Freedom from Fear: The American People in Depression and War, 1929–1945* (New York: Oxford University Press, 1999), 621; Paul A. C. Koistinen, *Arsenal of World War II: The Political Economy of American Warfare, 1940–1945* (Lawrence: University Press of Kansas, 2004), 305–11; Jim Lacey, *Keep from All Thoughtful Men: How U.S. Economists Won World War II* (Annapolis: Naval Institute Press, 2011), 103–15.

43. Robert Nathan to Brehon Somervell, September 17, 1942, Hopkins Papers; Nathan Interview; U.S. Civilian Production Administration, "Industrial Mobilization for War: History of the War Production Board and Predecessor Agencies, 1940–1945" (1947), 287–88; Bruce Catton, *The War Lords of Washington* (New York: Harcourt Brace, 1948), 42–43.

44. David Lilienthal to Felix Frankfurter, July 21, September 1, 1942, David E. Lilienthal Papers, Seeley G. Mudd Manuscript Library, Princeton University, Princeton, N.J.; *Washington Post,* December 11, 1942; *New York Times,* September 25, 1942.

45. Rick Atkinson, *An Army at Dawn: The War in North Africa, 1942–1943* (New York: Picador, 2002), 30–31; Leo J. Meyer, "The Decision to Invade North Africa (TORCH)," (Washington, D.C.: Center of Military History, 1990), 196.

46. John Egerton, *Speak Now against the Day: The Generation before the Civil Rights Movement in the South* (New York: Knopf, 1994), 173; *New York Times,* September 4, 25, 1942; Walter White to Martin Dies, September 25, 1942, President's Official Files 93, "Colored Matters"; *People's Voice,* October 3, 1942.

47. *Defender,* May 1942.

48. Southern Conference for Human Welfare, Nashville, Tennessee, full page ad, September 1942, President's Official Files 93, "Colored Matters."

49. *People's Voice,* June 6, 1942.

50. *Baltimore Afro-American,* October 3, 1942; *Crisis,* November 1942; A. Philip Randolph to John Bankhead, October 16, 1942, A. Philip Randolph Papers, Library of Congress; Cheryl Mullenbach, *Double Victory: How African American Women Broke Race and Gender Barriers to Help Win World War II* (Chicago: Chicago Review, 2013); Jason Morgan Ward, *Defending White Democracy: The Making of a Segregationist Movement and the Remaking of Racial Politics, 1936–1965* (Chapel Hill: University of North Carolina Press, 2011), 44; Danielle McGuire, *At the Dark End of the Street: Black Women, Rape, and Resistance—A New History of the Civil Rights Movement from Rosa Parks to Black Power* (New York: Knopf, 2010), 13–59.

51. *New York Times,* October 1, 1942.

52. "Chancellor Adolf Hitler's Address at the Opening of the Winter Relief Campaign, Berlin, September 30, 1942," www.ibiblio.org.

Chapter 10. October

1. *New York Times,* October 2, 3, 1942.

2. Presidential Press Conference #848, October 1, 1942, www.fdrlibrary.marist.edu; *New Yorker,* October 24, 1942.

3. *Washington Evening-Star,* October 3, 1942; *New York Times,* October 3, 1942; "FDR Day by Day," October 2, 1942, fdrlibrary.marist.edu; Office of Price Administration Report, January 19, 1943, James F. Byrnes Papers, Special Collections Library, Clemson University.

4. Evans Clark, ed., *Wartime Facts and Postwar Problems: A Study and Discussion Manual* (New York: Twentieth Century Fund, 1943), 99; Stuart Altman and David

Shactman, *Power, Politics, and Universal Healthcare: The Inside Story of a Century-Long Battle* (Amherst, N.Y.: Prometheus Books, 2011), 101.

5. Samuel Rosenman, ed., *Humanity on the Defensive,* vol. 11 of *The Public Papers and Addresses of Franklin D. Roosevelt* (New York: Harper and Bros., 1950), 396–404.

6. *New York Times,* October 4, 1942; Harold Ickes Diary, October 4, 1942, Library of Congress, Washington, D.C.; David Robertson, *Sly and Able: A Political Biography of James F. Byrnes* (New York: Norton, 1994), 318–19; Paul A. C. Koistinen, *Arsenal of World War II: The Political Economy of American Warfare, 1940–1945* (Lawrence: University Press of Kansas, 2004), 420–25; William Lasser, *Benjamin V. Cohen: Architect of the New Deal* (New Haven: Yale University Press, 2002), 255–57; Kenneth S. Davis, *FDR: The War President, 1940–1943* (New York: Random House, 2000), 622–27.

7. Alfred Lewis Baker to FDR, October 6, 1942, President's Official Files, Franklin D. Roosevelt Presidential Library, Hyde Park, N.Y.

8. *New York Times,* October 28, 31, 1942. FDR to Morgenthau, October 27, 1942, Henry Morgenthau Jr. Papers, FDR Library.

9. *People's Voice,* June 6, 1942; Postwar Problems Survey, September 1942, roper center.cornell.edu.

10. *Wall Street Journal,* October 31, 1942; Richard Polenberg, *One Nation Divisible: Class, Race, and Ethnicity in the United States since 1938* (New York: Viking, 1980), 61–62.

11. *New York Times,* November 15, 1942, December 1, 2010; Address by James F. Byrnes on CBS, November 16, 1942, Byrnes Papers.

12. Henry Morgenthau to James F. Byrnes, November 10, 1942, Leon Henderson Papers, FDR Library; *New York Times,* October 6, 7, 1942.

13. Office of War Information, "Intelligence Report: Rubber and Nationwide Gasoline Rationing," October 5, 1942, Oscar Cox Papers, FDR Library; J. B. Conant to Bernard Baruch, November 25, 1942, Bernard M. Baruch Papers, Seeley G. Mudd Manuscript Library, Princeton University, Princeton, N.J.; *New York Times,* October 7, 1942; Meg Jacobs, *Pocketbook Politics: Economic Citizenship in Twentieth-Century America* (Princeton: Princeton University Press, 2005), 193–97.

14. Louise Ames to Harold Ickes, September 24, 1942, John R. Richards to Louise Ames, October 30, 1943, Office of Price Administration Records, RG 188, National Archives, Washington, D.C.

15. Mrs. Jack Adams to Eleanor Roosevelt, September 15, 1942, Office of Price Administration Records; Burdette Marvin to Bernard Baruch, October 17, 1942, Baruch Papers.

16. *New York Times,* October 17, 1942.

17. Melvyn Dubofsky and Warren B. Van Tine, *John L. Lewis: A Biography* (Urbana: University of Illinois Press, 1986), 297–302; Walter Galenson, *The CIO Challenge to the AFL: A History of the American Labor Movement, 1935–1941* (Cambridge, Mass.: Harvard University Press, 1960), 72–75; *Chicago Daily Tribune,* October 8, 1942.

18. Rosenman, *Humanity on the Defensive*, 428; Antonio Thompson, *Men in German Uniform: POWs in America during World War II* (Knoxville: University of Tennessee Press, 2010), 77–81.

19. *New York Times*, October 8, 1942.

20. Jason Morgan Ward, *"Hanging Bridge": Racial Violence and America's Civil Rights Century* (New York: Oxford University Press, 2016), 5, 91–102; Timothy B. Tyson, *The Blood of Emmett Till* (New York: Simon and Schuster, 2017), 68–69.

21. *New York Amsterdam Star-News*, October 24, 1942.

22. *Defender*, October 18, 31, 1942; *Chicago Daily Tribune*, October 18, 1942; *Daily Worker*, April 23, 1943; Ward, *"Hanging Bridge,"* 115–16.

23. *New York Times*, October 21, 1942; John H. Sengstacke to FDR, October 14, 1942, President's Official Files 93, "Colored Matters," FDR Library; A. Philip Randolph to Allen Knight Chalmers, October 30, 1942, A. Philip Randolph Papers, Library of Congress; Gene Roberts and Hank Klibanoff, *The Race Beat: The Press, the Civil Rights Struggle, and the Awakening of a Nation* (New York: Vintage, 2007), 23.

24. "Paris, Illinois," Lynching File, NAACP Papers, Library of Congress; *New York Times*, July 14, 1943; *Terre Haute Tribune-Star*, October 21, 2012; ancestry.com.

25. "Southern Conference on Race Relations, Durham, North Carolina, October 20, 1942"; Raymond Gavins, *The Perils and Prospects of Southern Black Leadership: Gordon Blaine Hancock, 1884–1970* (Durham: Duke University Press, 1977), 120–27; *Daily Princetonian*, September 30, October 22, 1942.

26. U.S. Department of Justice, *Report to the Congress of the United States: Review of Restrictions on Persons of Italian Ancestry during World War II* (Washington, D.C.: U.S. Department of Justice, November 2001); *New York Times*, October 13, 1942; Constantine Panunzio, "Italian Americans, Fascism, and the War," *Yale Review* 31 (June 1942): 782; Stephen Fox, *The Unknown Internment: An Oral History of the Relocation of Italian Americans during World War II* (Boston: Twayne, 1990), xii, 100, 136; Mary Elizabeth Basile Chopas, *Searching for Subversives: The Story of Italian Internment in Wartime America* (Chapel Hill: University of North Carolina Press, 2017), 2.

27. Statistical Analysis Branch, OPA, "Effects of World War II on the Civilian Economy: United States Compared with Great Britain," December 1942, Office of Price Administration Records; *Chicago Daily Tribune*, October 22, 1942; Michael Lind, *Land of Promise: An Economic History of the United States* (New York: HarperCollins, 2012), 405.

28. Jay Winik, *1944: FDR and the Year That Changed History* (New York: Simon and Schuster, 2015), 354.

29. Office of War Information, *Battle Stations for All: The Story of the Fight to Control Living Costs* (Washington, D.C.: Office of War Information, February 1943), 30–31; *New York Times*, October 21, 1942; *Wall Street Journal*, October 19, 1942; Arthur H. Kent, "The Revenue Act of 1942," *Columbia Law Review* 18 (January 1943): 1–41; Roy C. Blakey and Gladys C. Blakey, "The Federal Revenue Act of 1942," *American Political Science Review* 36 (December 1942): 1069–82; *Newsweek*, November 2, 1942.

30. *New York Times,* October 21, 1942; *New Yorker,* November 7, 1942. The highest tax bracket rate reached during the war was 94 percent in 1944, which remains the highest since federal income taxes were introduced in 1913, taxfoundation.org.

31. Beardsley Ruml, "The Pay-as-You-Go Income Tax Plan," *Bulletin of the National Tax Association* 28 (March 1943): 166–71; *New York Times,* September 1, 1942; John Morton Blum, *V Was for Victory: Politics and American Culture during World War II* (San Diego: Harcourt Brace Jovanovich, 1976), 242–43.

32. *Wall Street Journal,* October 19, 21, 1942; *New York Times,* October 19, 1942.

33. *New York Times,* October 27, November 1, 1942.

34. Leon Henderson, "Our Full Share of Responsibility," speech before the Research Institute of America, September 8, 1942, ibiblio.org.

35. *New York Times,* October 17, 1942; *San Jose Evening News,* October 20, 1942; *Life,* September 14, 1942; Ickes Diary, September 19, 26, 1942.

36. Maury Klein, *A Call to Arms: Mobilizing America for World War II* (New York: Bloomsbury, 2013), 393–94.

37. Victor Davis Hanson, *The Second World Wars: How the First Global Conflict Was Fought and Won* (New York: Basic Books, 2017), 144–45.

38. Memo, FDR to Donald Nelson, October 29, 1942, Henry Harley Arnold Papers, Library of Congress; R. W. Goldsmith to Robert Nathan, October 26, 1942, Henderson Papers.

39. *New York Times,* October 2, 24, 1942; Statement by Clare Boothe Luce to Catholic Clergymen, October 20, 1942, Luce Papers; John W. Jeffries, *Testing the Roosevelt Coalition: Connecticut Society and Politics in the Era of World War II* (Knoxville: University of Tennessee Press, 1979), 118–35.

40. "Notes on the Congressional Campaign of Mrs. Clare Boothe Luce," Clare Boothe Luce Papers, Library of Congress.

41. "Notes on the Congressional Campaign of Mrs. Clare Boothe Luce"; U.S. Census, 1940, "Characteristics of Population by County, Connecticut."

42. Robert A. Caro, *The Path to Power: The Years of Lyndon Johnson* (New York: Knopf, 1982), 606–64.

43. *PM,* December 8, 1942; Robert Dallek, *Franklin D. Roosevelt: A Political Life* (New York: Viking, 2017), 498–99.

44. *Newsweek,* October 19, 1942

45. *Life,* November 16, 1942; *St. Petersburg Times,* September 20, 1942; Thomas Fleming, *The New Dealers' War: FDR and the War within World War II* (New York: Basic Books, 2001), 155.

46. For my father's early military history, I relied on World War II Enlistment Records located at ancestry.com, and his honorable discharge papers.

Chapter 11. November

1. *New York Times,* October 31, November 1, 12, 1942; *Chicago Daily Tribune,* November 1, 1942; *Williamsport (Pa.) Gazette,* November 12, 1942.

2. James M. McPherson, *Battle Cry of Freedom: The Civil War Era* (New York: Oxford University Press, 1988), 560–62; David Herbert Donald, *Lincoln* (New York: Simon and Schuster, 1995), 380–84.

3. *Chicago Daily Tribune*, November 1, 1942; *New York Times*, November 1, 1942.

4. *New York Times*, November 1, 1942; "Notes on the Congressional Campaign of Mrs. Clare Boothe Luce," Clare Boothe Luce Papers, Library of Congress, Washington, D.C.

5. *New York Times*, November 4, 5, 1942; Jim Newton, *Justice for All: Earl Warren and the Nation He Made* (New York: Riverhead Books, 2006), 160.

6. *New York Times*, November 3, 4, 5, 1942; Robert R. McCormick to Clare Boothe Luce, November 12, 1942, Luce Papers; John W. Jeffries, *Testing the Roosevelt Coalition: Connecticut Society and Politics in the Era of World War II* (Knoxville: University of Tennessee Press, 1979), 135–38.

7. Grant Rice to George W. Norris, October 7, 1942, George W. Norris Papers, Library of Congress; *New York Times*, November 4, 5, 8, 1942; *Newsweek*, November 16, 1942; *Wall Street Journal*, November 5, 1942; Nancy Beck Young, *Why We Fight: Congress and the Politics of World War II* (Lawrence: University Press of Kansas, 2013), 75–76. The turnout for the 2014 congressional elections was 35.9 percent.

8. *New York Times*, November 8, 1942; *Chicago Daily Tribune*, November 5, 1942; *Nation*, November 14, 1942; *Newsweek*, December 14, 1942.

9. *Time*, November 30, 1942; Gallup poll, November 1942, ropercenter.cornell.edu.

10. *Chicago Daily Tribune*, October 24, 1942; Harold Ickes Diary, November 22, 1942, Library of Congress; John Morton Blum, *V Was for Victory: Politics and American Culture during World War II* (San Diego: Harcourt Brace Jovanovich, 1976), 233; Samuel Rosenman, ed., *Humanity on the Defensive*, vol. 11 of *The Public Papers and Addresses of Franklin D. Roosevelt* (New York: Harper and Bros., 1950), 448.

11. *Life*, December 7, 1942.

12. *New York Times*, November 15, 1942.

13. John Harding, "The 1942 Congressional Elections," *American Political Science Review* 38 (February 1944): 41–58; Molly Guptill Manning, "Fighting to Lose the Vote: How the Soldier Voting Acts of 1942 and 1944 Disenfranchised America's Armed Forces," *New York University Journal of Legislation and Public Policy* 19 (2016): 335–79; Christopher H. Achen and Larry M. Bartels, *Democracy for Realists: Why Elections Do Not Produce Responsive Government* (Princeton: Princeton University Press, 2016), 4; Michael X. Delli Karpini and Scott Ketter, *What Americans Know about Politics and Why It Matters* (New Haven: Yale University Press, 1997), 17.

14. Statement by President Franklin D. Roosevelt Announcing Opening of Second Front Attacks in French North and West Africa, November 7, 1942, Washington, D.C., www.ibiblio.org/1942; Rick Atkinson, *An Army at Dawn: The War in North Africa, 1942–1943* (New York: Picador, 2002), 31; Carlo D'Este, *Eisenhower: A Soldier's Life* (New York: Henry Holt, 2002), 352–55.

15. David M. Kennedy, *Freedom from Fear: The American People in Depression and War, 1929–1945* (New York: Oxford University Press, 1999), 582–84; Jay Winik, *1944:*

FDR and the Year That Changed History (New York: Simon and Schuster, 2015), 60–61; Robert Dallek, *Franklin D. Roosevelt: A Political Life* (New York: Viking, 2017), 494–95.

16. *Life*, November 23, 1942.

17. Victor Davis Hanson, *The Second World Wars: How the First Global Conflict Was Fought and Won* (New York: Basic Books, 2017), 318–21; John Keegan, *The Second World War* (New York: Penguin, 1989), 230.

18. Hanson, *The Second World Wars*, 195–96; Joseph Wheelan, *Midnight in the Pacific: Guadalcanal—The World War II Battle That Turned the Tide of War* (Boston: Da Capo, 2017), 219–46.

19. FDR to Mr. and Mrs. T. F. Sullivan, February 1, 1943, fdrlibrary.marist.edu.

20. Rosenman, *Humanity on the Defensive*, 470–71; Gallup poll, October 1942, ropercenter.cornell.edu; Keith E. Eiler, *Robert P. Patterson and the War Effort, 1940–1945* (Ithaca: Cornell University Press, 1997), 297.

21. Gallup poll, October 1942, ropercenter.cornell.edu.

22. *New York Times*, November 15, 1942.

23. *New York Times*, November 22, 1942.

24. "The Platform of the Class Struggle," National Platform of the Workers (Communist) Party, 1928, 45; *New York Times*, November 15, 22, 1942; *Wall Street Journal*, October 28, 1942.

25. *New York Times*, November 18, 1942.

26. Statement by Chairman Peale, November 13, 1942, "Committee for Constitutional Government," Henry J. Kaiser Papers, Bancroft Library, University of California, Berkeley.

27. Edward J. Smith, *The $10,000 Issue*, June–July 1942, George W. Norris Papers, Library of Congress; *New York Times*, December 1, 2010.

28. Alistair Cooke, *The American Home Front, 1941–1942* (New York: Grove, 2006), 140–41.

29. *New York Times*, November 17, 1942.

30. Dorothy Sue Cobble, *The Other Women's Movement: Workplace Justice and Social Rights in Modern America* (Princeton: Princeton University Press, 2005), 97–106; James B. Atleson, *Labor and the Wartime State: Labor Relations and the Law during World War II* (Urbana: University of Illinois Press, 1998), 166; 1940census.archives.gov; *New York Times*, November 8, 26, 29, 1942.

31. *Time*, November 2, 1942.

32. *New York Times*, November 25, 1942.

33. "Summary of Report of War Production Board, November 24, 1942," "Statement Made by Robert Nathan Before WPB, November 24, 1942," Harry L. Hopkins Papers, Franklin D. Roosevelt Presidential Library, Hyde Park, N.Y.; *Daily Press* (Newport News, Va.), November 13, 1942.

34. Henry Morgenthau to James Byrnes, November 10, 1942, Henry Morgenthau Jr. Papers, FDR Library.

35. Glenda Elizabeth Gilmore, *Defying Dixie: The Radical Roots of Civil Rights, 1911–1950* (New York: Norton, 2008), 337; Young, *Why We Fight*, 173–82. In the House,

southerners chaired the Agriculture (Fulmer), Banking (Steagall), and Ways and Means (Doughton) committees.

36. *Chicago Daily Tribune,* October 13, 1942.

37. *New York Times,* November 18, 1942; *People's Voice,* October 31, 1942; Steven F. Lawson, *Black Ballots: Voting Rights in the South, 1944–1969* (Lanham, Md.: Lexington Books, 1999), 62–68; Keith M. Finley, *Delaying the Dream: Southern Senators and the Fight against Civil Rights* (Baton Rouge: Louisiana State University Press, 2008), 59–71.

38. Alben W. Barkley, *That Reminds Me: The Autobiography of the Veep* (Garden City: Doubleday, 1954), 157–58; FDR to Barkley, January 8, 1943, box 63, Alben W. Barkley Papers, Special Collections Research Center, University of Kentucky, Lexington; Ickes Diary, October 25, November 15, 1942; James K. Libbey, *Alben Barkley: A Life in Politics* (Lexington: University Press of Kentucky, 2016), 23–25.

39. Charles E. Simons to George W. Norris, September 21, 1942, Norris Papers.

40. *New York Times,* November 22, 24, 1942; *Chicago Daily Tribune,* November 18, 24, 1942; *People's Voice,* November 28, 1942; Finley, *Delaying the Dream.* Other poll-tax bills proposed in 1944 and 1946 failed to get past filibusters as well. The poll tax was finally outlawed by the ratification of the Twenty-Fourth Amendment in 1964.

41. *New York Times,* November 28, 1942; Charles C. Whitaker, *Race Work: The Rise of Civil Rights in the American West* (Lincoln: University of Nebraska Press, 2007), 74–75.

42. *Popular Science Monthly,* November 1942, 66–72.

43. Edna St. Vincent Millay, "Thanksgiving, 1942" from *The New York Times* (November 22, 1942). Copyright 1942, © 1969 by Edna St. Vincent Millay and Norma Millay Ellis. Reprinted with the permission of The Permissions Company, Inc., on behalf of Holly Peppe, Literary Executor, The Edna St. Vincent Millay Society. www.millay.org. James Holland, *The Allies Strike Back, 1941–1943: The War in the West* (New York: Atlantic Monthly, 2017), 225.

44. *New York Times,* November 27, 1942.

45. *New York Times,* November 29, 1942; Studs Terkel, *"The Good War": An Oral History of World War II* (New York: Pantheon, 1984), 324.

46. *Boston Sunday Globe,* November 29, 1942; *New York Times,* November 29, 30, 1942; See Erich Lindemann, "Symptomatology and Management of Acute Grief," *American Journal of Psychiatry* 101 (September 1944): 141–48; and Alexandra Adler, "Neuropsychiatric Complications in Victims of Boston's Cocoanut Grove Disaster," *Journal of the American Medical Association* 123 (December 25, 1943): 1098–1101.

47. *New York Times,* December 6, 1942.

Chapter 12. December

1. *St. Louis Post-Dispatch,* December 15, 1942, December 16, 2012; *New York Times,* November 15, 1942; *Chicago Daily Tribune,* December 15, 1942.

2. *New York Times Magazine*, December 2, 1963. Wigner won the Nobel Prize in physics in 1963.

3. *New York Times*, December 9, 1942; *Nation*, November 21, 1942; Eric Larrabee, *Commander in Chief: Franklin Delano Roosevelt, His Lieutenants, and Their War* (New York: Harper and Row, 1987), 425–26; Rick Atkinson, *An Army at Dawn: The War in North Africa, 1942–1943* (New York: Picador, 2002), 3–4, 260–62; Victor Davis Hanson, *The Second World Wars: How the First Global Conflict Was Fought and Won* (New York: Basic Books, 2017), 136.

4. AIPO Gallup poll, December 2, 1942, *Public Opinion Quarterly* (Spring 1943).

5. *St. Petersburg (Fla.) Evening Independent*, December 18, 1942; *New York Times*, December 12, 1942; *Afro-American*, December 15, 1942.

6. "Notes on the Congressional Campaign of Mrs. Clare Boothe Luce," Clare Boothe Luce Papers, Library of Congress, Washington, D.C.

7. Alan Brinkley, *The End of Reform: New Deal Liberalism in Recession and War* (New York: Knopf, 1995), 138–41.

8. "Issuance of Questionnaires by Governmental Agencies," Hearings Before the Joint Committee on Reduction of Non-Essential Federal Expenditures, 77th Congress, 2nd session, December 1942; Harold Ickes Diary, December 20, 1942, Library of Congress; *New York Times*, December 2, 4, 1942, October 3, 1971; Thomas Ford to Edward J. Flynn, August 8, 1942, President's Official Files, Franklin D. Roosevelt Presidential Library, Hyde Park, N.Y.

9. *New York Times*, December 10, 1942, January 5, 6, 1943.

10. Richard V. Gilbert to Leon Henderson, November 26, 1942, Richard V. Gilbert Papers, FDR Library; *New York Times*, December 8, 1942.

11. *New York Times*, December 14, 1942; "FDR Day by Day," December 2, 1942, www.fdrlibrary.marist.edu.

12. *100 Million Questions*, CBS Radio, December 10, 1942, at archive.org. *New York Times*, December 19, 1942.

13. *New York Times*, December 16, 1942.

14. Leon Henderson to FDR, December 15, 17, 1942, FDR to Henderson, December 17, 1942, President's Official Files; Ickes Diary, December 27, 1942.

15. *New York Times*, December 18, 1942.

16. *Wall Street Journal*, December 19, 1942; *Charlotte Observer*, December 18, 1942.

17. Lydell Peck to FDR, December 18, 1942, Minnie Morgan Webster to Henderson, December 17, 1942, President's Official Files.

18. Dabney Yarbrough to Henderson, December 25, 1942, President's Official Files; *Nation*, December 26, 1942; *New York Times*, May 7, 1943; Eliot Janeway, *The Struggle for Survival: A Chronicle of Economic Mobilization in World War II* (New Haven: Yale University Press, 1951), 199.

19. *New York Times*, June 29, November 1, 1943, March 17, 1945; "FDR Day by Day," fdrlibrary.marist.edu.

20. Studs Terkel, *"The Good War": An Oral History of World War II* (New York: Pantheon, 1984), 325; Adam Tooze, *The Wages of Destruction: The Making and Breaking of the Nazi Economy* (New York: Penguin, 2006), 552–89.

21. Office of Price Administration Report, January 19, 1943, James F. Byrnes Papers, Special Collections Library, Clemson University; *Time,* December 28, 1942; Milton Friedman and Anna Jacobsen Schwartz, *A Monetary History of the United States, 1867–1960* (Princeton: Princeton University Press, 1963), chs. 8–10; "Consumer Price Index, 1913–," www.minneapolisfed.org.

22. FDR Press Conference #864, December 1, 1942, www.fdrlibrary.marist.edu; *New York Times,* December 2, 1942; *Newsweek,* December 14, 1942.

23. *New York Times,* December 6, 1942; Gallup poll, December 1942, ropercenter. cornell.edu. The $25,000 salary tax ended in March 1943, when the House agreed to raise the federal debt limit but demanded the president "forget" his executive order on the tax issue. Mark H. Leff, "The Politics of Sacrifice on the American Home Front in World War II," *Journal of American History* 77 (March 1991): 1299; *New York Times,* March 26, 1943.

24. Evans Clark, ed., *Wartime Facts and Postwar Problems: A Study and Discussion Manual* (New York: Twentieth Century Fund, 1943), 1.

25. Samuel Rosenman, ed., *Humanity on the Defensive,* vol. 11 of *The Public Papers and Addresses of Franklin D. Roosevelt* (New York: Harper and Bros., 1950), 505–6; *New York Times,* December 28, 1942; Nick Taylor, *American-Made: The Enduring Legacy of the WPA: When FDR Put the Nation to Work* (New York: Bantam, 2008); and Jason Scott Smith, *Building New Deal Liberalism: The Political Economy of Public Works, 1933–1956* (Cambridge: Cambridge University Press, 2006), 222–31.

26. *New York Times,* December 8, 11, 27, 1942; Melissa A. McEuen, *Making War, Making Women: Femininity and Duty on the American Home Front, 1941–1945* (Athens: University of Georgia Press, 2011), 187.

27. *New York Times,* December 26, 1942; Rhaina Cohen, "Who Took Care of Rosie the Riveter's Kids?" *Atlantic,* November 18, 2005.

28. Oscar Cox to Harry Hopkins, December 11, 1942, Oscar Cox Papers, FDR Library.

29. Sir William Beveridge, "Social Insurance and Allied Services, November 1942," bl.uk/onlinegallery; *Nation,* December 12, 19, 1942; Elizabeth Borgwardt, *A New Deal for the World: America's Vision for Human Rights* (Cambridge, Mass.: Belknap Press of Harvard University Press, 2005), 49–50.

30. "American Nationwide Round-up," December 1, 2, 4, 5, 1942," American Division of Ministry of Information, William Beveridge Papers, Women's Library Reading Room, London School of Economics; Lord Beveridge, *Power and Influence* (London: Hadden and Stoughton, 1943), 320; Robert R. Nathan, *Mobilizing for Abundance* (New York: McGraw-Hill, 1944), 46; *Atlanta Constitution,* December 3, 1942; *New York Journal-American,* December 3, 1942; *Seattle Times,* December 3, 1942.

31. Ralph J. Watkins, "The Framework of an Economy of Plenty," November 27, 1942, Wayne Coy Papers, FDR Library.

32. War Production Board, "Civilian Consumption and Output in the United States: Review of 1942 and Prospects for 1943," Harry L. Hopkins Papers, FDR Library; War Production Board, "Official Munitions Production," December 1, 1942, Hopkins Papers; Donald Nelson to FDR, May 31, 1943, President's Secretary's Files, box 11, FDR Library; U.S. Civilian Production Administration, "Industrial Mobi-

lization for War: History of the War Production Board and Predecessor Agencies, 1940–1945" (1947), 426, 533; Gallup poll, December 1942, ropercenter.cornell. edu; John R. Craf, *A Survey of the American Economy, 1940–1946* (New York: North River, 1947), 178; Interview with Robert Nathan by Tracy Campbell, June 9, 1995, Arlington, Va., Edward F. Prichard, Jr. Oral History Project, Special Collections, University of Kentucky, Lexington; John Keegan, *The Second World War* (New York: Penguin, 1989), 219.

33. Victor Davis Hanson, *The Second World Wars: How the First Global Conflict Was Fought and Won* (New York: Basic Books, 2017), 188–90.

34. U.S. Department of Commerce, Bureau of Economic Analysis, "GDP and Other Major NIPA Series, 1929–2012: II," 183, at bea.gov; Federal Reserve Economic Data, "Unemployment Rate for the United States," Federal Reserve Bank of St. Louis, fred.stlouisfed.org; Kiran Klaus Patel, *The New Deal: A Global History* (Princeton: Princeton University Press, 2016), 262.

35. "Treasury Department Press Release, December 28, 1942," Henry Morgenthau Jr. Papers FDR Library; Michael C. C. Adams, *The Best War Ever: America and World War II* (Baltimore: Johns Hopkins University Press, 1994), 117.

36. *New York Times*, December 6, 8, 12, 1942, January 6, 1943; "Civilian Consumption and Output in the United States," War Production Board Report 227 (February 1943), Nelson Papers; *Chain Store Age*, January 1943; Stephen Daggett, "Costs of Major U.S. Wars," *Congressional Research Service* (June 2010); Max Hastings, *Inferno: The World at War, 1939–1945* (New York: Random House, 2011), 351; Maury Klein, *A Call to Arms: Mobilizing America for World War II* (New York: Bloomsbury, 2013), 515–16.

37. War Department, Foreign Industrial Information Section, "Report on German Controlled Materials Plan—Up to Date," February 5, 1943, Nelson Papers; Lutz Budraft, Jonas Scherner, and Jochen Streb, "Demystifying the German 'Armament Miracle' during World War II: New Insights from the Annual Audits of German Aircraft Producers," Yale University Economic Growth Center Paper 905, January 2005, 1–40; Tooze, *The Wages of Destruction*, 495–96.

38. Thomas Piketty, *Capital in the Twenty-First Century* (Cambridge, Mass.: Belknap Press of Harvard University Press, 2014), 118, 275: Jefferson Cowie, *The Great Exception: The New Deal and the Limits of American Politics* (Princeton: Princeton University Press, 2016), 142; Joseph E. Stiglitz, *The Price of Inequality: How Today's Divided Society Endangers Our Future* (New York: Norton, 2012), 28–32; Edward N. Wolff, *A Century of Wealth in America* (Cambridge, Mass.: Belknap Press of Harvard University Press, 2017), 562–66, 598–601.

39. *New York Times*, December 27, 1942; *Williamsport (Pa.) Gazette*, November 12, 1942.

40. *Time*, January 4, 1943; Stephen B. Adams, *Mr. Kaiser Goes to Washington: The Rise of a Government Entrepreneur* (Chapel Hill: University of North Carolina Press, 1997), 116.

41. Henry Wallace, "America's Part in World Reconstruction," radio address, December 28, 1942, Beveridge Papers.

42. *Fortune*, December 1942; *Life*, February 17, 1941; *Time*, December 14, 1942; Alan Brinkley, *The Publisher: Henry Luce and His American Century* (New York: Vintage, 2010), 152–53.

43. Address by Governor Frank M. Dixon Before the Southern Society of New York, broadcast by WABC, December 11, 1942, www.ibiblio.org/1942; John Egerton, *Speak Now against the Day: The Generation before the Civil Rights Movement in the South* (New York: Knopf, 1994), 499.

44. *Life*, December 21, 1942.

45. *JAHCO News*, December 24, 1942; *Life*, March 22, 1943.

46. *New York Times*, December 9, 23, 26, 1942; Rosenman, *Humanity on the Defensive*, 532–33; Carol Boggess, *James Still: A Life* (Lexington: University Press of Kentucky, 2017), 194.

47. *New York Times*, December 26, 1942.

48. *New York Daily News*, August 14, 2017; *New York Times*, July 4, 1943.

49. Robert E. Sherwood, *Roosevelt and Hopkins: An Intimate History* (New York: Harper, 1948), 665; *Spokane Daily Chronicle*, January 1, 1943; *New York Times*, January 1, 1943; *Chicago Daily Tribune*, January 1, 1943.

Epilogue

1. Steven Levitsky and Daniel Ziblatt, *How Democracies Die* (New York: Crown, 2018), 92–96, 192–93.

2. John Hope Franklin, "History—Weapon of War and Peace," *Phylon* 5 (Third Quarter, 1944): 257.

BIBLIOGRAPHY

Archival Collections

Archive of Folk Culture, American Folklife Center, Library of Congress, Washington, D.C.
  World War II Rumor Project Collection
Bancroft Library, University of California, Berkeley
  Japanese-American Evacuation and Resettlement Records
  Henry J. Kaiser Papers
Bedford Historical Society, Bedford, Ohio
  Jack and Heintz Company Records
Center for Jewish History, Lillian Goldman Reading Room, New York, N.Y.
  The American Jewish Yearbooks
Franklin D. Roosevelt Presidential Library, Hyde Park, N.Y.
  Oscar Cox Papers
  Wayne Coy Papers
  Mordecai Ezekiel Papers
  Richard V. Gilbert Papers
  Leon Henderson Papers
  Harry L. Hopkins Papers
  Henry Morgenthau Jr. Papers
  President's Official Files
  President's Secretary's File
  Records of the President's Rubber Survey Committee
  Eleanor Roosevelt Papers
Huntington Library, San Marino, Calif.
  Donald M. Nelson Papers
Library of Congress, Washington, D.C.

Henry Harley Arnold Papers
Raymond Clapper Papers
Cordell Hull Papers
Harold L. Ickes Diary
Robert H. Jackson Papers
Frank Knox Papers
William D. Leahy Papers
Clare Boothe Luce Papers
Margaret Mead Papers
NAACP Papers
George W. Norris Papers
A. Philip Randolph Papers
London School of Economics, Women's Library Reading Room
William Beveridge Papers
National Archives, Washington, D.C.
Office of Censorship Records, RG 216
Office of Price Administration Records, RG 188
War Damage Corporation Records, RG 234
New-York Historical Society, New York, N.Y.
Leonard Larsen Papers
New York Public Library, New York, N.Y.
National Board of Review of Motion Picture Records
Schomburg Center for Research in Black Culture, New York Public Library, New York, N.Y.
Universal Negro Improvement Association Records
Seeley G. Mudd Manuscript Library, Princeton University, Princeton, N.J.
Bernard M. Baruch Papers
Ferdinand Eberstadt Papers
David E. Lilienthal Papers
Harry Dexter White Papers
Special Collections Library, Clemson University, Clemson, S.C.
James F. Byrnes Papers
Special Collections Research Center, University of Kentucky, Lexington, Ky.
Alben W. Barkley Papers
Yale University Library, Manuscripts and Archives, New Haven, Conn.
Henry L. Stimson Papers

Newspapers

Afro-American
Atlanta Constitution
Baltimore Sun
Beacon Light

Boston Herald
Boston Sunday Globe
Brooklyn Daily Eagle
Cedar Valley (Iowa) Courier
Charlotte Observer
Chicago Daily Tribune
Cleveland News
Cleveland Plain Dealer
Crisis
Daily Princetonian
Daily Worker
Defender
Harvard Crimson
Houston Post
Indianapolis Recorder
Labor Action
Liberty
Los Angeles Times
Louisiana Weekly
Louisville Courier-Journal
Miami Daily News
Miami Herald
National Geographic
New Bedford (Mass.) Standard-Times
New York Amsterdam Star-News
New York Daily News
New York Journal-American
New York Post
New York Times
Paducah (Ky.) Sun-Democrat
People's Voice
Philadelphia Inquirer
PM
San Francisco Chronicle
San Jose Evening News
Seattle Times
Sikeston (Mo.) Herald
Sikeston (Mo.) Standard
Spokane Daily Chronicle
St. Louis Post-Dispatch
Texarkana Gazette
Tribune-Star (Terre Haute, Ind.)
Wall Street Journal
Washington Evening-Star

Washington Post
Williamsburg (Pa.) Gazette

Periodicals

America
American Mercury
American Unity: A Monthly Educational Guide
Atlantic Monthly
Banking
Barnard Alumnae
Catholic Telegraph-Register
Chain Store Age
Christian Century
Chronicle of Higher Education
Economist
Editor and Publisher
Fortune
JAHCO News
Leo Weekly
Life
Mountain Life and Work
Nation
Newsweek
New Yorker
Phylon
Popular Mechanics
Popular Science Monthly
Reader's Digest
Saturday Evening Post
Social Justice
Southern California Business
Survey Graphic
Time
Vogue

Books

Adams, Michael C. C. *The Best War Ever: America and World War II*. Baltimore: Johns
  Hopkins University Press, 1994.
Adams, Stephen B. *Mr. Kaiser Goes to Washington: The Rise of a Government Entrepre-
  neur*. Chapel Hill: University of North Carolina Press, 1997.
Allport, Gordon W., and Leo Postman. *The Psychology of Rumor*. New York: Russell
  and Russell, 1947.

Ames, Jessie Daniel. *The Changing Character of Lynching: Review of Lynching, 1931–1941.* Atlanta: Commission on Interracial Cooperation, 1942.

Atkinson, Rick. *An Army at Dawn: The War in North Africa, 1942–1943.* New York: Picador, 2002.

Bailey, Stephen Kemp. *Congress Makes a Law: The Story behind the Employment Act of 1946.* New York: Columbia University Press, 1957.

Baldwin, Neil. *Henry Ford and the Jews: The Mass Production of Hate.* New York: Public Affairs, 2001.

Bannai, Lorraine K. *Enduring Conviction: Fred Korematsu and His Quest for Justice.* Seattle: University of Washington Press, 2015.

Benton, Thomas Hart. *Year of Peril: A Series of War Paintings.* Chicago: Abbott Laboratories, 1942.

Biddle, Francis. *In Brief Authority.* Garden City: Doubleday, 1962.

Blum, John Morton. *V Was for Victory: Politics and American Culture during World War II.* San Diego: Harcourt Brace Jovanovich, 1976.

Borgwardt, Elizabeth. *A New Deal for the World: America's Vision for Human Rights.* Cambridge, Mass.: Belknap Press of Harvard University Press, 2005.

Breitman, Richard, and Allan J. Lichtman. *FDR and the Jews.* Cambridge, Mass.: Belknap Press of Harvard University Press, 2013.

Brinkley, Alan. *The End of Reform: New Deal Liberalism in Recession and War.* New York: Knopf, 1995.

Brokaw, Tom. *The Greatest Generation.* New York: Random House, 1998.

Brooks, Christopher A., and Robert Sims. *Roland Hayes: The Legacy of an American Tenor.* Bloomington: Indiana University Press, 2015.

Brownlee, W. Elliot, ed. *Funding the Modern American State, 1941–1995: The Rise and Fall of the Era of Easy Finance.* Cambridge: Cambridge University Press, 1996.

Burns, James MacGregor. *Roosevelt: The Soldier of Freedom, 1940–1945.* San Diego: Harcourt Brace Jovanovich, 1970.

Campbell, D'Ann. *Women at War with America: Private Lives in a Patriotic Era.* Cambridge, Mass.: Harvard University Press, 1984.

Catton, Bruce. *The War Lords of Washington.* New York: Harcourt Brace, 1948.

Chafe, William H. *The Paradox of Change: American Women in the Twentieth Century.* New York: Oxford University Press, 1991.

Cobble, Dorothy Sue. *The Other Women's Movement: Workplace Justice and Social Rights in Modern America.* Princeton: Princeton University Press, 2005.

Cook, Blanche Wiesen. *Eleanor Roosevelt.* Vol. 3: *The War Years and After, 1939–1962.* New York: Penguin, 2016.

Cooke, Alistair. *The American Home Front, 1941–1942.* New York: Grove, 2006.

Cowie, Jefferson. *The Great Exception: The New Deal and the Limits of American Politics.* Princeton: Princeton University Press, 2016.

Craf, John R. *A Survey of the American Economy, 1940–1946.* New York: North River, 1947.

Curtis, Brian. *Fields of Battle: Pearl Harbor, the Rose Bowl, and the Boys Who Went to War.* New York: Flatiron Books, 2016.

Dallek, Matthew. *Defenseless under the Night: The Roosevelt Years and the Origins of Homeland Security.* New York: Oxford University Press, 2016.

Dallek, Robert. *Franklin D. Roosevelt: A Political Life.* New York: Viking, 2017.

Davis, Kenneth S. *FDR: The War President, 1940–1943.* New York: Random House, 2000.

D'Este, Carlo. *Eisenhower: A Soldier's Life.* New York: Henry Holt, 2002.

Dobbs, Michael. *Saboteurs: The Nazi Raid on America.* New York: Knopf, 2004.

Dolinar, Brian. *The Black Cultural Front: Black Writers and Artists of the Depression Generation.* Jackson: University Press of Mississippi, 2012.

Dunn, Susan. *A Blueprint for War: FDR and the Hundred Days That Mobilized America.* New Haven: Yale University Press, 2018.

Equal Justice Initiative. *Lynching in America: Confronting the Legacy of Racial Terror.* 3rd ed. Montgomery, Ala.: Equal Justice Initiative, 2017.

Feldman, Glenn. *The Irony of the Solid South: Democrats, Republicans, and Race, 1865–1944.* Tuscaloosa: University of Alabama Press, 2013.

———. *Politics, Society, and the Klan in Alabama, 1915–1949.* Tuscaloosa: University of Alabama Press, 1999.

Finley, Keith M. *Delaying the Dream: Southern Senators and the Fight against Civil Rights.* Baton Rouge: Louisiana State University Press, 2008.

Fox, Stephen. *America's Invisible Gulag: A Biography of German American Internment and Exclusion in World War II.* New York: Peter Lang, 2000.

———. *The Unknown Internment: An Oral History of the Relocation of Italian Americans during World War II.* Boston: Twayne, 1990.

Franklin, John Hope. *Mirror to America: The Autobiography of John Hope Franklin.* New York: Farrar, Straus and Giroux, 2005.

Freedman, Lawrence. *The Future of War: A History.* New York: Public Affairs, 2017.

Friedman, Milton, and Anna Jacobsen Schwartz. *From New Deal Banking Reform to World War II Inflation.* Princeton: Princeton University Press, 1980.

———. *A Monetary History of the United States, 1867–1960.* Princeton: Princeton University Press, 1963.

Gabler, Neal. *Walt Disney: The Triumph of the American Imagination.* New York: Random House, 2006.

Gannon, Michael. *Operation Drumbeat: The Dramatic True Story of Germany's First U-Boat Attacks along the American East Coast in World War II.* New York: HarperCollins, 1990.

Gavins, Raymond. *The Perils and Prospects of Southern Black Leadership: Gordon Blaine Hancock, 1884–1970.* Durham: Duke University Press, 1977.

Gillon, Steven M. *Pearl Harbor: FDR Leads the Nation into War.* New York: Basic Books, 2011.

Gilmore, Glenda Elizabeth. *Defying Dixie: The Radical Roots of Civil Rights, 1911–1950.* New York: Norton, 2008.

Goodwin, Doris Kearns. *No Ordinary Time: Franklin and Eleanor Roosevelt: The Home Front in World War II.* New York: Simon and Schuster, 1994.

Gordon, Robert J. *The Rise and Fall of American Growth: The U.S. Standard of Living since the Civil War.* Princeton: Princeton University Press, 2016.

Hamilton, Nigel. *The Mantle of Command: FDR at War, 1941–1942*. Boston: Houghton Mifflin Harcourt, 2014.

Hanson, Victor Davis. *The Second World Wars: How the First Global Conflict Was Fought and Won*. New York: Basic Books, 2017.

Hastings, Max. *Inferno: The World at War, 1939–1945*. New York: Random House, 2011.

Herman, Arthur. *Freedom's Forge: How American Business Produced Victory in World War II*. New York: Random House, 2012.

Herring, George C. *From Colony to Superpower: U.S. Foreign Relations since 1776*. New York: Oxford University Press, 2008.

Hill, Robert A., ed. *The FBI's RACON: Racial Conditions in the United States during World War II*. Boston: Northeastern University Press, 1995.

Holland, James. *The Allies Strike Back, 1941–1943: The War in the West*. New York: Atlantic Monthly, 2017.

Hooks, Gregory. *Forging the Military-Industrial Complex: World War II's Battle of the Potomac*. Urbana: University of Illinois Press, 1991.

Ichioka, Yuji, ed. *Views from Within: The Japanese American Evacuation and Resettlement Study*. Los Angeles: Asian American Studies Center, 1989.

Irons, Peter H. *Justice at War: The Story of the Japanese American Internment Cases*. Berkeley: University of California Press, 1983.

Jacobs, Meg. *Pocketbook Politics: Economic Citizenship in Twentieth-Century America*. Princeton: Princeton University Press, 2005.

Janeway, Eliot. *The Struggle for Survival: A Chronicle of Economic Mobilization in World War II*. New Haven: Yale University Press, 1951.

Jeansonne, Glen. *Gerald L. K. Smith: Minister of Hate*. Baton Rouge: Louisiana State Press, 1977.

Jeffries, Hasan Kwame. *Bloody Lowndes: Civil Rights and Black Power in Alabama's Black Belt*. New York: New York University Press, 2009.

Jeffries, John W. *Wartime America: The World War II Home Front*. Lanham, Md.: Rowman and Littlefield, 2018.

Katznelson, Ira. *Fear Itself: The New Deal and the Origins of Our Time*. New York: Norton, 2013.

Keane, John. *The Life and Death of Democracy*. London: Simon and Schuster, 2009.

Keegan, John. *The Second World War*. New York: Penguin, 1989.

Kennedy, David M. *Birth Control in America: The Career of Margaret Sanger*. New Haven: Yale University Press, 1970.

———. *Freedom from Fear: The American People in Depression and War, 1929–1945*. New York: Oxford University Press, 1999.

Keyssar, Alexander. *The Right to Vote: The Contested History of Democracy in the United States*. New York: Basic Books, 2000.

Kiernan, Denise. *The Girls of Atomic City: The Untold Story of the Women Who Helped Win World War II*. New York: Simon and Schuster, 2013.

Klein, Maury. *A Call to Arms: Mobilizing America for World War II*. New York: Bloomsbury, 2013.

Klingaman, William K. *The Darkest Year: The American Home Front, 1941–1942*. New York: St. Martin's, 2019.

Koistinen, Paul A. C. *Arsenal of World War II: The Political Economy of American Warfare, 1940–1945*. Lawrence: University Press of Kansas, 2004.

Koppes, Clayton R., and Gregory D. Black. *Hollywood Goes to War: Patriotism, Movies and the Second World War from "Ninotchka" to "Mrs. Miniver."* New York: Free Press, 1987.

Kruse, Kevin M., and Stephen Tuck, eds. *Fog of War: The Second World War and the Civil Rights Movement*. New York: Oxford University Press, 2012.

Lacey, Jim. *Keep from All Thoughtful Men: How U.S. Economists Won World War II*. Annapolis: Naval Institute Press, 2011.

Lang, Clarence. *Grassroots at the Gateway: Class Politics and the Black Freedom Struggle in St. Louis, 1936–1975*. Ann Arbor: University of Michigan Press, 2009.

Larrabee, Eric. *Commander in Chief: Franklin Delano Roosevelt, His Lieutenants, and Their War*. New York: Harper and Row, 1987.

Leff, Mark. *The Limits of Symbolic Reform: The New Deal and Taxation, 1933–39*. Cambridge: Cambridge University Press, 1984.

Leuchtenburg, William E. *The FDR Years: On Roosevelt and His Legacy*. New York: Columbia University Press, 1995.

Levitsky, Steven, and Daniel Ziblatt. *How Democracies Die*. New York: Crown, 2018.

Libbey, James K. *Alben Barkley: A Life in Politics*. Lexington: University Press of Kentucky, 2016.

Lichtenstein, Nelson. *Labor's War at Home: The CIO in World War II*. Philadelphia: Temple University Press, 2008.

Lind, Michael. *Land of Promise: An Economic History of the United States*. New York: HarperCollins, 2012.

Love, Spencie. *One Blood: The Death and Resurrection of Charles R. Drew*. Chapel Hill: University of North Carolina Press, 1996.

Lowe, Keith. *The Fear and the Freedom: How the Second World War Changed Us*. New York: St. Martin's, 2017.

McEuen, Melissa A. *Making War, Making Women: Femininity and Duty on the American Home Front, 1941–1945*. Athens: University of Georgia Press, 2011.

Michaeli, Ethan. *"The Defender": How the Legendary Black Newspaper Changed America*. New York: Houghton Mifflin, 2016.

Moore, Deborah Dash. *GI Jews: How World War II Changed a Generation*. Cambridge, Mass.: Belknap Press of Harvard University Press, 2004.

Morris, Sylvia Jukes. *Rage for Fame: The Ascent of Clare Boothe Luce*. New York: Random House, 1997.

Mullenbach, Cheryl. *Double Victory: How African American Women Broke Race and Gender Barriers to Help Win World War II*. Chicago: Chicago Review, 2013.

Myrdal, Gunnar. *An American Dilemma: The Negro Problem and Modern Democracy*. New York: Harper, 1944.

Nathan, Robert R. *Mobilizing for Abundance*. New York: McGraw-Hill, 1944.

Neal, Arthur. *National Trauma and Collective Memory: Extraordinary Events in the American Experience*. Armonk: M. E. Sharpe, 2005.

Nelson, Donald M. *Arsenal of Democracy: The Story of American War Production.* New York: Harcourt Brace, 1946.

Odum, Howard W. *Race and Rumors of Race: The American South in the Early Forties.* Chapel Hill: University of North Carolina Press, 1943.

Offley, Ed. *The Burning Shore: How Hitler's U-Boats Brought World War II to America.* New York: Basic Books, 2014.

Olson, Lynne. *Those Angry Days: Roosevelt, Lindbergh, and America's Fight over World War II.* New York: Random House, 2014.

Overy, Richard. *Why the Allies Won.* New York: Norton, 1995.

Petillo, Carol M. "Douglas MacArthur and Manuel Quezon: A Note on the Imperial Bond." In William M. Leary, ed., *MacArthur and the American Century: A Reader.* Lincoln: University of Nebraska Press, 2001.

Phillips-Fein, Kim. *Invisible Hands: The Businessmen's Crusade against the New Deal.* New York: Norton, 2010.

Piketty, Thomas. *Capital in the Twenty-First Century.* Cambridge, Mass.: Belknap Press of Harvard University Press, 2014.

Polenberg, Richard, ed. *America at War: The Home Front, 1941–1945.* Englewood Cliffs, N.J.: Prentice-Hall, 1968.

———. *One Nation Divisible: Class, Race, and Ethnicity in the United States since 1938.* New York: Viking, 1980.

———. *War and Society: The United States, 1941–1945.* Philadelphia: J. B. Lippincott, 1972.

Reagan, Leslie J. *When Abortion Was a Crime: Women, Medicine, and Law in the United States, 1867–1973.* Berkeley: University of California Press, 1997.

Reed, Merl E. "Black Workers, Defense Industries, and Federal Agencies, 1941–1945." In Joe William Trotter and Eric Ledell Smith, eds., *African Americans in Pennsylvania: Shifting Historical Perspectives.* University Park: Pennsylvania State University Press, 1997.

———. *Seedtime for the Modern Civil Rights Movement: The President's Committee on Fair Employment Practices, 1941–46.* Baton Rouge: Louisiana State University Press, 1991.

Reeves, Richard. *Infamy: The Shocking Story of the Japanese American Internment in World War II.* New York: Picador, 2015.

Rhodes, Richard. *Hedy's Folly: The Life and Breakthrough Inventions of Hedy Lamarr, the Most Beautiful Woman in the World.* New York: Random House, 2012.

Roberts, Gene, and Hank Klibanoff. *The Race Beat: The Press, the Civil Rights Struggle, and the Awakening of a Nation.* New York: Vintage, 2007.

Robertson, David. *Sly and Able: A Political Biography of James F. Byrnes.* New York: Norton, 1994.

Robinson, Greg. *A Tragedy of Democracy: Japanese Confinement in North America.* New York: Columbia University Press, 2009.

Roeder, George H., Jr. *The Censored War: American Visual Experience during World War II.* New Haven: Yale University Press, 1993.

Roosevelt, Eleanor. *The Autobiography of Eleanor Roosevelt.* New York: Harper and Brothers, 1961.

Rosenman, Samuel, ed. *Humanity on the Defensive*. Vol. 11 of *The Public Papers and Addresses of Franklin D. Roosevelt*. New York: Harper and Bros., 1950.

Schivelbusch, Wolfgang. *The Culture of Defeat: On National Trauma, Mourning, and Recovery*. Translated by Jefferson Chase. New York: Picador, 2004.

Scott, James M. *Target Tokyo: Jimmy Doolittle and the Raid That Avenged Pearl Harbor*. New York: Norton, 2015.

Sherman, Richard B. *The Case of Odell Waller and Virginia Justice, 1940–42*. Knoxville: University of Tennessee Press, 1992.

Sherwood, Robert E. *Roosevelt and Hopkins: An Intimate History*. New York: Harper, 1948.

Shlaes, Amity. *The Forgotten Man: A New History of the Great Depression*. New York: Harper, 2007.

Smith, Jason Scott. *Building New Deal Liberalism: The Political Economy of Public Works, 1933–1956*. Cambridge: Cambridge University Press, 2006.

Smith, Richard Norton. *An Uncommon Man: The Triumph of Herbert Hoover*. New York: Simon and Schuster, 1984.

Sparrow, James T. *Warfare State: World War II Americans and the Age of Big Government*. New York: Oxford University Press, 2011.

Stewart, Maxwell S. *After the War?* Public Affairs Pamphlet no. 73 (1942).

Stiglitz, Joseph E. *The Price of Inequality: How Today's Divided Society Endangers Our Future*. New York: Norton, 2012.

Stone, Geoffrey R. *Perilous Times: Free Speech in Wartime, from the Sedition Act of 1796 to the War on Terrorism*. New York: Norton, 2004.

Sugrue, Thomas J. *The Origins of the Urban Crisis: Race and Inequality in Postwar Detroit*. Princeton: Princeton University Press, 1996.

———. *Sweet Land of Liberty: The Forgotten Struggle for Civil Rights in the North*. New York: Random House, 2008.

Terkel, Studs. *"The Good War": An Oral History of World War II*. New York: Pantheon, 1984.

Thompson, Antonio. *Men in German Uniform: POWs in America during World War II*. Knoxville: University of Tennessee Press, 2010.

Tooze, Adam. *The Wages of Destruction: The Making and Breaking of the Nazi Economy*. New York: Penguin, 2006.

Vatter, Harold G. *The U.S. Economy in World War II*. New York: Columbia University Press, 1985.

Virtue, John. *The Black Soldiers Who Built the Alaska Highway: A History of Four U.S. Army Regiments in the North, 1942–1943*. Jefferson, N.C.: McFarland, 2013.

Vogel, Steve. *The Pentagon: A History*. New York: Random House, 2007.

Ward, Jason Morgan. *Defending White Democracy: The Making of a Segregationist Movement and the Remaking of Racial Politics, 1936–1965*. Chapel Hill: University of North Carolina Press, 2011.

———. *"Hanging Bridge": Racial Violence and America's Civil Rights Century*. New York: Oxford University Press, 2016.

Ware, Caroline F. *The Consumer Goes to War: A Guide to Victory on the Home Front*. New York: Funk and Wagnalls, 1942.

Watkins, T. H. *Righteous Pilgrim: The Life and Times of Harold L. Ickes, 1874–1952.* New York: Henry Holt, 1990.

Watts, Steven. *The People's Tycoon: Henry Ford and the American Century.* New York: Vintage, 2006.

Weatherford, Doris. *American Women and World War II.* Edison, N.J.: Castle Books, 1990.

Weintraub, Stanley. *Pearl Harbor Christmas: A World at War, December 1941.* Cambridge, Mass.: Da Capo, 2011.

Wheelan, Joseph. *Midnight in the Pacific: Guadalcanal—The World War II Battle That Turned the Tide of War.* Boston: Da Capo, 2017.

Wills, Garry. *John Wayne's America: The Politics of Celebrity.* New York: Simon and Schuster, 1997.

Wilson, Mark R. *Destructive Creation: American Business and the Winning of World War II.* Philadelphia: University of Pennsylvania Press, 2016.

Winik, Jay. *1944: FDR and the Year That Changed History.* New York: Simon and Schuster, 2015.

Winkler, Allan M. *Home Front U.S.A.: America during World War II.* Arlington Heights: Harlan Davidson, 1986.

Witte, John F. *The Politics and Development of the Federal Income Tax.* Madison: University of Wisconsin Press, 1985.

Wolff, Edward N. *A Century of Wealth in America.* Cambridge, Mass.: Belknap Press of Harvard University Press, 2017.

Wortman, Marc. *1941: Fighting the Shadow War: A Divided America in a World at War.* New York: Atlantic Monthly, 2016.

Wynn, Neil A. *The African American Experience during World War II.* Lanham, Md.: Rowman and Littlefield, 2010.

Young, Nancy Beck. *Why We Fight: Congress and the Politics of World War II.* Lawrence: University Press of Kansas, 2013.

Zieger, Robert H. *The CIO: 1935–1955.* Chapel Hill: University of North Carolina Press, 1997.

Articles

Adler, Alexandra. "Neuropsychiatric Complications in Victims of Boston's Cocoanut Grove Disaster." *Journal of the American Medical Association* 123 (December 25, 1943): 1098–1101.

Allport, Gordon W., and Leo Postman. "An Analysis of Rumor." *Public Opinion Quarterly* (Winter 1946): 501–17.

Bellafaire, Judith A. "The Women's Army Corps: A Commemoration of World War II Service." Center for Military History, #72-15 (1993).

Blakey, Roy C., and Gladys C. Blakey. "The Federal Revenue Act of 1942." *American Political Science Review* 36 (December 1942): 1069–82.

Budraft, Lutz, Jonas Scherner, and Jochen Streb. "Demystifying the German 'Armament Miracle' during World War II: New Insights from the Annual Audits of

German Aircraft Producers." Yale University Economic Growth Center Paper 905, January 2005, 1–40.

Cohen, Rhaina. "Who Took Care of Rosie the Riveter's Kids?" *Atlantic*, November 18, 2005.

Corn, Jacqueline Karnell, and Jennifer Starr. "Historical Perspectives on Asbestos: Policies and Protective Measures in World War II Shipbuilding." *American Journal of Industrial Medicine* 11 (1987): 359–73.

Cushman, Robert E. "The Case of the Nazi Saboteurs." *American Political Science Review* 36 (December 1942): 1082–91.

Du Bois, W. E. B. "A Chronicle of Race Relations." *Phylon* 3 (First Quarter 1942).

Ervin, Keona K. "We Rebel: Black Women, Worker Theater, and Critical Unionism in Wartime St. Louis." *Souls: A Critical Journal of Black Politics, Culture, and Society* 18 (June 2016).

Fisher, Louis. "Detention and Military Trial of Suspected Terrorists: Stretching Presidential Power." *Journal of National Security Law and Policy* 2 (2006): 1–51.

Franke, Kara, and Dennis Paustenbach. "Government and Navy Knowledge Regarding Health Hazards of Asbestos: A State of the Science Evaluation, 1900 to 1970." *Inhalation Toxicology* 23, no. 53 (2011): 1–20.

Graham, W. A. "Martial Law in California." *California Law Review* 31 (December 1942): 6–15.

Guglielmo, Thomas A. "'Red Cross, Double Cross': Race and America's World War II–Era Blood Donor Service." *Journal of American History* (June 2010): 63–90.

Guttmacher, Alan F. "The Genesis of Liberalized Abortions in New York: A Personal Insight." *Case Western Reserve Law Review* 23 (1972): 756–64.

Heller, Steven. "The Almost-Forgotten Jewish Artist Who Propagandized Against Hitler." *Atlantic*, May 29, 2014.

Henderson, Leon, and Donald M. Nelson. "Prices, Profits, and Government." *Harvard Business Review* (Summer 1941): 389–404.

Huntington, Samuel P. "Democracy's Third Wave." *Journal of Democracy* 2 (Spring 1991).

Huq, Aziz Z., and Tom Ginsburg. "How to Lose a Constitutional Democracy." *UCLA Law Review* 65 (2018).

Jack, William S. "Jack and Heintz: Blueprint for Labor Relations." *Public Opinion Quarterly* 7 (Autumn 1943): 413–30.

Kimble, James J., and Lester C. Olson. "Visual Rhetoric Representing Rosie the Riveter: Myth and Misconception in J. Howard Miller's 'We Can Do It' Poster." *Rhetoric and Public Affairs* 9 (Winter 2006): 533–70.

Knapp, Robert H. "A Psychology of Rumor." *Public Opinion Quarterly* 8 (Spring 1944).

Koistenen, Paul A. C. "Mobilizing the World War II Economy: Labor and the Industrial-Military Alliance." *Pacific Historical Review* 42 (November 1973): 443–78.

Leff, Mark H. "The Politics of Sacrifice on the American Home Front in World War II." *Journal of American History* 77 (March 1991): 1299–1306.

Lieberman, Sanford R. "The Evacuation of Industry in the Soviet Union during World War II." *Soviet Studies* 35 (January 1983): 90–102.

Lucano, Stefano. "Contested Loyalties: World War II and Italian-Americans' Ethnic Identity." *Italian Americana* 30 (Summer 2012): 151–67.

Manning, Molly Guptill. "Fighting to Lose the Vote: How the Soldier Voting Acts of 1942 and 1944 Disenfranchised America's Armed Forces." *New York University Journal of Legislation and Public Policy* 19 (2016): 336–77.

Markel, Howard. "The Real Story behind Penicillin." *PBS Newshour,* September 27, 2013.

Mead, Margaret. ". . . To Keep Our Children Safe from Fear." *Guild Teacher,* February–March 1942.

Meyer, Leo J. "The Decision to Invade North Africa (TORCH)." Washington, D.C.: Center of Military History, 1990.

Nyhan, Brendan, and Jason Reifler. "When Corrections Fail: The Persistence of Political Misperceptions." *Political Behavior* 32 (June 2010).

Oatman, Eric. "The Drug That Changed the World." *P&S,* Columbia University College of Physicians and Surgeons (Winter 2005).

Panunzio, Constantine. "Italian Americans, Fascism, and the War." *Yale Review* 31 (June 1942): 771–82.

Philippon, Thomas, and Ariell Reshef. "Wages and Capital in the U.S. Financial Industry, 1909–2006." *Quarterly Journal of Economics* 127 (November 2012): 1551–1609.

Rockoff, Hugh. "Price and Wage Controls in Four Wartime Periods." *Journal of Economic History* 41 (June 1981).

Roosevelt, Eleanor. "Race, Religion, and Prejudice." *New Republic,* May 11, 1942.

Ruml, Beardsley. "The Pay-as-You-Go Income Tax Plan." *Bulletin of the National Tax Association* 28 (March 1943): 166–71.

Simpson, William M. "A Tale Untold? The Alexandria, Louisiana, Lee Street Riot." *Louisiana History* 35 (Spring 1994): 133–49.

Smith, Susan L. "Mustard Gas and American Race-Based Human Experimentation in World War II." *Journal of Law, Medicine, and Ethics* (Fall 2008).

Sutton, Matthew Avery. "Was FDR the Antichrist? The Birth of Fundamentalist Anti-liberalism in a Global Age." *Journal of American History* 98 (March 2012).

Taylor, David A. "During World War II, the U.S. Saw Italian-Americans as a Threat to Homeland Security." Smithsonian.com, February 2, 2017.

Ugland, Richard M. "Viewpoints and Morale of Urban High School Students during World War II: Indianapolis as a Case Study." *Indiana Magazine of History* 77 (June 1981): 150–78.

Warner, Edward. "What Airplanes Can Do: Present Limitations and Possible Developments." *Foreign Affairs* 20 (January 1942): 339–58.

Theses, Dissertations, and Unpublished Documents

Bartels, Andrew H. "The Politics of Price Control: The Office of Price Administration and the Dilemmas of Economic Stabilization, 1940–1946." Ph.D. diss., Johns Hopkins University, 1980.

Knapp, Robert H. "Serial Reproduction and Related Aspects of Rumor." Ph.D. diss., Harvard University, 1947.

Mak, Stephen Seng-hua. "America's Other Internment: World War II and the Making of Modern Human Rights." Ph.D. diss., Northwestern University, 2009.

Mansfield, Harvey C., and Associates, "A Short History of OPA." OPA Office of Temporary Controls, 1947.

Schmitz, John Eric. "Enemies among Us: The Relocation, Internment, and Repatriation of German, Italian, and Japanese Americans during the Second World War." Ph.D. diss., American University, 2007.

Court Cases

Ex parte Quirin, 317 U.S. 1 (1942)

Hirabayashi v. United States, 320 U.S. 81 (1943)

Korematsu v. United States, 323 U. S. 214 (1944)

Matlaw Corporation v. War Damage Corporation, 164 F.2d 281 (1947)

Tileston v. Ullman, 129 Conn. 84 (1942)

Tileston v. Ullman, 318 U.S. 44 (1943)

Trump v. Hawaii, 17-965, 585 U.S.___. (2018)

U.S. v. McWilliams, 54 F. Supp. 791 (D.D.C., 1944)

Government Documents

Budget of the United States Government for the Fiscal Year Ending June 30, 1943. Washington, D.C.: Government Printing Office, 1942.

Bureau of the Budget. *The United States at War: Development and Administration of the War Program by the Federal Government.* Washington, D.C.: Government Printing Office, 1946.

Bureau of the Census. *Statistical Abstract of the United States, 1950.* Washington, D.C.: Government Printing Office, 1950.

Office of War Information. *Battle Stations for All: The Story of the Fight to Control Living Costs.* Washington, D.C.: Office of War Information, February 1943.

U.S. Department of Justice. *Report to the Congress of the United States: Review of Restrictions on Persons of Italian Ancestry during World War II.* Washington, D.C.: U.S. Department of Justice, November 2001.

U.S. House of Representatives. *Report of the Select Committee Investigating National Defense Migration, March 19, 1942.* Washington, D.C.: Government Printing Office, 1942.

U.S. Selective Service System. *Selective Service in Peacetime, 1940–41: First Report of the Director of Selective Service.* Washington, D.C.: U.S. Government Printing Office, 1942.

Vital Statistics of the United States, 1942, part 1. Washington, D.C.: U.S. Government Printing Office, 1944.

Websites

ancestry.com
archives.gov/federal-register/executive-orders/1942.html
bea.gov
cfr.org
Eleanor Roosevelt FBI file, vault.fbi.gov
"FDR Day by Day," fdrlibrary.marist.edu
FOIA Reading Room, cia.gov
fred.stlouisfed.org
Gallup polls, ropercenter.cornell.edu
ibiblio.org/1942/
measuringworth.com
millercenter.org
minneapolisfed.org
piketty.pse.ens.fr/files/capital21c/
taxpolicycenter.org
ticdata.treasury.gov
woodrow.org

INDEX